COOKBOOK
OF THE
YEAR

Don Collins

Seattle, WA

Published by
Hara Publishing
P.O. Box 19732
Seattle, WA 98109

ISBN: 1-883697-35-2

Library of Congress Catalog Card Number:
96-078299

Manufactured in the United States
10 9 8 7 6 5 4 3 2

Contributing Editor: Cherie Tucker
Cover Design: Ron DeWilde
Desktop Publishers: Eric Mead and Shael Anderson

With Gratitude

To Sally, Jim, and Michael for being generous, gracious and adventuresome human beings. You were the first to follow the map and take this journey.

But most of all, thanks for being first in friendship!

Tom & Linda

Wishing you many celebrations around your evening meal – buon appetito!

[illegible]

FOREWORD

To put it plainly, COOKBOOK OF THE YEAR is simplifying my life! Knowing that each week I can take a pre-planned grocery list to the store, purchase supplies for the full week, and simply follow each day's recipe without having to plan, is both exciting and calming! This book is not only a boon to the tired and harried middle-aged career cook, but a welcome gift for newlyweds, recent graduates, those working on weight control, and couples who unhappily buy "take out" most of the week.

It's been my good fortune to dine at the Collins' household on many occasions. Some years ago I asked Don if he'd ever considered putting the many creative meals he served into a cookbook. His refreshing approach to putting out a meal at the end of a busy day has always been inspiring - and enviable. My own approach has always been to think about dinner on the way home from work! At this point, of course, I'm tired and uninspired about putting together a nutritious meal and usually end up fixing one of only a few quick recipes I know. This book, which I'm so grateful to Don for writing, has been life-changing! Now, no matter how busy the day, I look forward to an evening meal with little THOUGHT or effort on my part!

Don's emphasis on a healthy complex-carbohydrate diet guides us through many dishes using pasta, beans, potatoes, and rice, along with lots of vegetables and salads. The liberal use of nonfat, plain yogurt in his recipes also gives us some luscious "cream" sauces, as well as a much needed calcium boost. You'll be using fish on a regular basis too: something I always think I'll fix, but don't. And, look forward to trying tasty recipes with bits of tofu (suprisingly good!) and lesser-known vegetables such as kale and broccoflower (*I love it*!). On top of all the nutritional elements in the recipes, COOKBOOK OF THE YEAR offers the crowning achievement - the food is delicious! (If you have skeptics in your household, they won't realize that you've gone "healthy" on them!)

COOKBOOK OF THE YEAR serves up large quantities of wellness. Don's research tips on health and nutrition are fun and informative, and his recipes give us a sense of control by showing that we CAN cook and put together nutritious and delicious meals on a regular basis. His suggestions about enjoying the meal with candles, good music, etc., all lead us to a calmer place within a frazzled, fast-paced world.

With this daily planner look forward to the adventure of cooking again, eating delicious meals, working with whole foods, and enjoying them in your own home. The deli and fast (*fat*) food approaches will be a thing of the past! Take the grocery lists provided in this book, purchase everything listed, and know that you have finished buying (and puzzling over) food for the rest of the week! Whether you purchase this book in January, February, June or July...pick your week and month of choice and start letting COOKBOOK OF THE YEAR carry you along.

Thank you, Don, for peace of mind and for the discovery that the evening meal can be fun!

Priscilla Hake Lauris

(Ms. Lauris is the Wellness Director for Washington Mutual Bank, headquartered in Seattle, WA.)

INTRODUCTION

In writing this book, I've discovered that the recipes I created 20 years ago have evolved. The food is similar to the "comfort food" of my youth, but far more adventuresome in variety and flavor and reflects a growing awareness of a healthier lifestyle.

I've always navigated the nutritional pathways and led the weekly shopping excursions in my home. A number of years ago, at the urging of my family and friends, I began mapping out a cookbook. As the chief cook, I seldom used recipes. (Maybe it's a guy thing - like asking for directions!) I wanted to put a <u>complete</u> meal on the table, and cookbook recipes offered only an entree or a side dish. In this book, my recipes reflect the way I've always cooked, with several activities under way at one time culminating in the presentation of a complete meal.

As you follow this road map to good eating, a few explanations may make the journey easier. First, **the format**. Ingredients are grouped and shaded to clearly identify the order they are to be used. Ingredient items are often followed by *italicized* instructions describing basic preparation. Assembly instructions follow in bold print. When you've finished the assembly, you'll have a complete meal on the table.

Preparation may exceed stated times until you develop a routine of organization and get used to the flow of activity. Stay with it! Once you've prepared a few recipes you'll breeze through these meals like a seasoned chef.

Organization is the key! Be sure you've set all ingredients on the counter before you begin cooking. If canned goods are used, open the cans before you start. (I usually, pre-measure liquids and have them ready to go.) If you prepare ingredients as directed before you start, recipes will go together smoothly, i.e., *cut broccoli in 2" lengths, smash and chop garlic,* etc. You will notice a symbol just underneath the date box at the upper outside corner of the page. This symbol indicates an early preparation step which requires about 5 minutes in the morning. These directions usually involve "quick cooked" rice or preparations for "time bake." You may also be reminded to pick up a fresh loaf of bakery bread or fresh fish during the day. ***Glance at the recipe in the morning to see if there's an early preparation step.***

In case you're not familiar with the terms *smashed and chopped*, as it applies to **garlic preparation**, allow me to explain. Place the flat side of a large chopping knife over a clove of unpeeled garlic *(sharp edge of the knife facing away from you)*, and smack the flat side of the blade with the palm of your hand - *smashed*. The papery skin is now separated from the meat of the garlic. Pick up the skin and throw it away. The easy part is next - *chopped.*

You will note that many of my recipes use boneless, skinless chicken breasts. They are a bit more expensive, but skinless white meat is much lower in fat than dark meat and boneless breasts prepare and cook quickly. However, breasts are fairly easy to skin and bone, so feel free to save money by preparing them yourself. *I refer to a serving size as <u>one breast</u>. However, a complete breast is really the full upper carcass of a chicken (wings and back removed). My reference to one serving of chicken breast is actually <u>one half</u> of a full chicken breast. (Packages of frozen breasts are usually prepared in these 1/2 breast, or single serving, portions.)*

A commonly used seasoning in my recipes is Tabasco® sauce. I use this brand name product because of the overriding olive oil flavor it adds to dishes. The spicy "hit" adds interest while the olive oil essence allows me to reduce or eliminate oil in the recipes.

Weekly grocery lists are presented each Saturday. This single, well-planned shopping trip prepares you for each day of the coming week. In some instances I suggest buying items like fresh fish or fresh baked bread on the day it will be used. For convenience, and in the interest of keeping this book intact, I have duplicated **weekly grocery lists in the back of the book**. Remove the corresponding list and take it to the store with you. The back of each removable list also provides room for additional items you may need. It may seem that you are spending more money during the weekly shopping trips. However, if you tally the little trips you currently make plus the money spent eating out, you'll be spending far less.

So off you go to explore new avenues of nutrition and adventures in flavor. Just a little planning and every evening becomes a celebration. Best wishes for a successful journey!

GETTING STARTED

JANUARY

Preparing for a productive time in the kitchen requires a well organized trip to the grocery store. You may already have many of these items. See duplicate grocery lists in the back of the book.

Produce

1 lb. fresh broccoli
12-15 baby red potatoes
2 heads garlic
one 6" zucchini
2 medium yellow onions
2 large carrots
1/2 lb. white mushrooms
5-6 tart apples
1 head iceberg lettuce
1 head red leaf lettuce
10-12 Roma tomatoes
2 green bell peppers
2 red bell peppers
1 cucumber
pine nuts
1 fresh lemon

Canned or Dry Foods

12 oz. dry spaghetti
12 oz. dry spiral pasta
16 oz. brown rice
two 15 oz. cans chicken broth
one 29 oz. can tomato sauce
1 small jar Dijon mustard
1 small jar honey mustard
1 bottle low or nonfat salad dressing
Tabasco® sauce
chili powder
cumin powder
dry basil leaves
dry oregano leaves
one 16 oz. box corn starch
5 lb. unbleached flour
5 lb. white sugar
1 C. package pecan halves
one 17 oz. bottle olive oil
one 6 oz. bottle sesame oil
one 17 oz. bottle white vinegar
one 17 oz. bottle balsamic vinegar
6 oz. vegetable oil spray *(pump style)*
1 liter white cooking wine
breakfast cereal
1 large thin-crust Boboli®
1 loaf whole wheat bread

Notes

Frozen Foods

one 12 oz. can orange juice
12 oz. frozen peas
12 oz. frozen corn

Meat/Fish/Poultry

2 boneless, skinless chicken breasts
1 lb. Italian chicken or turkey sausage links
2 fresh snapper fillets
1 lb. turkey breast fillets

Chilled Foods and Dairy

1/2 gallon nonfat milk
32 oz. plain, nonfat yogurt
14 oz. fresh salsa
6 oz. fancy-shred Parmesan
3 oz. sharp cheddar cheese
7 oz. fresh pesto
1 package whole wheat tortillas
8 oz. fresh egg fettuccine

MONDAY
January/Week One

Notes

Don's Fajita Pollo (Chicken Fajitas)

This first meal is casual following the hectic holidays. It also conforms to the schedule in many households of January 1st football games.

Preparation time: 30 minutes
Servings: 2-4
Ingredients:

1 lb. turkey breast fillets *(sliced in 1/8" strips)*
1 T. olive oil
2 cloves garlic *(smashed and chopped)*
1 tsp. chili powder
1/4 tsp. ground cumin

1/4 C. chicken broth
1/2 green bell pepper *(seeded and cut in 1" chunks)*
1 red bell pepper *(seeded and cut in 1" chunks)*
3 slices medium sweet onion *(quartered)*
1 tsp. chili powder
1/4 tsp. ground cumin

1 package whole wheat flour tortillas

4 ripe Roma tomatoes *(chopped)*
1/2 head iceberg lettuce *(chopped)*
6 oz. grated cheddar cheese
salsa
1 C. plain, nonfat yogurt *(stirred smooth)*

- **Place turkey over medium-high heat in shallow 10" non-stick fry pan with oil, garlic, 1 tsp. chili powder, and 1/4 tsp. ground cumin. Sauté 5 minutes.**
- **Remove meat from pan and set aside.**
- **Add broth, peppers, onion, and remaining spices to same pan and sauté 3 minutes. Set aside.**
- **Warm 2 tortillas per person in microwave by placing all tortillas between two serving plates and cooking two 40 second cycles, or warm in 350 degree oven 10 minutes in shallow, covered pan.**

Set out chopped tomatoes, lettuce, grated cheese, salsa, yogurt, meat filling, and veggie filling in separate bowls.

Let people build their own fajitas.

Buenos!

Basic Pasta Marinara

TUESDAY

January/Week One

Always a favorite! It doesn't get much easier. Plus, you will have extra Red Sauce for another meal.

Preparation time: 25 minutes
Servings: 2
Ingredients:

Red Sauce

one 29 oz. can tomato sauce
1 T. olive oil *(optional)*
2 cloves garlic *(smashed and chopped) or 1 tsp. commercially prepared chopped garlic*
1 T. dry oregano
1 1/2 T. dry basil leaves
4 thin slices medium yellow onion *(chopped)*
a few dashes of Tabasco® sauce *(optional)*

8 oz. fresh egg fettuccine or 1/2 of a 12 oz. package of dry pasta

Salad

5-6 red or green lettuce leaves *(pat dry with paper towel)*
6 thin slices green bell pepper *(seeded)*
8-10 slices peeled cucumber *(sliced in rounds)*
2 chopped Roma tomatoes *(about 1" chunks)*

2-4 T. fancy-shred Parmesan cheese

- **Place large kettle filled 2/3 full of water over high heat.**
- **Place all Red Sauce ingredients in sauce pan. Bring to boil over medium-high heat. Cover. Reduce heat to low. Simmer 10 minutes.**
- **Drop pasta into boiling water.** *Set timer for 8 minutes if cooking dry pasta, or 3 minutes for fresh fettuccine.* **Drain and rinse with warm water in colander.**
- **Make green salads while pasta is cooking.**
- **Divide pasta on two plates.**
- **Cover each serving with 1/2 to 3/4 C. Red Sauce. Sprinkle 1-2 T. Parmesan cheese over each serving.**

Serve with green salad and your favorite low or nonfat dressing.

Notes

WEDNESDAY

January/Week One

Notes

Mustard-Glazed Chicken Breasts

The always-popular "meat and potatoes" approach.

Preparation time: 30 minutes
Servings: 2
Ingredients:

10 small baby red potatoes
1 T. olive oil

2 boneless, skinless chicken breasts
1/2 C. chicken broth
1 large clove garlic *(smashed and chopped)*
1 tsp. honey or Dijon mustard
1/4 C. white wine

1/2 lb. fresh broccoli *(cut in 2" lengths)*

2 tart apples *(cored and thinly sliced)*
2 lemon wedges

- **Preheat oven to 400 degrees.**
- **Place potatoes face down on oiled cookie sheet on center rack of oven. Cook 25 minutes.**
- **Place chicken breasts in small non-stick fry pan over medium-high heat with 1/4 C. of the broth and chopped garlic. When broth boils, cook 3 minutes before turning. Add remaining broth and cook other side 3 minutes.** *(As broth cooks away, breast will brown slightly on either side.)* **Reduce heat to low, turn breasts final time, and spread with mustard. Add 1/4 C. wine to pan, cover, and cook an additional 5-10 minutes.** *(If breasts are thin, cook five minutes. If they're large, cook 10 minutes.)*
- **Place broccoli in steamer basket in large, covered sauce pan with a little water. When chicken is nearly done, turn burner on high under broccoli and cook, covered, 3 minutes after water boils.**

Serve chicken breasts flanked by potatoes and broccoli. Line edge of plate with sliced apple. Place wedge of lemon on each plate for broccoli.

Light a candle and put on some nice music. Perhaps a glass of white wine is in order.

Spiral Pasta with Pesto "Cream" Sauce

THURSDAY

January/Week One

Another variation on pasta, this time with light cream sauce. It's so nice to eat a cream sauce that doesn't require an angioplasty procedure the next day!

Preparation time: 30 minutes
Servings: 3
Ingredients:

2 C. dry spiral pasta

1 carrot *(peeled and sliced)*
1 C. chicken broth
6 medium mushrooms *(sliced)*
2 slices medium yellow onion *(quartered)*
1/2 green bell pepper *(cut into 1" chunks)*
1 clove garlic *(smashed and chopped) or 1 tsp. prepared chopped garlic*
fresh-ground black pepper
one 6"- 8" long zucchini *(cut into 1/4" rounds)*

1/4 C. plain, nonfat yogurt *(stirred smooth)*
2 T. pesto
dash of Tabasco® *(optional)*

2 T. corn starch dissolved into 1/8 C. water

2-4 T. fancy-shred Parmesan
2 T. toasted pine nuts *(chopped)*
1 large Roma tomato *(chopped into 1" chunks)*

- **Place pasta water on to boil in large, heavy-bottomed kettle. When water boils, add dry pasta and cook.** *Set timer for 8 minutes.* **Drain and rinse.**
- **In same kettle you used for pasta, sauté carrot in 1/4 C. broth 2 minutes.**
- **Add mushrooms, onions, green pepper, and garlic. Sauté 2 minutes. Season with about 4 turns of fresh-ground pepper.**
- **Add zucchini and sauté another 2 minutes.** *If pan cooks dry, add another 1/4 cup broth.*
- **Remove all vegetables from kettle with perforated spoon and set aside. Add remaining broth to kettle and bring to boil over high heat.**
- **Mix yogurt, pesto and Tabasco® in small bowl.**
- **Thicken liquid in kettle with corn starch/water mixture, reduce heat to low, and cook 2-3 minutes. Remove from heat and add pesto/yogurt mixture.**
- **Add all vegetables and cooked pasta to thickened sauce and gently stir over medium-high heat until coated. Cover and remove from heat. <u>Do not boil.</u>**
- **Divide into 2-3 servings on individual plates.**

Garnish with Parmesan, chopped pine nuts, and tomato. Favoloso!

Notes

FRIDAY
January/Week One

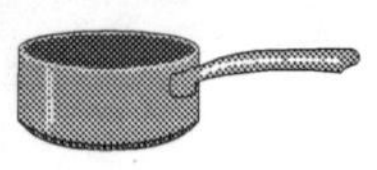

Notes

Red Snapper with Pesto

Fish should be an important part of your diet. It is always delicious when prepared properly. Versatile snapper lends itself to many delicious variations. In the Eastern U.S. it is truly red snapper. In the West it may be called rock fish or Pacific snapper.

Preparation time: 25 minutes
Servings: 2
Ingredients:

8 pecan halves *(toasted under the oven broiler and chopped)*
3 slices medium yellow onion *(chopped)*
1 1/2 C. rice *("quick cooked" this morning)*
1/2 C. chicken broth

1/2 lb. fresh broccoli *(cut into 2" lengths)*

1 large clove garlic *(smashed and chopped) or 1 tsp. prepared chopped garlic*
1/4 C. white wine
6 thin slices red bell pepper

1 large or 2 small red snapper (or Pacific snapper) fillets
2 tsp. fresh pesto

1/2 fresh lemon *(cut in wedges)*

- **Place pecan halves in shallow baking pan or on cookie sheet under broiler in oven. Watch closely!** *The whole process will take about 2 minutes.* **When pecans start to brown, turn them over and toast other side.** *Don't leave them, as you may forget them!* **Remove from oven and chop.**
- **Place pecans, onions, and rice in bowl with broth and microwave, covered, 3 minutes on high.**
- **Place broccoli in steamer in saucepan with 3/4 C. water. Set aside.**
- **Place garlic, wine, and bell pepper in non-stick fry pan over high heat and sauté 2 minutes. Lift red pepper out and set aside.**
- **Slide fish into wine and garlic mixture over high heat. When wine boils, cook 3 minutes per side.** *Set timer so you don't forget.* **If wine boils away, add another 1/3 C. liquid** *(wine, water, or broth).*
- **Turn burner on high under broccoli. When water boils, cover and cook 3 minutes.**
- **Turn fish, spread with pesto, and lay pepper strips over fish fillets.**
- **Fish and broccoli should be done at the same time.**

Arrange fish on individual serving plates flanked by broccoli and rice and garnish with lemon wedge. Light a candle and enjoy a lovely dinner.

"Quick Cooked" Rice

Place 1 C. long grain brown rice in a pan with 2 1/4 C. cold water. Cover and bring to boil over high heat. When water boils, turn off heat. Leave pan on burner. Do not lift cover! It will be ready to eat when you get home tonight.

SHOPPING DAY

SATURDAY

January/Week Two

Get ready for another week of celebrations around the evening meal. More delicious, "no guilt" eating is on the way.

Try to avoid impulse buying. Be particularly disciplined about snack foods as they are expensive and usually loaded with fat.

Do consider picking up a couple candles and bouquet of flowers (or a single flower) to add a touch of elegance to the table.

You will notice wine on the grocery list from time to time. You may substitute non-alcoholic wine or broth for wine in any recipe.

The grocery list on this page is duplicated in the back of the book. You may remove the list for January/Week Two and take it to the store with you.

Notes

GROCERY LIST

Produce

2 medium russet potatoes
3 medium white potatoes
8-10 baby red potatoes
2 medium yellow onions
1 lb. fresh mushrooms
1 green bell pepper
1 red bell pepper
3 large carrots
1/2 lb. fresh broccoli
green salad fixings
one bunch chard
6-8 Roma tomatoes
4 tart apples
1 fresh lemon
ginger root

Frozen Foods

1 package frozen spinach

Meat/Fish/Poultry

1 lb. ground turkey breast
1 package thin sliced turkey breast fillets
2 frozen halibut fillets *(If you prefer fresh fish, buy on the day you plan to cook it.)*

Canned or Dry Foods

one 29 oz. can tomato sauce
one 15 oz. can chicken broth
one 6 oz. can sliced water chestnuts
one 6 oz. can sliced bamboo shoots
8 oz. fresh fettuccine
8 oz. fresh (or dry) cheese tortellini
1 box old fashioned rolled oats
1 C. package shelled walnut halves
graham crackers
raisins
dried fennel seed
ground nutmeg
ground anise
red cooking wine

Chilled Foods and Dairy

1 dozen eggs

Buy if you're out

1 head garlic
frozen corn
12-16 oz. brown rice

SUNDAY

January/Week Two

Notes

"Bogus Pork" Medallions

You'd swear this was a delicious pork dinner! It is reminiscent of Sunday dinner from somewhere in bygone years.

Preparation time: 40 minutes
Servings: 3
Ingredients:

3 slices medium yellow onion *(quartered)*
2 medium *(unpeeled)* russet potatoes *(sliced in 1/2" slices)*
1 T. olive oil

one 12 oz. package frozen corn
4 thin slices red bell pepper *(chopped)*
1/4 C. water

1 lb. turkey breast fillets *(sliced)*
1/4 C. flour
1 T. olive oil
2 large cloves garlic *(smashed and chopped) or 1 tsp. chopped prepared garlic*
1/4 C. chicken broth
fresh-ground black pepper

1/4 C. white wine
1 large tart apple *(peeled, quartered, cored, and sliced in thin slices)*
1 T. brown sugar
1/8 tsp. cinnamon

- **Preheat oven to 400 degrees.**
- **Place onion and potatoes on cookie sheet oiled with 1 T. olive oil. Place in oven on center rack for 15 minutes. Turn and return to oven until dinner is ready.**
- **Place corn, red pepper, and water in sauce pan and set aside.**
- **Dredge sliced fillets in flour until well coated.**
- **Put remaining 1 T. oil and garlic in 10" fry pan over medium-high heat. When garlic begins to sizzle, add floured fillets. Cook until golden brown** *(3-4 minutes per side). If pan gets too dry, add a little chicken broth.* **Season each side with fresh-ground black pepper.**
- **Lift fillets out of fry pan and set in oven with potatoes.**
- **Add wine to fry pan and rub bottom of pan gently with fork to lift up any drippings.**
- **Add apple slices, brown sugar, and cinnamon. Reduce heat to low, cover pan, and cook 5 minutes, stirring occasionally.**
- **While sauce is cooking, turn on burner under corn. When water boils, cover and cook 3 minutes.**

Serve fillets on individual plates covered with apples and sauce. Serve corn and potatoes on either side of fillets. Delicious!

Pasta Bolognese

MONDAY

January/Week Two

We are keeping it simple: a pasta with meat sauce. The new twist is that you will create your own Italian sausage from ground turkey.

Preparation time: 30 minutes
Servings: 2-3
Ingredients:

Italian Turkey Sausage
- 1 T. olive oil
- 1 lb. ground turkey breast
- 2 slices medium yellow onion *(chopped)*
- 2 tsp. dry basil leaves
- 1 tsp. dry oregano leaves
- 1/2 tsp. ground anise
- 2 large cloves garlic *(smashed and chopped)*
- dash of Tabasco® sauce
- 1/8 C. red wine

green salad fixings

- 1 1/2 C. Red Sauce *(If you have leftovers use them. If not, whip up a new batch as shown on page 3.)*
- 1/4 C. red wine

8 oz. fresh fettuccine

3 T. fancy-shred Parmesan

Notes

- **Place pasta water on to boil in large kettle.**
- **Pour oil in non-stick fry pan.**
- **Place all Italian Turkey Sausage ingredients** *(including red wine)* **in fry pan and cook 10 minutes** *(until browned)* **over medium-high heat.** *Stir gently from time to time to ensure even cooking. The recipe makes more than you will use. Separate 1/3 of the Italian Sausage for tonight's recipe and reserve the rest for a future meal.*
- **Make green salads on individual plates while sausage is cooking.**
- **Combine 1 1/2 C. Red Sauce with wine and 1/3 of the Italian Sausage. Return to boil. Remove from heat.** *Reserve remaining Red Sauce for another meal.*
- **Drop fresh pasta into water to cook 2 1/2 minutes after water returns to boil. Drain and rinse.**
- **Spoon Bolognese Sauce over cooked pasta on individual plates.**

Garnish with Parmesan cheese and serve fresh green salad on the side.
Gusta Bravo! (It tastes great!)

TUESDAY

January/Week Two

Notes

"Quick cook" some rice as you get ready for work this morning. *(see page 6)*

Loaded Rice

This is one of my favorite recipes. A real "carbo-load!"

Preparation time: 25 minutes
Servings: 2
Ingredients:

8-10 baby red potatoes or 1 large russet potato
1 T. olive oil

1/2 lb. mushrooms *(sliced)*
1/4 red bell pepper *(thin-sliced)*
1 T. olive oil
1 large clove garlic *(smashed and chopped)*
1/4 C. white wine
2 slices medium onion *(quartered)*

3/4 C. chicken or vegetable broth
3 T. corn starch dissolved in 1/8 C. cold water

1 C. plain, nonfat yogurt
1 T. pesto
dash of Tabasco®

1 1/2 C. cooked brown rice

2 Roma tomatoes *(chopped)*

- **Preheat oven to 400 degrees.**
- **Wash and halve baby red potatoes. If using russet potato, wash and slice** *(unpeeled)* **in 1/2" slices. Place potatoes, flat side down, on cookie sheet oiled with one tablespoon olive oil.**
- **Sauté sliced mushrooms and bell pepper in oil with garlic, wine, and onion** *(about 4 minutes).* **When done, remove mushroom mixture from pan with perforated spoon. Set aside.**
- **Add broth to pan. Return to boil.**
- **If cooking russet potato slices, turn them now.**
- **Slowly stir corn starch mixture into boiling liquid. Reduce heat to low. Cook 5 minutes, stirring often.**
- **Add mushrooms to thickened mixture. Return to boil. Remove from heat.**
- **Stir yogurt, pesto, and Tabasco® together until smooth. Microwave 30 seconds on high. Stir again.**
- **Warm 1 1/2 C. cooked rice 2 minutes on high in microwave on individual serving plates.**
- **Remove potatoes from oven. If using baby reds, push them into rice on individual plates. If using russets, chop into 1" pieces before sprinkling over rice.**
- **Stir yogurt mixture into thickened mushroom sauce.**

Pour sauce over potato/rice mixture and garnish with fresh chopped tomatoes. Enjoy!

Cheese Tortellini with Red Sauce

Very simple and very quick. You will use some of your leftover Red Sauce from Monday.

Preparation time: 20 minutes
Servings: 2
Ingredients:

8 oz. fresh tortellini or 1 1/2 C. dry tortellini
green salad fixings
1 C. leftover Red Sauce
3 T. fancy-shred Parmesan

Notes

- **Place pasta water on to boil in large kettle.**
- **Drop tortellini into boiling water.** *Set a timer so it doesn't overcook.*

  Fresh tortellini will cook in 10-12 minutes.
  Dry tortellini will cook in about 20 minutes.

- **Drain and rinse pasta.**
- **Make green salads.**
- **Heat Red Sauce 2 minutes on high in microwave.**
- **Divide tortellini on two plates and top with Red Sauce.**

Garnish with Parmesan. Now this was almost too easy!

THURSDAY

January/Week Two

Notes

Did you buy fresh fish or frozen fish on Saturday? Do you need to pick up fresh fish on the way home from work tonight? You"ll need about 1/2 lb.

Baked Halibut

You may use halibut fillets or halibut steaks. Whichever you use, you only need about 4 oz. per serving. I often buy bags of fresh frozen halibut steaks at the local warehouse store and keep them in the freezer.

Preparation time: 30 minutes
Servings: 2
Ingredients:

3 medium white potatoes *(unpeeled, washed, and quartered)*
1/4 tsp. dried fennel seed
3/4 C. water

1 small clove garlic *(smashed and chopped)*
1/4 tsp. grated ginger
1/8 C. plain, nonfat yogurt

two 4-6 oz. fresh or frozen halibut fillets *(thaw before cooking)*
fresh-ground black pepper

one bunch chard *(washed, drained, stems removed, leaves coarsely chopped)*
2 T. balsamic vinegar
2 tsp. olive oil
1/4 C. broth
1/4 red bell pepper *(sliced in thin strips)*
3 thin slices medium yellow onion *(quartered)*
1/4 C. raisins *(optional)*

- **Preheat oven to 400 degrees.**
- **Place potatoes, fennel seeds, and water in medium sauce pan over medium-high heat. When water boils, reduce heat to low and cook, covered, 15 minutes.**
- **Mix garlic and ginger with yogurt.**
- **Place halibut in oiled pan or oven-proof dish.**
- **Grind fresh pepper over halibut.**
- **Spread yogurt mixture over halibut, cover dish with foil, and place on center rack of 450 degree oven.** *(Set timer for 15 minutes.)*
- **Combine all chard ingredients in deep heavy-bottomed kettle. Sauté over medium-high heat until chard is thoroughly wilted. Continue tossing occasionally over medium heat 5 minutes. Cover and set aside until plates are served. Lift out with perforated spoon and swirl on plates with fork.**

Serve halibut flanked by potatoes and chard. Serve with a nice glass of Fumé Blanc.

Omelet with Italian Turkey Sausage and Spinach

FRIDAY

January/Week Two

You will be using some of your leftover Italian Sausage from Monday.

Preparation time: 20 minutes
Servings: 2
Ingredients:

6 eggs
1/4 C. plain, nonfat yogurt
black pepper
several dashes of nutmeg

1 package frozen spinach *(thawed and drained)*

4 fresh mushrooms *(sliced)*
2 slices of a medium onion *(chopped)*
1 clove garlic *(smashed and chopped)*
1/4 C. chicken broth

1 T. olive oil

1/2 C. leftover Italian sausage
3 T. fancy-shred Parmesan

1 teaspoon pesto
1 teaspoon butter
2 slices of bread for toast

1/2 C. Red Sauce *(If no leftovers, see page 3.)*

Notes

- **Break 2 eggs into medium-sized bowl. Separate remaining eggs, discarding yolks and adding whites to bowl with whole eggs. Beat 30 seconds with wire whisk.**
- **Stir yogurt and beat into eggs. Season with black pepper and dash of nutmeg and set aside.**
- **Drain spinach in strainer. Press spinach to side of strainer with large spoon to force water out.**
- **Sauté mushrooms, onion, and garlic in broth, in 10" non-stick fry pan over medium heat 3 minutes. Remove from pan and set aside.**
- **Wash pan, dry thoroughly, and reheat with 1 T. olive oil.**
- **Beat egg mixture one more time with whisk and pour into heated pan.**
- **Cook 3 minutes over medium-high heat lifting edges and letting uncooked egg run underneath until all egg is firm. Reduce heat to low.**
- **Place filling** *(meat, vegetable mixture and Parmesan)* **down center of omelet. Fold edges over filling and cook 2 more minutes.**
- **Place a dinner plate over omelet pan and turn pan upside down while holding plate over top. You have now turned omelet out onto plate. Slide omelet back into pan so that folded seam of omelet is now on the hot surface. Cook another 3 minutes.**
- **Mix pesto and butter and spread on freshly toasted bread.**
- **Warm Red Sauce in microwave** *(1 minute on full power)* **or in a small pan on stove top.**

Halve omelet and remove from pan to two serving plates. Spread Red Sauce over each half. Garnish with a sprinkle of Parmesan.

SATURDAY

January/Week Three

SHOPPING DAY AND MUFFINS IN THE MORNING

Notes

Carrot Muffins

- **Preheat oven to 375 degrees. Spray muffin tins with vegetable oil spray.**
- Mix the following in one bowl: **1 1/4 C. unbleached flour, 1/2 C. whole wheat flour, 1/2 C. old-fashioned oats, 1/2 package graham crackers (crushed fine), 1/8 tsp. ginger, 1/8 tsp. ground cloves, 1 tsp. cinnamon, 1 tsp. baking powder, 1 tsp. baking soda, 2 medium or 1 large carrot (ground fine), 1/4 C. chopped walnuts, 1/2 C. raisins.**
- **In a separate, smaller bowl mix: 1 egg (beaten), 1 1/4 C. milk, 2 T. white vinegar, 3 T. vegetable oil, 1/3 C. molasses.**
- **Stir all ingredients together (wet to dry) in large bowl, and place in muffin tins *(makes a dozen).***

Bake 30-35 minutes. *Serve with nonfat cream cheese. (If you stir the cream cheese thoroughly and serve in a separate dish, no one will know it's nonfat.)*

Do you pack a lunch? *You could probably save $500 a year if you did. Figure it out yourself. There are approximately 240 work days in a year. How much do you spend a day on lunch? A "brown bag" from home will cost you about 1/3 of what you spend eating out.*

I often purchase *a large quantity of chicken/turkey sausage with sun-dried tomatoes at the local warehouse store. I cut them into individual lengths and freeze them in a ziplock-style freezer bag. As needed, I set them out (in the fridge) to thaw the morning I plan to use them. If I forget, I thaw frozen sausages in a covered dish in the microwave for 1 1/2 minutes at maximum power just prior to cooking them.*

GROCERY LIST

Produce

one 6" zucchini
1 medium yellow onion
1 lb. fresh mushrooms
1 green bell pepper
1 red bell pepper
3 large carrots
1 head broccoflower
green salad fixings
one large cucumber
4 Roma tomatoes
one bunch fresh cilantro
one bunch fresh parsley
1 fresh lemon
one lime

Frozen Foods

one package large, shelled, cooked shrimp

Meat/Fish/Poultry

2 frozen orange roughy fillets *(keep frozen)*
2 Italian turkey sausage links

Canned or Dry Foods

one 29 oz. can tomato sauce
one 29 oz. can "Ready-cut" tomatoes
two 15 oz. cans chicken broth
one pound dry white beans *or three 15 oz. cans white beans*
16 oz. dry whole wheat spaghetti
12 oz. dry penne pasta
12 oz. dry spinach spiral pasta
1 C. package pecan halves

Chilled Foods and Dairy

plain, nonfat yogurt

Buy if you're out

1 head garlic
brown rice
white cooking wine
red cooking wine

White Beans and Red Sauce

SUNDAY

January/Week Three

This dish is actually very Italian. I find it a refreshing alternative to pasta dishes. If you don't wish to cook beans, buy two 15 oz. cans cooked navy beans. If using canned beans, be sure to drain and rinse them thoroughly. Save 1 1/2 C. (or one can) beans for Thursday's recipe.

Preparation time: 20 minutes *(after beans are cooked)*
Servings: 2
Ingredients:

2 C. cooked white beans

Red Sauce
one 29 oz. can tomato sauce
1 T. dry basil
2 tsp. dry oregano
4 slices medium onion *(chopped)*
2 cloves garlic *(smashed and chopped) or 1 tsp. prepared chopped garlic*
dash of Tabasco®

1 each: fresh cucumber, tomato, and sweet onion *(5 thin slices of each per serving)*
low or nonfat Italian dressing

2-4 T. fancy-shred Parmesan

Notes

- **Start cooking beans in morning.**
- **Wash and sort 2 cups navy beans and place in large kettle 2/3 full of water. Bring to boil and turn off heat. Let stand** *(covered)* **3-4 hrs.**
- **Drain beans. Add 8 cups fresh water and bring to boil.** *(Leave uncovered to prevent pan from boiling over.)* **Once boiling, reduce heat to low. After about 10 minutes, cover. Cook over low heat 2 hours or until tender. Remove from heat. Drain and rinse before serving.**
- **Place tomato sauce, spices, onion, garlic and Tabasco® in covered sauce pan. Cook 10 minutes over medium heat.**
- **Overlap cucumber, tomato, and onion in alternating slices along edge of each serving plate. Dress with 1 T. low or nonfat Italian dressing per serving.**
- **Prior to serving, rewarm beans in microwave** *(1 minute on high),* **or pour boiling water over beans in large bowl, let stand five minutes and drain.**

Today you will cook beans from scratch. The process is quite easy and can be done while you go about your normal activities.

Spoon one cup cooked beans per serving in center of individual plates with sliced vegetables along edge and cover beans with 1/2 C. Red Sauce per serving. Garnish with Parmesan.

MONDAY
January/Week Three

Notes

"Creamy" Spinach Spirals Prima Vera

Here's another variation on "cream sauce" pasta that won't increase your waistline.

Preparation time: 25 minutes
Servings: 3
Ingredients:

2 T. toasted pine nuts *(chopped)*

1 carrot *(peeled and sliced)*
1 C. vegetable broth or chicken broth

6 medium mushrooms *(sliced)*
2 slices medium yellow onion *(quartered)*
1 large clove garlic *(smashed and chopped) or 1/2 tsp. prepared chopped garlic*
fresh-ground black pepper

1/2 green pepper *(chopped in 1" squares)*
1/2 red bell pepper *(chopped in 1" squares)*
one 6" long zucchini *(cut in 1/4" rounds)*

2 1/2 C. dry spinach spiral pasta

1/2 C. white wine
3 T. corn starch *(dissolved in 1/8 C. water)*
2 dashes of Tabasco®

3/4 C. plain, nonfat yogurt
2 T. pesto

3 T. fancy-shred Parmesan
1 large Roma tomato *(chopped, use for garnish)*

- **Place pasta water on to boil in large kettle.**
- **Toast pine nuts in shallow pan under broiler. It will take only a few minutes, so stay with them.** *(Toast extra! They store, unrefrigerated, in any container with tight-fitting lid.)*
- **Sauté carrot in 1/4 C. broth 2 minutes. Remove from pan.**
- **Sauté mushrooms, onions, and garlic 2 minutes in same pan. Season with 4 turns of fresh ground pepper. Remove from pan and set aside with carrots.**
- **Sauté peppers and zucchini using another 1/8 C. broth if needed. Sauté 1 minute. Remove from pan and set aside with other veggies.**
- **Drop pasta into boiling water and cook 8 minutes. Drain and rinse.**
- **Pour white wine, leftover broth from sauté pan, and any remaining broth into pasta kettle and bring to boil. Reduce heat and gradually stir in corn starch mixture. It will thicken. Add Tabasco® and cook over low heat 5 minutes.**
- **Stir yogurt and pesto together until smooth. Microwave 20 seconds on high to take chill off, and stir once more.**
- **Add all vegetables and pasta to thickened sauce. Return to boil and remove from heat.**
- **Blend yogurt mixture into vegetable sauce.**
- **Spoon onto individual serving plates in generous portions.**

Garnish with Parmesan, tomatoes, and toasted pine nuts. Favoloso!

Orange Roughy with Dill

Orange roughy! What a delicate, versatile fish this is. Caught off the coast of New Zealand, processed and frozen within minutes of being caught, these frozen fillets have a very delicate and fresh quality.

TUESDAY

January/Week Three

Preparation time: 25 minutes
Servings: 2
Ingredients:

Notes

1/4 C. roasted pecans *(chopped)*
1/4 C. white wine
2 slices medium onion *(chopped)*
3 T. chopped parsley *(fresh or dried)*
2 cups cooked rice

1 large or 2 medium carrots *(peeled and sliced diagonally)*
1 head broccoflower *(cut into 2" pieces)*

1/2 C. white wine
1 clove garlic *(smashed and chopped)*
2 small roughy fillets or 2/3 lb. roughy
fresh-ground black pepper
a couple pinches of dill weed

1/2 fresh lemon *(cut in wedges)*

- **Preheat oven to 400 degrees.**
- **Add nuts, wine, onion, and parsley to rice. Cover and microwave on high 2 1/2 minutes.**
- **Place carrots and broccoflower in steamer basket in medium sauce pan with 3/4 C. water.** *Do not begin cooking yet!*
- **Place wine and garlic in sauté pan and bring to boil.**
- **Slide fish fillets into boiling mixture and season with a few turns fresh-ground black pepper. Cook about 3 minutes per side. Turn fillets and sprinkle dill weed over each fillet.** *Watch liquid in pan. If it cooks away, add another 1/4 C. wine, chicken broth, or water.*
- **Turn heat on under carrot mixture. Bring to boil and steam** *(covered)* **3 minutes. Serve immediately!**

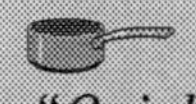

"Quick cook" rice in the morning before work. See page 6. Cook a double recipe. You'll use the other half Thursday.

Serve fillets flanked by vegetables and nutty rice in individual serving plates with a wedge of lemon for the broccoflower and carrots.

WEDNESDAY
January/Week Three

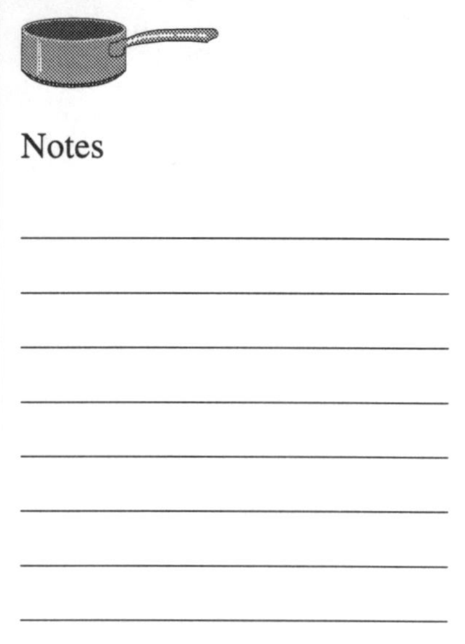

Notes

Pick up a loaf of hearty bread today.

Spaghetti with Italian Turkey Sausage

We're still keeping it simple. This is very similar to Pasta Bolognese.

Preparation time: 30 minutes
Servings: 2
Ingredients:

- a loaf of your favorite crusty bread
- 2 links Italian turkey sausage
- 1 1/2 C. Red Sauce *(see page 15)*
- 1/4 C. red wine
- 1/2 package dry whole wheat spaghetti
- green salad fixings
- 3 T. fancy-shred Parmesan

- **Wrap bread in foil and place in 200 degree oven.**
- **Place pasta water on to boil in large kettle.**
- **Prick sausages 5-10 times with fork. Wrap sausage links in paper towel and place in shallow bowl or pie plate. Cover bowl and microwave for 1 1/2 minutes at full power. Repeat 2 times.** *If you don't have a microwave, simply prick the sausages and sauté over medium-high heat for 10-12 minutes. Turn them often as they cook. Reduce heat to medium, add 1/2 C. water, cover and cook 5 minutes. Discard liquid left over after cooking.*
- **If you have Red Sauce use it. If not, make some now and add wine to 1 1/2 C. Red Sauce. Cook in covered pan 5 minutes over medium heat.** *Save extra for another meal. It also freezes well.*
- **Drop pasta into water and cook 8-10 minutes.** *Set timer so you don't forget.*
- **Make green salads on individual plates.**
- **Drain and rinse pasta, divide on two plates. Place one sausage on each serving and spoon Red Sauce over pasta and meat.**

Garnish with Parmesan cheese. Serve with crusty bread and crisp green salad.

Cajun White Beans and Rice

THURSDAY

January/Week Three

A slightly spicy and delicious meal if you have cooked beans and left-over rice.

Preparation time: 30 minutes *(once beans are cooked)*
Servings: 3-4
Ingredients:

1/2 green bell pepper *(chopped)*
8 medium mushrooms *(sliced)*
2 thin slices medium onion *(chopped)*
1 clove garlic *(smashed and chopped) or 1/2 tsp. prepared chopped garlic*
1 T. olive oil *(optional)*
1/4 C. broth

3/4 C. Red Sauce *(leftovers)*
1 T. chili powder
1 T. dry oregano leaves
1 tsp. cumin
2 T. fresh cilantro *(washed and chopped)*
2 T. lime juice
a couple dashes of Tabasco®

2-4 tortillas

1 C. cooked brown rice *(leftovers)*
1 1/2 C. cooked white beans or one 15 oz. can *(drained and rinsed)*

Optional:
6 medium cooked frozen shrimp *(thawed)*
1/2 C. frozen corn
plain, nonfat yogurt *(stirred smooth)*

Notes

- **Sauté vegetables 3 minutes in large heavy-bottomed sauce pan with garlic, oil, and broth. Remove from pan and set aside in bowl.**
- **Place Red Sauce, spices, lime juice, and Tabasco® in same sauce pan. Cook 10 minutes over medium heat.**
- **Warm tortillas in microwave** *(30 seconds, covered, on high)*
- **Add rice, beans, vegetables, and** *(optional)* **shrimp and corn to Red Sauce in sauce pan. Mix thoroughly and reheat over medium-high heat stirring constantly. Serve immediately.**

You may choose to add a dollop of plain, nonfat yogurt to each serving. Serve warm tortillas on the side.

FRIDAY

January/Week Three

Notes

Leftovers

This is the night to grab a quick meal from leftovers in the fridge. I call leftovers the ultimate in fast food. It's right at your fingertips and the price is definitely right.

Preparation time: 15-20 minutes
Servings: 3-4
Ingredients:

leftover White Beans and Rice
leftover pasta
leftover Red Sauce

- **You may need to put some pasta water on to boil if you're short of cooked pasta. Most leftovers warm well in the microwave. Warm them at maximum power in 1 1/2 minute bursts, stirring them between bursts. Be sure to cover them loosely.** *If you don't have a microwave, use your stove top and small sauce pans. It will go almost as fast.*
- **Make a green salad to go with leftover pasta.**

A tip to liven up leftovers:

Sauté some fresh vegetables in a little leftover broth.

1/4 C. broth
1 clove garlic *(smashed and chopped)*
1 carrot *(peeled and sliced)*
1 slice medium onion *(quartered)*
1/2 green pepper *(cut in 1" cubes)*
4-5 sliced mushrooms
1 chopped Roma tomato
1 tsp. pesto

- **Sauté vegetables in order listed adding each vegetable at one minute intervals i.e., garlic and carrot - one minute, add onion - one minute, add pepper, etc.**
- **Remove from heat. Toss them with 1 tsp. pesto and serve on the side.**

A tip for reheating pasta:

Boil water. Put leftover pasta in a bowl and cover with boiling water. Let stand 3-5 minutes while getting other leftover items together. Drain pasta in colander just prior to serving.

SHOPPING DAY

SATURDAY

January/Week Four

Do you bring your own cloth bags to the grocery store? Most stores will add a five cent or more credit for every bag you bring with you. They'll even credit you for reusing paper bags.

The grocery list calls for two large Russet baking potatoes (one per person) for Thursday. If you're cooking for 3 or 4, adjust the quantity accordingly. Do the same with broccoli. Add about 1/4 lb. per serving.

Notes

Make some quark! *This is a great substitute for sour cream and can also be used as a "cheese" spread on crackers. Follow these directions:*

- **Place a large coffee filter in a strainer and set strainer over a bowl.**
- **Spoon one pint nonfat, plain yogurt into filter.**
- **Set in fridge overnight.**

In the morning you will have a thick "cheese-like" yogurt in the filter. This is quark. Store the quark in a covered container in the fridge. Save the water that has drained off the yogurt. It's full of nutrients and can be used in future food preparations. Add it to soups, sauces or substitute for broth and wine when cooking.

GROCERY LIST

Produce

one 6" zucchini
2 large russet baking potatoes
1 medium yellow onion
1 lb. fresh mushrooms
1/8 lb. fresh snow peas
1 green bell pepper
1 red bell pepper
1 large carrot
3/4 lb. fresh broccoli
green salad fixings
4-6 Roma tomatoes
one medium ripe tomato
1 fresh lemon

Frozen Foods

frozen snow peas *(if fresh aren't available)*

Meat/Fish/Poultry

4 oz. smoked salmon
2-4 boneless, skinless chicken breasts
1 Italian chicken or turkey sausage link
5-6 large frozen, cooked, shelled, and deveined shrimp

Canned or Dry Foods

one 29 oz. can "Ready-cut" tomatoes
two 15 oz. cans chicken broth
one 15 oz. can black beans
one 6 oz. can sliced water chestnuts
one 6 oz. can chopped black olives
one 6 oz. can sliced bamboo shoots
12 oz. dry bow tie pasta
12 oz. dry multi-colored, spiral pasta
1 box fortune cookies
8 oz. fresh fettuccine

Chilled Foods and Dairy

plain, nonfat yogurt
fresh salsa
whole wheat flour tortillas
shredded Parmesan
3-4 oz. extra-sharp cheddar cheese

Buy if you're out

1 head garlic
frozen corn
chili powder
cumin powder
sesame oil
low-sodium soy sauce
Tabasco®
brown rice
cornmeal

SUNDAY

January/Week Four

Notes

Smoked Salmon Pasta

This is truly one of my favorite pastas!

Preparation time: 25 minutes
Servings: 2
Ingredients:

8 mushrooms (*sliced*)
1/2 red bell pepper (*cut into thin 1" long strips*)
2 slices medium yellow onion (*chopped*)
2 cloves garlic (*smashed and chopped*) *or 1/2 tsp. prepared garlic*
1 T. olive oil
1/4 C. dry white wine

1/2 C. chicken or vegetable broth
2 T. corn starch dissolved in about 1/8 C. water

fixings for a green salad

4 oz. smoked salmon (*skin removed and broken into bite-sized pieces*)
1 package frozen snow peas, or 1/8 lb. fresh snow peas

2 T. pesto
3/4 C. plain, nonfat yogurt

8 oz. fresh fettuccine

3 T. fancy-shred Parmesan cheese
3 Roma tomatoes (*chopped*)

- **Place pasta water on to boil in large kettle.**
- **Sauté mushrooms, red bell pepper, onion, and garlic in oil and wine over medium-high heat 2 minutes. Remove from pan with slotted spoon and set aside.**
- **Add broth to remaining white wine in pan. Bring to boil. Reduce heat to medium.**
- **Stir corn starch mixture into boiling liquid. Reduce heat to low and cook 5 minutes. Stir occasionally.**
- **Make green salads.**
- **Add salmon and snow peas to thickened sauce. Return to boil and cook 1 minute.**
- **Return mushroom mixture to sauce. Cook 1 minute and remove pan from heat.**
- **Mix pesto and yogurt until smooth. Microwave 30 seconds on high to take chill off. Stir again.**
- **Drop pasta into boiling water. When water returns to boil, cook 2 minutes** *(set a timer so you don't forget),* **drain, and rinse.**
- **In same kettle used to cook pasta, mix salmon mixture and yogurt over low heat. DO NOT BOIL!**
- **Toss pasta with sauce in large kettle until pasta is well coated.**
- **Serve on individual plates garnished with Parmesan cheese and fresh tomatoes.**

Serve green salad on the side.
Oh yes!!

Hot and Sour Stir Fry

Here's a spicy stir fry that will warm your bones on a winter night.

Preparation time: 30 minutes
Servings: 3-4
Ingredients:

1 T. olive oil
1/4 tsp. sesame oil
3 thin slices medium onion *(chopped)*
2 cloves garlic *(smashed and chopped)*
1 boneless, skinless chicken breast *(chopped into 1/2" cubes)*

1/8 lb. broccoli *(cut in 2" lengths)*
2 T. low-sodium soy sauce
1/4 C. chicken broth
6 mushrooms *(sliced)*

1 1/4 C. chicken broth
1/8 tsp. cayenne pepper
1 T. white sugar
5 T. white vinegar
3 T. corn starch mixed with 1/4 C. water

5-6 deveined, cooked shrimp *(thawed)*

1 1/2 C. cooked rice

1 medium tomato *(chopped)*

- **Place oils in large heavy-bottomed sauce pan over high heat. Sauté onion, garlic, and chicken 5 minutes, stirring constantly.**
- **Toss in broccoli, soy sauce, and 1/4 C. broth. Sauté 2 more minutes.**
- **Add mushrooms. Sauté another minute.**
- **Remove all ingredients from pan with perforated ladle or spoon and set aside.**
- **Using same pan, mix remaining broth, cayenne, sugar, and vinegar and return to heat. Bring to boil and stir in corn starch/water mixture. Reduce heat to low, add shrimp, and cook 3-4 minutes. Stir occasionally.**
- **Warm 3/4 C. rice per serving in microwave for 2 minutes on high, or warm rice over medium-high heat in shallow sauce pan with about 1/8 C. of water.** *Keep an eye on it so it doesn't cook down.*
- **Return vegetables and chicken to broth and add tomatoes. Toss over medium heat until everything is thoroughly coated. Serve immediately over warm rice.**

Plan to eat this meal with chopsticks, it tastes so much better that way! It's also fun to have a fortune cookie and tea to finish the meal.

MONDAY

January/Week Four

Notes

"Quick cook" rice in the morning before work. See page 6. Cook a double recipe. You'll use the left-overs tomorrow.

TUESDAY

January/Week Four

Notes

Mexican Chicken Breasts

A delicious "south-of-the-border" style meal.

Preparation time: 30 minutes
Servings: 2
Ingredients:

1/4 C. Red Sauce *(see page 15) Use 1/4 C. in this recipe and save the rest.*
1 T. chili powder
1/2 tsp. cumin
1 tsp. oregano

Coating for Chicken
5 T. flour
2 T. cornmeal
1 T. chili powder
1 tsp. oregano
1/2 tsp. cumin
1/8 tsp. black pepper

2 boneless, skinless chicken breasts
1 T. olive oil
2 cloves garlic *(smashed and chopped)*
3 slices medium yellow onion *(chopped)*

1/4 red bell pepper *(chopped)*
1/4 green bell pepper *(chopped)*
1 thin slice onion *(chopped)*
1 T. chili powder
1/2 C. broth
1/2 C. frozen corn
1/2 C. cooked rice *(leftovers)*

one 15 oz. can black beans *(drained and rinsed)*
1/4 C. salsa

2 thin slices extra-sharp cheddar cheese
flour tortillas

- **To 1/4 C. prepared Red Sauce, add 1 T. chili powder, 1/2 tsp. cumin, and 1 tsp. oregano in small bowl and microwave on high 1 1/2 minutes, or bring to boil in small sauce pan over medium-high heat. Remove from heat. Set aside.**
- **In a plastic bag, mix flour, cornmeal, 1 T. chili powder, 1 tsp. oregano, 1/2 tsp. cumin, and black pepper. Shake to mix thoroughly.**
- **Drop chicken breasts into bag and shake until coated.**
- **Preheat sauté pan with oil over medium-high heat. Place coated breasts, garlic, and all but 1 T. onion in pan and cook until breasts are golden brown on both sides. Reduce heat to medium-low, cover, and cook 5 minutes.**
- **While breasts are cooking, put red and green pepper, onion, chili powder, and broth in bottom of shallow sauce pan. Bring to boil and cook 1 minute. Add corn, boil 2 more minutes** *(stirring occasionally),* **and stir in cooked rice. Reduce heat to low and continue cooking 2 minutes** *(again, stirring occasionally)*.
- **Place rinsed beans in sauce pan with salsa over low heat.**
- **Turn breasts and cover with previously prepared Red Sauce. Place cheese slice over each breast. Cover, reduce heat to low, and cook 5 minutes.**

Serve on individual plates with the breast in the center flanked by black beans and rice. Serve a warm, rolled tortilla on the side.

Pasta Prima Vera with Red Sauce

WEDNESDAY
January/Week Four

This is another way to fix a delicious prima vera pasta. You'll have leftovers.

Preparation Time: 30 minutes
Servings: 2
Ingredients:

2 1/2 C. dry spiral pasta

1 T. olive oil
1/2 tsp. crushed garlic
1 large carrot *(peeled and sliced)*
2 slices medium onion *(quartered)*

1/4 C. broth *(use vegetable if you are cooking vegetarian)*
1/2 medium green pepper *(cubed in 1" chunks)*
1 small zucchini 6" long *(cut in 1/8" rounds)*
6 medium mushrooms *(sliced in 1/4" slices)*

1 1/2 C. Red Sauce *(leftover from last night) Save 1/2 C. for Friday's meal.*

2 Roma tomatoes *(cut in 1" chunks)*

2-4 T. fancy-shred Parmesan cheese
4 T. chopped black olives

Notes

- **Place pasta water on to boil in large sauce pan.**
- **Drop dry pasta into boiling water and cook 8 minutes.** *(Set a timer so you don't forget.)*
- **Measure olive oil and garlic into sauté pan over medium-high heat. Start with carrot and onion. Sauté 1 minute. Add broth, green pepper, zucchini, and mushrooms — sauté 2 minutes. Remove veggies from pan and set aside.**
- **Drain and rinse pasta.**
- **Pour 1 1/2 C. leftover Red Sauce into same pan used to cook pasta. Bring to boil.**
- **Add all vegetables** *(including Roma tomatoes)* **to sauce and remove from heat.**
- **If necessary, microwave cooked pasta 1 minute on high to reheat, or measure 1 to 1 1/2 C. per serving and place in bowl with boiling water for 1 minute prior to serving. Drain and rinse in colander.**
- **Divide onto separate plates and ladle veggie sauce over it.**

Garnish with Parmesan and chopped olives and serve immediately.

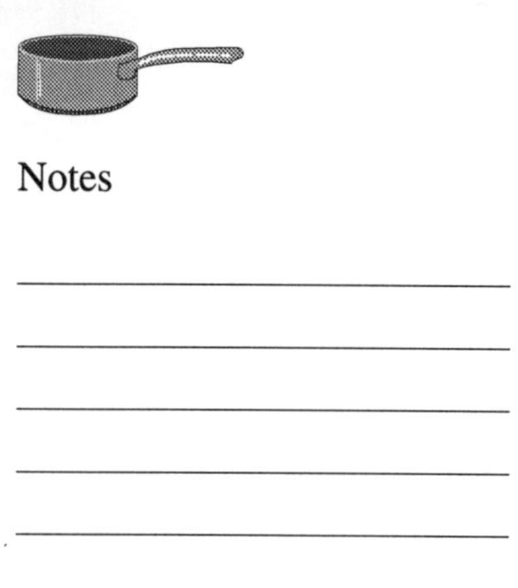

THURSDAY

January/Week Four

Notes

Baked Potato with Broccoli

Baked potatoes are truly a wonder meal! You'll supply your body with valuable potassium and vitamins with the potato and lots of calcium and vitamin C when you add the broccoli. The condiments used to dress the potato won't hurt you either!

Preparation time: 15-20 minutes
Servings: 2
Ingredients:

- 2 large russet baking potatoes *(washed, rubbed with olive oil, and pricked with a fork)*
- 1/2 lb. fresh broccoli *(cut in 2" lengths)*
- 1/2 C. frozen corn
- 3/4 C. plain, nonfat yogurt *(stirred smooth)*
- sharp cheddar cheese
- salsa
- lemon

- **Prepare potatoes in the morning prior to work and set your oven for "time bake" so that they will have been cooking for 1 hour when you arrive home in the evening.** *(You may also cook them in the microwave. Cook for three 5-minute cycles at full power. Turn the potatoes to a different position after each cycle.)*
- **Place broccoli in steamer basket in sauce pan with a little water. Bring to boil, cover, and cook 3 minutes.** *Set timer so you don't forget.* **Remove pan and uncover when timer goes off.**
- **Measure 1/2 C. frozen corn into glass dish. Cover and thaw in microwave 1 minute at full power.**
- **Stir yogurt, set out cheese (with grater), and salsa while broccoli is cooking.**

Split potatoes and place on serving plates. Top with corn, yogurt, and salsa. Garnish with a few gratings of sharp cheddar cheese. Serve broccoli on same plate with a wedge of lemon.

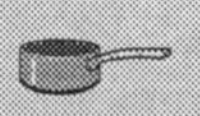

If you have "time bake" on your oven, you may wish to wash potatoes, prick them with a fork, rub them with olive oil, and place them in a shallow pan in the oven before work today. Set the oven temperature at 400 degrees so that it turns on 1 hour before you are to arrive home.

Bow Tie Pasta with Chunky Red Sauce

FRIDAY

January/Week Four

A slightly different twist for Red Sauce pasta.

Preparation time: 25 minutes
Servings: 2-3
Ingredients:

a loaf of your favorite hearty bread

Chunky Red Sauce
one 29 oz. can "Ready-cut" tomatoes
1/4 C. red wine
2 cloves garlic *(smashed and chopped) or 1 tsp. commercially prepared chopped garlic*
2 slices medium yellow onion *(chopped)*
1 1/2 T. dry basil leaves
1 T. dry oregano leaves
dash of Tabasco®
1/2 C. Red Sauce

1 Italian sausage link *(cooked and sliced in rounds)*

12 oz. dry bow tie pasta

green salad fixings

2-4 T. fancy-shred Parmesan cheese

- **Wrap bread in foil and place in warm oven.**
- **Place large kettle on stove filled 2/3 full of water. Turn heat on high and cover.**
- **Set colander over sauce pan. Pour chopped tomatoes into colander and drain liquid into sauce pan. Set tomato chunks aside in bowl.**
- **Add all Chunky Red Sauce ingredients** *(except tomato chunks)* **to juice from tomatoes in sauce pan. Bring to boil. Reduce heat to low. Cover and cook 5 minutes.**
- **Prick Italian sausage, wrap in paper towel, and place in covered bowl. Microwave two 2-minute bursts on high. Let cool.**
- **Pour dry pasta into boiling water. Cook 10 minutes. Drain and rinse.**
- **Make green salads while pasta cooks.**
- **Press sausage firmly with flat side of fork while wrapped in paper towels to force out excess fat. Slice in rounds and place on fresh paper towel. Place rounds in shallow pan and brown slightly over high heat.** *This will only take a few minutes.*
- **Add tomato chunks to Red Sauce and bring to boil. Remove from heat.**
- **Spoon sauce over pasta on individual serving plates. Lay sausage rounds over top of servings and sprinkle with 1-2 T. Parmesan cheese.**

Serve with warm bread and salad on side.

Notes

Pick up a loaf of your favorite hearty bread today.

SATURDAY
January/February

Notes

SHOPPING DAY

It's shopping day again! *You'll have a number of new recipes to try this month. One of my favorites comes up this Sunday.*

Always check *your grocery list against what you may already have in stock. Particularly things like rice, pasta, and frozen vegetables.*

It has been said *that one should never go to the grocery store hungry. I think that's true. If you can go right after breakfast or lunch, you'll do better at resisting unnecessary high-fat snack foods.*

Some people do better shopping alone. *Shopping with children or spouse can sometimes lead to buying too many superfluous items.*

The four worst kitchen time-wasters: *starting to cook before you read the entire recipe, pulling out ingredients as you go, using dull knives (which is also dangerous), and working on a cluttered countertop.*

McCall's, 110 5th Ave., New York, NY 10011-5601

GROCERY LIST

Produce

1 medium yellow onion
8-10 baby red potatoes
1/2 lb. fresh mushrooms
1 green bell pepper
1 red bell pepper
1 large carrot or 2 medium carrots
1 bunch celery
1/2 lb. fresh broccoli
1 bunch red leaf lettuce
one head iceberg lettuce
one bunch green onions
green salad fixings
8 Roma tomatoes
1 large tart apple
1 bunch fresh basil
1 fresh lemon

Frozen Foods

1 package frozen spinach

Meat/Fish/Poultry

1 1/2 lb. ground turkey breast
1 boneless, skinless chicken breast
6-8 slices barbecued pork

Canned or Dry Foods

one 29 oz. can tomato sauce
two 15 oz. cans chicken broth
one 15 oz. can vegetable broth
one 6 oz. can sliced bamboo shoots
12 oz. dry penne or mastaciolli pasta
8 oz. fresh cheese tortellini

Chilled Foods and Dairy

plain, nonfat yogurt
4 oz. sharp cheddar cheese
whole wheat flour tortillas
or corn tortillas

Buy if you're out

1 head fresh garlic
frozen corn
frozen peas
sesame oil
low-sodium soy sauce
brown rice
saltine crackers
fresh pesto
fresh salsa
eggs

Apple Sausage and Red Potatoes

A most interesting variation for ground turkey.

Preparation time: 40-45 minutes
Servings: 3
Ingredients:

SUNDAY
January/February

8-10 baby red potatoes *(with 1 T. olive oil for cookie sheet)*

Apple Sausage Mixture

1 lb. ground turkey breast	1 clove garlic *(smashed and chopped)*
1 egg *(beaten)*	3 slices medium onion *(chopped fine)*
1/2 T. cinnamon	3/4 C. low-salt soda crackers *(crushed fine)*
dash of nutmeg	1/2 tsp. dry basil leaves

1 large apple *(cored and chopped into very small pieces)*

1 T. olive oil

1/2 C. white wine
1/2 C. chicken broth
2 T. flour mixed with 1/4 C. nonfat milk
4-5 turns fresh-ground black pepper
2 dashes ground nutmeg

1 large or 2 medium carrots *(peeled and sliced)*
1/2 lb. fresh broccoli *(cut in 3" stems)*

1/2 C. plain, nonfat yogurt *(stirred smooth)*

juice from 1/2 lemon mixed with 1 tsp. melted butter

Notes

- **Place potatoes, flat side down, on oiled cookie sheet in preheated 400 degree oven for 30 minutes.**
- **In large bowl, mix all Apple Sausage ingredients.** *You may mix thoroughly with hands or use food processor.*
- **Shape mixture into tubular lengths approximately 1" X 3" in size.** *(Don't expect the shaped sausages to be perfect in appearance, as the mixture will be a bit soft and sticky.)*
- **Place shaped sausages on large plate and microwave for 3 minutes. This will bind them so that they won't fall apart while browning.** *(If you don't have a microwave, set the shaped sausages in a shallow pan and bake them in the oven for 10 minutes with potatoes.)*
- **Place sausages in shallow fry pan with 1 T. oil and brown over medium-high heat.** *Be sure to turn them often.*
- **When thoroughly browned** *(5-10 minutes)* **lift out of pan and set aside.**
- **Add wine and chicken broth to fry pan and bring up any drippings over medium-high heat** *(gently rub bottom of pan with fork when wine comes to boil.).*
- **Shake flour and milk vigorously in container with tight-fitting lid until will blended. Slowly stir into broth mixture. It will thicken. Season with black pepper and nutmeg. Reduce heat and cook 5 minutes stirring often.**
- **Put carrots and broccoli in steamer basket in sauce pan with 1/2 C. water and steam 2 minutes, covered.**
- **Remove white sauce from heat and stir in yogurt.**
- **Serve on individual plates with 2 sausages on each plate and white sauce spooned over each sausage. Flank with potatoes and carrot/ broccoli mixture.**

Dress carrots and broccoli with lemon/butter mixture.

MONDAY

January/February

Fried Rice with Barbecued Pork

Here's a quick and delicious meal. Hopefully you will have "quick cooked" rice in the morning before work.

Preparation time: 20 minutes

Servings: 2-3

Ingredients:

1 tsp. sesame oil
1/2 C. broth
2 C. cooked rice
6-8 slices barbecued pork *(chopped into small chunks)*
2 stalks celery *(washed and chopped)*
4-5 green onions *(chopped)*
1 large clove garlic *(smashed and chopped) or 1 tsp. prepared garlic*
1 6 oz. can bamboo shoots *(drained)*
4 T. low-salt soy sauce
1/4 C. frozen corn
1/4 C. frozen peas
5-6 mushrooms *(sliced)*
2 Roma tomatoes *(chopped)*

- **Chop all vegetables and pork before you start.**
- **Place oil, broth, rice, pork, celery, onions, and garlic in large non-stick fry pan or wok and stir 2 minutes over high heat.**
- **Add bamboo shoots, soy sauce, frozen corn and peas and stir 2 minutes.**
- **Add mushrooms and stir 2 minutes.**
- **Stir in tomatoes just before serving.**

If you can, eat with chopsticks.

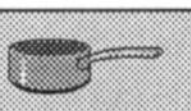

"Quick cook" some rice in the morning before work. *(see page 6)*

Do you have 6-8 slices barbecued pork? You can find barbecued pork at most grocery delis.

Leftover Night

It's time to clean out the leftover "goods" while they're still good!

TUESDAY

January/February

Preparation time: 20 minutes
Servings: 2-3
Ingredients:

leftover Red Sauce
leftover pasta
Fried Rice
leftover Apple Sausage
whatever you have in the fridge

Notes

- **If you need to cook a little extra pasta, put some water on to boil.**
- **Perhaps a couple fresh green salads will freshen up the leftovers.**
- **Enhance some leftover pasta with "Pesto Toast"**
  Mix 1 tsp. pesto and 1 tsp. butter in small bowl.
  Spread over 3 slices of toast.

A tip for heating up leftover pasta:

Boil some water. Put leftover pasta in a bowl and cover with boiling water. Let stand for 3-5 minutes while getting other leftover items together. Drain pasta in a colander just prior to serving.

Pasta side dish from leftovers:

- **Cook 2 C. dry pasta or noodles. Drain and rinse.**
- **In large bowl, mix 1 T. olive oil, 1/4 C. chicken broth, 3 chopped green onions, 1 clove garlic** *(smashed and chopped),* **and 3 fresh basil leaves** *(chopped).*
- **Microwave, covered, at full power 1 minute.**
- **Chop 1 Roma tomato and add to liquid.**
- **Toss pasta in liquid until well coated.**

Enjoy your leftover evenings. It saves you piles of money and reduces waste. Whatever you do, don't go out to dinner tonight! This is the best of "fast food" and it's free.

A trivia note:

80% of Americans eat at a fast-food restaurant once a month.

25% of us eat there every day.

Source: *CSPI Fast-Food Guide, Revised* (Center for Science in the Public Interest), Suite 300, 1875 Connecticut Ave. NW, Washington DC, 20009

WEDNESDAY
January/February

Notes

Taco Salad

Taco Salad at your local restaurant is possibly one of the fattest choices on the menu. This version goes together quickly and won't round out your day.

Preparation time: 15-20 minutes
Servings: 3-4
Ingredients:

1/4 C. Red Sauce *(see page 15)*

1/2 lb. ground turkey breast
1 T. olive oil
2 slices medium yellow onion *(chopped)*
1 clove garlic *(smashed and chopped)*
1 tsp. oregano leaves
1/2 tsp. ground cumin
1 T. mild chili powder
dash of Tabasco®

1/2 green pepper *(cut in 1" cubes)*
1 clove garlic *(smashed and chopped)*
2 slices yellow onion *(quartered)*
1 T. chili powder
1/4 C. broth or water

6-8 leaves washed red leaf lettuce
1/2 head chopped iceberg lettuce

sharp cheddar cheese
2-3 Roma tomatoes *(chopped)*

flour or corn tortillas

1/2 C. plain, nonfat yogurt *(stirred smooth)*
salsa

- **Make a fresh batch of Red Sauce.** *(Use 1/4 C. for this meal and reserve the rest.)*
- **Sauté ground turkey in olive oil along with onion, garlic, and spices in large non-stick fry pan over medium-high heat. Sauté 5 minutes stirring constantly. Add 1/4 C. Red Sauce. Cover, reduce heat to low, and cook an additional 5 minutes.**
- **When meat is done, remove from pan, place in bowl, and set aside.**
- **Using same fry pan sauté green pepper, garlic, and onions with chili powder and broth. Sauté 2 minutes over high heat. Remove from pan and set aside.**
- **Place 2 washed leaves red leaf lettuce on each plate as bed for salad. Top with chopped iceberg lettuce.**
- **Divide meat and sautéed vegetables onto beds of lettuce.**
- **Garnish with a grating of sharp cheese and chopped tomato.** *Go easy on the cheese! Only two or three draws across the grater per salad are needed.*
- **Warm tortillas by setting them, one at a time, in large fry pan** *(for about 30 seconds per side)* **over medium-high heat.**
- **Spoon yogurt and salsa over salad to suit your taste.**

Serve with tortillas on the side.

Tortellini with Pesto "Cream" Sauce

THURSDAY

January/February

Here's a new twist for tortellini. Once again, the cream sauce isn't so rich that it makes you feel overstuffed at the end of the meal.

Preparation time: 25 minutes
Servings: 2-3
Ingredients:

8 oz. fresh tortellini or 1 1/2 C. dry

1 C. broth
1 slice onion *(chopped)*
2 cloves garlic *(smashed and chopped)*
3 T. corn starch dissolved in 1/4 C. water
2 T. Parmesan cheese
dash of Tabasco®

green salad fixings

1/2 C. plain, nonfat yogurt *(stirred smooth)*
1 1/2 T. pesto

3 Roma tomatoes *(chopped)*
3-4 T. fancy-shred Parmesan cheese

- **Place pasta water on to boil in large kettle.**
- **Drop tortellini into boiling water.** *Cook fresh tortellini 10-12 minutes. Note: If you're using fresh tortellini, make sauce before cooking tortellini. If you're using dry tortellini, put tortellini on to cook before preparing sauce.*
- **Place broth, onion, and garlic in small sauce pan and bring to boil. Reduce heat to low and cook 5 minutes. Thicken with corn starch/water mixture. Add Parmesan and Tabasco®. Cook, uncovered, an additional 5 minutes. Remove from heat.**
- **Make green salads while sauce and pasta cook.**
- **Drain and rinse pasta.**
- **Stir yogurt and pesto until smooth and add to thickened broth. Do not return to heat.**
- **Serve on individual plates with white sauce spooned over top of tortellini.**

Garnish with fresh chopped tomatoes and Parmesan. Not bad for a 25 minute effort! Serve with green salad on the side.

Notes

FRIDAY
January/February

Notes

Pasta with Tomato/Basil "Cream" Sauce

Similar to marinara but using fresh basil and fresh tomato. Most refreshing!

Preparation time: 25 minutes
Servings: 2-3
Ingredients:

Sauce
- 1 C. vegetable broth
- 2 cloves garlic *(smashed and chopped) or 1 tsp. commercially prepared chopped garlic*
- 1 T. dry oregano
- 1/4 C. fresh basil leaves *(chopped)*
- 2 thin slices medium yellow onion *(chopped)*
- a few dashes of Tabasco® sauce *(optional)*

- 2 T. corn starch dissolved in 1/3 C. water

- one boneless, skinless chicken breast
- one clove garlic *(smashed and chopped)*
- 1 T. olive oil
- 1/2 C. water

- fixings for green salad

- 2 C. dry penne pasta *(whole wheat if you can find it)*

- 6-8 Roma or slicing tomatoes *(chopped)*
- 1/2 C. plain, nonfat yogurt *(stirred smooth)*

- 2-4 T. fancy-shred Parmesan cheese
- 2 T. fresh parsley *(chopped)*

- **Place large kettle filled 2/3 full of water over high heat.**
- **Mix first six ingredients in sauce pan. Bring to boil over medium-high heat.**
- **Reduce heat to medium. Thicken sauce with corn starch mixture. Cook 5 minutes.**
- **Sauté chicken breast and garlic in oil over medium-high heat until brown on both sides. Reduce heat to medium, add 1/2 C. water, cover, and cook 5 minutes.**
- **While breast is cooking, throw together salads. (Make them on individual plates.)**
- **Slip dry pasta into boiling water. Cook 8 minutes. Drain and rinse.**
- **Stir chopped tomatoes into sauce.**
- **Remove chicken breast from pan and chop. Add to sauce.**
- **Stir yogurt until creamy smooth. Add to sauce, blending thoroughly, and remove from heat.**
- **Divide pasta on two** *(or three)* **plates.**

Cover each serving with 1/2 to 3/4 cup sauce. Sprinkle 1-2 T. Parmesan cheese and fresh, chopped parsley over each serving.

SHOPPING DAY

SATURDAY

February/Week One

It's shopping day!

I will occasionally make an excursion to my local warehouse food store for a very disciplined shopping trip. I buy boneless, skinless chicken breasts in 4 lb. bags, as well as large bags of frozen, cooked shrimp, and chicken/turkey sausage. I also pick up jumbo (5 oz.) containers of dried oregano and basil leaves and large bags of fancy-shred Parmesan cheese.

If you try this bulk shopping idea, take the following steps when you arrive home. Cut the sausages into individual links and freeze them in a large zipper-top freezer bag.

Put some of the Parmesan in the fridge in a 1 pint storage container with a tight-fitting lid and freeze the rest. This is much cheaper than buying Parmesan at the grocery store.

The large bags of shrimp and chicken are most handy to have around and, once again, offer substantial savings when bought in this manner.

The dry spices will keep for next to eternity!

If you buy some items in bulk, be sure to cross them off the weekly list.

Notes

GROCERY LIST

Produce

one 6" zucchini
2 large russet baking potatoes
2 medium yellow onions
1 1/2 lb. fresh mushrooms
2 green bell peppers
2 red bell peppers
1 large carrot
1/8 lb. fresh broccoli
one bunch celery
one head bok choy
green salad fixings
8 Roma tomatoes
2 fresh lemons
1-2 tart apples

Frozen Foods

Meat/Fish/Poultry

1 lb. turkey breast fillets
1 lb. boneless, skinless chicken breasts

Canned or Dry Foods

six 15 oz. cans chicken broth
one 6 oz. can sliced water chestnuts
one 6 oz. can sliced bamboo shoots
1 lb. dry navy beans
12 oz. dry multi-colored spiral pasta
one large thin-crust Boboli®
1/2 C. package whole, blanched almonds
a loaf of your favorite hearty bread

Chilled Foods and Dairy

plain, nonfat yogurt
4-6 oz. sharp cheddar cheese

Buy if you're out

1 head garlic
white pepper
ground cloves
brown rice
whole wheat tortillas

SUNDAY
February/Week One

Notes

White Bean Chili

This is a delicious and unique chili. I'm offering it as a weekend entree because it will take 1 1/2 - 3 hours cooking time. Once you have beans cooked, the preparation time will only be about 30 minutes. Like all soups, it's best when it has time to "rest" before eating. (Save 1 1/2 C. chili for Tuesday's dinner)

Preparation time: 30-40 minutes *(once beans are cooked)*
Servings: 3-6
Ingredients:

4 C. cooked white navy beans
a loaf of your favorite hearty bread

1 lb. turkey breast fillets *(cubed)*
3 cloves garlic *(smashed and chopped) or 2 tsp. prepared garlic*
45 oz. chicken broth *(3 cans)*

1 medium onion *(chopped)*
1 green bell pepper *(chopped)*
1 red bell pepper *(chopped)*
2 T. dried oregano leaves
2 tsp. ground white pepper
1 T. ground cumin
1/4 tsp. ground cloves

4 T. flour mixed with 1/2 C. nonfat milk

Red Paste
1 C. Red Sauce
1 T. chili powder
2 tsp. ground cumin
1/4 tsp. cayenne pepper
1 clove garlic *(smashed and chopped)*

2 C. plain, nonfat yogurt *(stirred smooth)*

- **Cook beans as described.** *(see page 15)*
- **Wrap bread in foil and place in warm oven.**
- **Brown turkey with 1 tsp. of the garlic and 1/4 C. of broth in large heavy-bottomed kettle. It will take about 7 minutes over medium-high heat. When liquid boils away, keep stirring until turkey meat is golden brown.**
- **Remove pan from heat. Add all remaining broth, beans, onion, peppers, and spices. Return kettle to burner and bring to boil over high heat. Reduce heat to low and cook 1/2 hour.**
- **Shake flour and milk in container with tight lid until all lumps have disappeared. Turn up heat under kettle and return chili to boil. Slowly add flour mixture to boiling chili, stirring constantly. Once thickened, reduce heat to low and cook 10 minutes.**
- **Make "Red Paste" by mixing all ingredients in small bowl and cooking, covered, in microwave 2 minutes.** *If you don't have a microwave, mix ingredients in small sauce pan and cook over medium-low heat 5 minutes. Stir occasionally to prevent burning.*
- **When ready to serve, remove kettle from heat and stir in yogurt. Serve in individual bowls with a swirl** *(1 heaping tablespoon)* **of "Red Paste" per bowl.**

Serve with a slice of your favorite warm bread.

Chicken Almond Stir Fry

A most satisfying stir fry! You will use "quick cooked" rice prepared this morning before work.

Preparation time: 30 minutes
Servings: 3-4
Ingredients:

2 boneless, skinless chicken breast *(chopped into 1/2" cubes)*
1 T. vegetable oil
1/4 tsp. sesame oil
3 slices medium onion *(sliced in 1/8" thick slices and chopped)*
2 cloves garlic *(smashed and chopped)*

1/8 lb. broccoli *(cut in 2" lengths)*
2 stalks bok choy *(cubed)*
one 6 oz. can sliced water chestnuts *(drained)*
2 T. low-sodium soy sauce
one 6 oz. can sliced bamboo shoots *(drained)*
one 15 oz. can low-sodium chicken broth

6 mushrooms *(sliced)*

1/4 C. whole almonds *(toasted under broiler)*

5 T. corn starch mixed with 1/4 C. water

2-3 C. cooked rice

- **Chop raw chicken and set aside in bowl. *Important note: thoroughly wash, rinse and dry cutting board after chopping chicken before continuing to chop vegetables. I usually pour boiling water over the board after chopping raw meat.***
- **Place oils in large heavy-bottomed sauce pan or wok over high heat. Sauté onion, garlic, and chopped chicken** *(about 5 minutes)* **stirring constantly.**
- **Toss in broccoli, bok choy, drained water chestnuts, 1 T. soy sauce, bamboo shoots, and 1/4 C. broth. Sauté 2 more minutes.**
- **Add mushrooms and a little more broth. Sauté another minute.**
- **Remove all ingredients from pan with perforated ladle or spoon and set aside.**
- **Toast almonds.**
- **Using same pan, mix remaining broth and 1 T. soy sauce. Bring to boil and thicken with corn starch/water mixture. Reduce heat and cook 3-4 minutes.**
- **Add vegetables, meat and almonds to sauce and toss until everything is thoroughly coated. Serve immediately over warmed rice on individual plates.**

Remember! Stir fry tastes better with chopsticks!

Notes

"Quick cook" some rice before work this morning. *(see page 6)*

TUESDAY
February/Week One

Notes

Baked Potato with Chili

A theme and variation on an old standby.

Preparation time: 15-20 minutes
Servings: 2
Ingredients:

2 large russet baking potatoes
(washed, rubbed with olive oil and poked with a fork)
frozen corn
1 C. leftover White Bean Chili from Sunday
3/4 C. plain, nonfat yogurt *(stirred smooth)*
sharp cheddar cheese

- **Prepare potatoes in the morning prior to work and set your oven for "time bake" so they will have been cooking for 1 hour when you arrive home in the evening.** *(You may also cook them in the microwave. Cook for three 5-minute cycles at full power. Turn the potatoes to a different position after each cycle.)*
- **Place corn in sauce pan with a little water over medium-high heat. Bring to boil, cover and remove from heat, or microwave in covered dish 1 1/2 minutes on high.**
- **Warm leftover White Bean Chili.**
- **Stir yogurt and set out cheese with grater.**

Top split potatoes with chili, yogurt and corn. Garnish with a few gratings of sharp cheddar cheese.

If you have "time bake" on your oven, wash potatoes and place in oven this morning before work. Set to begin cooking 1 hour before you arrive home tonight.

Spiral Pasta with Pesto "Cream" Sauce

WEDNESDAY

February/Week One

Another variation on cream sauce pasta. Save 1/2 cup of sauce for tomorrow night.

Preparation time: 25 minutes
Servings: 3
Ingredients:

Notes

1 carrot *(peeled and sliced)*
1 C. vegetable broth or chicken broth
1/2 C. white wine

6 medium mushrooms *(sliced)*
2 slices medium yellow onion *(quartered)*
1 large clove garlic *(smashed and chopped)*
- or - 1/2 tsp. prepared chopped garlic
fresh-ground black pepper

1/2 green pepper and 1/2 red bell pepper *(chopped in 1" squares)*
one 6" long zucchini *(cut in 1/4" rounds)*

1 1/2 C. dry multi-colored spiral pasta

1/2 C. broth
2 T. corn starch *(dissolved in 1/8 cup water)*
2 dashes of Tabasco®

3/4 C. plain, nonfat yogurt
2 T. pesto

3 T. fancy-shred Parmesan
1 large Roma tomato *(chopped) use for garnish*

- **Place pasta water on to boil in large kettle.**
- **Sauté carrot in 1/4 C. broth and wine. Sauté 3 minutes. Remove from pan.**
- **Sauté mushrooms, onions, and garlic 2 minutes in same pan. Season with 4 turns of fresh-ground pepper. Remove from pan and set aside with carrots.**
- **Sauté peppers and zucchini using another 1/8 C. broth if needed. Sauté 3 minutes, remove from pan, and set aside with other veggies.**
- **Drop pasta into boiling water and set timer for 8 minutes. Drain and rinse.**
- **Put leftover broth from sautéing and any remaining broth into pasta kettle and bring to boil. Reduce heat and gradually stir in corn starch mixture. It will thicken. Add Tabasco® and cook over low heat 5 minutes.**
- *Reserve 1/2 C. thickened White Sauce and place in container with tight fitting lid in fridge.*
- **Stir yogurt and pesto together until smooth. Microwave mixture 25 seconds on high to remove chill, and stir once more.**
- **Add all vegetables and pasta to thickened sauce. Return to boil and remove from heat.**
- **Stir yogurt mixture into vegetable sauce. Blend thoroughly.**
- **Spoon onto individual serving plates in generous portions.**

Garnish with Parmesan and tomatoes. Encore!

THURSDAY
February/Week One

Notes

White Pizza and Salad

You'll be glad you saved the White Sauce from last night.

Preparation time: 25 minutes
Servings: 2
Ingredients:

1 cooked, boneless, skinless chicken breast *(sliced in thin slices)*
1 T. olive oil
1 large clove garlic *(smashed and chopped)*
or 1/2 tsp. prepared chopped garlic

1 Boboli® shell or frozen pizza shell

1/2 C. leftover White Sauce
2 T. fancy-shred or grated Parmesan cheese
1 tsp. dry oregano leaves
1/2 tsp. dry basil leaves
1 dash of Tabasco®

2 slices medium yellow onion *(quartered)*
1/2 red bell pepper *(sliced in thin slices and chopped)*
6 medium mushrooms *(sliced)*
5 T. fancy-shred Parmesan cheese

fixings for a green salad

- **Preheat oven to 400 degrees.**
- **Sauté chicken breast in oil and garlic over medium-high heat in small sauté pan.**
- **Cook about 5 minutes per side turning every 2 minutes to prevent burning. If it starts to get too dark, add 1/4 cup water to pan and reduce heat. When cooked, set breast on cutting-board and slice in thin slices.**
- **Place Boboli® directly on oven rack in center of oven and cook 3 minutes.** *(Set a timer so you don't forget.)*
- **Place White Sauce in a bowl with 2 T. Parmesan, spices, and Tabasco®. Cover bowl and cook in microwave 1 minute on high.**
- **Remove Boboli® from oven and spread White Sauce on crust.**
- **Top with chicken, veggies, and remaining Parmesan. Return to oven 8-10 minutes.**
- **Prepare green salads on individual plates while pizza is cooking.**
- **Remove pizza from oven and cut in 8 wedges while hot.**

Serve the Pizza on individual serving plates two slices at a time with salad on the side.

Leftover Night

Let's do leftovers again!

Preparation time: 20 minutes
Servings: 2-3
Ingredients:

leftover White Chili
leftover pasta
leftover Chicken/Almond Stir Fry
whatever you have in the fridge

- ***Perhaps a couple fresh green salads will freshen up the leftovers.*** *If you make green salads, core and chop a tart apple. Sprinkle 1/2 chopped apple over each salad.*

- ***A fresh loaf of your favorite hearty bread*** *is always a hit with leftovers.*

Friday works well for leftover night if you're planning to go out to a movie or an evening of socializing.

FRIDAY

February/Week One

Notes

SATURDAY

February/Week Two

SHOPPING DAY

***When buying mushrooms**, put them in a paper bag for storage in the fridge. They will stay fresh longer stored in paper.*

***Drink a large glass of water** just before you go to the grocery store. It will curb your appetite.*

***Many people overlook the value of walking** as a means of aerobic exercise. Thirty minutes of walking before dinner can be most helpful to release the tensions of the day. It will also serve to stimulate your metabolism. Drink a large (16 oz.) glass of water shortly before you begin the walk and, if you're hungry, eat half an apple.*

***Leave the TV off during dinner.** Studies have shown that watching TV actually slows down the metabolism.*

Notes

GROCERY LIST

Produce

8-10 baby red potatoes
2 medium russet potatoes
2 medium yellow onions
1 large carrot
1 lb. fresh mushrooms
2 green bell peppers
2 red bell peppers
1/8 lb. broccoli
1 head Romaine lettuce
1 head red or green leaf lettuce
6-8 Roma tomatoes
one large cucumber
1 tart apple
1 ripe banana *(save for next Sat. muffin recipe)*
1 lemon

Frozen Foods

frozen concentrated apple and orange juice
16 oz. frozen green beans
vanilla nonfat frozen yogurt
frozen pie cherries *(if canned are unavailable)*

Meat/Fish/Poultry

1/2 lb. turkey breast fillets
turkey bacon
1/2 lb. ground turkey breast
5 boneless, skinless chicken breasts

Canned or Dry Foods

one 29 oz. can tomato sauce
two 15 oz. cans chicken broth
two 15 oz. cans white beans
one 16 oz. can sour pie cherries
12-16 oz. dry lasagna noodles
16 oz. dry penne pasta
8 oz. fresh fettuccine
old-fashioned oatmeal
wheat germ
1/2 C. package chopped walnuts
1/2 C. package sliced almonds
vanilla extract
dried rosemary
one 6 oz. bottle cherry juice or
12 oz. cranberry juice
4-6 oz. chocolate sauce
a loaf of hearty Italian bread

Chilled Foods and Dairy

1 dozen eggs
1 pint part skim Ricotta cheese
8 oz. part-skim mozzarella cheese

Buy if you're out

1 head garlic
1 bunch fresh parsley
sesame oil
low-sodium soy sauce

Lasagna

SUNDAY

February/Week Two

Here is a good weekend recipe. It will take about 40 minutes to assemble and about 45 minutes to cook. Let the lasagna cool for about 15 minutes before cutting and serving.

Preparation time: 40 minutes *(45 minutes cooking time)*
Servings: 4-6
Ingredients:

Italian Turkey Sausage
1 T. olive oil
1 lb. ground turkey breast
2 slices medium yellow onion *(chopped)*
2 tsp. dry basil leaves
1 tsp. dry oregano leaves
1/2 tsp. ground anise
2 large cloves garlic *(smashed and chopped)*
dash of Tabasco® sauce

1 C. ground Italian Turkey Sausage *(see above)*

1 1/2 C. Red Sauce *(see page 15)*

five 18" dry lasagna noodles or 7 standard dry noodles

1/2 C. plain, nonfat yogurt
1/2 C. part skim or lowfat Ricotta cheese
1 egg
1 tsp. corn starch

1 T. olive oil
8 sliced fresh mushrooms
6 oz. part-skim mozzarella
3 oz. shredded Parmesan

fixings for a green salad

a loaf of your favorite Italian bread

Notes

- **Place large kettle filled 2/3 full of water on to boil.**
- **Cook Italian sausage while you wait for water to boil.**
- **Assemble Red Sauce if you don't have leftovers.**
- **Slide noodles into boiling water and set timer for 10 minutes.**
- **Remove sausage from heat when cooked and set aside.**
- **Blend yogurt, Ricotta cheese, egg, and corn starch with electric mixer, or in food processor.**
- **Rub a 9" X 13" glass baking dish with olive oil and layer ingredients as follows:**
  1 layer of noodles
  1/2 C. Italian Sausage
  1/2 C. Red Sauce
  1/2 C. Ricotta cheese mixture
  all mushrooms
  another layer of noodles
  5 oz. of the mozzarella
  1/2 C. sausage
  1/2 C. Red Sauce
  1/2 C. Ricotta cheese mixture
  another layer of noodles
  1/2 C. Red Sauce
  remaining mozzarella and Parmesan
- **Cook on center rack of oven, uncovered, 40 minutes at 350 degrees.**
- **Make green salads while lasagna is cooking.**
- **Remove lasagna from oven and cool for 15 minutes before cutting.**
- **Wrap bread in foil and place in oven while lasagna cools.**

Light some candles and have a nice glass of red wine.

MONDAY
February/Week Two

Notes

Pick up a loaf of your favorite hearty bread today.

Hot Chicken Salad

Lighter fare after last night's heavy Italian dinner.

Preparation time: 20 minutes
Servings: 2
Ingredients:

1 boneless, skinless chicken breast
1 T. olive oil
1 clove garlic *(smashed and chopped)*

1/4 C. broth
1/8 lb. broccoli *(chopped in 1" pieces)*

Dressing
1/4 C. orange juice
1 clove garlic *(smashed and chopped)*
1/2 tsp. basil leaves
2 T. olive oil
1 T. balsamic vinegar
1/2 tsp. sesame oil

4 leaves Romaine lettuce
4 leaves green or red leaf lettuce
1/2 green pepper *(cut in thin slices)*
2 slices yellow onion *(quartered)*
2-3 Roma tomatoes *(chopped)*
1 tart apple *(cored, and chopped in small pieces)*

a loaf of hearty bread

- **Sauté chicken breast in oil and garlic in non-stick pan over medium-high heat 4 minutes per side.**
- **Add broth and chopped broccoli. Sauté another 2 minutes. Remove pan from heat and set aside.**
- **Assemble dressing in glass bowl. Cover and microwave on high 40 seconds.**
- **Tear lettuce into large bite-sized pieces on two dinner plates and top with raw vegetables and apple.**
- **Slice chicken into thin strips and arrange on salads with hot broccoli.**

Top with warm salad dressing and serve with a slice of your favorite bread.

Tyrolean Stew

TUESDAY
February/Week Two

Time to warm your bones on a cold winter night.

Preparation time: 30 minutes
Servings: 3-4
Ingredients:

2 medium russet potatoes *(unpeeled and quartered)*
1 T. olive oil

1/2 lb. turkey breast fillet *(cubed)*
1 T. olive oil
1 clove garlic *(smashed and chopped)*

hearty bread *(leftovers from last night)*

1 C. leftover Red Sauce
1/8 teaspoon dried rosemary leaves *(crushed)*
1 large carrot *(peeled and sliced diagonally in 1/8" rounds)*
2 slices medium yellow onion *(quartered)*
1/2 green bell pepper *(cut in 1" cubes)*
1/2 red bell pepper *(cut in 1" cubes)*

Notes

- **Place potatoes on oiled cookie sheet in 400 degree oven.** *Set timer for 10 minutes.*
- **In large, heavy-bottomed sauce pan sauté cubed, raw turkey with oil and garlic over medium-high heat 5 minutes or until browned. Remove from pan and set aside to cool.**
- **Turn potatoes to another flat side and continue cooking.**
- **Wrap bread in foil and place in oven.**
- **Measure Red Sauce into same pan used for cooking turkey and add crushed rosemary leaves.**
- **Add carrot, bring to boil and cook 2 minutes, stirring occasionally.**
- **Add onion and boil 1 minute.**
- **Add peppers and boil 1 minute.**
- **Add cooked turkey and potatoes, cook 1 more minute.**

Serve in bowls with a roll or a slice of your favorite bread.

WEDNESDAY
February/Week Two

Notes

Chicken Breasts with Sour Cherry Sauce

What a lovely little Valentine's Day celebration. The quantities shown assume you're cooking for two.

Preparation time: 30 minutes
Servings: 2
Ingredients:

10 baby red potatoes
1 T. olive oil

2 boneless, skinless chicken breasts
1 clove garlic *(smashed and chopped)*
1 T. olive oil

1/2 lb. frozen green beans
1/2 red bell pepper *(cut in thin strips)*
1 T. lemon juice
1/4 C. chicken broth

1/4 C. dry white wine
1/4 C. juice from cherries *(if you use canned cherries)*
1/4 C. cherry or cranberry juice
Use extra 1/2 C. juice if using frozen cherries.
2 T. corn starch dissolved in 1/8 C. water
1/2 C. sour pie cherries

3 T. sliced almonds *(toasted under broiler)*

- **Place potatoes face down on oiled cookie sheet and slide into 400 degree oven. Cook 25 minutes.**
- **Sauté chicken breasts in garlic and oil in non-stick fry pan over medium-high heat** *(about 5 minutes per side).* **If pan gets dry, add water or white wine** *(about 1/4 C).* **When browned, place on an oven-safe plate in oven with potatoes** *(no more than 10 minutes).* **Set pan aside - you will use it as is.**
- **Place green beans, red pepper, lemon juice, and broth in heavy-bottomed sauce pan.** *Do not turn on burner yet.*
- **Pour wine into pan in which chicken was cooked. Rub bottom gently with fork over medium-high heat until wine boils. Add cherry or cranberry juice and return to boil.**
- **Thicken sauce with corn starch mixture and reduce heat to low. Cook 3 minutes.**
- **Add cherries and cook 1 more minute.**
- **Turn heat on high under beans now. When water boils, cook 7 minutes.**
- **Remove potatoes from oven and use oven to toast almonds.**
- **Stir almonds into beans.**
- **Serve breasts on individual serving plates. Spoon cherry sauce over breasts and flank breasts with potatoes on one side and beans on the other.**

Finish the meal with a dish of frozen nonfat vanilla yogurt. Go ahead and splurge! Put a tablespoon of your favorite chocolate sauce over it.

White Beans and Red Sauce

THURSDAY

February/Week Two

Following is a repeat performance of a wonder meal with a slightly different twist.

Preparation time: 20 minutes
Servings: 2
Ingredients:

Red Sauce
one 29 oz. can tomato sauce
1 T. dry basil
2 tsp. dry oregano
cayenne pepper to taste *(optional)*
4 slices medium onion *(chopped)*
2 cloves garlic *(smashed and chopped)*

1/2 red bell pepper *(chopped)*
1/2 green bell pepper *(chopped)*
3 slices medium yellow onion *(chopped)*

two 15 oz. cans white beans *(rinsed)*

2-4 T. fancy-shred Parmesan

fresh cucumber, tomato and sweet onion *(5 slices each per serving)*
low or nonfat salad dressing

Notes

- **Use leftover Red Sauce if you have it, or place tomato sauce, spices, onion, and garlic in covered sauce pan. Cook 10 minutes over medium-low heat.** *Measure 2 C. for this recipe and reserve the rest for another meal.*
- **Add peppers and onion to 2 C. sauce. Bring to boil and cook 2 minutes. Remove from heat.**
- **Warm beans in microwave** *(set for 1 minute on high),* **or pour boiling water over beans in large bowl and let stand five minutes. Drain.**

Spoon one cup cooked beans per serving in center of individual plates and cover beans with 1/2-3/4 C. Red Sauce per serving. Garnish with Parmesan. Overlap cucumber, tomato, and onion along edge of plate and dress with lowfat salad dressing.

FRIDAY
February/Week Two

Notes

Pasta "Donaldo"

This pasta has about 1/4 the fat of a conventional "Alfredo" style cream sauce: If you eat meat, you'll love the option with bacon. If you don't, you'll love the version with toasted pine nuts.

Preparation Time: 30 minutes
Servings: 4
Ingredients:

2 slices turkey bacon *(cooked crispy and chopped) You may substitute 5 T. chopped, toasted pine nuts if you are cooking vegetarian.*

16 oz. dry penne pasta *(you may also use mostaciolli or rigatoni)*

1/2 lb. mushrooms *(sliced)*
3 cloves garlic *(smashed and chopped)*
1/4 C. white wine

3/4 C. chicken or vegetable stock
1 T. butter

3 T. flour *(shaken with 1/3 C. nonfat milk)*

1/4 tsp. ground nutmeg
1/4 C. shredded part-skim mozzarella
1/4 C. fancy-shred Parmesan

fixings for green salad

1 C. plain, nonfat yogurt *(stirred smooth)*

fresh-ground black pepper to taste
1 T. fresh parsley *(chopped)*

- **Place pasta water in large kettle over high heat.**
- **Cook bacon as indicated.**
- **Place pasta in boiling water and cook 8 minutes.** *Set a timer so you don't forget.* **Drain and rinse.**
- **Sauté mushrooms in garlic and wine. Cook 2 minutes. Remove from pan. Set aside.**
- **Add stock to pan. Bring to boil. Add butter. Drain excess liquid from mushroom mixture into pan.**
- **Mix flour and milk in container with tight-fitting lid. Shake vigorously 30 seconds.**
- **Pour flour paste into boiling liquid, stirring constantly. Return to boil. Turn heat to low. Add bacon, nutmeg, and cheeses** *(reserve 4 T. Parmesan for garnish),* **and continue cooking 10 minutes. Stir occasionally.**
- **Prepare green salads.**
- **Stir yogurt until smooth. Microwave 20 seconds on high to bring to room temperature.**
- **Gently stir yogurt mixture into the cheese sauce.**
- **Re-rinse pasta with warm water to make sure it doesn't stick together. Drain thoroughly and stir into sauce.**

Serve on 4 individual plates and garnish with remaining Parmesan, fresh-ground black pepper, and parsley. Serve with crisp green salad on the side.

Cooking bacon

Wrap bacon slices in paper towel, set on plate and microwave two 2-minute cycles at high setting until crispy but not burned. If you don't have a microwave, put bacon in shallow pan covered with foil and bake 20 minutes in 400 degree oven. Lay bacon on fresh paper towel after cooking.

SHOPPING DAY

SATURDAY

February/Week Three

Check your larder. Let's go shopping! Be sure you are keeping up on staples like rice and dry pasta.

This Saturday I have included a dinner for 4, a wonderful opportunity to entertain.

TRIVIA QUIZ

Q: *What are America's favorite vegetables?*

A: *Listed in their order of popularity: potatoes, iceberg lettuce, tomatoes, onions and carrots.*

U. S. Food and Drug Administration, Rockville, MD.

Notes

Banana/Walnut Muffins *(makes 1 dozen)*

- Preheat oven to 375 degrees.
- Mix in large bowl: 1 1/2 C. unbleached flour, 1/4 C. wheat germ, 1/2 C. old-fashioned oats, 1/4 C. granulated sugar, 2 tsp. baking powder, 1/2 C. chopped walnuts.
- In a separate, smaller bowl beat 1 egg plus 2 egg whites, 2/3 C. milk, 2 T. vegetable oil, 1 tsp. vanilla extract, 1 ripe *(mashed)* banana and 1/8 tsp. grated lemon rind.
- Stir all ingredients together *(wet to dry)* and place in muffin tins which have been sprayed with vegetable oil spray. (Makes a dozen.)

Bake 30-35 minutes. *Serve with nonfat cream cheese. Stir cream cheese thoroughly and serve in a separate dish.*

GROCERY LIST

Produce

8-10 baby red potatoes
one large russet potato
6 medium russet potatoes
2 medium yellow onions
1 lb. fresh mushrooms
2 red bell peppers
4 large carrots
1/2 lb. fresh broccoli
green salad fixings
2 bags prewashed spinach
one bunch fresh parsley
4 Roma tomatoes
fresh ginger root
celery
1 fresh lemon
10-12 dried apricots

Frozen Foods

Meat/Fish/Poultry

15-16 oz. fresh halibut fillets (3 fillets)
6 boneless, skinless chicken breasts
1 lb. ground turkey breast
1/2 lb. turkey breast fillets

Canned or Dry Foods

one 29 oz. can tomato sauce
four 15 oz. cans chicken broth
one 6 oz. can baby shrimp
one 6 oz. can minced clams
one 6 oz. can apricot nectar
12 oz. dry whole wheat penne pasta
8 oz. fresh fettuccine
1 small jar capers
1/2 C. package slivered almonds
1 small jar Italian or Greek olives
1 bottle beer

Chilled Foods and Dairy

shredded Parmesan
fresh pesto

Buy if you're out

1 head fresh garlic
frozen corn
brown rice
ground anise
powdered mustard
paprika

SUNDAY

February/Week Three

Notes

Jaegersnitzel

A delicious old-world supper on a Sunday evening.

Preparation time: 40 minutes
Servings: 2-3
Ingredients:

2-3 C. cooked rice

1 turkey breast fillet *(cut into 1" cubes)*
1 T. olive oil
2 cloves garlic *(smashed and chopped)*

1/2 medium onion *(sliced in 1/2" slices - quartered)*

one 15 oz. can chicken broth
1 large carrot *(peeled and sliced in 1/8" rounds)*
8-10 mushrooms *(thick sliced)*

1 T. paprika
1/4 tsp. white pepper
1/8 tsp. cayenne pepper
1/4 tsp. crushed rosemary leaves
1/4 tsp. dry mustard
1/4 C. beer

3 T. corn starch dissolved in 1/4 C. water

3/4 C. plain, nonfat yogurt *(stirred smooth)*

- **Place rice on to cook as you begin preparations.**
- **In large, heavy-bottomed sauce pan, sauté cubed turkey with oil and garlic. Sauté over medium-high heat 5 minutes - until golden brown.**
- **Add onions and sauté another 2 minutes. Remove from pan and set aside.**
- **Add broth and carrots to same pan. Bring to boil and cook 2 minutes. Add mushrooms and cook 1 more minute. Remove from pan and set aside with meat.**
- **Add all spices and beer to broth and boil 2 minutes. Thicken with corn starch mixture.**
- **Return meat and vegetables to broth mixture and cook 5 minutes on low heat, stirring occasionally.**
- **Remove from heat. Stir in yogurt.**

Serve over cooked rice on individual plates.

Gingered Halibut

You'll find this fish dinner easy to prepare and most satisfying. Cook an extra fillet for later in the week.

Preparation time: 30 minutes
Servings: 2
Ingredients:

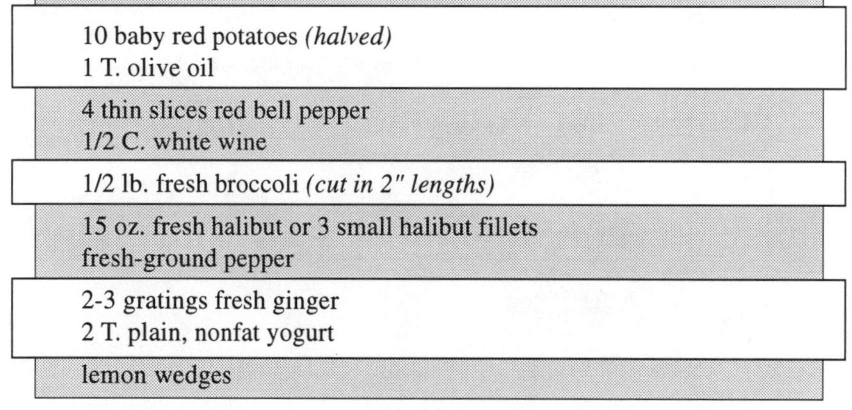

10 baby red potatoes *(halved)*
1 T. olive oil
4 thin slices red bell pepper
1/2 C. white wine
1/2 lb. fresh broccoli *(cut in 2" lengths)*
15 oz. fresh halibut or 3 small halibut fillets
fresh-ground pepper
2-3 gratings fresh ginger
2 T. plain, nonfat yogurt
lemon wedges

- **Place potatoes on oiled cookie sheet in 400 degree oven. Set timer for 20 minutes.**
- **Sauté pepper slices in wine 1 minute. Remove peppers from pan and set aside.**
- **Place broccoli in steamer basket over water in medium-sized, covered sauce pan.** *Do not turn on burner yet!*
- **Place fillets in wine left over from sautéing peppers. Season with fresh-ground black pepper and poach over medium-high heat 4 minutes per side.**
- **Stir ginger into yogurt.**
- **Turn halibut in pan and spread yogurt mixture over two fillets. Top with red pepper strips. If pan is dry, add 1/2 C. water or white wine. Cover and cook 4 minutes.**
- **Turn heat on high under broccoli. When water boils, cook only 2 minutes, covered.**

Serve halibut on center of plate flanked by broccoli and potatoes. Garnish with lemon wedge. Save one fillet for fish chowder on Wednesday.

MONDAY

February/Week Three

Notes

If you've waited to buy fresh halibut fillets, pick them up on the way home from work today.

TUESDAY
February/Week Three

Penne Pasta with Mushroom Sauce

Ah, the wonders of mushrooms! A great vitamin-laden pasta dish with both mushrooms and red bell pepper.

Preparation time: 30 minutes
Servings: 2-3
Ingredients:

1/2 lb. dry penne pasta

1/2 lb. mushrooms *(sliced - chop 4 mushrooms into tiny pieces)*
3 cloves garlic *(smashed and chopped)*
1/2 red bell pepper *(sliced in thin slices about 1" long)*
2 thin slices medium yellow onion *(chopped fine)*
1/4 C. white wine

1 C. chicken or vegetable stock
3 T. flour *(shaken with 1/2 C. nonfat milk)*
fresh-ground black pepper

green salad fixings

3 T. shredded Parmesan

1/2 C. plain, nonfat yogurt
dash of Tabasco®

2 T. Parmesan
1 T. fresh parsley *(chopped)*

- **Cook pasta in large heavy-bottomed kettle 8-10 minutes. Drain and rinse.**
- **Use pasta kettle to sauté all mushrooms, garlic, pepper, and onion in wine. Sauté 3 minutes and lift mushroom mixture out of pan.**
- **Add broth and bring to boil.**
- **Place flour and milk in small container with tight-fitting lid and shake vigorously for 30 seconds until well blended.**
- **Slowly pour flour mixture into boiling liquid, stirring constantly. Season with a few turns black pepper. Cook 5 minutes.**
- **Prepare green salads on individual plates.**
- **Add Parmesan and mushrooms to white sauce. Return to boil.**
- **Remove white sauce from heat. Add pre-stirred yogurt and Tabasco®.**

Gently stir pasta into white sauce. Serve immediately with green salad. Garnish with Parmesan and parsley.

Notes

Fish Chowder

Use the leftover piece of halibut from Monday night.

Preparation time: 30 minutes
Servings: 3-4
Ingredients:

a loaf of your favorite bread

two 15 oz. cans chicken broth
1 clove garlic *(smashed and chopped)*
1 medium russet potato *(cubed in 1/2" pieces)*
1 small yellow onion *(chopped)*
2 stalks celery *(chopped)*
1/4 C. frozen corn
1 large carrot *(chopped)*
one 6 oz. can minced clams
one 6 oz. can baby shrimp or 4 oz. frozen shrimp
leftover halibut
1 bay leaf
1 tsp. dry oregano leaves
several dashes Tabasco®

4 T. flour *(shaken with 1/4 C. nonfat milk)*

green salad fixings

1 C. yogurt *(stirred smooth)*

- **Wrap bread in foil and place in warm oven.**
- **Place broth, garlic, all vegetables, seafood** *(with juice from cans)*, **spices, and Tabasco® in large 8-quart sauce pan over high heat and bring to a boil. Reduce heat to medium-low. Cover and cook 10 minutes.**
- **Shake flour and milk mixture in small container with tight-fitting lid for 30 seconds to blend thoroughly. Stir flour mixture slowly into broth. Cover and cook another 10 minutes.**
- **Make a crisp green salad.**
- **Stir in yogurt just prior to serving.**

Don't forget the warm bread.

WEDNESDAY

February/Week Three

Notes

Pick up a loaf of your favorite hearty bread today.

THURSDAY

February/Week Three

Notes

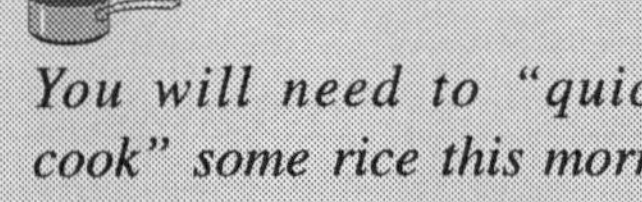

You will need to "quick cook" some rice this morning before work. (see page 6)

Loaded Rice

An encore of one of my favorite recipes.

Preparation time: 25 minutes
Servings: 2
Ingredients:

8-10 baby red potatoes or 1 large russet potato
1 T. olive oil

1/2 lb. mushrooms *(sliced)*
1/4 red bell pepper *(thin-sliced)*
1 T. olive oil
1 large clove garlic *(smashed and chopped)*
1/4 C. white wine
2 slices medium onion *(quartered)*

3/4 C. chicken or vegetable broth
3 T. corn starch dissolved in 1/8 C. cold water

1 C. plain, nonfat yogurt
1 T. pesto
dash of Tabasco®

1 1/2 C. cooked brown rice

2 Roma tomatoes *(chopped)*

- **Preheat oven to 400 degrees.**
- **Wash and halve baby red potatoes. If using russet potato, wash and slice** *(unpeeled)* **in 1/2" slices. Place potatoes, flat side down, on cookie sheet oiled with one tablespoon olive oil.**
- **Sauté sliced mushrooms and bell pepper in oil with garlic, wine, and onion** *(about 4 minutes).* **When done, remove mushroom mixture from pan with perforated spoon. Set aside.**
- **Add broth to pan. Return to boil.**
- **If cooking russet potato slices, turn them now.**
- **Slowly stir corn starch mixture into boiling liquid. Reduce heat to low. Cook 5 minutes, stirring often.**
- **Add mushrooms to thickened mixture. Return to boil. Remove from heat.**
- **Stir yogurt, pesto, and Tabasco® together until smooth. Microwave 30 seconds on high. Stir again.**
- **Warm 1 1/2 C. cooked rice 2 minutes on high in microwave on individual serving plates.**
- **Remove potatoes from oven. If using baby reds, push them into rice on individual plates. If using russets, chop into 1" pieces before sprinkling over rice.**
- **Stir yogurt mixture into thickened mushroom sauce.**

Pour sauce over potato/rice mixture and garnish with fresh chopped tomato. Enjoy!

Pasta Putanesca

FRIDAY

February/Week Three

This pasta is similar to Bolognese. Just a few extra goodies to give it a kick.

Preparation time: 30 minutes
Servings: 2-3
Ingredients:

Italian Turkey Sausage
- 1 T. olive oil
- 1 lb. ground turkey breast
- 2 slices medium yellow onion *(chopped)*
- 2 tsp. dry basil leaves
- 1 tsp. dry oregano leaves
- 1/2 tsp. ground anise
- 2 large cloves garlic *(smashed and chopped)*
- dash of Tabasco®

green salad fixings

- 1 1/2 C. Red Sauce *Use leftovers or make a new batch.* *(see page 47)*
- 1/8 C. red wine
- 2 cloves garlic *(smashed and chopped)*
- 2 T. green capers *I like the larger capers, they're softer and more flavorful.*
- 5 Italian or Greek olives *(chopped)*

8 oz. fresh egg fettuccine

3 T. fancy-shred Parmesan

Notes

- **Place pasta water on to boil in large kettle.**
- **Place all Italian Sausage ingredients in fry pan and cook until browned over medium-high heat** *(about 10 minutes)*. **Remove from heat and set aside.**
- **Prepare green salads on individual plates.**
- **To 1 1/2 C. Red Sauce, add wine, 1/3 of cooked Italian Sausage, extra 2 cloves garlic, capers, and olives.** *Reserve remainder of sausage for another time.*
- **Cover sauce and place over low heat while finishing dinner preparations.**
- **Drop fresh pasta into boiling water. Cook 2 1/2 minutes. Drain and rinse.**
- **Divide pasta onto plates and cover with Putanesca Sauce.**

Garnish with Parmesan cheese. You've done it again!

SATURDAY

February/March

Elegant Dinner for Four

Saturday night and a chance to entertain at home.

Preparation time: 40 minutes
Servings: 4
Ingredients:

10 dried apricots *(leave 4 whole and chop the rest)*

6 medium russet potatoes *(peeled and quartered)*
2 cloves garlic *(smashed/peel removed-no need to chop)*
3/4 C. water

4 boneless, skinless chicken breasts
1 T. olive oil
2 cloves garlic *(smashed and chopped)*

1 tsp. butter
1/8 C. nonfat milk

1/4 C. white wine
1/2 C. apricot nectar
2 T. corn starch mixed with 1/8 C. water

1/2 C. slivered almonds *(toasted under broiler)*

1/4 C. chicken broth
juice from 1/2 lemon
2 bags prewashed spinach
1 red bell pepper *(cut in thin strips)*

paprika

- **Place all apricots in small covered dish with 1/2 C. water. Cook at full power in microwave 1 minute. Set aside.** *If you don't have a microwave, put all ingredients in a small sauce pan. Bring it to a boil over high heat. Remove immediately from heat, cover and set aside.*
- **Place potatoes, garlic, and water in large kettle. Bring to boil, reduce heat to medium and cook, covered, 15 minutes.**
- **In large fry pan, brown chicken breasts over medium-high heat with oil and garlic. Reduce heat to low, cover and cook 5 minutes per side. Turn often so they don't get too dark.**
- **Mash cooked potatoes** *(with garlic)* **in cooking kettle with butter and milk. Cover.**
- **Remove chicken breasts from pan and turn heat up to medium-high. Add wine to pan. As wine begins to boil, rub bottom of pan gently with fork to bring up brown drippings. Add apricots** *(with water)* **and nectar. When liquid returns to boil, thicken with corn starch/water mixture. Return breasts to pan. Reduce heat to low and cook 5 minutes.**
- **Toast almonds under broiler and set aside.**
- **Mix broth and lemon in large, heavy-bottomed kettle. Sauté 1 bag spinach at a time with half the red pepper strips. Turn until thoroughly wilted. Remove from pan. Repeat. Serve immediately. Sprinkle with toasted almonds.**

Serve on individual plates with a generous swirl of spinach in the center flanked by chicken and a large helping of potatoes. Spoon apricot sauce over breasts (with one whole apricot on each breast). Garnish potatoes with a dash of paprika. Light a candle and open a bottle of your favorite Chardonnay. This is a meal worth celebrating!

Notes

____
____
____
____
____
____
____
____

A change in routine

Here's a lovely dinner for two couples or for the family. The change in shopping day and routine should be welcome as well.

SHOPPING DAY

SUNDAY
February/March

Tonight is leftover night! *You probably have lots to use up, so be sure you don't procrastinate.*

The recipe for Monday calls for hazelnut tortellini. This is a specialty tortellini featured by one of the fine vendors in Seattle, Washington. If you can't find it, don't worry. The recipe works quite well with cheese tortellini. Buy 6-8 hazelnuts, toast them lightly under the broiler, chop, and sprinkle over the top of the pasta.

You will notice that I suggest brown rice when buying rice. Brown rice has twice as much fiber as white rice. In addition, it beats white rice in nearly every nutrient including zinc, magnesium, protein, vitamin B6 and selenium.

Are you trying to lose weight *and having difficulty succeeding?*
Two suggestions:

- *You might be ignoring the "trigger foods." Do you have a weakness for certain fattening foods like ice cream or potato chips? If so, find lowfat substitutes like nonfat frozen yogurt or pretzels. Also, think back to your childhood when you developed your eating habits. What occasions "trigger" cravings for fat-filled foods? Once you've sorted this out, it may be easier to recognize and resist the cravings.*
- *If you are attending a social gathering where alcohol is served, try having one drink and then switch to soda water or non-alcoholic beer.*

Notes

GROCERY LIST

Produce

2 medium yellow onions
1/2 lb. fresh mushrooms
2 green bell peppers
2 red bell peppers
2 large carrots
celery
1/8 lb. fresh broccoli
one head green cabbage
iceberg lettuce
one bunch green onions
green salad fixings
10-12 Roma tomatoes
1 large slicing tomato
1 fresh lemon

Frozen Foods

frozen concentrated orange juice
16 oz. frozen peas

Meat/Fish/Poultry

1 lb. turkey breast fillets
5 boneless, skinless chicken breasts
2 frozen orange roughy fillets *(do not thaw)*
6 frozen scallops *(do not thaw)*

Canned or Dry Foods

one 29 oz. can tomato sauce
two 15 oz. cans chicken broth
12 oz. dry whole wheat spiral pasta
8 oz. fresh cheese or hazelnut tortellini
1/2 C. package pecan halves
6-8 hazelnuts
a loaf of your favorite Italian bread

Chilled Foods and Dairy

4 oz. sharp cheddar cheese
whole wheat tortillas
plain, nonfat yogurt

Buy if you're out

1 head garlic
fresh ginger root
1 bunch fresh parsley
brown rice
brown sugar
red cooking wine
white cooking wine
fresh pesto

MONDAY
February/March

Notes

Hazelnut Tortellini

Something special in tortellini if you can find it. If you can't find it, use cheese tortellini and 6-8 hazelnuts from the bulk food section. Toast nuts, chop fine, and sprinkle over pasta as a garnish.

Preparation time: 20 minutes
Servings: 2
Ingredients:

a loaf of Italian bread

1 C. broth
1/4 C. white wine
1 slice onion *(chopped)*
1 clove garlic *(smashed and chopped)*

3 T. corn starch dissolved in 1/8 C. water

2 T. fancy-shred Parmesan cheese
dash of nutmeg

1/3 C. plain, nonfat yogurt *(stirred smooth)*

8 oz. fresh hazelnut or cheese tortellini

green salad fixings

3 Roma tomatoes *(chopped)*
3-4 T. fancy-shred Parmesan cheese
6-8 hazelnuts *(toasted and chopped)*
Use hazelnuts if cooking cheese tortellini.

- **Wrap bread in foil and place in warm oven.**
- **Place pasta water on to boil in large kettle.**
- **Place broth, wine, onion, and garlic in small sauce pan and bring to boil. Cook 5 minutes. Thicken with 3 T. corn starch mixed with 1/8 C. water. Cook 5 more minutes. Stir in Parmesan and season with dash of nutmeg. Return to boil and remove from heat.**
- **Stir yogurt into thickened broth. Do not return to heat.**
- **Drop tortellini into boiling water. Reduce heat to medium.** *Fresh tortellini will cook in 7-10 minutes. Set a timer so you don't overcook.* **Drain and rinse.**
- **Make green salads while tortellini cooks.**
- **Serve on individual plates with White Sauce spooned over top.**

Garnish with fresh-chopped tomatoes, Parmesan, (and chopped hazelnuts). Serve with warm Italian bread and crisp salad on the side.

Don's Fajita Pollo (Chicken Fajitas)

TUESDAY

February/March

This casual meal remains a favorite. It works well if people are eating in shifts or on the run.

Preparation time: 30 minutes
Servings: 2-4
Ingredients:

1 lb. turkey breast fillets *(sliced in 1/8" strips)*
1 T. olive oil
2 cloves garlic *(smashed and chopped)*
1 tsp. chili powder
1/4 tsp. ground cumin

1/4 C. chicken broth
1/2 green bell pepper *(seeded and cut in 1" chunks)*
1 red bell pepper *(seeded and cut in 1" chunks)*
3 slices medium sweet onion *(quartered)*
1 tsp. chili powder
1/4 tsp. ground cumin

1 package whole wheat flour tortillas

4 ripe Roma tomatoes *(chopped)*
1/2 head iceberg lettuce *(chopped)*
6 oz. grated cheddar cheese
salsa
1 C. plain, nonfat yogurt *(stirred smooth)*

Notes

- **Place turkey strips over medium-high heat in shallow 10" non-stick fry pan with oil, garlic, 1 tsp. chili powder, and 1/4 tsp. ground cumin. Sauté 5 minutes.**
- **Remove meat from pan and set aside.**
- **Add broth, peppers, onion, and remaining spices to same pan and sauté 3 minutes. Set aside.**
- **Warm 2 tortillas per person in microwave by placing all tortillas between two serving plates and cooking two 40-second cycles, or warm in 350 degree oven10 minutes in shallow, covered pan.**

Set out chopped tomatoes, lettuce, grated cheese, salsa, meat filling, veggie filling, and yogurt in separate bowls. Let people build their own fajitas.

Buenos!

WEDNESDAY
February/March

Notes

Pasta with Scallops

Very simple. Like pasta marinara only with scallops.

Preparation time: 30 minutes
Servings: 2-3
Ingredients:

6 frozen scallops *(thaw just prior to cooking)*
1 T. olive oil
3 slices medium onion *(quartered)*
1 clove garlic *(smashed and chopped)*
2 stalks celery *(chopped in 1" pieces)*
1/4 C. chicken broth

1 1/2 C. Red Sauce *(use leftovers or whip up a new batch, page 47)*
dash of Tabasco®
1/4 C. red wine

green salad fixings

8 oz. fresh fettuccine

3 T. fancy-shred Parmesan

- **Place pasta water on to boil in large kettle.**
- **Place scallops in large fry pan with oil, onion, garlic, celery, and broth. Sauté 3 minutes over medium-high heat.**
- **Add 1 1/2 C. Red Sauce, Tabasco®, and wine. Return to boil. Remove from heat.**
- **Prepare green salads.**
- **Drop pasta into water to cook. Cook 2 1/2 minutes. Drain and rinse.**

Divide pasta onto plates. Spoon Red Sauce with scallops over each serving. Garnish with Parmesan cheese and serve with crisp green salad.

Gusta Bravo! (It tastes great!)

Teriyaki Chicken

THURSDAY

February/March

Here's a new recipe for your enjoyment. I love the taste of teriyaki and this one is low in both fat and salt. Save some rice for tomorrow's meal.

Preparation time: 30 minutes
Servings: 2-3
Ingredients:

Teriyaki Sauce
- 1/2 C. white wine
- 1/4 C. orange juice
- 2 cloves garlic *(smashed and chopped)*
- 2 thin slices onion *(chopped very fine)*
- 6 T. low-sodium soy sauce
- 1 tsp. sesame oil
- 1/2 tsp. freshly grated ginger
- 2 T. brown sugar

- 2-3 C. cooked brown rice *("quick cooked" this morning)*
- 1/8 C. water

- 2-3 boneless, skinless chicken breasts
- 1 T. vegetable oil
- 1/2 C. water

- 1/2 head cabbage *(cored and chopped)*
- 2 large carrots *(peeled and sliced diagonally)*
- 1/8 lb. broccoli *(cut in 2" pieces)*
- 2 slices medium onion *(quartered)*
- 1/4 C. orange juice
- 1/4 C. Teriyaki Sauce *(from recipe above)*

- 1 T. fresh parsley *(chopped)*

Notes

"Quick cook" some rice before work this morning. Make a double batch and save half for tomorrow. *(see page 6)*

- **Measure all Teriyaki Sauce ingredients into small sauce pan. Place over medium-high heat and bring to boil. Reduce heat to low and cook, covered, 5 minutes.** *Set aside 1/4 C. to dress vegetables.*
- **Place cooked rice plus 1/8 C. water in covered, oven-safe, bowl in 250 degree oven.**
- **Place chicken breasts in sauté pan with vegetable oil over medium-high heat. Baste chicken with Teriyaki Sauce. Cook 3 minutes and turn breasts. Reduce heat to medium and baste again. Add 1/2 C. water to pan, cover, and set timer for 5 minutes.**
- **Place vegetables in medium-sized sauce pan with 1/4 C. orange juice. Bring to boil. Add 1/4 C. Teriyaki Sauce. Stir to coat all vegetables with sauce. Reduce heat and cook, uncovered, 5 minutes - stirring often.**
- **Turn chicken breasts and baste again with Teriyaki Sauce. Cook 2 minutes.**

Serve on individual plates with 1 C. rice per serving in center and chicken and vegetables on either side. Sprinkle fresh parsley over rice.

FRIDAY

February/March

Notes

Orange Roughy with Pesto

Remember the days when families had fish on Friday? Well, it's Friday, so, for the sake of nostalgia, we'll have fish. Here's another variation on orange roughy. I love this fish!

Preparation time: 25 minutes
Servings: 2
Ingredients:

8 pecan halves *(toasted under broiler)*
4 green onions *(chopped)*
1 1/2 C. rice *(extra from yesterday)*
1/2 C. chicken broth

1/2 lb. frozen peas
1 tsp. butter
1/4 C. chicken broth

6 thin slices red bell pepper
1 large clove garlic *(smashed and chopped)*
1/4 C. white wine

2 roughy fillets *(thawed)*

2 tsp. fresh pesto

- **Place pecans, onions, and rice in bowl with broth and cook, covered, in microwave 3 minutes on high.**
- **Place peas, butter, and broth in covered sauce pan.** *(No need to add extra butter.) Wait to turn on burner.*
- **Place bell pepper, garlic, and wine in non-stick fry pan over medium-high heat and sauté 2 minutes. Lift red pepper out and set aside.**
- **Slide fish into wine/garlic mixture over medium-high heat. When liquid boils, cook 3 minutes per side.** *Set timer so you don't forget.* **If wine boils away, add another 1/3 C. liquid** *(wine, water or broth)*.
- **Turn burner on high under peas. When water boils, cover and cook 2 minutes. Remove from heat.**
- **Turn fish, spread with pesto, lay pepper strips over fillets and cook 2 more minutes.** *Add another 1/3 C. liquid if necessary.*
- **Arrange fish on individual serving plates flanked by peas on one side and rice on the other.**

Light a candle and enjoy a lovely dinner.

SATURDAY
March/Week One

SHOPPING DAY PLUS LEFTOVERS

It's shopping day!

You probably have lots of leftovers! Usually Saturday is a free night to cook whatever you wish, but tonight, use up those leftovers.

This week you will have a bean dish. Beans are an important staple for your diet. They're high in fiber, an excellent source of protein and loaded with important nutrients. The bonus is that they are inexpensive and have no fat.

Beans are particularly important in the diet of diabetics. They have complex sugars and digest slowly, thus controlling insulin production in the body.

My mother began my introduction to cooking by asking me to help cook beans. She left me a note with instructions on draining and rinsing. If you have a child at home, this is a great introduction.

Since you're cooking beans on Sunday, you can try a practice session with your helper to see how it goes.

When buying dry pasta, I often look for amaranth spaghetti. Amaranth is a most nutritious grain and the pasta is delicious. Try some if you can find it.

Notes

GROCERY LIST

Produce

one 6" zucchini
1 medium yellow onion
1 1/2 lb. fresh mushrooms
1 green bell pepper
1 red bell pepper
1 large carrot
1 acorn squash
1/2 lb. fresh broccoli
green salad fixings
8 Roma tomatoes
2 oranges
1 tart apple
2 fresh lemons
1 bunch fresh cilantro

Frozen Foods

Meat/Fish/Poultry

1 1/2 fresh true cod fillets *(you may wish to buy fresh fish on Thursday.)*
1 lb. turkey breast fillets
1/2 lb. ground turkey breast

Canned or Dry Foods

one 29 oz. can tomato sauce
one 15 oz. can chicken broth
one 6 oz. can chopped black olives
16 oz. dry whole wheat spaghetti
16 oz. whole wheat spiral pasta
1 lb. dry black beans *or two 15 oz. cans black beans*
one large thin-crust Boboli®

Chilled Foods and Dairy

plain, nonfat yogurt
nonfat milk

Buy if you're out

1 head garlic
1 bunch fresh parsley
frozen corn
1 jar garlic dill pickles
Worcestershire sauce
balsamic vinegar
whole wheat flour tortillas

SUNDAY

March/Week One

Notes

Black Bean Casserole

You will need cooked black beans for this meal. If you were unable to cook them during the day today, use canned black beans. One 15 oz. can will yield about 1 1/2 cups beans. When using canned beans, be sure to rinse them thoroughly to eliminate excess salt. Store 1/2 C. cooked beans in the fridge for Thursday's meal.

Preparation time: 30 minutes *(after beans are cooked)*
Servings: 3-4
Ingredients:

1/2 lb. ground turkey breast
1/2 medium yellow onion *(chopped)*
2 cloves garlic *(smashed and chopped)*
1 T. olive oil

1 C. tomato sauce
2 T. chili powder
1/2 tsp. ground cumin
1/8 C. fresh parsley *(chopped)*
1/8 C. fresh cilantro *(chopped)*

2-3 C. cooked black beans or two 15 oz. cans cooked black beans
save 1/2 C. beans for Thursday
1 C. cooked brown rice
1/2 green bell pepper *(chopped)*

whole wheat flour tortillas

2 Roma tomatoes *(chopped)*

2 oranges *(sliced for garnish)*

- **In large fry pan or cast iron skillet, sauté turkey, onion, and garlic in oil 5 minutes over medium-high heat.**
- **Add tomato sauce and all spices. Cover and cook another 5 minutes.**
- **Add beans, rice, and green pepper to tomato/meat sauce. Reduce heat to low and cook 5 minutes, stirring occasionally.**
- **Warm two tortillas per person 20 seconds at full power in microwave while bean mixture cooks.**
- **Add tomatoes to casserole just before serving.**
- **Serve on individual plates with sliced oranges on sides of plate as garnish.**

Serve with warm tortillas.

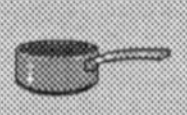

"Quick cook" rice during the day today. *(See "Quick Cooked" rice, page 6.)*

Cook beans during the day today. Follow the preparation steps for cooking beans *on page 15.*

Whole Wheat Pasta Prima Vera

MONDAY

March/Week One

Pasta prima vera with a slight variation. Tonight we will use whole wheat or amaranth pasta.

Preparation Time: 30 minutes
Servings: 2
Ingredients:

Red Sauce
29 oz. can tomato sauce
2 cloves garlic *(smashed and chopped)*
1 T. dry oregano
1 1/2 T. dry basil leaves
4 slices medium yellow onion *(chopped)*
a few dashes of Tabasco® sauce *(optional)*

12 oz. dry whole wheat or amaranth pasta

1 T. olive oil
1/4 C. broth *(use vegetable if you are cooking vegetarian)*
1/2 tsp. crushed garlic
1 large carrot *(peeled and sliced)*
1/2 green pepper *(cubed in 1" chunks)*
1 small zucchini 6" long *(cut in 1/8" rounds)*
2 slices medium onion *(quartered)*
6 medium mushrooms *(washed and sliced in 1/4" slices)*

1 1/2 C. Red Sauce

2 Roma tomatoes *(cut in 1" pieces)*

2-4 T. fancy-shred Parmesan cheese
4 T. chopped black olives

Notes

- **Place pasta water on to boil in large sauce pan.**
- **Make Red Sauce in medium-sized, covered sauce pan. Cook, covered, 10 minutes.**
- **Drop dry pasta into boiling water and cook 8 minutes.** *(Set a timer so you don't forget.)* **Drain and rinse with warm water.**
- **Measure olive oil, broth, and garlic into sauté pan. Begin with carrots and sauté 1 minute. Add green pepper, zucchini, onion, and mushrooms and sauté 2 minutes. Remove from pan and set aside.**
- **Measure 1 1/2 C. Red Sauce into same pan pasta was cooked in and bring to boil.** *Reserve remaining sauce for another meal.*
- **Return veggies, including Roma tomatoes, to pan. Return to boil and remove from heat.**
- **Microwave cooked pasta 1 minute at full power to reheat.** *If you don't have a microwave, measure 1 1/2 C. per serving and place in bowl with hot tap water for 2 minutes. Drain.*
- **Divide into two portions on separate plates and ladle veggie sauce over it.**

Garnish with Parmesan and chopped olives and serve immediately.

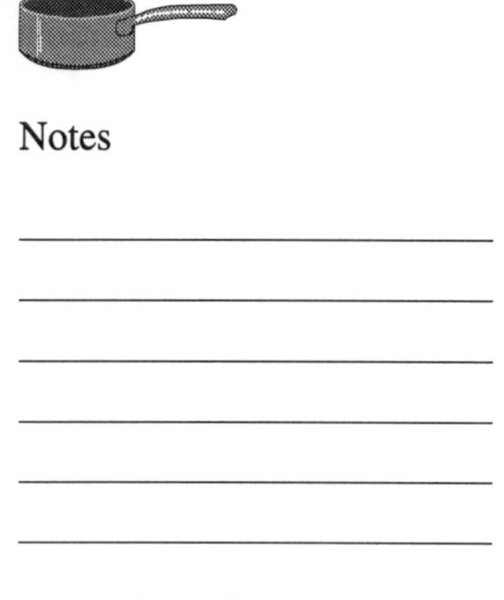

Notes

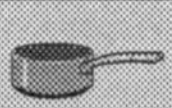

"Quick cook" some rice this morning before work. *(see page 6)*

Stroganoff

This is an example of homemade or "comfort food" that's low-in-fat yet tastes like the real deal. If you don't care for dill pickles, substitute 1/2 C. white wine for 1/2 C. broth. You may substitute egg noodles for the rice. On Saturday I asked you to purchase 1 lb. turkey breast fillets. It's easier to find in 1 lb. packages. This recipe uses only 1/2 lb. Freeze the remainder (if not previously frozen) for Irish Stew on page 78.

Preparation time: 30 minutes
Servings: 2-3
Ingredients:

1/2 lb. turkey breast fillets *(thin sliced)*
1 small yellow onion *(chopped)*
2 cloves garlic *(smashed and chopped)*
1 T. olive oil

1/4 lb. mushrooms *(sliced)*

1/2 lb. broccoli *(cut in 2" lengths)*

1/2 C. chicken broth *(Substitute 1/2 C. wine if not using dill pickles.)*
3/4 C. nonfat milk
3 T. flour shaken with 1/4 C. nonfat milk
1 1/2 T. paprika
2 large or 3 small dill pickles *(chopped)*

2 C. cooked brown rice or 2 C. cooked egg noodles

1 T. lemon juice

1/2 C. plain, nonfat yogurt *(stirred smooth)*

1/2 lemon *(cut in wedges)*

- **If you're having egg noodles with this dish, put water on to boil now.**
- **In large fry pan or cast iron skillet, sauté turkey, onion, and garlic in oil 5 minutes over medium-high heat.**
- **Add mushrooms. Sauté another 2 minutes.**
- **Remove mixture from pan and set aside. Set pan on cool burner.**
- **Place broccoli in steamer basket over water in covered sauce pan. Set aside.**
- **Pour broth in fry pan over medium-high heat and swirl with fork to bring up drippings.**
- **Add 3/4 C. milk and bring to boil. Reduce heat to medium and remove pan from heat while you shake flour and milk mixture.**
- **Return pan to heat, bring to boil, and slowly stir in flour mixture.**
- **Add paprika and pickle. Reduce heat to low and cook 5 minutes. Stir occasionally.**
- **Warm rice or cook noodles now.**
- **Turn on burner under broccoli. When water boils, cover and cook 2 minutes.**
- **Add meat mixture and lemon juice to sauce. Cook 3 minutes. Stir occasionally.**
- **Stir yogurt into sauce just before serving.**

Serve over rice or noodles on individual plates with broccoli on the side. Place a wedge of lemon on each plate for broccoli.

Spiral Pasta with Mushroom Red Sauce

WEDNESDAY

March/Week One

Theme and variation on marinara sauce. Use whole wheat spirals if you can find them.

Preparation time: 25 minutes
Servings: 2-3
Ingredients:

Notes

16 oz. dry spiral pasta

3/4 lb. mushrooms *(sliced, select 4-6 and chop finely)*
1 clove garlic *(smashed and chopped)*
2 thin slices medium yellow onion *(quartered)*
1/8 C. white wine

1 C. leftover Red Sauce
1 clove garlic *(smashed and chopped)*

green salad fixings

2 T. Parmesan
2 T. fresh chopped parsley *(optional)*

- **Cook pasta in large heavy-bottomed kettle 8-10 minutes. Drain and rinse.**
- **Use pasta kettle to sauté all mushrooms, garlic, and onion in wine. Sauté 3 minutes over medium-high heat and remove with perforated spoon.**
- **Add leftover Red Sauce and garlic to pan. Bring to boil.**
- **Return mushrooms to pan with Red Sauce. Bring to boil and remove from heat.**
- **Make green salads on individual plates.**
- **Gently stir cooked pasta into Red Sauce with mushrooms.**
- **Serve immediately on individual plates.**

Garnish with Parmesan and parsley and serve with green salad.

Un risultato soddisfacente!

THURSDAY

March/Week One

Notes

True Cod with Black Bean Sauce

True cod is a delicious, robust fish. The bean sauce is a nice compliment to the flavor.

Preparation time: 35 minutes
Servings: 2
Ingredients:

10 baby red potatoes *(quartered)*

1 acorn squash

2 slices medium onion *(quartered)*
1/2 finely-chopped tart apple
2 T. lemon juice
1 tsp. brown sugar
dash of cinnamon

Black Bean Sauce
1/2 C. black beans *(held over from last Sunday)*
1 clove garlic *(smashed and chopped)*
1 thin slice medium yellow onion *(chopped)*
1 T. Worcestershire sauce
1/4 C. broth

1/2 lb. true cod fillets
1/2 C. white wine

- **Preheat oven to 400 degrees.**
- **Mix quartered potatoes and Potato Seasoning** *(see shaded insert)* **in medium-sized bowl. Toss with fork until well coated. Lift potatoes out of liquid and place on oiled cookie sheet in 400 degree oven.** *Set timer for 15 minutes.* **Turn potatoes when timer goes off and return to oven.**
- **Place whole squash in microwave and cook 2 minutes on high. Remove and pierce squash numerous times with fork. Return to microwave on plate and cook 5 minutes at full power. Let cool 5 minutes before continuing.**
- **Cut squash in half and remove seeds and pulp. Fill cavity with onion and apple. Drizzle lemon juice over each half and sprinkle with brown sugar and cinnamon. Microwave for 3 minutes at full power.** *If you don't have a microwave, cut in quarters, place in shallow pan, cover with apple/onion mixture, sprinkle with lemon juice, sugar, and cinnamon, cover with foil, and place in oven with potatoes. Cook 35-40 minutes until tender.*
- **Place all black bean sauce ingredients in blender or food processor. Blend thoroughly.** *You may also mash beans with a fork and blend in other ingredients by hand.* **Pour into small sauce pan. Bring to boil. Remove from heat.**
- **Place fish fillets in sauté pan with white wine. Bring to boil over high heat. Season with black pepper and cook 2 minutes. Turn fillets and cook 2 minutes. If pan cooks dry, add another 1/2 C. wine.** *If fillets are more than 1/2" thick, you may have to cook 3-4 minutes per side.* **Cover pan and remove from heat.**

Arrange fish on individual serving plates. Spoon 2 T. black bean sauce over each fillet. Place squash and potatoes on either side.

Potato Seasoning

1 tsp. chili powder
1/4 tsp. ground cumin
1/4 tsp. crushed oregano leaves
1 clove garlic (smashed and chopped)
1 thin slice medium yellow onion (chopped)
1 T. balsamic vinegar
1 T. olive oil

You may need to pick up fresh fish today.

Pizza and Salad

FRIDAY

March/Week one

This should use the last of your leftover Red Sauce.

Preparation time: 25 minutes
Servings: 2
Ingredients:

1 link Italian turkey or chicken sausage *(sliced into 1/8" rounds)*
large Boboli® shell or frozen pizza shell

3/4 C. Red Sauce
1 large clove garlic *(smashed and chopped)*
2 T. fancy-shred Parmesan cheese
1 dash of Tabasco®

2 slices medium yellow onion *(quartered)*
4-6 black olives *(chopped)*
6 medium mushrooms *(sliced in 1/4" slices)*
4 T. fancy-shred Parmesan
fixings for a green salad

Notes

- **Preheat oven to 400 degrees.**
- **Prick sausage several times with fork and wrap in paper towel. Place sausage in covered dish and microwave 2 minutes on high. Repeat.**
- **Place Boboli® directly on oven rack in center of oven and cook 3 minutes.** *(Set a timer so you don't forget.)* **Remove from oven.**
- **Place Red Sauce in small bowl with garlic, 2 T. Parmesan and Tabasco®. Cover bowl. Cook in microwave 2 minutes at full power.** *If you don't have a microwave, put ingredients in a small sauce pan and bring to a boil over medium-high heat. When it boils, cover and remove from heat.*
- **Spread Red Sauce on Boboli® crust.**
- **Arrange onions, olives, and mushrooms on top of Red Sauce and top with remaining Parmesan. Return to oven 8-10 minutes.**
- **Prepare green salads.**
- **Remove pizza from oven and cut in wedges while hot.**

Let cool 5 minutes before eating.

Serve Pizza on large serving plate in center of table with salads on the side. Light a candle and enjoy a nice glass of Chianti.

SATURDAY
March/Week Two

SHOPPING DAY

There is a rather interesting week of cooking ahead. You may wonder why the heavy emphasis on potatoes? It's in honor of St. Patrick's Day.

Actually there are few foods which give more nutritional value than a potato. One 6 oz. potato provides nearly twice as much potassium as a banana, over a third of the USRDA for vitamin C, and two thirds of the iron. Of course, it's a treasure chest of complex carbohydrates.

Continue that thought as you consider the baked potato and broccoli dinner scheduled for Friday. One cup of broccoli gives you 164% of the USRDA for vitamin C, 42% of the vitamin A, 24% of the folic acid, and 18% calcium.

Are you buying candles and flowers to enhance the celebration of your evening meal? Candlelight and color add such life to a table.

You ***are*** *reading the shopping list correctly. You'll need more chicken broth than usual this week.*

Notes

____

____

____

____

____

____

____

____

GROCERY LIST

Produce

one 6" zucchini
6 large russet potatoes
8-10 baby red potatoes
3 medium yellow onions
1 lb. fresh mushrooms
2 green bell peppers
2 red bell peppers
3 large carrots
1 lb. fresh broccoli
green salad fixings
1/2 lb. Roma tomatoes
1 lemon
1 lime

Frozen Foods

Meat/Fish/Poultry

4-6 oz. sirloin tip steak
turkey bacon
1 boneless, skinless chicken breast
6 large, cooked, shelled, frozen shrimp

Canned or Dry Foods

one 29 oz. can tomato sauce
five 15 oz. cans chicken broth
12 oz. dry whole wheat spiral pasta
8 oz. fresh fettuccine
1 lb. dry kidney beans *If you don't wish to cook beans, one 15 oz. can will do.*

Chilled Foods and Dairy

1 dozen eggs
shredded Parmesan
nonfat milk
fresh salsa

Buy if you're out

1 head garlic
celery
1 bunch fresh parsley
frozen corn
sesame oil
brown rice
stone-ground cornmeal
bay leaf
red cooking wine

Cajun Red Beans and Rice with Corn Bread

SUNDAY

March/Week Two

A slightly spicy and delicious meal to prepare when you have cooked beans and leftover rice. Today you'll cook all ingredients and you'll have extra beans, rice, and Red Sauce for another time. All three freeze beautifully.

Preparation time: 45 minutes *(after cooking beans and rice)*
Servings: 3-4
Ingredients:

1/2 green bell pepper *(chopped)*
8 medium mushrooms *(sliced)*
2 slices of a medium onion *(quartered)*
1 clove fresh garlic *(smashed and chopped)*
1 T. olive oil
1/4 C. broth

1/2 C. Red Sauce
a couple dashes of Tabasco®
1 T. chili powder
1 tsp. oregano
1 tsp. cumin

1 C. cooked brown rice
1 C. cooked red kidney beans

Optional:
6 medium cooked frozen shrimp
1/2 C. frozen corn

plain, nonfat yogurt

- **Begin cooking beans in morning.** *(page 15)*
- **Quick cook rice in morning.** *(page 6) Make a double batch. You'll use the leftovers on Tuesday.*
- **Make a batch of Red Sauce.** *(page 65)*
- **Prepare some corn bread.** *(See recipe insert this page.)*
- **Sauté vegetables together in large, heavy-bottomed sauce pan with garlic, oil, and broth 3 minutes. Remove from heat and set aside.**
- **Place 1/2 C. Red Sauce and Tabasco® in large sauce pan with spices. Cook over medium-low heat 10 minutes.**
- **Add rice, beans, and vegetables to pan with Red Sauce. Mix thoroughly, cover, and place over low heat.**
- **Add optional ingredients at this time.**
- **Add a dollop of plain, nonfat yogurt to each serving.** *(Stir yogurt prior to serving.)*

Serve with corn bread on the side.

Notes

Old-Fashioned Corn Bread

Place an oiled 10" cast iron skillet (or similar size baking pan) on center rack of preheated 400 degree oven. (Remove in 5 minutes or if pan begins to smoke.)
Mix the following together:
2 C. cornmeal
1- 1 1/4 C. nonfat milk
2 tsp. baking powder
1 egg
1 1/2 T. vegetable oil
- ***Pour batter into hot skillet.***
- ***Bake 20-25 minutes.***

Serves 4-6
Dense and tasty!

MONDAY

March/Week Two

Notes

Pick up a loaf of hearty bread today.

Potato Soup

What can I say! It's the week of St. Patrick's day. So we're into potatoes this week.

Preparation time: 30 minutes
Servings: 3-4
Ingredients:

hearty bread

4 large russet potatoes *(peeled and cut in 1" chunks)*
2 pieces cooked turkey bacon
1 clove garlic *(smashed and chopped)*
1 medium yellow onion *(chopped)*
1 large carrot *(chopped)*
2 stalks celery *(chopped)*
1/2 red bell pepper *(chopped)*
1 bay leaf
3 dashes Tabasco® sauce
1/4 C. frozen corn
two 15 oz. cans chicken or vegetable broth

1 C. nonfat milk
1 T. butter
5 T. flour mixed with 1/4 C. milk *(shaken until smooth)*

fresh-ground black pepper
2 T. fresh parsley *(chopped fine)*

3/4 C. plain, nonfat yogurt *(stirred smooth)*

- **Wrap bread in foil and place in warm oven.**
- **Place potatoes and all items above** *(in first box)* **in large heavy-bottomed sauce pan. Bring to boil over high heat. Reduce heat to low, cover, and cook 20 minutes.**
- **Add milk and butter - return to boil. Thicken with flour/milk mixture by slowly pouring it into liquid while stirring constantly.**
- **Add pepper and parsley. Reduce heat and cook 5 minutes.**
- **Stir yogurt in just prior to serving.**

Serve with hearty bread. Irish soda bread if you can find it.

Loaded Rice

TUESDAY

March/Week Two

Here's a new twist for Loaded Rice.

Preparation time: 25 minutes
Servings: 2
Ingredients:

8-10 baby red potatoes
1 T. olive oil

1 boneless, skinless chicken breast
1 T. olive oil
1 large clove garlic *(smashed and chopped)*
4 slices medium onion *(quartered)*

3/4 C. chicken or vegetable broth
1/4 C. white wine

3 T. corn starch dissolved in 1/8 C. cold water
dash of Tabasco®
1/2 red bell pepper *(chopped)*

1 C. plain, nonfat yogurt
1 T. pesto

1 1/2 C. cooked brown rice *(leftover from Sunday)*

2 Roma tomatoes *(chopped)*

Notes

- **Preheat oven to 400 degrees.**
- **Wash and halve baby red potatoes. If using russet potato, wash and slice** *(unpeeled)* **in 1/2" slices. Place potatoes, flat side down, on cookie sheet oiled with one tablespoon olive oil.**
- **Sauté chicken breast in oil with garlic and onion** *(about 4 minutes).* **When browned, remove chicken/onion mixture from pan. Set aside.**
- **Add broth and wine to pan. Return to boil.**
- **If cooking russet potato slices, turn them now.**
- **Slowly stir corn starch mixture into boiling liquid. Reduce heat to low, add Tabasco® and bell pepper. Cook 5 minutes - stirring often.**
- **Add chicken, garlic and onions to thickened mixture. Return to boil. Reduce heat to low, cover, and cook 5 minutes. Remove from heat.**
- **Stir yogurt and pesto until smooth. Microwave 30 seconds on high. Stir into thickened sauce.**
- **Warm 1 1/2 C. cooked rice 2 minutes on high in microwave on individual serving plates.**
- **Remove potatoes from oven. If using baby reds, push them into rice on individual plates. If using russets, chop into 1" pieces before sprinkling over rice.**

Pour sauce over potato/rice mixture and garnish with fresh chopped tomato.

Enjoy!

WEDNESDAY
March/Week Two

Notes

Leftover Night

Clean out the leftovers from last week!

Preparation time: 20 minutes
Servings: 2-3
Ingredients:

Red Beans and Rice
Potato Soup
leftover hearty bread

- **If you have leftover hearty bread, make some toast.**

Be sure to take advantage of leftover night. It's money in the bank. We're talking free food!

If you have leftover Stroganoff but no rice, use some leftover noodles. If cooking noodles, it's only 15 minutes 'til mealtime.

Are you having trouble finding fresh fish? *Don't worry! The safest fish you can buy is frozen fillets of cod, halibut, pollack, or other white fish like roughy. These fish live in cold, clean, deep ocean waters where they collect few toxins. Their harvest often is monitored for cleanliness, and the fish usually is frozen on board the boat. They are also low in fat.*
Working Woman, 230 Park Avenue, New York, NY 10169

Be careful about hot-dogs! *A foot-long hot dog sold in a convenience store has 520 calories and 27 gm. of fat. Hot dogs are also one of the leading causes of choking in toddlers.*
Good Ideas for Diet and Exercise, 1115 Broadway, New York, NY 10010
William Sears, MD , SanClemente, CA

Steak Strips and Pasta

THURSDAY

March/Week Two

Although I seldom eat red meat, this is one of my favorite pastas.

Preparation time: 25 minutes
Servings: 2-3
Ingredients:

2 thin slices medium yellow onion *(quartered)*
2 cloves garlic *(smashed and chopped)*
1/2 lb. fresh mushrooms *(sliced)*
1/2 C. chicken broth
1/4 C. red wine

8 oz. fresh fettuccine

1/2 tsp. sesame oil
1 T. olive oil
4-6 oz. steak *(cut into thin strips)*

green salad fixings

3 Roma tomatoes *(chopped)*
2 T. Parmesan
2 T. fresh chopped parsley *(optional)*

Notes

- **Place pasta water over high heat in large heavy-bottomed kettle.**
- **Place onions, garlic, and mushrooms in broth and wine. Sauté 3 minutes and remove all ingredients from pan. Set aside.**
- **Place pasta in boiling water and cook 2 1/2 minutes. Drain and rinse.**
- **Spread oils thoroughly around hot pan. Add steak strips and sauté over medium-high heat until browned** *(about 5 minutes).*
- **Prepare green salads.**
- **Return mushroom mixture to pan and reheat. Add pasta and toss** *(over heat)* **until liquid thoroughly coats pasta.**

Serve immediately on individual plates. Sprinkle tomato over each serving. Garnish with Parmesan and parsley, and serve with green salad.

Splendido!

FRIDAY

March/Week Two

Notes

Baked Potato with Broccoli

One last time this week. You guessed it. Potatoes!

Preparation time: 15-20 minutes
Servings: 2
Ingredients:

2 large russet baking potatoes
(washed, rubbed with olive oil, and poked with a fork)
2 slices turkey bacon *(cooked and chopped)*
1/2 lb. fresh broccoli *(cut in 2" lengths)*
3/4 C. plain, nonfat yogurt *(stirred smooth)*
salsa
sharp cheddar cheese
1/2 lemon *(cut in wedges)*

- **Bake potatoes 1 hour at 400 degrees or in microwave for three 5-minute cycles at full power.** *(Turn potatoes to a different position after each cycle.)*
- **Cook bacon.** *(see insert)*
- **Place broccoli in steamer basket in sauce pan with a little water. When water boils, cover pan and cook 3 minutes.** *Set a timer so you don't forget.* **Remove pan and uncover when timer goes off. Serve immediately.**

Split hot potatoes and place on serving plates. Top with bacon, yogurt, and salsa. Garnish with a few gratings of sharp cheddar cheese. Serve broccoli on same plate with a wedge of lemon.

Put potatoes in oven and set "time bake" in the morning before work. If you don't have "time bake," how about washing potatoes, rubbing them with oil, poking them with a fork, placing them in a shallow pan in oven, and leaving instructions for your helper to turn on the oven 1 hour before you arrive home.

If you have neither of the above, microwave the potatoes when you get home.

Cooking Bacon

Cook all the bacon in package.
Place 2 layers paper towel on serving plate.
Lay 4 strips bacon on towel.
Cover bacon with another towel.
Lay another 4 strips on towel. Repeat until you have 4 layers.
Cover with a second serving plate.
Microwave two 2-minute cycles on high, turning plate 90 degrees after each cycle.
Flip plates over so bottom plate is now on top and cook one more 2-minute cycle.
Lay bacon on fresh paper towels after cooking.
Select all under-cooked strips and cook one more minute.
Freeze extra cooked bacon in plastic bag.

SHOPPING DAY

SATURDAY

March/Week Three

On Wednesday evening I suggest cooking extra salmon, which will be used for the following night's meal. Be sure to set the extra cooked fish aside. I call these "purposeful leftovers."

What are your evening dining habits?
If you're a family, how often do you eat dinner together? How much time do you devote to eating dinner in the evening? This can be a valuable time to connect with each other and share some of the day's successes or frustrations. The following bits of trivia come from an article by Cari Nierenberg in the June '94 issue of Cooking Light magazine.

- *"Slightly more than half of American families eat dinner together every day."*
- *"In the average American household, dinner lasts about 30 minutes, and, in many families, less than 20."*
- *"A little more than 40% of families eat dinner together two to three times per week."*

How often do you eat dinner with the television on in the same room?
I do not feel television and dinner should be synonymous. Don't get me wrong, there are special events or programs when dinner and television can be companions. These should be the exception not the rule.

Yes, you are buying lots of spinach this week! *The frozen is for Tuesday's Thai Lime Fry, and the fresh is for spinach salad on Thursday.*

Notes

GROCERY LIST

Produce

2 large russet potatoes
2 medium russet potatoes
one 6" zucchini
3 medium yellow onions
1/2 lb. fresh mushrooms
1 green bell pepper
2 red bell peppers
4 large carrots
celery
1/4 lb. fresh green beans
1/2 lb. broccoli
2 bunches fresh spinach *(or 1 package fresh, prewashed spinach)*
green salad fixings
one large cucumber
one bunch green onions
one bunch fresh cilantro
one bunch fresh parsley
6-8 Roma tomatoes
1 tart apple
2 dozen pistachios
1 ripe cantaloupe
1 lemon
1 lime
1 package plain, firm tofu
hearty bread

Frozen Foods

frozen spinach

Meat/Fish/Poultry

1 1/2 lb. turkey breast fillets
1 lb. boneless, skinless chicken breasts
1 1/4 lb. fresh salmon fillets
(You may wish to buy fresh fish the day it is to be cooked.)

Canned or Dry Foods

four 15 oz. cans chicken broth
one 6 oz. can sliced water chestnuts
12 oz. dry spinach spiral pasta
8 oz. fresh cheese tortellini
1 small jar Italian or Greek olives
a loaf of hearty bread

Chilled Foods and Dairy

1 dozen eggs
plain, nonfat yogurt

Buy if you're out

1 head garlic
1/2 C. pine nuts
frozen peas
brown rice
dry dill weed
cayenne pepper
Dijon mustard

SUNDAY
March/Week Three

Notes

Irish Stew

I'm part Irish and this dish tastes a lot like the stew I remember eating when I was young. The difference being, that stew was made with beef. You're cooking a double recipe, since this dish tastes even better as leftovers.

Preparation time: 45 minutes
Servings: 3-4
Ingredients:

a loaf of your favorite hearty bread

1 lb. turkey breast fillets *(cut into 1" cubes)*
1 medium yellow onion *(coarsely chopped)*
3 cloves garlic *(smashed and chopped)*
2 T. olive oil

two 15 oz. cans chicken broth

1 green bell pepper *(chopped)*
2 large carrots *(cut in 1/4" thick rounds)*
2 stalks celery *(chopped in 1/2" pieces)*
2 large russet potatoes *(chopped in 1" cubes)*
1/4 lb. fresh green beans *(ends removed and cut in 1" lengths)*
1/4 tsp. dry rosemary leaves *(crushed fine)*
1 tsp. dry oregano leaves
1 tsp. dry basil leaves
1 large bay leaf

6 T. flour
1/2 C. milk
fresh-ground black pepper

SAINT PATRICKS DAY

- **Wrap bread in foil and place in warm oven.**
- **In large, heavy-bottomed sauce pan, sauté turkey, onion and garlic in oil 10 minutes. Sauté until golden brown.**
- **Remove meat from pan and set aside. Add broth and stir to bring drippings up from bottom of pan.**
- **Add vegetables and spices to broth, return meat to pan and bring to boil. Reduce heat to low. Cover and cook 20 minutes.**
- **Lift meat and vegetables out of pan and place in bowl. Return liquid to boil over medium-high heat. Thicken with flour/milk mixture which has been shaken together until smooth. When liquid thickens, reduce heat, season with generous amount of fresh-ground black pepper and cook 5 minutes.**
- **Remove bay leaf from broth. Return meat and vegetables to broth. Cover and cook over low heat 10 minutes.**

Serve in bowls with a warm slice of your favorite bread.

"Creamy" Spinach Spirals Prima Vera

MONDAY

March/Week Three

Tonight we revisit this delicious prima vera recipe.

Preparation time: 25 minutes
Servings: 3
Ingredients:

2 T. toasted pine nuts *(chopped)*

1 carrot *(peeled and sliced)*
1 C. vegetable broth or chicken broth

6 medium mushrooms *(sliced)*
2 slices medium yellow onion *(quartered)*
1 large clove garlic *(smashed and chopped)*
or 1/2 tsp. prepared chopped garlic
fresh-ground black pepper

1/2 green pepper *(chopped in 1" squares)*
1/2 red bell pepper *(chopped in 1" squares)*
one 6" long zucchini *(cut in 1/4" rounds)*

2 C. dry spinach spiral pasta

1/2 C. white wine
3 T. corn starch *(dissolved in 1/8 C. water)*
2 dashes of Tabasco®

3/4 C. plain, nonfat yogurt
2 T. pesto

3 T. fancy-shred Parmesan
1 large Roma tomato *(chopped, use for garnish)*

Notes

- **Place pasta water on to boil in large kettle.**
- **Toast pine nuts in shallow pan under broiler. It will take only a few minutes, so stay with them.** *(Toast extra! They store, unrefrigerated, in any container with tight-fitting lid.)*
- **Sauté carrot in 1/4 C. broth 2 minutes. Remove from pan.**
- **Sauté mushrooms, onions, and garlic 2 minutes in same pan. Season with 4 turns of fresh-ground pepper. Remove from pan and set aside with carrots.**
- **Sauté peppers and zucchini using another 1/8 C. broth if needed. Sauté 1 minute. Remove from pan and set aside with other veggies.**
- **Drop pasta into boiling water and cook 8 minutes. Drain and rinse.**
- **Pour white wine, leftover broth from sauté pan, and any remaining broth into pasta kettle and bring to boil. Reduce heat and gradually stir in corn starch mixture. It will thicken. Add Tabasco® and cook over low heat 5 minutes.**
- **Stir yogurt and pesto together until smooth. Microwave 20 seconds on high to take chill off, and stir once more.**
- **Add all vegetables and pasta to thickened sauce. Return to boil and remove from heat.**
- **Blend yogurt mixture into vegetable sauce.**
- **Spoon onto individual serving plates in generous portions.**

Garnish with Parmesan, tomatoes, and toasted pine nuts. Favoloso!

TUESDAY

March/Week Three

Notes

"Quick cook" rice in the morning before work. (see page 6)

Set spinach out to thaw in the morning before work.

Thai Lime Fry

This is a delicious and slightly exotic dish.

Preparation time: 30 minutes
Servings: 2
Ingredients:

1/2- 3/4 C. turkey breast fillets *(chopped fine)*
1 clove garlic *(smashed and chopped)*
1 T. vegetable oil

2 stalks celery *(chopped)*
2 slices medium onion *(chopped)*
1 large clove garlic *(smashed and chopped)*
1/2 C. broth
1/2 tsp. sesame oil

1/4 green pepper *(cut into cubes)*
1/4 red pepper *(cut into cubes)*
6 medium mushrooms *(sliced)*

1/4 C. cilantro *(chopped)*
juice from 1/2 lime
2 dozen pistachios *(shelled and chopped)*
1 package frozen spinach *(thawed and drained)*
a dash of cayenne pepper *(more if you like it hotter)*

2 C. cooked brown rice

2 Roma tomatoes *(chopped)*

- **Sauté chopped meat and garlic in oil 5 minutes over medium-high heat in large fry pan or wok until brown.**
- **Add celery, onion, garlic, broth, and sesame oil. Sauté 1 minute.**
- **Add peppers and mushrooms and sauté another 2 minutes. Remove from pan with perforated spoon and set aside.**
- **Add cilantro, lime juice, pistachios, spinach and cayenne to liquid in pan. Sauté 3 minutes.**
- **Prior to serving, warm rice on serving plates in microwave 1 minute on high.**
- **Return all ingredients to pan. Toss thoroughly.**
- **Add tomato just before serving.**

Serve over rice.

Poached Salmon with Baked Potato Fries

WEDNESDAY
March/Week Three

Another quick and delicious fish dinner with an extra piece of fish for tomorrow.

Preparation time: 30 minutes
Servings: 2
Ingredients:

Notes

2 medium russet potatoes
(with skins and cut in 1/2" thick French fry-shaped strips)
1 T. olive oil

1 large carrot *(peeled and chopped)*
1/4 C. broth

1 1/4 lb. fresh salmon fillet
1/2 C. white wine
1 clove garlic *(smashed and chopped)*

1/4 tsp. dry dill weed

3/4 C. frozen peas
2 T. fresh parsley *(chopped)*

- **Place potatoes on cookie sheet oiled with 1 T. olive oil. Place in 400 degree oven and set timer for 15 minutes.**
- **Place carrot in sauce pan with broth.** *Do not turn on heat yet.*
- **When timer goes off, turn potatoes over and return to oven.**
- **Divide salmon into 3 pieces and slide fillets into sauté pan with wine and garlic. Turn heat on high and cook 2 minutes when wine begins boiling. Add more liquid if necessary.**
- **Turn heat on high under carrots now. When water boils, cover, and cook 1 minute.**
- **Turn salmon with spatula and sprinkle two fillets with dry dill weed. Cover, reduce heat to medium, and cook 4 minutes.**
- **Add frozen peas and 1 T. fresh parsley to carrots. Return to boil and cook 1 minute. Cover and remove from heat.**

You may need to pick up a piece of fresh salmon on the way home from work tonight.

Serve salmon in center of individual plates. Sprinkle with leftover parsley. Place potatoes on one side and vegetables on the other. Save unseasoned fillet for tomorrow night.

THURSDAY

March/Week Three

Notes

Stop at the bakery today and pick up a fresh loaf of your favorite hearty bread.

Spinach Salad with Cold Salmon

Delicious light fare. I prepare this salad without eggs. A good substitute is thin slices of lightly sautéed tofu. Don't turn up your nose! Try it first! If you don't like it, no need to do it again! However, I find the tofu a satisfying substitute.

Preparation time: 25 minutes
Servings: 2
Ingredients:

hearty bread

2 bunches fresh spinach *(washed carefully and patted dry)*
You may also substitute one bag of prewashed spinach if your store carries it.
1/2 cucumber *(peeled, sliced in 1/4" rounds and quartered)*
3 green onions *(washed and chopped)*
1/2 red bell pepper *(thin sliced and quartered)*
4 Roma tomatoes *(chopped)*

1/2 C. tofu *(chopped)*
1 tsp. Dijon mustard
1/4 C. broth

Dressing
2 strips cooked turkey bacon *(chopped - use cooked bacon in freezer)*
2 T. balsamic vinegar
1 clove garlic *(smashed and chopped)*
2 tsp. Dijon mustard
6 T. chicken or vegetable broth
2 T. olive oil
2 T. white wine
fresh-ground black pepper *(to taste)*
1/2 tsp. sesame oil

1 tart apple *(cored and sliced)*
3-6 oz. leftover cooked salmon *(broken into pieces)*
2-3 T. fancy-shred Parmesan

- **Wrap hearty bread with foil and place in warm oven.**
- **Toss vegetables in large bowl.**
- **Sauté tofu with mustard and broth in small non-stick fry pan over medium-high heat. Sauté 2 minutes. Remove from pan with perforated spoon and place in bowl with vegetables. Toss.**
- **Combine dressing ingredients in same pan used to sauté tofu. Cook over medium-high heat 2 minutes. Let cool 5 minutes.**
- **Pour warm dressing into bowl with vegetables and toss again.**
- **Core and slice a tart apple and serve 1/2 sliced apple on small plate to the side of each salad.**
- **Serve salads on large individual plates topped with crumbled salmon and Parmesan.**

Serve with a warm slice of hearty bread.

Mustard-Glazed Chicken Breasts

FRIDAY

March/Week Three

I love this recipe! It's a little different than the last time you fixed it.

Preparation time: 30 minutes
Servings: 2
Ingredients:

5 medium russet potatoes *(peeled and quartered)*
3/4 C. water
1 large clove garlic *(peeled)*

2 boneless, skinless chicken breasts
1/2 C. chicken broth
1 large clove garlic *(smashed and chopped)*
1 tsp. honey or Dijon mustard
1/4 C. white wine

1/2 lb. fresh broccoli *(cut in 2" lengths)*

1/2 cantaloupe *(sliced in thin slices)*

1 tsp. butter
1/4 C. nonfat milk

1 lemon
paprika

- **Place potatoes, water, and garlic in large, covered sauce pan. Cook 20 minutes over medium heat.** *Check water at 10 minutes. If necessary, add another 1/2 C. water.*
- **Place chicken breasts in small, non-stick fry pan over medium-high heat with 1/4 C. of the broth and chopped garlic. When broth boils, cook 3 minutes before turning. Add remaining broth and cook other side 3 minutes.** *(As broth cooks away, breast will brown slightly on either side.)* **Reduce heat to low, turn breasts final time, and spread with mustard on 2 of the 3 breasts. Add 1/4 C. wine to pan, cover, and cook an additional 5-10 minutes.** *(If breasts are thin, cook five minutes. If they're large, cook 10 minutes.)*
- **Place broccoli in steamer basket in large covered sauce pan with a little water.** *Do not turn on heat yet.*
- **Prepare cantaloupe and set thin slices on side of each plate.**
- **Mash potatoes and garlic with water left in pan. Add butter and milk.**
- **Turn burner on high under broccoli and cook, covered, 3 minutes after water boils. Remove from heat, uncover, and serve immediately.**

Serve chicken breasts flanked by mashed potatoes and broccoli. Place wedge of lemon on each plate for broccoli. Garnish potatoes with a dash of paprika. (Save 1 cooked breast for tomorrow's brunch recipe). Light a candle, put on some good music, and enjoy with a glass of white wine.

Notes

Before storing leftovers

Potato Patties
Mix 1 1/2 - 2 C. leftover mashed potatoes with 4 T. chopped green onions and one beaten egg white.

Form into 4-6 patties, place on plate and microwave 3 minutes on high. Cool, cover, and store in fridge for next Sunday's meal.

SATURDAY

March/Week Four

Notes

SHOPPING DAY PLUS BRUNCH

There are several new recipes coming up next week. Once again, you will use leftovers from earlier recipes as you prepare meals later in the week.

How do you stack up? Or should I say stock up? *Here are five items Americans buy most at the grocery store: Coca-Cola, Pepsi-Cola, Kraft processed cheese, Campbell's soup, and Budweiser beer.*

Health, 301 Howard St. Suite, 1800, San Francisco, CA 94105

Did you know that some sugared soft drinks *have up to 12 teaspoons of sugar in one 12 oz. serving?*

Read the labels on prepared or canned foods. *Take special note of the nutritional data. Is there a high sodium content? Are more than 30 percent of the calories in the product derived from fat?*

Baked Eggs and Muffins

Preheat oven to 350 degrees.
Prepare muffins *(see page 14). Wait to put them in oven with eggs.*
In a medium-sized mixing bowl, beat the following ingredients thoroughly:
2 eggs, 4 egg whites, 1 T. Worcestershire sauce, and 1/4 C. nonfat milk
Add :
1/2 C. finely chopped tofu *(I swear, you won't know it's there!)*
1/2 C. chopped broccoli *(you may use leftovers if you have them)*
2 slices onion *(chopped)*
1/2 C. cooked, chopped chicken *(leftover from last night)*
1/4 tsp. black pepper
2 T. shredded Parmesan
Place in a small casserole dish sprayed with vegetable oil spray.
Garnish with 1 T. chopped parsley.
Place in oven with muffins. Cook 35 minutes.
Slice an orange or grapefruit to have with the muffins and eggs.
Serves 2-4

GROCERY LIST

Produce

one 6" zucchini
2 medium yellow onions
1/2 lb. fresh mushrooms
1 green bell pepper
1 red bell pepper
3 large carrots
1/4 lb. fresh broccoli
1/8 lb. fresh green beans
one head Romaine lettuce
green salad fixings
iceberg lettuce
one bunch green onions
one large cucumber
6-8 Roma tomatoes
4 lemons

Frozen Foods

Meat/Fish/Poultry

3 fresh halibut fillets
turkey bacon
2 boneless, skinless chicken breasts

Canned or Dry Foods

one 29 oz. can tomato sauce
one 29 oz. can chopped tomatoes
one 29 oz. can "Ready-cut" tomatoes
two 15 oz. cans chicken broth
four 15 oz. cans vegetable broth
16 oz. dry whole wheat penne pasta
12 oz. dry spiral pasta or spaghetti *(get whole wheat if you can find it)*
one 15 oz. can garbanzo beans
one 15 oz. can kidney beans
a loaf of your favorite hearty bread

Chilled Foods and Dairy

1 dozen eggs
fancy-shred Parmesan
fresh pesto

Buy if you're out

1 head garlic
celery
frozen corn
frozen peas
sesame oil
low-sodium soy sauce
brown rice
dry red wine
fumé blanc (wine)
butter

Grilled Halibut with Potato Patties

SUNDAY

March/Week Four

You may use halibut fillets or halibut steaks. Whichever you use, you only need about 4 oz. per serving. You will be cooking an extra piece of fish for Wednesday's meal.

Preparation time: 30 minutes
Servings: 2
Ingredients:

leftover potato patties from Friday
1 T. olive oil

three 4 oz. halibut fillets or three medium halibut steaks
1/2 C. broth or white wine
1 small clove garlic *(smashed and chopped)*
3 T. Worcestershire sauce

1 1/2 C. frozen peas
1/4 C. water
juice of 1/2 lemon
1 tsp. butter *(melted)*

Notes

- **Place potato patties in oiled, preheated pan over medium-high heat and brown each side. Set aside.**
- **Place halibut in sauté pan with 1/4 C. of the broth and garlic. Cook over high heat 2 minutes. Turn and add remaining broth. Spread Worcestershire sauce over each fillet. Cover, lower heat to medium. Cook 3 minutes.** *(Yes, you have cooked one too many servings of halibut! Set one aside in a covered dish in the fridge. You'll use it Wednesday evening.)*
- **Measure peas into sauce pan with water. Bring to boil, cover and turn off heat. Add lemon juice and butter, stir to coat and remove from heat.**

Serve on two plates, flanking halibut with potato patties and peas. Serve with a nice glass of Fume Blanc.

MONDAY

March/Week Four

Notes

Pasta "Prosciutto" Americano

Enjoy an encore of one of my favorite pastas. Prosciutto is actually an Italian version of smoked ham. To be more precise, it should be called pancetta or bacone, but prosciutto has a familiar ring to it. The leftover Red Sauce from the fridge is important as it gives a nice consistency to the Chunky Red Sauce. However, if you don't have leftover Red Sauce, the recipe will survive without it!

Preparation time: 30 minutes
Servings: 2-3
Ingredients:

Chunky Red Sauce
- one 29 oz. can "Ready-cut" tomatoes
- 2 cloves garlic *(smashed and chopped)*
- 1 T. dry oregano leaves
- 1 1/2 T. dry basil leaves
- 1/4 C. dry red wine
- 2 slices medium yellow onion *(chopped)*
- a few dashes of Tabasco® sauce *(optional)*
- 1/2 C. leftover Red Sauce

- a loaf of your favorite crusty bread

- 3 slices cooked turkey bacon *(chopped - use leftover bacon in freezer)*
- 1 1/2 C. Chunky Red Sauce from above recipe

- 3 C. dry penne pasta

- green salad fixings

- 2-4 T. fancy-shred Parmesan cheese

- **Place a large kettle 2/3 full of water on stove. Turn heat on high and cover.**
- **Strain juice from "Ready-cut" tomatoes through colander into sauce pan. Set tomato chunks aside on plate.**
- **Place all Chunky Red Sauce ingredients** *(except tomato chunks)* **in sauce pan. Bring to boil over medium-high heat and cook, covered, 8 minutes.**
- **Wrap bread in foil and place in warm oven.**
- **Add tomato chunks. Return to boil and remove from heat. Set aside.** *You will have a little over 3 C. sauce. Retain 1 1/2 C. in sauce pan for this recipe. Reserve the rest for another meal.*
- **Add chopped bacon to 1 1/2 C. Chunky Red Sauce retained in sauce pan. Return to boil, cover, and remove from heat.**
- **Drop dry pasta into boiling water and cook 8 minutes. Drain and rinse with warm water.** *Set 1/2 C. cooked pasta aside for tomorrow's recipe.*
- **Prepare green salads on individual plates.**
- **Divide remaining pasta between two plates. Cover each serving with 1/2 to 3/4 C. "Prosciutto" Americano Sauce. Sprinkle 1-2 T. Parmesan cheese over each serving.**

Serve with a crisp green salad and crusty bread.

Minestrone Soup

A great stand-by. This soup goes together easily, and freezes well for a fast meal when you're in a hurry.

Preparation time: 25 minutes
Servings: 2
Ingredients:

1 loaf of your favorite hearty bread

one 29 oz. can chopped tomatoes
three 15 oz. cans vegetable broth
1/2 medium yellow onion *(chopped)*
2 cloves garlic *(smashed and chopped)*
1 stalk celery *(chopped)*
dash of Tabasco®
3 T. dry sweet basil leaves
1 T. dry oregano leaves
1/8 lb. fresh green beans *(cut in 1" lengths)*
1/2 green bell pepper *(chopped)*
1 medium carrot *(sliced)*
1 small zucchini *(chopped)*
5-6 mushrooms *(sliced)*
one 15 oz. can garbanzo beans *(drain and use 1/2 can)*
1 small can red kidney beans *(drain and use 1/2 can)*
1/2 C. frozen corn

1/2 C. cooked pasta *(reserved from last night)*

fixings for a green salad

shredded Parmesan cheese

- **Wrap bread in foil and place in 200 degree oven.**
- **Place large kettle on burner over high heat. In order listed, add all ingredients in box above. Bring to boil. Cover and cook 10 minutes.**
- **Remove from heat, add cooked pasta, cover, and let stand 5-10 minutes.**
- **Prepare green salads.** *Sprinkle a few leftover garbanzo and kidney beans over salads.*
- **Garnish each bowl of soup with 2 T. shredded Parmesan.**

Don't forget the warm bread.

Notes

If you're out of hearty bread, pick some up today.

Whole Wheat Pasta with Halibut

Another theme and variation on marinara sauce. Use whole wheat spaghetti or spirals if you found them on shopping day. Use leftover halibut from Sunday.

Preparation time: 25 minutes
Servings: 2-3
Ingredients:

Notes

2 thin slices medium yellow onion *(quartered)*
1 clove garlic *(smashed and chopped)*
1 stalk celery *(chopped in 1/2" pieces)*
1 T. olive oil

1 1/2 C. leftover Chunky Red Sauce

12 oz. dry pasta

green salad fixings

6 medium mushrooms *(sliced)*
1 cooked halibut fillet or steak
(broken into pieces with bones and skin removed)

2 T. Parmesan
2 T. fresh chopped parsley *(optional)*

- **Place pasta water on stove over high heat in large heavy-bottomed kettle.**
- **Sauté onions, garlic, and celery in oil 3 minutes over medium-high heat in large fry pan.**
- **Add leftover Chunky Red Sauce and bring to boil. Cover, and remove from heat.**
- **Drop pasta into boiling water and cook 7-9 minutes.**
- **Prepare green salads.**
- **Add mushrooms and broken halibut to Chunky Red Sauce. Return to boil, cover and reduce heat to low.**
- **Drain and rinse pasta when cooked.**
- **Serve immediately on individual plates covered with Halibut Sauce.**

Garnish with Parmesan and parsley and serve with green salad.

Molti bravi!

Hot Vegetable Nest

This is a very interesting creation. I like it meatless - true to its name. However, if you wish to add meat, throw in 6 to 8 shrimp or 1 chopped, cooked chicken breast while you are sautéing the vegetables.

Preparation time: 25 minutes
Servings: 2
Ingredients:

Notes

1 loaf of your favorite hearty bread

1 large carrot *(sliced in rounds)*
1 T. olive oil
1/4 C. vegetable broth
1 clove garlic *(smashed and chopped)*

2 thin slices medium onion *(quartered)*
1 1/2 C. broccoli *(chopped)*

6 medium mushrooms *(sliced)*

1/4 head iceberg lettuce *(shredded)*

1 tsp. Dijon mustard
1/2 C. plain, nonfat yogurt *(stirred smooth)*

2 Roma tomatoes *(chopped)*

1 T. toasted pine nuts *(chopped) Use previously stored nuts, or toast fresh. (page 79)*

Pick up some hearty bread or rolls today.

- **Wrap bread in foil and place in warm oven.**
- **Start by placing carrots, oil, broth, and garlic in sauté pan or medium-sized, heavy-bottomed sauce pan over medium-high heat. Sauté 2 minutes**
- **Add onion and broccoli. Sauté 1 minute.**
- **Add mushrooms. Sauté 1 minute. Remove from heat and set aside.**
- **Arrange shredded lettuce in nest shape on individual serving plates.**
- **Combine mustard and yogurt and microwave 20 seconds on high.**
- **Return sauté pan with vegetables to heat and add yogurt sauce. Blend thoroughly and remove from heat. *Do not boil.***
- **Add tomatoes, and spoon vegetable mixture over lettuce. Serve immediately.**

Top with pine nuts. Serve with warmed bread.

Notes

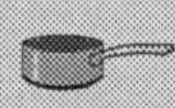

"Quick cook" rice before work this morning. *(see page 6)*

Garlic/Lemon Chicken Breasts

A truly delicious meal! Reminiscent of Asian-style lemon chicken.

Preparation time: 30 minutes
Servings: 2
Ingredients:

1/4 C. chicken broth
1/2 tsp. sesame oil
1 T. low-sodium soy sauce
1 1/2 C. cooked rice
3 green onions *(chopped)*
1 stalk celery *(finely chopped)*
1/2 red bell pepper *(chopped)*

2 boneless, skinless chicken breasts
1 T. olive oil
2 cloves garlic *(smashed and chopped)*
1/2 C. chicken broth

2 medium carrots *(peeled and sliced in 1/8" rounds)*

1/4 C. white wine
juice from 1 lemon
2 T. white sugar

3 T. corn starch mixed with 1/3 C. water

- **Preheat oven to 350 degrees.**
- **In an oven-safe bowl, mix 1/4 C. chicken broth, sesame oil, and soy sauce.**
- **Add rice, onions, celery, and red bell pepper. Stir thoroughly, cover, and place in preheated oven on center rack. Set timer for 20 minutes.**
- **Brown chicken breasts over medium-high heat in oil and garlic. Add broth, cover, and cook 5 minutes.**
- **Place carrots in steamer basket over a little water in medium sauce pan with tight-fitting lid.** *Do not turn on heat yet.*
- **Remove chicken from pan and set aside.**
- **Add wine, lemon, any remaining broth, and sugar to sauté pan. Stir until boiling and all drippings have come up from bottom of pan.**
- **Quickly stir in corn starch mixture and cook 2 minutes over medium-high heat.**
- **Return chicken breasts to pan with sauce, reduce heat to low, and cover.**
- **Turn heat on high under carrots. When water boils, reduce heat and cook, covered, 2 minutes.**

Serve meal on individual plates, spooning lemon sauce over chicken. If you wish, spoon sauce over rice and carrots as well.

SHOPPING DAY

SATURDAY
March/April

Fat consumption is down! *Today Americans get 34% of their calories from fat compared with 36% ten years ago. The recommended level is no more than 30%.*
The National Center for Health Statistics, Hyattsville, MD

It you're staying the course with this book, you should be maintaining a fat consumption level well below the recommended level of 30%.

You'll make Hot and Sour Bean Soup on Sunday. This recipe gets rave reviews from diners each time I make it.

Dried beans and peas *are excellent sources of folic acid, soluble fiber and compounds called saponins, which lower blood cholesterol levels. They're also low in fat, high in protein, and have been linked to reduced rates in prostate cancer and breast cancer.*
Vegetarian Times, "Blue Chip Foods", by Winifred Yu, June 1996

There is a 6 oz. can of black olives on the grocery list this week. Sometimes I buy 6-8 black olives at the salad bar instead of buying a whole can. It's an inexpensive way to pick up a few olives.

Notes

GROCERY LIST

Produce
one 6" zucchini
one 6" crooked neck squash
3 medium russet potatoes
3 medium yellow onions
1 1/2 lb. fresh mushrooms
1 green bell pepper
2 red bell peppers
1 yellow bell pepper
1 large carrot
bok choy
1/2 lb. fresh broccoli
green salad fixings
1 head red or green leaf lettuce
1 cucumber
8-10 Roma tomatoes
one bunch fresh parsley
2 oranges
1 lemon
1 lime
1 package firm, plain tofu

Frozen Foods
1 package cooked, shelled, large shrimp
(buy frozen shrimp if fresh are unavailable)

Meat/Fish/Poultry
1 lb. boneless, skinless chicken breasts
1 Italian sausage link
2 chorizo sausage links
5 large raw shrimp *(you may wish to pick up on Friday)*

Canned or Dry Foods
one 29 oz. can tomato sauce
four 15 oz. cans chicken broth
one 15 oz. can vegetable broth
saffron threads
one 6 oz. can sliced water chestnuts
one 6 oz. can sliced bamboo shoots
white rice
1 lb. dry navy beans
or four 15 oz. cans beans
12 oz. dry multi-colored spiral pasta
8 oz. fresh cheese ravioli
one 6 oz. can black olives
8 oz. roasted cashews
one box fortune cookies
a loaf of hearty bread

Chilled Foods and Dairy
pesto sauce

Buy if you're out
1 head garlic
celery
frozen corn
sesame oil
low-sodium soy sauce
white vinegar
white cooking wine

SUNDAY

March/April

Notes

Hot and Sour Bean Soup

Here is a delicious, nutritious bean soup recipe that provides leftovers for future meals.

Preparation time: 45 minutes *(once beans are cooked)*
Servings: 6-8
Ingredients:

1 lb. dry white beans *(Navy or Great Northern)*
3 quarts water
You may substitute canned, cooked beans if you wish.
Be sure to rinse them thoroughly to get rid of excess salt.
You will need four 15 oz. cans.

a loaf of your favorite hearty bread

three 15 oz. cans chicken or vegetable broth
1/2 medium yellow onion *(chopped)*
2 stalks celery *(chopped)*
1 red bell pepper *(chopped)*
1 yellow bell pepper *(chopped)*
1 green bell pepper *(chopped)*
2 cloves garlic *(smashed and chopped)*

1/4 C. white sugar
1/2 C. white vinegar
1/4 to 1/2 tsp. cayenne pepper *(to taste)*

- **Wash dry beans and soak overnight in 3 quarts water in large kettle.** *(If using canned beans, start at the *.)*
- **Discard water in morning and add another 3 quarts water.**
- **Bring beans to a boil and reduce heat to low. Cook over low heat for 1 1/2 hours.**

* **Remove one cup cooked beans from kettle. Mash and set aside.**

- **Wrap bread in foil and place in warm oven.**
- **Add broth, vegetables, and garlic. Bring to boil. Reduce heat to low and cook 1/2 hour.**
- **Add sugar, vinegar and cayenne.**
- **Add mashed beans to kettle. Stir to blend thoroughly.**
- **Cover and cook another ten minutes on low heat.**

Serve with a loaf of warm bread. Mmmm! Mmmmm! Delicious!

Spiral Pasta with Sliced Italian Sausage

Another delicious pasta variation.

MONDAY
March/April

Preparation time: 25 minutes
Servings: 2-3
Ingredients:

Notes

Red Sauce
one 29 oz. can tomato sauce
(Makes 3 1/2 C. Reserve 1 1/2 C. for today's recipe and freeze the rest for later use.)
2 cloves garlic *(smashed and chopped)*
1/4 C. red wine
1 T. dry oregano
1 1/2 T. dry basil leaves
4 slices medium yellow onion *(chopped)*
a few dashes of Tabasco® sauce *(optional)*

one link Italian sausage *(any kind)*

2 1/2 C. dry spiral pasta *(whole wheat if you can find it)*

Salad
5-6 washed leaves red or green leaf lettuce *(pat dry with paper towel)*
6 slices green bell pepper
8-10 slices peeled cucumber
2 chopped Roma tomatoes *(about 1" chunks)*

6 medium mushrooms *(sliced)*
2 slices medium onion *(quartered)*
4 black olives *(sliced) or 2 T. sliced olives*

2-4 T. fancy-shred Parmesan cheese

- **Place large kettle on stove filled 2/3 full of water. Turn heat on high and cover.**
- **Make Red Sauce in sauce pan. Bring all ingredients to boil. Cover, reduce heat to low and cook 10 minutes.**
- **Place sausage in shallow dish on top of some paper towel. Prick skin 6 or 7 times with fork. Cover dish and microwave three 1 1/2-minute bursts on high.**
- **Press sausage with fork to get as much fat to drain off as possible.**
- **Slice sausage into rounds and place slices on fresh paper towels.**
- **Drop pasta into boiling water and set timer for 8 minutes. Drain and rinse.**
- **Prepare green salads.**
- **Measure 1 1/2 C. Red Sauce into pasta kettle. Add mushrooms, onion, olives, and sausage. Return sauce to boil. Cook 1 minute and remove from heat.**
- **Mix pasta and Red Sauce mixture in pasta kettle. Divide between two plates and sprinkle 1-2 T. Parmesan cheese over each serving.**

Serve with green salad.

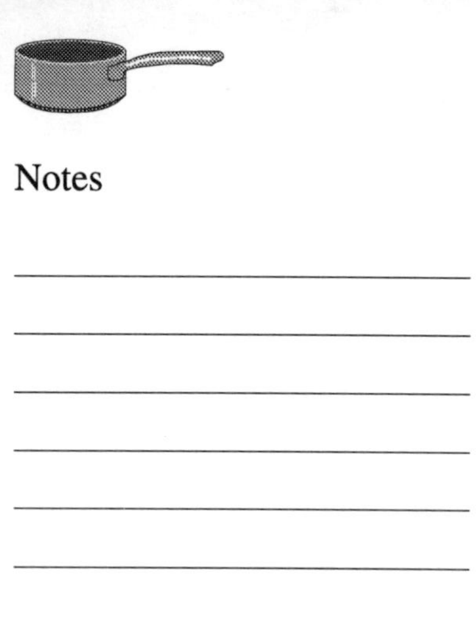

Notes

Broccoli/Cashew Stir Fry

A stir fry loaded with nutrients. This is a most rewarding meatless meal.

Preparation time: 30 minutes
Servings: 2-3
Ingredients:

1 T. olive oil
1/4 tsp. sesame oil
1/4 C. vegetable broth *(open one 15 oz. can)*
3 slices medium onion *(chopped)*
2 cloves garlic *(smashed and chopped)*
1/2 lb. broccoli *(cut in 1" pieces)*

6 mushrooms *(sliced)*
1/2 C. roasted cashews
1/2 red bell pepper *(cubed)*
1/2 C. sliced, peeled water chestnuts
1/2 C. sliced bamboo shoots
2 T. low-sodium soy sauce

1 1/4 C. vegetable broth *(remainder of can)*
2 T. corn starch mixed with 1/4 C. water

1 medium tomato *(chopped)*

1 1/2 C. cooked rice

- **Place oils and broth in large heavy-bottomed sauce pan or wok over high heat. Sauté onion, garlic, and broccoli 2 minutes stirring constantly.**
- **Add mushrooms, cashews, red pepper, water chestnuts, bamboo shoots, and soy sauce. Sauté an additional 2 minutes.**
- **Remove all ingredients from pan with perforated ladle or spoon and set aside on large plate.**
- **Using same pan, add remaining broth and bring to boil.**
- **Thicken with corn starch, water mixture. Reduce heat and cook 3-4 minutes.**
- **Return vegetables to pan and add tomatoes. Stir to coat with sauce and remove from heat.**
- **Warm 3/4 cup rice per serving in microwave 2 minutes. If you don't have a microwave, warm rice over medium-high heat in shallow sauce pan with 1/8 C. water. Keep an eye on it so it doesn't cook down.**
- **Spoon stir fry over rice on individual plates and serve immediately.**

Have you tried eating with chopsticks yet? Try it tonight! Your stir fry will taste better once you have gotten the hang of it. It's also fun to have a fortune cookie and tea to finish the meal.

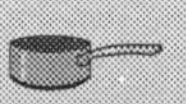

You will need to "quick cook" some rice before work

"Quick Cooked" Rice
Place 1 C. long grain brown rice in a pan with 2 1/4 C. cold water. Cover and bring to boil over high heat. When water boils turn off heat. Leave pan on burner. Do not lift cover! It will be ready to eat when you get home tonight.

Chicken Breasts with Mushroom Sauce

WEDNESDAY
March/April

You'll find this sauce a special treat.

Preparation time: 35 minutes
Servings: 2
Ingredients:

3-4 medium potatoes *(peeled and quartered)*
3/4 C. water
1 clove garlic *(peeled)*

1/2 lb. fresh white mushrooms *(sliced - select 4-6 and chop fine)*
2 thin slices medium yellow onion *(quartered)*
1 clove garlic *(smashed and chopped)*
1/4 C. white wine

3 boneless-skinless chicken breasts
1/2 C. chicken broth
1 clove garlic *(smashed and chopped)*

1/2 C. broth
1/4 tsp. crushed, dry rosemary leaves
1/4 C. white wine
3 T. corn starch *(dissolved in 1/4 C. water)*

1/8 C. nonfat milk
2 tsp. butter

one 6" zucchini *(coarsely chopped)*
one 4-6" yellow crooked neck *(coarsely chopped)*
1/2 red bell pepper *(chopped)*
2 slices medium onion *(quartered)*
1 T. olive oil

1 T. pesto mixed with 3 T. broth
2 Roma tomatoes *(chopped in large pieces)*

1 T. Parmesan

Notes

- **Place potatoes in medium sauce pan with water and garlic. Bring to boil, cover, reduce heat and cook 15 minutes.** *Check them in 5 minutes to be sure the water hasn't boiled away.*
- **In large fry pan, sauté mushrooms, onion, and garlic in wine 3 minutes. Remove veggies from pan with perforated spoon. Set aside.**
- **Place chicken breasts in same pan with 1/4 C. of the chicken broth and garlic. Sauté over medium-high heat 3 minutes turning once. Add remaining broth and sauté another 3 minutes until lightly browned. Reduce heat to low, add a little water to pan, cover, and cook 5 minutes per side.**
- **Remove chicken from pan. Add broth, rosemary, and wine. Bring to boil and stir to bring up drippings.**
- **Thicken with corn starch mixture. Reduce heat to low, and cook 5 minutes.**
- **Return mushrooms and chicken to sauce, cover, and turn off heat.**
- **Mash potatoes and garlic with milk and butter. Cover and set aside.**
- **Sauté green and yellow squash, red pepper, and onion in oil 3 minutes.**
- **Mix pesto and broth. Add pesto mixture and tomatoes to zucchini mixture. Toss over heat 1 minute.**

Serve chicken breast and a scoop of potatoes covered with mushroom sauce. Spoon zucchini mixture next to chicken and top zucchini with Parmesan.

Ravioli and Red Sauce with Pesto Toast

A special treat will add interest to this meal — pesto toast!

Preparation time: 20 minutes
Servings: 2 *(or more)*
Ingredients:

- 8 oz. fresh ravioli
  (I like cheese, but there are many varieties from which to choose.)
- green salad fixings
- 1 1/2 C. leftover Red Sauce
  or freshly made Red Sauce (page 93)
- 1/2 tsp. pesto
- 1/2 tsp. butter
- 3-4 T. fancy-shred Parmesan cheese

- **Put pasta water on to boil in large kettle.**
- **Drop ravioli in boiling water.** *Fresh ravioli will cook in 8-10 minutes. Set a timer so you don't overcook it.* **Drain and rinse.**
- **Prepare green salads.**
- **Warm Red Sauce in small pan on stove or in covered dish in microwave while pasta is cooking.**
- **Mix pesto and butter together and spread on toast.**
- **Serve ravioli on individual plates with Red Sauce over top.**

Garnish with Parmesan and serve with green salad and Pesto Toast on the side.

Notes

Paella

FRIDAY

March/April

The following recipe is a staple in Spanish cooking. Although it takes longer to cook, it goes together easily and is one of the more delicious rice dishes you will ever eat. If you can't find fresh shrimp, use large frozen shrimp. If you want your paella very hearty use both shrimp and one or two sausages. True, the saffron is pricey, but you don't have this dish that often.

Notes

Preparation time: 1 hour
Servings: 2-4
Ingredients:

6-8 raw, shelled shrimp
2 chopped, spicy sausage links *(chorizo if you can find them)*
2 T. olive oil
3 cloves garlic *(smashed and chopped)*
1 medium yellow onion *(chopped)*
1/2 red and 1/2 green bell pepper *(chopped)*
1/2 C. white wine
1 1/2 C. uncooked white rice
2 C. vegetable or chicken broth
dash of cayenne pepper
2 tsp. saffron threads *(crumbled)*
6 medium white mushrooms *(sliced)*
1/2 C. frozen peas
juice from one lime
a loaf of hearty bread
2 oranges *(sliced)*
4 Roma tomatoes *(chopped)*

- **Preheat oven to 400 degrees.**
- **Clean and devein shrimp by making a slice along the back to remove vein. Rinse well to remove all shell and eggs.**
- **If using uncooked sausage, prick thoroughly with fork, wrap in paper towel and cook at full power in microwave for two 2-minute bursts. Cool and chop.**
- **Place oil and garlic in large oven-safe pan.** *A cast-iron skillet will work if you have a tight-fitting lid.* **Sauté shrimp lightly in garlic and oil. Lift out of pan. Sauté chorizo sausage in oil** *(about 2 minutes)*. **Add onions, bell peppers, and wine. Sauté 2 minutes.**
- **Add rice, broth, cayenne pepper, and saffron. Bring to boil over high heat. Reduce heat to medium. Cook, uncovered, 15 minutes stirring often.**
- **After rice has cooked 15 minutes, distribute mushrooms, shrimp, and peas around top of rice. Sprinkle with lime juice, cover, and cook 20 minutes in oven.**
- **Wrap bread in foil. Place in oven with Paella for the final 5 minutes of cooking.**
- **Slice oranges to serve on side.**
- **Remove pan from oven and sprinkle with tomatoes. Return to oven and cook another 5 minutes - uncovered.**

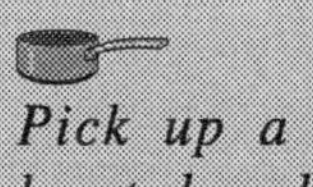

Pick up a loaf of hearty bread today.

Set pan in middle of table and let people help themselves. Serve with warm bread and sliced oranges.

SATURDAY

April/Week One

Notes

SHOPPING DAY

Are you still eating too much? *The Third National Health and Nutrition Examination Survey found that Americans' consumption of fat as a percentage of calories is down to 34%, and blood-cholesterol levels are down 8% since 1960. But our daily calorie intake is up an average of 231 calories.*
Vitality Magazine, July 1994

If you budget the fat in your diet, *you'll need to save up in a big way if you eat the fare at the ballpark. A foot-long hot dog with ketchup and mustard has 360 calories and 34 gm. of fat, (that's saturated fat), and a chili dog weighs in at 660 calories and 48 gm. of fat.*
The Fat Counter by Annette B. Natow, PhD.,R.D., and Jo-Ann Heslin, M.A., R.D., Pocket Books, 1989

Are you worried about the fat in your baked goods?
Try substituting 2 egg whites for 1 whole egg. Example: If a recipe calls for 3 eggs, use 1 whole egg and 4 egg whites.
Substitute 1/2 applesauce for the oil in any baking recipe. Example: If the recipe calls for 1/2 cup oil, use 1/4 C. oil and 1/4 C. applesauce. Some folks substitute all applesauce for oil. However, baked goods like pie crust or butter cookies need all the shortening or butter indicated.

This week you'll start off with Lentil Soup. As part of the legume family, lentils are among the richest in iron. Lentils are also very low in fat, (about 5% of total calories), contain no cholesterol, are an excellent source of fiber and are very high in potassium.

GROCERY LIST

Produce

2 large russet potatoes
3 medium white potatoes
2 medium yellow onions
1/2 lb. fresh mushrooms
1 green bell pepper
1 red bell pepper
2 large carrots
1/2 lb. broccoli
one bunch fresh asparagus
green salad fixings
6-8 Roma tomatoes
dried apricots
2-3 crisp delicious apples
1 fresh lemon

Frozen Foods

Meat/Fish/Poultry

1 boneless, skinless chicken breast
1 link Italian turkey sausage
2 fresh snapper fillets

Canned or Dry Foods

one 29 oz. can tomato sauce
five 15 oz. cans chicken broth
1 lb. package dry lentils
8 oz. fresh cheese tortellini
1 large, thin-crust Boboli®
a loaf of your favorite hearty bread

Chilled Foods and Dairy

plain, nonfat yogurt
3 oz. sharp Cheddar cheese
fresh salsa

Buy if you're out

1 head garlic
celery
frozen corn
balsamic vinegar
dried dill weed
dried fennel seed
whole dry bay leaf
dry red wine
shredded Parmesan

Lentil Soup

Wash lentils and pick out any foreign matter that may be mixed in with them. Place 2 cups of washed lentils in a large kettle with 8 cups of water. You're ready to start.

Preparation time: 20 minutes *(cooking time 1 hour)*
Servings: 4-6
Ingredients:

2 C. dry lentils

1 medium onion *(finely chopped)*
2 cloves garlic *(smashed and chopped)*
1 bay leaf
3 stalks celery *(diced in small pieces)*

1 link cooked Italian turkey sausage *(optional)*
2 medium carrots *(chopped)*
1/2 red bell pepper *(chopped)*
three 15 oz. cans chicken or vegetable broth
1/2 tsp. ground cumin
1 tsp. dry oregano leaves
dash of Tabasco® *(optional)*

a loaf of your favorite hearty bread

2 large delicious apples *(sliced)*

1 C. plain, nonfat yogurt *(stirred smooth)*

- **Bring lentils to a boil. Reduce heat and cook 1/2 hour.**
- **Add onions, garlic, bay leaf and celery. Cook 15 minutes.**
- **Add meat, carrots, red bell pepper, broth, spices, and Tabasco®. Continue cooking 15 minutes.**
- **Wrap bread in foil and place in warm oven.**
- **Remove bay leaf from soup.**
- **Slice apples.**
- **Stir yogurt. Swirl 2 T. yogurt into each serving of soup.**

Don't forget the warm bread! Serve apple slices on a plate in the center of the table.

Notes

MONDAY
April/Week One

Notes

Poached Snapper with Dill

More fish please! This recipe has a nice tangy bite to it. Any rock fish will do.

Preparation time: 25 minutes
Servings: 2
Ingredients:

3 medium white potatoes *(washed and quartered)*
3/4 C. water
1/2 tsp. dry fennel seed

one bunch asparagus

1/2 C. white wine
1 clove garlic *(smashed and chopped)*
1/2 - 3/4 C. chicken or vegetable broth

2 small snapper fillets *(2/3 lb.)*
black pepper
a couple pinches of dill weed

1/2 fresh lemon *(cut in wedges)*

- **Place potatoes in medium sauce pan with water and fennel seed. Bring water to boil, cover, reduce heat to medium-low, and cook 15 minutes. Remove from heat.**
- **Cut or snap off white ends of asparagus. Wash and place in steamer basket in large sauce pan with about 1/2 C. water.** *Do not turn on burner yet.*
- **Place wine, garlic, and 1/2 C. broth in sauté pan and bring to boil.**
- **Slide fish fillets into boiling mixture and season with black pepper. Cook about 3 minutes per side. When you turn fillets, sprinkle dill weed over each. If liquid in pan cooks away, add another 1/4 C. broth.**
- **Turn heat on under asparagus. Bring to a boil and steam** *(covered)* **1 minute. If asparagus is large,** *(the circumference of your finger)*, **steam 3 minutes.**

Serve fillets flanked by asparagus and potatoes on individual serving plates with a wedge of lemon on each plate.

White Pizza and Salad

TUESDAY
April/Week One

I love this pizza!

Preparation time: 25 minutes
Servings: 2
Ingredients:

1 cooked, boneless, skinless chicken breast *(thin-sliced)*
1 T. olive oil
1 large clove garlic *(smashed and chopped)*

1/2 C. chicken broth
1/4 C. white wine
1 small clove garlic *(smashed and chopped)*
2 slices medium yellow onion *(chopped)*
2 tsp. dry oregano leaves
1 T. dry basil leaves

4 T. flour shaken with 1/4 C. nonfat milk
4 T. fancy-shred Parmesan

dash of Tabasco®
1/4 C. plain, nonfat yogurt*(stirred smooth)*

1 large, thin-crust Boboli® shell or frozen pizza shell

2 slices medium yellow onion *(quartered)*
1/2 red bell pepper *(sliced in thin slices)*
6 medium mushrooms *(sliced)*
5 T. fancy-shred Parmesan

fixings for a green salad

Notes

- **Preheat oven to 400 degrees.**
- **Sauté chicken breast in oil and garlic over medium-high heat in small sauté pan. Cook about 5 minutes per side turning every 2 minutes to prevent burning. If it starts to get too dark, add 1/4 C. water to pan and reduce heat. When cooked, set breast on cutting-board and slice in thin slices.**
- **Place broth, wine, garlic, onion, and spices in sauce pan and bring to boil. Reduce heat and cook 5 minutes.**
- **Return liquid to boil and gradually stir in flour mixture to thicken. Reduce heat, add Parmesan, and cook another 5 minutes.**
- **Remove pan from heat and add Tabasco® and yogurt.**
- **Place Boboli® directly on oven rack in center of oven and cook 3 minutes.** *(Set a timer so you don't forget.)* **Remove from oven.**
- **Spread 3/4 C. White Sauce on Boboli® crust.**
- **Arrange onions, peppers, and mushrooms, on top of White Sauce and top with remaining Parmesan. Return to oven for 8-10 minutes.**
- **Prepare green salads.**
- **Remove pizza from oven and cut in 8 wedges while hot. Let cool a few minutes before serving.**

Serve the Pizza on individual serving plates with fresh green salad on the side.

Leftover Night

Its showtime! Enjoy your leftovers tonight and avoid the guilt of finding "funky green stuff" in your fridge next month.

Preparation time: 20 minutes
Servings: 2-3
Ingredients:

Whatever——
Red Sauce
leftover White Pizza
pasta
stir fry
Lentil Soup

- **If you need to cook a little extra pasta, put some water on to boil.**
- **Slice some fresh fruit to have on the side with leftover Lentil Soup.**

Notes

More trivia:

Americans spent $267 billion eating out in 1993, up from $250 billion in 1990. Forty-three cents of every dollar we spend on food is spent in restaurants.

The Journal of the American Dietetic Association, 216 West Jackson Blvd., Suite 800, Chicago, IL 60606

Tortellini with Red Sauce

THURSDAY

April/Week One

Very simple! I like fresh tortellini, but you can use dried as well. It just takes longer to cook.

Preparation time: 20-30 minutes
Servings: 2 *(or more if you wish)*
Ingredients:

a loaf of your favorite bread
green salad fixings
8 oz. fresh tortellini *(or 1 1/2 C. dry tortellini)*
1 1/2 C. leftover Red Sauce or freshly made Red Sauce *(see page 93)*
3-4 T. fancy-shred Parmesan

- **Wrap bread in foil and place in warm oven.**
- **Place pasta water on to boil in large kettle.**
- **Prepare green salads.**
- **Drop tortellini into boiling water.** *Fresh will cook in 8-10 minutes - dry will take 20+ minutes. Set a timer so you don't overcook it.*
- **Prepare Red Sauce now.**
- **Drain and rinse tortellini.**
- **Serve on individual plates with Red Sauce spooned over tortellini.**
- **Garnish with Parmesan.**

Once again, this was almost too easy! Serve crisp green salad on the side and pass the warm bread.

Notes

Pick up a fresh loaf of hearty bread today.

FRIDAY
April/Week One

Notes

Baked Potato with Broccoli

Here it comes again! "The wonder meal!" Enjoy! You'll be hard-pressed to do better for yourself.

Preparation time: 15-20 minutes
Servings: 2
Ingredients:

2 large russet baking potatoes
(washed, rubbed with olive oil, and pricked with a fork)

1/2 lb. fresh broccoli *(cut in 2" lengths)*

1/2 C. frozen corn

3/4 C. plain, nonfat yogurt *(stirred smooth)*
sharp cheddar cheese
salsa

lemon

- **Prepare potatoes in the morning prior to work and set your oven for "time bake" so that they will have been cooking 1 hour when you arrive home in the evening.** *(You may also cook them in the microwave. Cook for three 5-minute cycles at full power. Turn the potatoes to a different position after each cycle.)*
- **Place broccoli in steamer basket in sauce pan with a little water. Bring to boil, cover, and cook 3 minutes.** *Set timer so you don't forget.* **Remove pan and uncover when timer goes off.**
- **Measure 1/2 C. frozen corn into glass dish. Cover and thaw in microwave 1 minute at full power.**
- **Stir yogurt, set out cheese (with grater), and salsa while broccoli is cooking.**

Split potatoes and place on serving plates. Top with corn, yogurt, and salsa. Garnish with a few gratings of sharp cheddar cheese. Serve broccoli on same plate with a wedge of lemon.

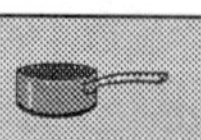

If you have "time bake" on your oven you may wish to wash potatoes in the morning, rub them with oil and set them on "time bake" for 1 hour at 400 degrees. Set "time bake" to start one hour before you will be arriving home.

SATURDAY

April/Week Two

Notes

SHOPPING DAY

Are you trying to lose weight? *The best way is to eat right, reduce fat intake and exercise. (Walking is one of the best forms of exercise.)*

Here are five of the worst reasons people try to lose weight:

To win a weight loss bet.
To try to look like Cindy Crawford.
To satisfy a weight chart.
To squeeze into a size 9 dress for a family wedding next month.
To make your spouse love you more.

Walking Magazine, March/April, 1994

A tip: *Don't discard the water that forms on the top of the yogurt in your yogurt container. Stir the liquid back into the yogurt. It contains B vitamins and minerals and is low-in-fat, (or has no fat if you use nonfat yogurt).*

University of California , Berkeley Wellness Letter, New York, NY10012

You could be suffering from a magnesium deficiency if you get cramps in your calves or thighs while lying in bed. Halibut, mackerel, rice, bran, tofu, and spinach are high in magnesium.

Stephen Subotnick, *D.P.M.,* a sports podiatrist, Hayward, CA

Marinade for "Wild Game" Breast of Turkey

Prepare marinade for Sunday when you return from shopping.

2-3 lb. turkey breast fillets

Marinade
(Mix all together)

1 C. dry red wine
1/4 C. balsamic vinegar
1 T. extra-virgin olive oil
1/2 tsp. sesame oil
2 T. Worcestershire sauce
2 tsp. oregano
1/2 tsp. thyme
1/2 tsp. crushed rosemary leaves
2 cloves garlic *(smashed and chopped)*
3 slices medium yellow onion *(chopped)*

Place turkey fillets in marinade and cover overnight in fridge. Turn in morning.

GROCERY LIST

Produce

6 medium russet potatoes
10 baby red potatoes
4-6 fresh turnips
one 6" zucchini
2 medium yellow onions
1 lb. fresh mushrooms
1 green bell pepper
1 red bell pepper
2 large carrots
green salad fixings
green leaf lettuce
one cucumber
3-4 bunches fresh spinach *or two bags prewashed spinach*
6-8 Roma tomatoes
1 head red cabbage
1 tart apple
1 fresh lemon

Frozen Foods

Meat/Fish/Poultry

1 lb. ground turkey breast
2-3 lb. turkey breast fillets

Canned or Dry Foods

two 29 oz. cans tomato sauce
three 15 oz. cans chicken broth
one 6 oz. can tuna packed in water
one 15 oz. can whole cranberries
8 oz. fresh fettuccine
12 oz. dry penne pasta
lowfat Italian salad dressing

Chilled Foods and Dairy

plain, nonfat yogurt
pesto sauce
butter

Buy if you're out

1 head garlic
toasted sunflower meats
sesame oil
extra-virgin olive oil
ground anise
brown rice
red cooking wine

SUNDAY
April/Week Two

"Wild Game" Marinated Breast of Turkey

This is a wonderfully adventuresome, special meal. The flavors are reminiscent of game or lamb dishes. It takes a bit longer to prepare, but it's worth it. An excellent holiday meal!

Preparation time: 2 hours
Servings: 4-6
Ingredients:

Notes

2-3 lb. boneless turkey breast fillets marinated overnight in fridge

6 medium-sized turnips *(peeled and quartered)*

6-8 medium-sized russet potatoes *(peeled and quartered)*
1 C. water
2 cloves garlic *(whole - peeled)*

3-4 bunches fresh spinach *(washed) or*
2 large packages prewashed fresh spinach
1/2 C. vegetable broth

4 T. flour shaken with 1/4 C. nonfat milk

1/8 tsp. nutmeg
1/2 C. plain, nonfat yogurt
4 Roma tomatoes *(chopped)*

1 T. butter
1/8 C. nonfat milk

2 T. corn starch mixed with 1/8 C. water

one 15 oz. can whole cranberries

- **Place marinated turkey and 1 C. of marinade in shallow roasting pan.**
- **Cover pan with foil and cook at 350 degrees for 1 hour.**
- **Add turnips and another 1/2 C. marinade to turkey in oven.**
- **Cook additional 1/2 hour.**
- **Place potatoes in large saucepan with 1 C. water and garlic. Cover and cook 15-20 minutes until potatoes are tender. Remove from heat. Do not drain.**
- **Bring washed spinach and broth to boil in large kettle. Sauté 3 minutes until spinach is thoroughly wilted.**
- **Lift spinach out with fork and thicken broth with flour mixture. Cook over medium-low heat 5 minutes.**
- **Return spinach to pan and cook over low heat 2-3 minutes.**
- **Stir in nutmeg, nonfat yogurt, and chopped tomatoes. Cover and remove from heat.**
- **Add 1 T. butter to potatoes and mash with 1/8 C. nonfat milk, cooking liquid, and garlic.**
- **Place one cup liquid from cooking turkey in shallow sauce pan. Bring to boil and thicken with corn starch mixture. Cook 5 minutes on low heat.**
- **Open can of whole cranberries and place in serving dish. Chop in dish to eliminate shape of can.**

Slice turkey in 1/2" slices and serve with thickened sauce spooned over top. Flank with potatoes, spinach, and turnips. Serve with cranberry sauce.

Tuna Salad

Time to lighten up after a big dinner yesterday. This is actually quite a meal. You won't feel deprived.

Preparation time: 25 minutes
Servings: 2
Ingredients:

a loaf of your favorite hearty bread

1 head green leaf lettuce *(washed and patted dry)*
1/2 cucumber *(peeled, sliced in 1/4" rounds and quartered)*
3 green onions *(washed and chopped)*
or two thin slices of a yellow onion *(quartered)*
1/4 red bell pepper *(thin sliced and quartered)*
1/4 green bell pepper *(thin sliced and quartered)*
1 medium carrot *(grated)*
1/4 C. finely chopped red cabbage

one 6 oz. can water-packed tuna *(drained)*
4 Roma tomatoes *(chopped)*
2 T. toasted sunflower seeds

1 tart apple *(cored and sliced)*

low or nonfat Italian dressing

- **Wrap bread in foil and place in warm oven.**
- **Arrange broken lettuce leaves on large individual dinner plates.**
- **Place cucumbers around edge of plate, sprinkle with onion, red and green pepper, grated carrot, and cabbage.**
- **Divide tuna over top and garnish with tomato and seeds.**
- **Serve 1/2 sliced apple on a small plate to the side of each salad.**

Serve your favorite hearty bread in a basket in the center of the table.

Notes

Pick up a loaf of your favorite bread on your way home from work.

TUESDAY

April/Week Two

Notes

Penne Pasta with "Creamy" Red Sauce

This is nearly as easy as pasta marinara.

Preparation time: 25 minutes
Servings: 2-3
Ingredients:

Red Sauce
one 29 oz. can tomato sauce
2 cloves garlic *(smashed and chopped)*
1 T. dry oregano leaves
1 1/2 T. dry basil leaves
2 slices medium yellow onion *(chopped)*
a few dashes of Tabasco® sauce *(optional)*

2 1/2 C. dry penne pasta or rigatoni

fixings for a green salad

1 1/2 C. Red Sauce *(from above recipe)*
1/2 C. plain, nonfat yogurt *(stirred smooth)*

2-4 T. fancy-shred Parmesan

- **Place pasta water on to boil in large kettle.**
- **Make Red Sauce.**
- **Drop dry pasta into boiling water and set timer for 8 minutes.**
- **Prepare green salads.**
- **When pasta is cooked, drain and rinse with warm water.**
- *Reserve all but 1 1/2 C. Red Sauce for a future meal.*
- **Stir yogurt into 1 1/2 C. Red Sauce. Remove from heat.**
- **Divide pasta on two plates.**
- **Cover each serving with 3/4 C. "Creamy" Red Sauce.**
- **Sprinkle 1-2 T. Parmesan cheese over each serving.**

Serve with crisp green salad.

Leftover Night

You've got a few things there — use 'em or lose 'em!

Preparation time: 20 minutes
Servings: 2-3
Ingredients:

WEDNESDAY
April/Week Two

leftover "Wild Game" Turkey Breast
leftover sauce from marinated turkey
potatoes
Red Sauce

Notes

- **If you need to cook a little extra pasta, put some water on to boil.**
- **Slice some fresh fruit to have on the side.**
- **If necessary, cook and mash some additional potatoes. Dice turkey, and stretch the marinade sauce with an extra 1/8 C. wine or broth. Drop diced turkey into the sauce and serve over potatoes.**

This is where you really get your money's worth!

More trivia:

According to the Sept. 1993 issue of Vitality Magazine, *one of the top ten fat burners is eating breakfast in the morning. Why? It starts your body's metabolism process.*

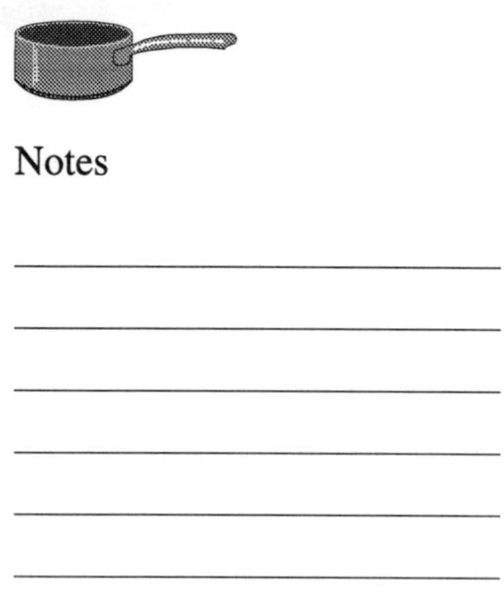

Loaded Rice

Time once again for my favorite "carbo-load."

Preparation time: 25 minutes
Servings: 2
Ingredients:

8-10 baby red potatoes or 1 large russet potato
1 T. olive oil

1/2 lb. mushrooms *(sliced)*
1/4 red bell pepper *(thin-sliced)*
1 T. olive oil
1 large clove garlic *(smashed and chopped)*
1/4 C. white wine
2 slices medium onion *(quartered)*

3/4 C. chicken or vegetable broth
3 T. corn starch dissolved in 1/8 C. cold water

1 1/2 C. cooked brown rice

1 C. plain, nonfat yogurt
1 T. pesto
dash of Tabasco®

2 Roma tomatoes *(chopped)*

- **Preheat oven to 400 degrees.**
- **Wash and halve baby red potatoes. If using russet potato, wash and slice** *(unpeeled)* **in 1/2" slices. Place potatoes, flat side down, on cookie sheet oiled with one tablespoon olive oil.**
- **Sauté sliced mushrooms and bell pepper in oil with garlic, wine, and onion** *(about 4 minutes).* **When done, remove mushroom mixture from pan with perforated spoon. Set aside.**
- **Add broth to pan. Return to boil.**
- **If cooking russet potato slices, turn them now.**
- **Slowly stir corn starch mixture into boiling liquid. Reduce heat to low. Cook 5 minutes, stirring often.**
- **Add mushrooms to thickened mixture. Return to boil. Remove from heat.**
- **Stir yogurt, pesto, and Tabasco® together until smooth. Microwave 30 seconds on high. Stir again.**
- **Warm 1 1/2 C. cooked rice 2 minutes on high in microwave on individual serving plates.**
- **Remove potatoes from oven. If using baby reds, push them into rice on individual plates. If using russets, chop into 1" pieces before sprinkling over rice.**
- **Stir yogurt mixture into thickened mushroom sauce.**

Pour sauce over potato/rice mixture and garnish with fresh chopped tomato.
Enjoy!

If you haven't any cooked rice in the fridge, "quick cook" some rice this morning before work.

"Quick Cooked" Rice
Place 1 C. long grain brown rice in a pan with 2 1/4 C. cold water. Cover and bring to boil over high heat. When water boils, turn off heat. Leave pan on burner. Do not lift cover! It will be ready to eat when you get home tonight.

Pasta Bolognese

FRIDAY

April/Week Two

A return to an old standby. Remember this one with your own Italian Turkey Sausage from ground turkey?

Preparation time: 30 minutes
Servings: 2-3
Ingredients:

8 oz. fresh fettuccine

Italian Turkey Sausage
1 T. olive oil
1 lb. ground turkey
2 slices medium yellow onion *(chopped)*
2 large cloves garlic *(smashed and chopped)*
2 tsp. dry basil leaves
1 tsp. dry oregano leaves
1/2 tsp. ground anise
dash of Tabasco® sauce
1/8 C. red wine

Red Sauce
one 29 oz. can tomato sauce
2 cloves garlic *(smashed and chopped)*
1/4 C. red wine
1 T. dry oregano
1 1/2 T. dry basil leaves
4 slices medium yellow onion *(chopped)*
a few dashes of Tabasco® sauce *(optional)*

1/3 lb. cooked Italian Sausage
1/8 C. red wine
1 1/2 C. Red Sauce

green salad fixings

3 T. fancy-shred Parmesan

Notes

- **Place pasta water on to boil in large kettle. Drop pasta into water and cook 2 1/2 minutes. Drain and rinse.**
- **Place oil in sauté pan over medium-high heat.**
- **Add ground turkey and the rest of the Italian Sausage ingredients.**
- **Prepare Red Sauce at the same time. Place all ingredients in medium sauce pan and bring to boil. Cover, reduce heat to low, and cook 10 minutes.** *(When Red Sauce is cooked, measure 1 1/2 C. for tonight's recipe and put remainder away in fridge.)*
- **Sauté sausage mix until browned.** *(Reserve 1/3 of the sausage for tonight's recipe and put remainder away in fridge.)*
- **Combine Italian Sausage, wine and Red Sauce in same pan used to cook Red Sauce.** *Bring to boil. Reduce heat to low and cover while finishing dinner preparations.*
- **Prepare green salads.**
- **Divide pasta on two plates and spoon Bolognese Sauce over each serving.**
- **Garnish with Parmesan cheese.**

Serve with crisp green salad. Pretty simple!

SATURDAY

April/Week Three

SHOPPING DAY

Notes

It's shopping day again! Check your supplies and head for the store! There are a number of new and delicious recipes coming up next week!

How are you doing with exercise? *The American Heart Association now includes inactivity among the most controllable risk factors for heart disease. The other factors are smoking, high cholesterol and high blood pressure.*
Health Scene, Katy Medical Center, Katy, TX

Ever try to pass a kidney stone? *More than a million Americans develop kidney stones every year. Eating less salt and drinking more orange juice may reduce your risk of developing this painful condition. (Reducing salt in your diet won't hurt your blood pressure either.)*
Research at the University of Texas Southwestern Medical Center, Dallas, TX

Are you still craving fast food? Check this out! *Jack in the Box's "Colossus," a half-pound burger with cheese and bacon has 1,095 calories, 75 grams fat, 225 mg. cholesterol, and 1,340 mg. sodium.*
Nutrition Action Health Letter, Washington, DC 20009

When you get home *from the store, put 2 cups dry navy beans in a pot with 10 cups water. Soak overnight.*

GROCERY LIST

Produce

- 2 medium yellow onions
- 10 baby red potatoes
- 6-8 small white potatoes
- 6 fresh mushrooms
- 2 green bell peppers
- 2 red bell peppers
- 1 yellow or orange bell pepper
- 2 large carrots
- 1/8 lb. fresh broccoli
- one head green cabbage
- green salad fixings
- 1 bunch beet greens *(or available greens)*
- 6-8 Roma tomatoes
- 1 lemon
- 1 lime
- 1 tart apple
- 1 bunch fresh parsley

Frozen Foods

- frozen orange juice
- 1 package large, shelled, cooked shrimp

Meat/Fish/Poultry

- 3 Italian turkey or chicken sausage links
- 2 frozen orange roughy fillets

Canned or Dry Foods

- one 29 oz. can tomato sauce
- one 29 oz. can "Ready-cut" tomatoes
- two 15 oz. cans chicken broth
- 1 lb. dry navy beans *ortwo 15 oz. cans white beans (Buy canned beans only ifyou are not cooking dry beans.)*
- 12 oz. dry bow tie pasta
- 8 oz. fresh cheese ravioli
- a loaf of hearty bread

Chilled Foods and Dairy

Buy if you're out

- 1 head garlic
- frozen peas
- corn starch
- brown sugar
- brown rice
- Dijon mustard
- red cooking wine
- shredded Parmesan
- plain, nonfat yogurt
- butter

White Beans, Red Sauce & Peppers

Bell peppers are in supply at a reasonable price. Their addition to this recipe adds a refreshing flair to a repeat performance. If yellow or orange peppers are too expensive, you can survive without them.

SUNDAY
April/Week Three

Preparation time: 20 minutes *(after beans are cooked)*
Servings: 2
Ingredients:

- a loaf of your favorite hearty bread
- 3 C. cooked white beans or *two 15 oz. cans rinsed white beans*
- 1 1/2 C. leftover Red Sauce *(leftover from Friday)*
- 3 slices yellow onion *(quartered)*
- 1/2 red, green, and yellow bell pepper *(chopped in 1" chunks)*
- fixings for green salad
- 2-4 T. fancy-shred Parmesan

Notes

- **Wrap bread in foil and place in warm oven.**
- **Start with beans cooked earlier in the day.** *(If you haven't cooked beans, use two 15 oz. cans rinsed beans.)*
- **Place leftover Red Sauce in medium-sized sauce pan and bring to boil.**
- **Add onion and chopped red, green and yellow peppers. Cook over low heat 5 minutes.**
- **Prepare green salads.**
- **Warm beans in microwave** *(1 minute on high).* **If you don't have a microwave, pour boiling water over beans in large bowl, let stand five minutes and drain.**

Measure 1 1/2 C. cooked beans per serving in center of individual plates and cover with 3/4 C. Red Sauce and Peppers. Garnish with Parmesan. Serve with crisp green salad and warm bread.

Begin cooking beans during the afternoon.

Pour off water from beans which were soaked overnight. Add 8 C. fresh water. Bring to boil. Reduce heat to low. When boiling slows, cover and cook over low heat 2 hours. Remove from heat and drain in colander. Return to pan, add 2 cups water, cover, and set aside until you're ready to prepare tonight's meal.

MONDAY
April/Week Three

Notes

Orange Roughy with Mustard Glaze

Continuing theme and variation on orange roughy!

Preparation time: 25 minutes
Servings: 2
Ingredients:

3-4 medium white potatoes *(washed and quartered)*
3/4 C. water

one bunch beet greens *(or available greens)*
1/2 C. broth
1/4 C. orange juice
4 T. balsamic vinegar
1/2 clove garlic *(chopped)*
2 slices medium onion *(quartered)*

3/4 C. white wine
1 clove garlic *(smashed and chopped)*
4 thin slices of a red bell pepper

2 medium orange roughy fillets or 2/3 lb. of roughy
black pepper
1 tsp. Dijon or honey mustard

1/2 tart apple *(chopped)*

1 tsp. butter
6 T. chicken broth
1 T. chopped fresh parsley

- **Wash potatoes and quarter. Place in medium sauce pan with water. Bring to boil over medium-high heat. Cover, reduce heat to low. Set timer for 15 minutes. When tender remove from heat.**
- **Wash greens and cut leaves away from stems. Set leaves aside. Chop stems in 1" pieces. Place stems, broth, orange juice, vinegar, garlic and onions in large heavy-bottomed kettle. Bring to boil, reduce heat to low. Simmer 7 minutes.**
- **Place 1/2 C. of the wine, garlic and red pepper in sauté pan and bring to boil. After 1 minute, lift red pepper out and set aside on plate.**
- **Slide fish fillets into boiling mixture and season with black pepper. Cook about 3 minutes per side. After turning fish, spread 1/2 tsp. mustard over each fillet and top with cooked red pepper. Add another 1/4 C. wine. Cook 2 more minutes.**
- **Add leaf portion of greens and apple to stems in large kettle. Toss over medium-high heat until wilted. Reduce heat and stir frequently for 5 minutes. If necessary, add a little broth to keep pan from cooking dry. Drain in colander just before serving.**
- **Remove potatoes from heat. Drain.** *I freeze leftover cooking water for use in soups.* **Add butter** *(only 1 tsp.)*, **broth, and chopped parsley. Gently toss over medium heat until well coated.**

Serve fillets flanked by greens and potatoes.

Ravioli with "Cream" Sauce

TUESDAY
April/Week Three

This is similar to tortellini with cream sauce. The sauce is successful over any kind of ravioli. Buy whichever kind "tickles your fancy."

Preparation time: 25 minutes
Servings: 2-3
Ingredients:

1 C. broth
1/4 C. white wine
1 slice onion *(chopped)*
2 cloves garlic *(smashed and chopped)*

3 T. corn starch dissolved in 1/4 C. water

2 T. Parmesan cheese
dash of Tabasco®

8 oz. fresh ravioli

green salad fixings

1/2 C. plain, nonfat yogurt *(stirred smooth)*
1 1/2 T. pesto

3 Roma tomatoes *(chopped)*
1 T. fresh chopped parsley
3-4 T. fancy-shred Parmesan

Notes

- **Boil pasta water in large kettle.**
- **Place broth, wine, onion, and garlic in small sauce pan and bring to boil. Cook 5 minutes over medium heat.**
- **Thicken with 3 T. corn starch mixed with 1/4 C. water. Cook 5 more minutes.**
- **Add Parmesan and Tabasco®. Cook, uncovered, an additional 5 minutes. Remove from heat.**
- **Place ravioli in boiling water.** *Fresh ravioli cooks in 7-9 minutes. Set a timer so you don't overcook it.* **Drain and rinse.**
- **Prepare green salads.**
- **Stir yogurt and pesto until smooth. Cook 30 seconds at full power in microwave to take off chill. Stir once more and add to thickened broth. Do not return to heat.**
- **Serve ravioli on individual plates with "Cream Sauce" spooned over the top.**

Garnish with fresh chopped tomatoes, parsley and Parmesan. Accompany with fresh green salads. Molti Bravi! You've done it again!

WEDNESDAY

April/Week Three

Notes

"Cossack" Red Potatoes and Sausage

Here is a delicious one-dish meal. I call it "Cossack" potatoes because I had a similar dish in a Russian cafe. I added the Parmesan cheese which makes it a little more international.

Preparation time: 30 minutes
Servings: 2-3
Ingredients:

10 baby red potatoes
1 T. olive oil

2 links Italian chicken or turkey sausage
2 T. broth

1/4 C. chicken broth with 2 dashes Tabasco® sauce
1 clove garlic *(smashed and chopped)*
1 large carrot *(peeled and sliced in 1/8" slices)*

1/2 green bell pepper *(chopped in 1" pieces)*
1/2 red bell pepper *(chopped in 1" pieces)*
one slice medium yellow onion *(quartered)*

2 T. pesto
3 T. broth
dash of Tabasco®

4 Roma tomatoes *(chopped in large pieces)*
4-6 T. fancy-shred Parmesan cheese

- **Preheat oven to 400 degrees.**
- **Wash potatoes, cut in half and place face down on oiled cookie sheet in oven.**
- **Prick sausage several times with fork. Wrap in paper towel, place in covered dish and microwave 2 minutes on high. Repeat process twice. Cool slightly and slice in 1/8" rounds.**
- **Place sausage in large fry pan and sauté with 2 T. broth 3 minutes.**
- **Add remaining broth** *(with Tabasco®)*, **garlic, and carrots. Sauté 2 minutes.**
- **Add peppers and onion and sauté an additional 3 minutes.**
- **Remove potatoes from oven and add to sausage/vegetable mixture.**
- **Mix pesto, broth, and Tabasco®.**
- **Stir chopped tomatoes and pesto mixture into sausage/vegetable/potato mixture.**

Serve immediately on individual plates and garnish with Parmesan cheese.

Teriyaki Shrimp and Rice

A new variation on teriyaki.

Preparation time: 30 minutes
Servings: 2-3
Ingredients:

THURSDAY

April/Week Three

Notes

Teriyaki Sauce
1/2 C. white wine
1/4 C. orange juice
2 cloves garlic *(smashed and chopped)*
2 thin slices onion *(chopped very fine)*
6 T. low-sodium soy sauce
1 tsp. sesame oil
1/2 tsp. freshly grated ginger
3 T. brown sugar

8-10 large cooked shrimp *(shelled and deveined)*
one slice medium onion *(chopped)*
1/4 C. Teriyaki Sauce

1/2 C. frozen peas
1 carrot *(peeled and cut in "shoe string" thin slices)*

2-3 cups cooked brown rice ("quick cooked" this morning)

1/2 head cabbage *(cored and chopped)*
1 large carrot *(grated)*
2 slices medium onion *(quartered)*
1/8 lb. broccoli *(cut in 1" pieces)*
3 T. orange juice
1/4 C. Teriyaki Sauce

If you haven't any cooked rice in the fridge, "quick cook" some rice this morning before work. *(see page 110)*

- **Place all teriyaki sauce ingredients in sauce pan over medium-high heat and bring to boil. Reduce heat to low and cook, covered, 5 minutes.**
- **Place shrimp, chopped onion, and 1/4 C. Teriyaki Sauce in sauté pan. Sauté over medium heat 1 minute. Remove shrimp from pan and set aside.**
- **Add peas and sliced carrots to pan. Sauté 2 more minutes. Stir in cooked rice while on burner. Cover, remove from heat.**
- **Place cabbage, grated carrot, onion, broccoli, and orange juice in medium sauce pan with Teriyaki Sauce. Bring to boil stirring constantly. Cook 3 minutes. Add shrimp, heat thoroughly, and serve.**

Serve on individual serving plates. Rice mixture one side with vegetable/shrimp mixture on the other.

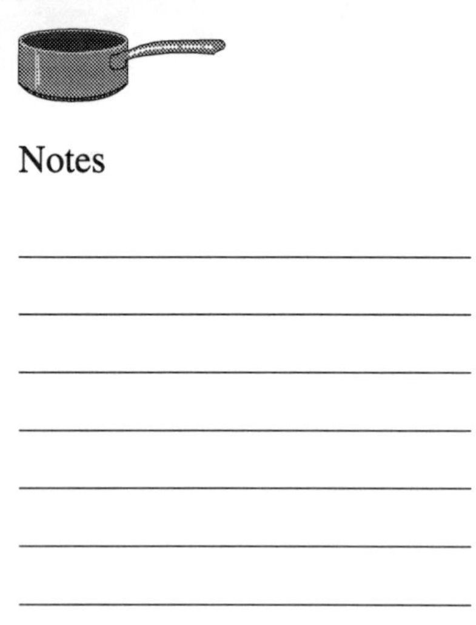

FRIDAY
April/Week Three

Notes

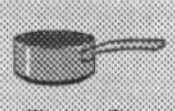

Pick up a loaf of hearty bread today.

Bow Tie Pasta with Chunky Red Sauce

A repeat of a delicious meatless pasta.

Preparation time: 25 minutes
Servings: 2-3
Ingredients:

a loaf of your favorite hearty bread

Chunky Red Sauce
one 29 oz. can "Ready-cut" tomatoes
1/4 C. red wine
2 cloves garlic *(smashed and chopped)*
or 1 tsp. commercially prepared chopped garlic
2 slices medium yellow onion *(chopped)*
1 1/2 T. dry basil leaves
1 T. dry oregano leaves
dash of Tabasco®
1/2 C. Red Sauce

1 Italian sausage link *(cooked and sliced in rounds)*

4 C. dry bow tie pasta

green salad fixings

2-4 T. fancy-shred Parmesan cheese

- **Wrap bread in foil and place in warm oven.**
- **Place large kettle on stove filled 2/3 full of water. Turn heat on high and cover.**
- **Set colander over sauce pan. Pour chopped tomatoes into colander and drain liquid into sauce pan. Set tomato chunks aside in bowl.**
- **Add all Chunky Red Sauce ingredients** *(except tomato chunks)* **to juice from tomatoes in sauce pan. Bring to boil. Reduce heat to low. Cover and cook 5 minutes.**
- **Prick Italian sausage several times with fork, wrap in paper towel, and place in covered bowl. Microwave two 2-minute bursts on high. Let cool.**
- **Pour dry pasta into boiling water. Cook 10 minutes. Drain and rinse.**
- **Make green salads while pasta cooks.**
- **Press sausage firmly with flat side of fork while wrapped in paper towels to force out excess fat. Slice in rounds and place on fresh paper towel. Place rounds in shallow pan and brown slightly over high heat.** *This will only take a few minutes.*
- **Add tomato chunks to Red Sauce and bring to boil. Remove from heat.**
- **Spoon sauce over pasta on individual serving plates. Lay sausage rounds over top of servings and sprinkle with 1-2 T. Parmesan cheese.**

Serve with warm bread and salad on side. Was it a little easier this time?

SHOPPING DAY

SATURDAY

April/May

Yes, I use a lot of red bell pepper! *While red bell peppers are considerably more expensive than green bell peppers, they are packed with vitamin A — 10 times more vitamin A than green peppers. More important, I relish the flavor it adds to nearly any dish. Don't be deterred by the price. The average-sized red pepper will probably add only $1.00 to your grocery bill.*

An average person *can burn 200-250 calories playing 18 holes of golf. However, one must walk the course. Sorry, no free ride to fitness.*

Are you recycling and watching the packaging on what you buy? *The average American produces 110,000 lb. of garbage by age 75.*

Health, 301 Howard St. , Suite 1800, San Francisco, CA 94105

A chocolate craving *may indicate your body needs magnesium. Good sources of magnesium are fruits, potatoes, whole grain cereals, and fresh vegetables.*

Women's Health Letter, 2245 E. Colorado Blvd., Suite 104, Pasadena, CA 91107

Notes

____

____

____

____

____

____

____

____

GROCERY LIST

Produce

- 6-8 baby red or white potatoes
- 2-4 medium baking potatoes
- 2 medium yellow onions
- 4 tart apples
- fresh ginger
- 1 green bell pepper
- 1 red bell pepper
- 1 yellow bell pepper
- 2 large carrots
- one bunch green onions
- green salad fixings
- 2 ripe kiwi
- 6-8 Roma tomatoes
- fresh parsley
- 4 oz. fresh snow peas
- 1 lemon
- 1 lime

Frozen Foods

- 1 package frozen snow peas *(if fresh snow peas are unavailable)*

Meat/Fish/Poultry

- 1 lb. ground turkey breast
- 1 package thin-sliced turkey fillets *(you may also use whole fillets and slice them yourself)*
- 6-10 boneless, skinless chicken breasts
- 8-10 large, cooked cocktail shrimp

Canned or Dry Foods

- one 29 oz. can tomato sauce
- two 15 oz. cans chicken broth
- one 15 oz. can black beans
- one small bottle barbecue sauce
- whole wheat or saltine crackers
- 8 oz. fresh cheese tortellini
- white cooking wine

Chilled Foods and Dairy

- 6 oz. sharp cheddar cheese
- nonfat milk
- tortillas

Buy if you're out

- garlic
- frozen corn
- one 15 oz. can navy beans *(if you have no leftover beans)*
- dried rosemary
- chili powder
- cumin powder
- sesame oil
- low-salt soy sauce
- corn starch
- balsamic vinegar
- cornmeal
- brown rice
- Parmesan cheese
- eggs
- plain, nonfat yogurt

SUNDAY
April/May

Notes

Grilled Chicken and Barbecued Beans

Here is a delicious early spring barbecue.

Preparation time: 30 minutes
Servings: 4
Ingredients:

8 baby red potatoes *(washed and halved)*
1 T. olive oil

Chicken Baste
3 T. balsamic vinegar
1 small clove garlic *(smashed and chopped) or* 1/2 tsp. chopped garlic
1/8 tsp. sesame oil
1/4 C. white wine

4-8 boneless, skinless chicken breasts

BBQ Sauce
1/3 C. tomato sauce
2 T. Worcestershire
dash Tabasco®
2 T. white vinegar
3 T. brown sugar
1 clove chopped garlic
1 T. chopped onion
1 tsp. dried oregano
2 tsp. chili powder

1/3 C. Barbecue Sauce *(make your own or use commercial)*
1/2 green bell pepper *(chopped)*
1/2 yellow bell pepper *(chopped)*
2 thin slices medium onion *(chopped)*
1 clove garlic *(smashed and chopped)*
1 1/2 C. cooked white beans *(thaw leftovers from freezer)*
3 Roma tomatoes *(chopped)*

- **Cook halved potatoes on oiled cookie sheet 25 minutes in 400 degree oven.**
- **Mix Chicken Baste in small bowl.**
- **Grill chicken while basting constantly, or sauté by adding 2 T. basting liquid at a time and sautéing until liquid boils away. Chicken will be cooked in 10 minutes.** *(I usually cook extra and freeze some for lunches or future meals.)*
- **Mix Barbecue Sauce ingredients in small sauce pan. Bring to boil, cover, reduce heat to low and cook 5 minutes.**
- **Place 1/3 C. Barbecue Sauce, peppers, onion, and garlic in sauce pan. Bring to boil. Cook 3 minutes.**
- **Add white beans, tomatoes, and cooked potatoes. Stir until heated through.**

Serve bean mixture in center of plate with chicken breast on the side. Save leftover basting liquid and Barbecue Sauce for future use.

Leftover Night

One final clean-up at the end of the month. Make sure you don't have things growing in there.

Preparation time: 20 minutes
Servings: 2-3
Ingredients:

Notes

leftover Beans, Red Sauce and Peppers
Chicken and Barbecued Beans
Red Sauce

- **If you need to cook a little extra pasta, put some water on to boil.**
- **Make a green salad to add freshness to leftovers.**

About low calorie diets:
Most diets don't work! Be particularly careful about low calorie diets. You need to consume 10 calories a day for every pound you weigh to keep your organs working properly.
Self, 350 Madison Ave., New York, New York 10017

Prepare Turkey Apple Loaf for tomorrow night's dinner

Turkey Apple Loaf

1 lb. ground turkey breast
1 C. crushed saltine crackers
1 clove garlic *(smashed and chopped)*
2 thin slices onion *(chopped very fine)*
2 egg whites
1/2 tsp. dry oregano leaves
1/2 tsp. ground black pepper
1/3 C. chicken broth
1 tart apple *(chopped)*
1/8 tsp. crushed rosemary leaves
1/4 tsp. cinnamon

- **Mix all ingredients thoroughly in large bowl and pack in small loaf pan.**
- **Place in 350 degree oven for one hour.** *(Set timer so you don't forget.) Remove from oven. Let cool for 1/2 hour. Remove from pan, wrap in foil and refrigerate until tomorrow evening.*

TUESDAY
April/May

Notes

Turkey Apple Loaf

This recipe is very similar to old fashioned meat loaf. I've added a Northwest flair.

Preparation time: 30 minutes *(prepare loaf the night before)*
Servings: 2-4
Ingredients:

2-4 medium-sized baking potatoes *(one per person)*

Turkey Apple Loaf *(prepared last night)*

Corn with Red Pepper
1/2 red bell pepper *(chopped)*
1/4 C. chicken broth
2 C. frozen whole kernel corn

Sauce for Turkey Apple Loaf
1/2 C. chicken broth
1/2 C. white wine
1 clove garlic *(smashed and chopped)*
1 thin slice medium onion *(chopped fine)*
1/2 tsp. cinnamon

2 T. corn starch mixed with 1/4 C. water

1/4 C. plain, nonfat yogurt

Baked Potato Topping
2 green onions *(chopped)*
1 C. plain, nonfat yogurt *(stirred)*

Set oven at 400 degrees on "time bake" so that it will begin cooking 1/2 hour before you arrive home. Prick baking potatoes with fork, rub with a little olive oil and place on center rack of oven.

- **If you weren't able to cook potatoes on "time bake," prick them with fork, place them on a plate and microwave three 5-minute bursts on high. Wrap them in foil and set aside.**
- **Place cooked, foil-wrapped meat loaf on center rack of oven. Heat at 400 degrees for 1/2 hour, or place in oven during final 1/2 hour while potatoes cook.**
- **Place chopped pepper, broth, and corn in small sauce pan.** *Do not turn on heat yet.*
- **Measure remaining broth and wine into sauce pan. Add garlic, onion and cinnamon. Bring to boil.**
- **Thicken with corn starch mixture. Cook 5 minutes over low heat. Remove from heat.**
- **Let stand a few minutes and add stirred yogurt.**
- **Turn heat on under corn. Bring to boil and cook 1 minute. Remove from heat.**
- **Stir green onions into yogurt.**
- **When potatoes are tender, remove from oven with meat loaf. Unwrap meat loaf and cool. Wait 5 minutes before slicing.**

Serve meat loaf with a couple spoonfuls of sauce over it. Flank meat with corn and split potato. Set yogurt/onion mixture on table to dress potatoes.

Cheese Tortellini with Red Sauce

WEDNESDAY
April/May

Let's revisit this simple, delicious recipe.

Preparation time: 20 minutes
Servings: 2
Ingredients:

Red Sauce *(see page 111)*
green salad fixings
8 oz. fresh tortellini or 1 1/2 C. dry tortellini
4 T. fancy-shred Parmesan cheese
2 T. fresh chopped parsley

- **Place pasta water in large kettle. Bring to boil.**
- **Prepare Red Sauce.** *(Save 1/4 C. for Friday's meal.)*
- **Fix green salads.**
- **Place tortellini in boiling water. Cook 7-9 minutes. Drain and rinse.**
- **Serve on individual plates with 1/2 - 3/4 C. Red Sauce per serving.**

Garnish with Parmesan and chopped parsley.

Notes

Garlic/Lime Sautéed Shrimp

I think you'll like this one. It's got a good spicy hit!

Preparation time: 30 minutes
Servings: 2
Ingredients:

2 C. cooked rice

1/4 C. white wine
8-10 cooked and deveined cocktail shrimp
juice from one lime
1 clove garlic *(smashed and chopped) or 1 tsp. prepared garlic*
1/4 tsp. fresh ginger

4 slices medium onion *(chopped)*
1 clove garlic *(smashed and chopped) or 1 tsp. prepared garlic*
1/2 C. broth
1 large carrot *(cut in thin strips 1" long)*

3 dashes cayenne pepper
4 oz. fresh or frozen snow peas

2 T. corn starch dissolved in 1/4 C. water

2 fresh kiwi fruits *(peeled and sliced in rounds)*
2 Roma tomatoes *(chopped)*

- **"Quick cook" rice in the morning or place 2 C. brown rice in 4 C. water on the stove when you come in from work. When it boils, cover and reduce heat to low, and cook 1/2 hour.** *You'll have left-over rice. Save it for tomorrow night.*
- **Place wine, shrimp, lime juice, garlic, and ginger in large fry pan. Sauté 2 minutes. Remove from pan with perforated spoon and place in bowl. Leave juice in pan.**
- **Place onion, 1 clove garlic, broth, and carrot strips in same pan and sauté 1 minute.**
- **Add cayenne pepper and snow peas and sauté 2 minutes.**
- **Use perforated spoon to lift vegetables out of pan. Leave juice. Return to boil.**
- **Thicken by slowly stirring corn starch mixture into liquid.**
- **Reduce heat and cook uncovered 5 minutes.**
- **Peel and slice kiwi. Overlay slices along edge of two serving plates.**
- **Return shrimp and vegetables to sauce.**

Add fresh chopped tomato, return to boil and serve immediately over bed of rice. ***Caution!*** *Do not overcook the dish at this point. The shrimp will get tough and the tomatoes mushy if cooked too long.*

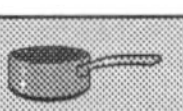

"Quick cook" some rice in the morning before work. (see page 110) Cook extra. You'll use it tomorrow evening.

Mexican Chicken Breasts

In honor of Cinco de Mayo.

Preparation time: 30 minutes
Servings: 2
Ingredients:

1/4 C. leftover Red Sauce
1 T. chili powder
1/2 tsp. cumin
1 tsp. oregano

Coating for Chicken

5 T. flour	1 tsp. oregano
2 T. cornmeal	1/2 tsp. cumin
1 T. chili powder	1/8 tsp. black pepper

2 boneless, skinless chicken breasts
1 T. olive oil
2 cloves garlic *(smashed and chopped)*
3 slices medium yellow onion *(chopped)*

1/4 red bell pepper *(chopped)*
1/4 green bell pepper *(chopped)*
1 thin slice onion *(chopped)*
1 T. chili powder
1/2 C. broth
1/2 C. frozen corn
1/2 C. leftover cooked rice

one 15 oz. can black beans *(drained and rinsed)*
1/4 C. salsa

2 thin slices extra-sharp cheddar cheese
flour tortillas

Notes

- **Mix Red Sauce, 1 T. chili powder, 1/2 tsp. cumin, and 1 tsp. oregano in small bowl and microwave on high 1 1/2 minutes, or bring to boil in small sauce pan over medium-high heat. Remove from heat. Set aside.**
- **In a plastic bag, mix flour, cornmeal, 1 T. chili powder, 1 tsp. oregano, 1/2 tsp. cumin, and black pepper. Shake to mix thoroughly.**
- **Drop chicken breasts into bag and shake until coated.**
- **Preheat sauté pan with oil over medium-high heat. Place coated breasts, garlic, and all but 1 T. onion in pan and cook until breasts are golden brown on both sides. Reduce heat to medium-low, cover, and cook 5 minutes.**
- **While breasts are cooking, put red and green pepper, onion, chili powder, and broth in bottom of shallow sauce pan. Bring to boil and cook 1 minute. Add corn, boil 2 more minutes** *(stirring occasionally)*, **and stir in cooked rice. Reduce heat to low and continue cooking 2 minutes** *(again, stirring occasionally)*.
- **Place rinsed beans in sauce pan with salsa over low heat.**
- **Turn breasts and cover with leftover Red Sauce. Place cheese slice over each breast. Cover, reduce heat to low, and cook 5 minutes.**

Serve on individual plates with the breast in the center flanked by black beans and rice mixture. Serve a warm, rolled tortilla on the side.

SATURDAY

May/Week One

Notes

SHOPPING DAY

You don't find many red meat recipes in this book. *One reason is that they're high in fat. Men should take special note. One study found that men who ate the most red meat had the highest risk of an advanced or fatal case of prostate cancer. Another companion study found that men who ate red meat 5 times or more a week had higher prostate cancer risks than those who ate red meat one to three times a month.*
Research at Harvard University, Cambridge, MA

Are you getting enough fiber? *Many people are not getting the recommended daily intake of 20-35 grams. The best sources of fiber are bran (some breakfast cereals), beans (all kinds), apples, carrots, corn, cucumbers, potatoes, and squash.*
The Cooper Aerobics Center, Dallas, TX

Fat intake, *not calorie intake, makes children obese. Doctors don't usually recommend that children go on diets. Instead, they encourage them to eat healthful lowfat meals and snacks.*
American Journal of Clinical Nutrition, 9650 Rockville Pike, Bethesda, MD 20814

Try putting raisins or banana *(or both) on your breakfast cereal. A banana has 569 mg. potassium and raisins (1/4 C.) have 271 mg. potassium. (Raisins are also an excellent source of iron.) Another great source of potassium is cantaloupe. Half a cantaloupe has 502 mg.*
New Body, 1700 Broadway, New York, NY 10019

If you eat vegetarian, *you can always substitute vegetable broth for chicken broth in my recipes.*

GROCERY LIST

Produce

8-10 baby red potatoes
 or 1 large russet potato
4 tart apples
2 yellow onions
1/2 lb. fresh broccoli
1 lb. fresh mushrooms
2 green bell peppers
2 red bell peppers
12 medium carrots
1 bunch green onions
2 bunches fresh spinach
or 1 package prewashed spinach
green salad fixings
1 cucumber
6-8 Roma tomatoes
one lemon
firm tofu

Frozen Foods

Meat/Fish/Poultry

1 lb. ground turkey breast
2 boneless, skinless chicken breasts
2 fresh snapper or cod fillets *(You will not cook the fish until Thursday. You may wish to wait and purchase fresh fish on Thursday.)*

Canned or Dry Foods

1/2 C. package sliced almonds
1/2 C. package pecan halves
one small bottle Greek or Italian olives
one small bottle capers
one small can sliced black olives
one 29 oz. can tomato sauce
five 15 oz. cans chicken broth
one 15 oz. can vegetable broth
12 oz. dry spiral or penne pasta
 (whole wheat if you can find it)
one loaf of your favorite hearty bread
2 large thin-crust Boboli® or frozen pizza shells

Chilled Foods and Dairy

1 dozen eggs

Buy if you're out

pine nuts
garlic
one package turkey bacon *(Check the freezer. You'll only need a couple pieces.)*
ground cinnamon
dry basil leaves
dry oregano leaves
dry tarragon leaves
ground anise
brown rice
Tabasco®
olive oil
Dijon mustard
red cooking wine
white cooking wine
plain, nonfat yogurt
fresh pesto
butter

Spinach Salad and Carrot/Apple Soup

SUNDAY

May/Week One

This is a nice theme and variation on spinach salad. Here is a meal absolutely loaded with nutrients, a most elegant, light fare. I prepared this soup for a dinner party of conservative eaters. They all loved it! One even commented that it was "one of the best soups" he had ever eaten.

Preparation time: 25 minutes
Servings: 2
Ingredients:

1 loaf of your favorite hearty bread

2 bunches fresh spinach
(washed, dried, stems removed and leaves broken into pieces)
1/2 cucumber *(peeled, sliced in 1/4" rounds and quartered)*
3 green onions *(chopped)*
1/2 red bell pepper *(thin sliced and quartered)*
4 Roma tomatoes *(chopped)*

1/2 C. tofu *(chopped)*
1 tsp. Dijon mustard
1/4 C. broth

Dressing
2 strips cooked turkey bacon *(chopped)*
(An option to bacon would be 2 T. chopped, toasted pine nuts.)
2 T. balsamic vinegar
2 T. olive oil
1 clove garlic *(smashed and chopped)*
2 tsp. Dijon mustard
5 T. chicken or vegetable broth
2 T. white wine
fresh-ground black pepper *(to taste)*
1/2 tsp. sesame oil

Carrot/Apple Soup *(prepared earlier)*
1/2 C. plain, nonfat yogurt *(stirred smooth)*
2 T. toasted pine nuts *(chopped)*

4 T. sliced almonds *(toasted)*
2-3 T. fancy-shred Parmesan

- **Wrap bread in foil and place in warm oven.**
- **Toss vegetables in large bowl.**
- **Sauté tofu with mustard and broth in a small non-stick fry pan over medium-high heat. Sauté 2 minutes. Remove from pan with perforated spoon and place in large bowl with vegetables.** *(Save liquid in pan.)* **Toss vegetables and tofu together.**
- **Add dressing ingredients to same pan used to sauté tofu. Bring to boil. Remove from heat. Let stand 5 minutes.**
- **Pour dressing into bowl with vegetables and toss again.**
- **Reheat soup prepared earlier today. When soup is hot, stir in yogurt and place in bowls. Garnish with chopped, toasted pine nuts.**
- **Serve salads on large individual plates garnished with sliced almonds, and Parmesan cheese.**

Serve with warm bread.

Notes

Do this minimal preparation during the day for tonight's meal. It will take about 30-40 minutes.

Carrot/Apple Soup
9 medium carrots *(washed and chopped)*
one 15 oz. can chicken *or vegetable broth*
1 small yellow onion *(chopped)*
2 large tart apples *(cored, peeled, and chopped)*
1 clove garlic *(smashed and chopped)*
1 tsp. cinnamon
one 15 oz. can broth *(second can)*

- ***Place carrots, one 15 oz. can broth, onion, apples and garlic in large sauce pan. Cook over medium heat 20-25 minutes.***
- ***Place cooked carrot mixture in food processor and blend thoroughly or beat on high speed with electric mixer until smooth.***
- ***Return to pan, add cinnamon and second can broth, and cook 15 minutes over low heat. Cover and remove from heat until ready to serve.*** *If more than 2 hours will pass before dinner, refrigerate.*

MONDAY

May/Week One

Pasta Putanesca

Tonight we'll revisit this spicy pasta which is destined to become a favorite. Experiment with the flavors. Add an extra clove of chopped garlic or give it an extra shot of Tabasco®. Maybe use a different kind of pasta.

Preparation time: 30 minutes
Servings: 2-3
Ingredients:

Notes

Italian Sausage
1 T. olive oil
1 lb. ground turkey breast
2 slices medium yellow onion *(chopped)*
2 tsp. dry basil leaves
1 tsp. dry oregano leaves
1/2 tsp. ground anise
2 large cloves garlic *(smashed and chopped)*
dash of Tabasco® sauce

1 1/2 C. Red Sauce
Use leftovers or make a new batch. *(page 111)*

green salad fixings

1/8 C. red wine
2 cloves garlic *(smashed and chopped)*
2 T. green capers *I like the larger capers, they're softer and more flavorful.*
5 Italian or Greek olives *(chopped)*

12 oz. dry whole wheat pasta

3 T. fancy-shred Parmesan
1 T. chopped parsley

- **Place pasta water on to boil in large kettle.**
- **Place all Italian Sausage ingredients in fry pan and cook until browned over medium-high heat** *(about 10 minutes)*. **Remove from heat and set aside.** *Use 1/3 of the Italian Sausage in tonight's recipe and save remainder for another time.*
- **Prepare Red Sauce.** *Reserve 1 1/2 C. for tonight's meal and save the rest for a future meal.*
- **Prepare green salads on individual plates.**
- **To 1 1/2 C. Red Sauce, add wine, 1/3 of the cooked Italian Sausage, extra 2 cloves garlic, capers, and olives.**
- **Cover sauce and place over low heat while finishing dinner preparations.**
- **Drop dry pasta into boiling water. Cook 8 minutes. Drain and rinse.**
- **Divide pasta onto plates and cover with Putanesca Sauce.**

Garnish with Parmesan cheese and chopped parsley.

You've done it again!

Chicken/Mushroom Omelet

Another variation on lowfat omelets. You'll cook an extra chicken breast. Don't eat it! Save it!

Preparation time: 20 minutes
Servings: 2
Ingredients:

6 eggs
1/4 C. plain, nonfat yogurt *(stirred smooth)*
black pepper
1/2 tsp. oregano leaves

2 sautéed boneless, skinless chicken breasts *(chopped)*
1 clove garlic *(smashed and chopped)*
1 T. olive oil

10-12 large white mushrooms *(chopped)*
2 slices of a medium onion *(chopped)*
1/2 C. broth
1/4 C. white wine

2 T. corn starch dissolved in 1/4 C. water

1/4 red bell pepper *(chopped)*
3 T. fancy-shred Parmesan

1 tsp. pesto
1 tsp. butter
2 slices of bread for toast

- **Break 2 eggs into medium-sized bowl. Separate whites from yolks of remaining eggs. Discard yolks and add whites to bowl with whole eggs. Beat about 30 seconds with wire whisk.**
- **Beat yogurt into eggs and season with black pepper and oregano. Set aside.**
- **Brown chicken breasts and garlic in oil in small fry pan** *(5 minutes per side).*
- **Remove from pan and let cool. Add a few T. water to pan and bring up drippings. Add to egg mixture.** *Chop one chicken breast and put one away in fridge.*
- **Sauté 1/2 the mushrooms and onion in broth and wine in 10" non-stick fry pan over medium heat. Sauté 3 minutes.**
- **Remove mushrooms from pan and thicken liquid with corn starch mixture and cook over reduced heat 5 minutes. Pour sauce over mushroom mixture in bowl.**
- **Important! Wash pan thoroughly, dry, coat with a little oil, and reuse.**
- **Pour egg mixture into pan and cook 1 minute. Lay uncooked mushrooms, red pepper, and chopped chicken down center of pan. Cook another 2 minutes. Sprinkle Parmesan over vegetable mixture and fold edges over vegetables. Hold folded portion in place with spatula for 1 minute.**
- **Slide omelet out onto a serving plate. Use plate to turn omelet over in pan.**
- **Reduce heat to low. Cook, covered, with folded portion down, 2 minutes.**
- **Mix pesto and butter in small cup.**
- **Toast bread and spread with pesto mixture.**
- **Rewarm mushroom sauce in microwave 1 minute on high prior to serving.**

Halve omelet and remove from pan to two serving plates. Spread mushroom sauce over each half and serve.

Notes

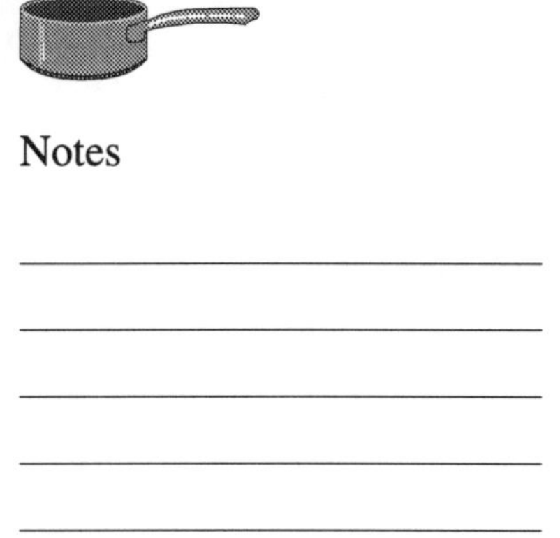

Notes

"Quick cook" some rice this morning before work. *(see page 110)* *Cook extra rice. Use 2 C. rice to 4 1/2 C. water.*

Loaded Rice

Have at it! It's time for this favorite! You'll make extra white sauce for Friday night's meal.

Preparation time: 25 minutes
Servings: 2
Ingredients:

8-10 baby red potatoes or 1 large russet potato
1 T. olive oil

1/2 lb. mushrooms *(sliced)*
1/4 red bell pepper *(thin-sliced)*
1 T. olive oil
1 large clove garlic *(smashed and chopped)*
1/4 C. white wine
2 slices medium onion *(quartered)*

3/4 C. chicken or vegetable broth
3 T. corn starch dissolved in 1/8 C. cold water

1 1/2 C. cooked brown rice

1/2 lb. fresh broccoli *(cut into 2" pieces)*

1 C. plain, nonfat yogurt
1 T. pesto
dash of Tabasco®

2 Roma tomatoes *(chopped)*

2 wedges lemon

- **Preheat oven to 400 degrees.**
- **Wash and halve baby red potatoes. If using russet potato, wash and slice** *(unpeeled)* **in 1/2" slices. Place potatoes, flat side down, on oiled cookie sheet.**
- **Sauté sliced mushrooms and bell pepper in oil with garlic, wine, and onion** *(about 4 minutes).* **When done, remove mushroom mixture from pan with perforated spoon. Set aside.**
- **Add broth to pan. Return to boil.**
- **If cooking russet potato slices, turn them now.**
- **Slowly stir corn starch mixture into boiling liquid. Reduce heat to low. Cook 5 minutes, stirring often.** *Set aside 1/2 C. white sauce mixture for Friday's meal.*
- **Add mushrooms to thickened mixture. Return to boil. Remove from heat.**
- **Warm 1 1/2 C. cooked rice 2 minutes on high in microwave on individual serving plates.** *Reserve remaining rice for tomorrow.*
- **Remove potatoes from oven. If using baby reds, push them into rice on individual plates. If using russets, chop into 1" pieces before sprinkling over rice.**
- **Place broccoli in steamer basket in covered sauce pan and turn heat on high. Steam, covered, 2 minutes.**
- **Stir yogurt, pesto, and Tabasco® together until smooth. Microwave 30 seconds on high. Stir again, and add to thickened mushroom sauce.**

Pour sauce over potato/rice mixture and garnish with fresh chopped tomato. Serve broccoli and lemon on side of plate. Enjoy!

Red Snapper with Pesto

THURSDAY

May/Week One

Time again for fish. Remember this delicious variation?

Preparation time: 25 minutes
Servings: 2
Ingredients:

8 pecan halves *(toasted under the oven broiler and chopped)*
3 slices medium yellow onion *(chopped)*
1 1/2 C. rice *(left over from yesterday)*
1/2 C. chicken broth

3 medium carrots *(sliced at an angle)*
1/4 C. broth
1 tsp. olive oil
1/8 tsp. tarragon

1 large clove garlic *(smashed and chopped)*
or 1 tsp. prepared chopped garlic
6 thin slices of a red bell pepper
1/2 C. white wine
1 large or 2 small red snapper *(or Pacific Snapper)* fillets

2 tsp. fresh pesto

Notes

- **Place pecans, onions, and rice in bowl with broth and cook, covered, in microwave 3 minutes.**
- **Place carrots in saucepan with broth, oil, and tarragon.** *Do not turn on heat yet.*
- **Place garlic, bell pepper, and wine in non-stick fry pan over medium-high heat. Sauté 2 minutes. Lift red pepper out and set aside on plate.**
- **Slide fish into wine and garlic mixture over high heat. When wine boils, cook 3 minutes per side.** *If wine boils away, add another 1/3 C. liquid (wine, water or broth).*
- **Turn burner on high under carrots. When water boils, cover and cook 2 minutes. Remove from heat.** *To serve, lift carrots out of remaining liquid with perforated spoon.*
- **Turn fish, spread with pesto, and lay pepper strips over fish fillets. Reduce heat to low, cover, and cook final 3 minutes.**
- **Fish and carrots should be done about the same time.**

You may need to pick up fresh fish today.

Arrange fish on individual serving plates flanked by carrots on one side and rice on the other.

FRIDAY

May/Week One

Notes

Red and White Pizza with Salad

You will use your leftover Red Sauce and Italian Sausage from Monday night, leftover chicken from Tuesday night, and leftover White Sauce from Wednesday.

Preparation time: 25 minutes
Servings: 2-4
Ingredients:

3/4 C. leftover Italian Turkey Sausage

2 Boboli® shells or frozen pizza shells

3/4 C. leftover Red Sauce
1 large clove garlic *(smashed and chopped)*
or1/2 tsp. prepared chopped garlic
2 T. fancy-shred Parmesan cheese
1 dash of Tabasco®

1/2 C. leftover white sauce
1/4 C. plain, nonfat yogurt *(stirred smooth)*

4-6 black olives *(chopped)*

3 slices medium yellow onion *(quartered)*
12 medium mushrooms *(sliced in 1/4" slices)*

1/2 red bell pepper *(chopped)*
1 leftover chicken breast *(thin sliced)*

8 T. fancy-shred Parmesan

fixings for a green salad

- **Preheat oven to 400 degrees.**
- **Thaw sausage in microwave or place in covered, oven-safe dish while oven preheats.**
- **Place Boboli® shells directly on center rack in oven. Cook 3 minutes and remove.**
- **Place Red Sauce in small bowl with 1/2 the garlic, 2 T. Parmesan, and Tabasco®. Cover bowl. Cook in microwave 2 minutes at full power or place in a small sauce pan and bring to a boil over medium-high heat. Cover, and remove from burner.**
- **Place leftover white sauce and remaining garlic in another pan over medium heat. When warm, stir in yogurt. Remove from heat.**
- **Spread Red Sauce on one crust and white sauce on other.**
- **Arrange sausage, olives, 1/2 the onion, and 1/2 the mushrooms on red pizza.**
- **Place remaining onion, mushrooms, red pepper, and chicken on white pizza.**
- **Divide Parmesan between pizzas and return to oven for 8-10 minutes.**
- **Prepare green salads.**
- **Remove pizzas from oven and cut in wedges while hot.**

Let Pizza cool for 5 minutes before eating. Serve with salad on the side.

SATURDAY

May/Week Two

SHOPPING DAY

You will need cooked black and white beans for the first recipe, "Black and White Chili." Try cooking your own beans. It is much cheaper than buying canned beans. You also have better control of the sodium content. If you use canned beans, be sure to rinse them well to eliminate salt.

To remove red table wine stains from clothing, *rub in table salt then launder with an appropriate bleach.*
The Good Housekeeping Household Encyclopedia, Hearst Books, 1993

No cry babies! *Chilling onions before chopping them will make your eyes water less. Teary eyes are caused by an enzyme in onion called allinase that bonds to the sulfur in onion when exposed to air. The enzyme irritates the tear ducts.*
Self, 350 Madison Avenue, New York NY 10017

If your spirit needs lifting, *take a walk or climb stairs. Even a 5 or 10 minute workout will boost your spirits and give you a new perspective on the day.*
Robert Thayer, MD, professor of psychology, California State University, Long Beach

Notes

GROCERY LIST

Produce

- 2 large russet potatoes
- one 6" zucchini
- 2 yellow onions
- 1/8 lb. fresh broccoli
- 1/2 lb. fresh mushrooms
- 2 green bell peppers
- one each - yellow and red bell pepper
- bok choy
- 1 orange
- 1/4 lb. dried cranberries
- green salad fixings
- 6-8 Roma tomatoes

Frozen Foods

- frozen corn

Meat/Fish/Poultry

- 1 lb. ground turkey breast
- 8-10 large frozen, cooked, shelled shrimp
- 2 boneless, skinless chicken breasts

Canned or Dry Foods

- 1/2 C. package chopped walnuts
- 1/2 C. package whole, blanched almonds
- one 6 oz. can sliced water chestnuts
- one 6 oz. can sliced bamboo shoots
- one 15 oz. can apple sauce
- one 29 oz. can tomato sauce
- two 29 oz. cans "Ready-cut" tomatoes
- two 15 oz. cans chicken broth
- 2 C. dry black beans *(or two 15 oz. cans black beans)*
- 2 C. dry navy beans *(or two 15 oz. cans navy beans)*
- 12 oz. dry whole wheat or spinach spaghetti
- 12 oz. dry multi-colored spiral pasta
- red cooking wine
- one loaf of your favorite hearty bread
- 1 box fortune cookies

Chilled Foods and Dairy

- 3 oz. sharp Cheddar cheese

Buy if you're out

- one head garlic
- dried thyme leaves
- ground cumin
- chili powder
- ground cloves
- old-fashioned oats
- plain, nonfat yogurt
- fancy shred Parmesan

Black and White Chili

SUNDAY

May/Week Two

Here is a great chili to throw together on a weekend. It goes together in about 20 minutes, but it should simmer for about 30 minutes following the assembly. Make some corn bread to go with it. You should have extra beans. Save one cup black beans in fridge for later in the week. The rest will keep nicely in the freezer.

Notes

Preparation time: 50 minutes *(20 to assemble, 30 to cook)*
Servings: 4-6
Ingredients:

- 1 lb. ground turkey breast
- 1 T. olive oil
- 1 medium onion *(chopped)*
- 2 cloves garlic *(smashed and chopped) or 2 tsp. prepared garlic*
- one 29 oz. can chopped tomatoes
- one 29 oz. can tomato sauce
- 1 green bell pepper *(chopped)*
- 2 cups cooked white navy beans
- 2 cups cooked black beans
- 2 T. chili powder
- 1/2 tsp. ground cloves
- 1 tsp. ground cumin
- 1/4 tsp. Tabasco®
- dash of cayenne pepper *(optional)*

a loaf of your favorite hearty bread or prepare corn bread *(see page 71)*

a grating of very sharp Cheddar cheese

- **Brown turkey in sauté pan with oil, onion and garlic.**
- **Combine turkey mixture, and all ingredients above, in 8 quart sauce pan.**
- **Cover and simmer 30 minutes.**
- **Wrap bread in foil and place in warm oven, or prepare corn bread.**
- *Freeze remaining beans, reserving 1 C. black beans for Tuesday's dinner.*
- **Grate sharp Cheddar cheese** *(about 1 T. per serving)* **over each bowl.**

Serve with bread or corn bread.

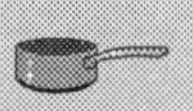

Cook black and white beans in separate kettles during the day.

- ***Drain water from pre-soaking beans.***
- ***Add 2 quarts fresh water to each kettle.***
- ***Cook slowly for 2 hours or until tender. Add a few cups additional water as needed.***

Whole Wheat Pasta with Chunky Red Sauce

A slightly more robust version of marinara. The whole wheat pasta (I suggested spaghetti, but you may use any kind) will add nice flavor and texture.

Preparation time: 25 minutes
Servings: 2-3
Ingredients:

Notes

Chunky Red Sauce
one 29 oz. can "Ready-cut" tomatoes
1/4 C. red wine
2 cloves garlic *(smashed and chopped)*
or 1 tsp. commercially prepared chopped garlic
2 slices medium yellow onion *(chopped)*
1 1/2 T. dry basil leaves
1 T. dry oregano leaves
dash of Tabasco®

1/2 C. Red Sauce *(see page 111)*

12 oz. whole wheat spaghetti

green salad fixings

2-4 T. fancy-shred Parmesan cheese

- **Place large kettle on stove filled 2/3 full of water. Turn heat on high and cover.**
- **Place colander over sauce pan and drain "Ready-cut" tomatoes. When liquid has drained, pour tomato chunks into bowl and set aside.**
- **Add remaining Chunky Red Sauce ingredients to tomato liquid in pan. Cover and cook 10 minutes over medium-high heat.**
- **Prepare a batch of Red Sauce.** *Measure 1/2 C. for tonight's meal and reserve remainder.*
- **Place dry pasta into boiling water and set timer for 10 minutes. Drain and rinse with warm water.**
- **Prepare green salads.**
- **Add 1/2 C. Red Sauce and chunky tomatoes to tomato liquid. Return to boil. Remove from heat.**
- **Divide pasta on two plates.**
- **Cover each serving with 1/2 to 3/4 cup of Chunky Red Sauce.** *Reserve remaining Chunky Red Sauce and Red Sauce for a future meal.*
- **Sprinkle 1-2 T. Parmesan cheese over each serving.**

Serve with a crisp green salad.

TUESDAY
May/Week Two

Notes

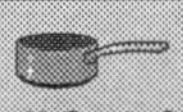

"Quick cook" some rice this morning before work. *(see page 110)* *Make a double batch. You'll use the remainder on Wednesday.*

Black Beans, Rice and Peppers

Here is a delicious use for leftover black beans from Sunday. You will have "quick cooked" rice this morning, if you didn't have leftovers.

Preparation time: 30 minutes
Servings: 3-4
Ingredients:

hearty bread

fixings for a green salad

1/2 green bell pepper *(chopped in 1" squares)*
1/2 red bell pepper *(chopped in 1" squares)*
1/2 orange or yellow bell pepper *(chopped in 1" squares)*
2 slices of a medium onion *(quartered)*
1 clove fresh garlic *(smashed and chopped)*
or 1 tsp. prepared chopped garlic
1/4 C. broth

1/2 C. Red Sauce or Chunky Red Sauce *(leftovers)*
a couple dashes of Tabasco®

1 C. cooked brown rice
1 C. cooked black beans *(leftover from Sunday)*

2-4 T. fancy-shred Parmesan cheese

- **Wrap bread in foil and place in warm oven.**
- **Prepare green salads.**
- **Sauté all vegetables together with garlic and broth 3 minutes over high heat in large, heavy sauce pan.**
- **Place Red Sauce and Tabasco® in same large pan with vegetables. Bring to boil. Cook 2 minutes. Remove from heat.**
- **Add rice and beans to vegetable/Red Sauce mixture. Warm over medium heat until thoroughly heated. Serve on individual plates.**
- **Garnish with Parmesan cheese.**

Serve with warmed bread and green salad.

Chicken Almond Stir Fry

Tonight we revisit this tasty stir fry. If you can't find the bok choy, try adding a can of drained, sliced bamboo shoots. If you like spicy food, add a couple dashes cayenne pepper to sauce when corn starch is added.

Preparation time: 30 minutes
Servings: 3-4
Ingredients:

2 boneless, skinless chicken breasts *(chopped into 1/2" cubes)*
1 T. vegetable oil
1/4 tsp. sesame oil
3 slices medium onion *(sliced in 1/8" thick slices and chopped)*
2 cloves garlic *(smashed and chopped)*

1/8 lb. broccoli *(cut in 2" lengths)*
2 stalks bok choy *(cubed)*
one 6 oz. can sliced water chestnuts *(drained)*
2 T. low-sodium soy sauce
one 6 oz. can sliced bamboo shoots *(drained)*
one 15 oz. can low-sodium chicken broth

6 mushrooms *(sliced)*

5 T. corn starch mixed with 1/4 C. water

2-3 C. cooked rice *(leftovers)*

1/4 C. whole almonds *(toasted under broiler)*

Notes

- **Chop raw chicken and set aside in bowl. *Important note: thoroughly wash, rinse and dry cutting board after chopping chicken, and before continuing to chop vegetables. I usually pour boiling water over the board after chopping raw meat.***
- **Prepare all vegetables before starting to cook.**
- **Place oils in large heavy-bottomed sauce pan or wok over high heat. Sauté onion, garlic and chopped chicken** *(about 5 minutes)* **stirring constantly.**
- **Toss in broccoli , bok choy, drained water chestnuts, 1 T. of the soy sauce, bamboo shoots, and 1/4 C. broth. Sauté 2 more minutes.**
- **Add mushrooms and a little more broth. Sauté another minute.**
- **Remove all ingredients from pan with perforated ladle or spoon and set aside.**
- **Using same pan, mix remaining broth and** *(1 T.)* **soy sauce. Bring to boil and thicken with corn starch/water mixture. Reduce heat and cook 3-4 minutes.** *(Add optional dashes cayenne pepper.)*
- **Warm 2-3 C. rice in covered dish 2 minutes on high in microwave.**
- **Add vegetables, meat and almonds to sauce and toss until everything is thoroughly coated. Serve immediately over warmed rice on individual plates.**

Have you learned how to use chopsticks? If not, try them out. Stir fry tastes better with chopsticks! It's true! Finish off the meal with tea and fortune cookies.

Notes

Cajun Spiral Pasta with Shrimp

Here is a delicious theme and variation on Red Sauce pasta which is sure to spice up your evening. Prepare the entire meal in one large, heavy-bottomed kettle.

Preparation time: 20 minutes
Servings: 2-3
Ingredients:

2 C. dry multi-colored spiral pasta

8 medium-sized mushrooms *(sliced)*
one 6" zucchini *(sliced in rounds)*
2 slices medium onion *(quartered)*
1/4 C. white wine

8-10 large, cooked, deveined shrimp
1 clove garlic *(smashed and chopped)*
1 T. chili powder
1/4 tsp. cumin

1 1/2 C. Red Sauce *(leftovers from Monday)*
1 clove garlic *(smashed and chopped)*
2 dashes of Tabasco®
1/4 tsp. dry oregano leaves
1/8 tsp. powdered cumin
1/8 tsp. dry thyme leaves
pinch of black pepper *(or white pepper if you have it)*
dash cayenne pepper *(more if you like things hotter)*

fixings for a green salad

2 T. fancy-shred Parmesan

- **Cook pasta in large heavy-bottomed kettle. Drain and rinse.**
- **Sauté mushrooms, zucchini, and onion in wine over medium-high heat** *(using same pan).* **Sauté 2 minutes. Lift mushrooms and zucchini out of liquid with perforated spoon. Set aside in dish.**
- **Add shrimp, garlic, and spices to liquid and sauté 1 minute. Set all ingredients in pan aside in separate bowl.**
- **Place Red Sauce, garlic, and spices in same pan. Cover and cook 5 minutes over medium heat.**
- **Prepare green salads.**
- **Add shrimp and vegetables to sauce. Heat until it returns to boil. Remove from heat.**
- **Rerinse pasta in warm water. Gently stir noodles into Red Sauce mixture and serve immediately.**

Garnish with Parmesan cheese and serve green salad on the side.

Baked Potato with Black & White Chili Topping

Wonderful! It's easy, delicious, and uses up leftovers!

FRIDAY

May/Week Two

Preparation time: 15-20 minutes
Servings: 2
Ingredients:

2 large russet baking potatoes
1 C. Black & White chili *(leftover from Sunday)*
1/2 C. frozen whole kernel corn
1/4 C. plain, nonfat yogurt *(stirred smooth)*
grating of sharp cheddar cheese.

Notes

- **If you weren't able to cook potatoes on "time bake," cook them now. You may also prick potatoes with a fork and microwave for three 5-minute cycles at full power, turning after each cycle.** *Wrap in foil and let stand for 5 minutes.*
- **Warm chili in microwave in small covered bowl 1 1/2 minutes at full power, or in a small sauce pan on stove top over medium-high heat. Stir constantly until it begins to boil, and remove from heat immediately.**
- **Add frozen corn to chili and continue heating 2 minutes. Do not boil.**
- **Stir yogurt until smooth.**

Cut potatoes in half, top with chili, and garnish with yogurt and a few gratings of sharp cheddar cheese.

If you have "time bake" on your oven, wash potatoes and place in oven this morning before work. Set to begin cooking 1 hour before you are to arrive home tonight.

SATURDAY

May/Week Three

Notes

SHOPPING DAY AND MUFFINS

How are you doing? *The American Dietetic Association (ADA) and the American Cancer Society are two of the organizations that recommend at least 5 servings of fruits and vegetables a day. (For optimum nutrition, ADA recommends up to nine servings.) A serving equals: 1 cup raw leafy vegetables; 1/2 cup raw chopped vegetables; 1/2 - 3/4 C. vegetable or fruit juice; 1 whole medium piece of fruit; 1/2 cup cooked or canned fruit, or 1/4 C. dried fruit.*

In case you're wondering, *there are 2-3 tablespoons of juice and 3 teaspoons of grated rind in one lemon. You'll need 5-6 lemons for 1 cup of juice.*

Cooking Light, 2100 Lakeshore Drive, Birmingham, AL 35209

Popcorn is still one of the best snack foods. *Americans consume 18 billion quarts of it a year. That's 71 quarts per person. One cup of plain, air-popped corn has 19 calories and no fat. That's provided you don't put butter on it. Be careful about microwave popcorn. It can be quite high in fat and sodium. It's always a good idea to read the labels on packages.*

American Popcorn Co., Sioux City, IA

Cranberry/Nut Muffins

Dry	Wet
1 C. white flour	3/4 C. nonfat milk
1 C. whole wheat flour	1 tsp. vanilla
1/2 C. oats	1 egg
1/4 C. chopped walnuts	1 T. vegetable oil
1/4 C. brown sugar	1/2 tsp. grated orange rind
1 tsp. baking powder	1/4 C. applesauce
2/3 C. dried cranberries	

- **Stir dry ingredients together in large bowl.**
- **Lightly beat wet ingredients together in separate bowl.**
- **Mix wet and dry ingredients together.**
- **Add cranberries.**
- **Spray muffin tins** *(makes 12)* **with vegetable spray.**
- **Place on center rack in oven at 375 degrees for 35 minutes.**

GROCERY LIST

Produce

4-5 baby red potatoes
3 medium white potatoes
3 large carrots
one parsnip
2 yellow onions
1 sweet onion
1/2 lb. fresh broccoli
3/4 lb. fresh mushrooms
2 green bell peppers
2 red bell peppers
1 cucumber
two 6" zucchini
fresh ginger root
one bunch fresh parsley
green salad fixings
one head red leaf lettuce
iceberg lettuce
3 oz. toasted sunflower seeds *(shelled)*
6-8 Roma tomatoes
1 lemon
1 orange

Frozen Foods

one 3 lb. package frozen, boneless, skinless chicken breasts
frozen halibut fillets or steaks
Buy if fresh halibut is too expensive.

Meat/Fish/Poultry

1 lb. turkey breast fillets
2 halibut fillets *You may wish to buy fresh fish on Wednesday.*

Canned or Dry Foods

dried fennel seeds
paprika
ground cumin
whole bay leaf
brown sugar
white cooking wine
red cooking wine
two 6 oz. cans chopped clams
one 29 oz. can tomato sauce
two 15 oz. cans chicken broth
one small can sliced black olives
8 oz. fresh or dry linguini
12 oz. dry spiral pasta *(multi-colored or spinach)*
one loaf of your favorite hearty bread

Chilled Foods and Dairy

3 oz. sharp cheddar cheese
plain, nonfat yogurt
nonfat milk
whole wheat tortillas
fresh salsa

Buy if you're out

one head garlic
dried thyme leaves
ground cumin
chili powder
ground cloves
old-fashioned oats
plain, nonfat yogurt
fancy-shred Parmesan

Hungarian Goulash

SUNDAY

May/Week Three

This is a hearty, one-dish meal.

Preparation time: 40 minutes
Servings: 3-4
Ingredients:

a loaf of your favorite hearty bread

4-5 baby red potatoes *(scrubbed and cut into quarters)*
1 medium parsnip *(peeled and cut into pieces the same size as potato)*
1/4 C. water
1/4 C. red wine

1 turkey breast fillet *(cut into 1" pieces)*
1 T. olive oil
1 clove garlic *(smashed and chopped)*

one 29 oz. can "Ready-cut" tomatoes
2 large carrots *(peeled and sliced into 1/2" rounds)*
2 cloves garlic *(smashed and chopped)*
1/2 medium onion *(chopped in large pieces)*
2 T. paprika
1 tsp. oregano leaves
1 bay leaf

one green bell pepper *(chopped into 1" chunks)*

Notes

- **Wrap bread in foil and place in warm oven.**
- **Place potatoes and parsnip in medium sauce pan over high heat with 1/4 C. water and 1/4 C. red wine. When liquid boils, reduce heat to medium and cook covered for 15 minutes.**
- **Sauté turkey breast pieces over medium-high heat with oil and garlic until brown.**
- **Drain juice from tomatoes into large sauce pan.** *(Set tomatoes aside in bowl.)* **Add carrots, garlic, onion, and spices. Bring to boil and cook 4 minutes at medium heat.**
- **Add cooked turkey and bell pepper. Cook 3 minutes.**
- **Add potatoes, parsnips, and tomato chunks. Reduce heat to low and cook, uncovered, 5 minutes.**

Ladle into bowls and serve with warm bread.

Notes

Linguini with Clam Sauce

A repeat performance. Remember this tasty, yet lowfat version of a classic clam sauce pasta? You'll have extra sauce for next Sunday's meal.

Preparation time: 30 minutes
Servings: 3
Ingredients:

12 medium-sized mushrooms *(sliced and chopped)*
1 small (6") zucchini *(split down the middle and sliced)*
1 clove garlic *(smashed and chopped)*
2/3 C. white wine

4 slices medium onion *(chopped)*
1 clove garlic *(smashed and chopped)*
1/2 C. broth
2 tsp. dry oregano
1 tsp. dry basil

two 6 oz. cans chopped clams *(with juice)*
3 dashes Tabasco®

4 T. flour
1/2 C. nonfat milk

4 T. Parmesan cheese

fixings for a green salad

8 oz. fresh linguini *(you may also use angel hair or spaghetti noodles)*

3/4 C. plain, nonfat yogurt *(stirred smooth)*

2 T. fancy-shred Parmesan cheese
1 T. chopped fresh parsley

- **Place pasta water on to boil in large kettle.**
- **In heavy sauce pan, sauté mushrooms, zucchini and garlic in white wine. Sauté 2 minutes. Remove veggies from pan with perforated spoon.**
- **Place onion, garlic, broth, oregano, and basil in sauce pan and bring to boil.**
- **Add clams** *(with juice)* **and Tabasco®. Return to boil.**
- **Shake flour and 1/2 C. milk in container with tight-fitting lid until mixture is smooth.**
- **When liquid returns to boil, slowly stir in flour mixture.**
- **Add 4 T. Parmesan. Reduce heat and cook, uncovered, 5 minutes.**
- **Prepare green salads.**
- **Slide pasta into boiling water.** *Cook linguini no more than 2 minutes.* **Drain and rinse with warm water.**
- **Stir yogurt into clam sauce and serve immediately over pasta.**

Garnish with shredded Parmesan and chopped parsley. Bravo! Pasta della mare!

Leftover Night

TUESDAY

May/Week Three

This should be an adventure!

Preparation time: 20 minutes
Servings: 2-3
Ingredients:

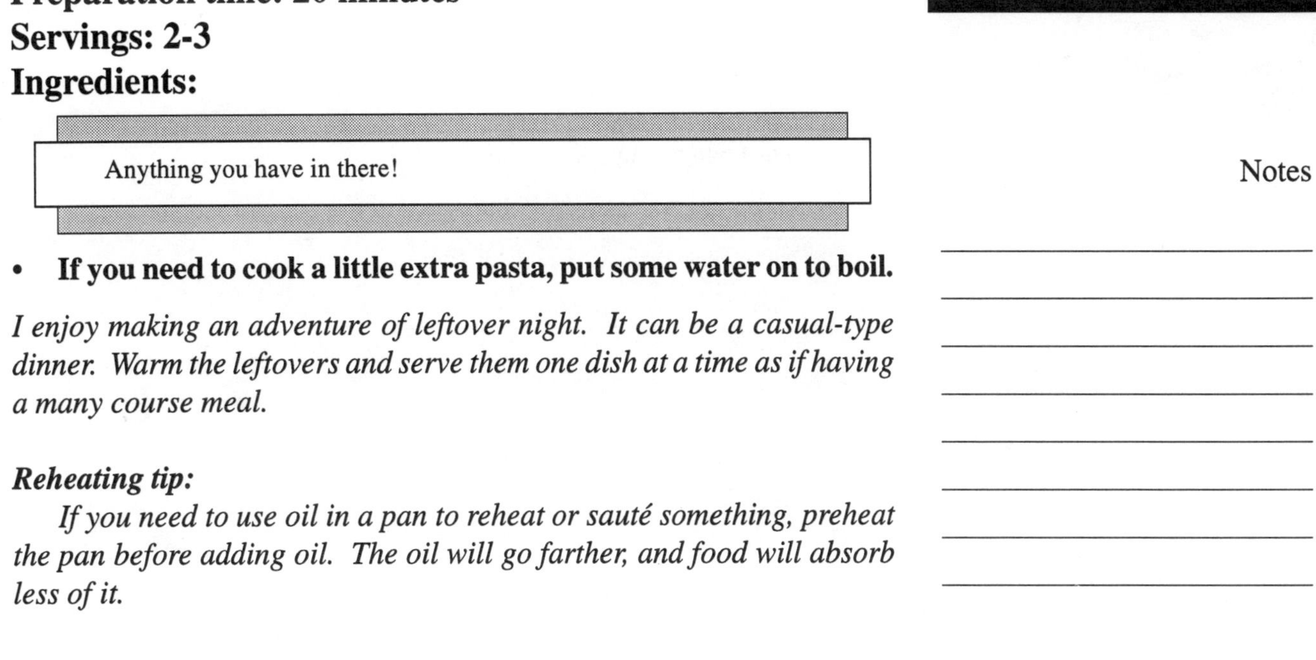

Anything you have in there!

Notes

- **If you need to cook a little extra pasta, put some water on to boil.**

I enjoy making an adventure of leftover night. It can be a casual-type dinner. Warm the leftovers and serve them one dish at a time as if having a many course meal.

Reheating tip:

If you need to use oil in a pan to reheat or sauté something, preheat the pan before adding oil. The oil will go farther, and food will absorb less of it.

WEDNESDAY

May/Week Three

Notes

You may wish to buy fresh fish today.

Gingered Halibut

Let's revisit this wonderful flavor combination.

Preparation time: 30 minutes
Servings: 2
Ingredients:

3 medium white potatoes *(quartered)*
3/4 C. water
1/4 tsp. dried fennel leaves
4 thin slices red bell pepper
1/2 C. white wine
1/2 lb. fresh broccoli *(cut in 2" lengths)*
15 oz. fresh halibut or 3 small halibut fillets
fresh-ground pepper
2-3 gratings fresh ginger
2 T. plain, nonfat yogurt
lemon wedges

- **Place potatoes in medium sauce pan with 3/4 C. water and dried fennel leaves. Bring to boil. Reduce heat to medium, cover, and cook 15 minutes. Remove from heat.** *Leave covered.*
- **Sauté pepper slices in wine,** *(1 minute).* **Remove peppers from pan and set aside.**
- **Place broccoli in steamer basket over a little water in medium-sized covered sauce pan.** *Do not turn on heat yet.*
- **Place fillets in wine remaining in sauté pan. Season with fresh-ground black pepper and poach over medium-high heat 4 minutes per side.** ***Important:*** *If liquid cooks away, add more wine or 1/2 C. water. Always maintain enough liquid to cover bottom of pan.*
- **Stir ginger into yogurt.**
- **Turn halibut in pan and spread yogurt mixture over each fillet. Place slices of red pepper over each fillet.** *If pan is dry, add 1/2 C. water or white wine.* **Cover pan and cook 4 minutes.**
- **Turn on heat under broccoli. Bring to boil. Cook, covered, 2 minutes.**
- **Place fish on individual serving plates with potatoes and broccoli served on either side.**

Place a wedge of fresh lemon on each plate for broccoli.

Hot Fajita Salad

THURSDAY

May/Week Three

A wonderful lighter fare. Theme and variation on fajitas. Use quark instead of sour cream.

Preparation time: 30 minutes
Servings: 2-4
Ingredients:

1 lb. turkey breast fillets *(cut in 1/8" strips)*
1 T. olive oil
2 cloves garlic *(smashed and chopped)*
or 1 tsp. commercially prepared chopped garlic
1 tsp. chili powder
1/4 tsp. ground cumin

1/4 C. broth
1 green bell pepper *(cut in 1" chunks)*
1 red bell pepper *(cut in 1" chunks)*
3 slices of a medium sweet onion *(quartered)*
1 tsp. chili powder
1/4 tsp. ground cumin

several leaves red leaf lettuce *(broken)*
1/2 head chopped iceberg lettuce
4 ripe Roma tomatoes *(chopped)*
8 slices peeled cucumber *(chopped)*

1 C. quark *(prepared this morning) stir before serving*
salsa

2 T. toasted sunflower seeds

4 whole wheat flour tortillas

- **Slice turkey breast fillets in thin (1/8") slices.**
- **Place poultry in shallow 10" non-stick fry pan with oil, garlic, chili powder, and 1/4 tsp. ground cumin over medium-high heat and sauté 5 minutes.**
- **Remove meat from pan and set aside.**
- **Add broth, peppers, onions, and remaining spices to same pan and sauté 3 minutes. Lift vegetables out with perforated spoon and set aside.**
- **Lay broken leaf lettuce on plates and top with chopped iceberg lettuce. Sprinkle with tomato and cucumber.**
- **Spoon fajita mixture over lettuce and sprinkle with tomato and cucumber.**
- **Top with quark and salsa to taste and garnish with a few toasted sunflower seeds.**
- **Warm tortillas in microwave by placing them between two serving plates and cooking 20 seconds on high, or warm in oven at 350 degrees 5 minutes in shallow, covered pan.**

Roll warmed tortillas and serve on side.

Notes

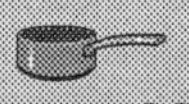

Make some quark

This morning before work, place 1 1/2 C. plain, nonfat yogurt in a sieve which has been lined with a coffee filter or paper towel. Set sieve over a dish to drain and place in fridge. Tonight you will have a thick version of yogurt reminiscent of rich sour cream.

FRIDAY
May/Week Three

Notes

Pasta Prima Vera with Red Sauce

Tonight it's time for Red Sauce-style prima vera again. You will need to make fresh Red Sauce.

Preparation Time: 30 minutes
Servings: 2 large adult portions *plus leftovers*
Ingredients:

2 1/2 C. dry spiral pasta

1 1/2 C. Red Sauce *(page 111)*

1 T. olive oil
1/2 tsp. crushed garlic
1 large carrot *(peeled and sliced)*
2 slices medium onion *(quartered)*

1/4 C. broth *(use vegetable if you are cooking vegetarian)*
1/2 medium green pepper *(cubed in 1" chunks)*
one 6" zucchini *(cut in 1/8" rounds)*
6 medium mushrooms *(sliced in 1/4" slices)*

2 Roma tomatoes *(cut in 1" chunks)*

2-4 T. fancy-shred Parmesan cheese
4 T. chopped black olives

- **Place pasta water on to boil in large sauce pan.**
- **Drop dry pasta into boiling water and cook 8 minutes.** *(Set a timer so you don't forget.)*
- **Make Red Sauce.**
- **Measure olive oil and garlic into sauté pan over medium-high heat. Add carrot and onion. Sauté 1 minute.**
- **Add broth, green pepper, zucchini, and mushrooms and sauté 2 minutes. Remove veggies from pan and set aside.**
- **Drain and rinse pasta.**
- **Pour 1 1/2 C. Red Sauce into same pan used to cook pasta. Bring to boil.**
- **Add all vegetables** *(including Roma tomatoes)* **to sauce and remove from heat.**
- **If necessary, microwave cooked pasta 1 minute on high to re-heat, or measure 1 to 1 1/2 C. per serving and place in bowl with boiling water for 1 minute prior to serving. Drain and rinse.**
- **Divide onto separate plates and ladle veggie sauce over it.**

Garnish with Parmesan and olives and serve immediately.

SHOPPING DAY

SATURDAY

May/Week Four

There are a number of lowfat and nonfat snack crackers on the market. *Read the labels on the carton. Some popular crackers have a fat content as high as 6 gm. per serving.*

Basil, chili powder, paprika, and parsley *are high in beta carotene, the antioxidant that may help prevent cancer and heart disease.*
First for Women, 270 Sylvan Avenue, Englewood Cliffs, NJ 07632

Chocolate bars can sabotage your diet: *think before you snack! A 3-4 oz. bar can pack 500 calories and 26 gm. fat. (That can pack it on to your thighs big time.)*
Nutrition Action Health Letter, 1875 Connecticut Ave., Suite 300, Washington, DC 20009

Shopping tip: *Shop for items on top and bottom shelves. Items placed at eye level are usually higher in price. Don't forget to check nutrition labels. Cheaper is not always better for you.*

If you're trying to stick to a budget, shop alone. It's harder to stick to a list when family members go along.

Notes

GROCERY LIST

Produce

6-7 large russet potatoes
one 6" zucchini
3 large carrots
2 yellow onions
1/2 lb. fresh broccoli
1/2 lb. fresh mushrooms
1 green bell pepper
2 red bell peppers
one bunch red seedless grapes
1 pink grapefruit
1 white grapefruit
2-3 tart apples
one bunch fresh parsley
green salad fixings
one head red leaf lettuce
iceberg lettuce
cucumber
6-8 Roma tomatoes
2 fresh lemons

Frozen Foods

Meat/Fish/Poultry

1 lb. turkey breast fillets
10 -12 boneless, skinless chicken breasts

Canned or Dry Foods

one 15 oz. can whole beets
two 6 oz. cans chopped clams
one 29 oz. can tomato sauce
one 15 oz. can chicken broth
12 oz. dry spinach linguini
12 oz. dry penne pasta *(whole wheat)*
or multi-colored spiral pasta
one large, thin-crust Boboli® shell
a loaf of your favorite crusty bread
You may wish to pick this up fresh from the bakery on Thursday.

Chilled Foods and Dairy

Buy if you're out

one head garlic
one 10 oz. package frozen corn
brown sugar
ground cinnamon
balsamic vinegar
Worcestershire sauce
honey
plain, nonfat yogurt
fancy-shred Parmesan

SUNDAY
May/Week Four

Notes

Clam Sauce Pizza and Salad

Now you will use the leftover Clam Sauce from last Monday night.

Preparation time: 25 minutes
Servings: 2
Ingredients:

1 Boboli® shell or frozen pizza shell

1 large clove garlic *(smashed and chopped)*
1/2 C. leftover Clam Sauce
dash of Tabasco®
1 T. fancy-shred Parmesan

2 slices medium yellow onion *(quartered)*
1/2 red bell pepper *(chopped)*
6 medium mushrooms *(sliced)*
5 T. fancy-shred Parmesan cheese

fixings for a green salad

- **Preheat oven to 400 degrees.**
- **Place Boboli® directly on oven rack in center of oven and cook 3 minutes.**
- **Place garlic, Clam Sauce, Tabasco®, and Parmesan in bowl. Cover and microwave 1 minute on high or warm in small sauce pan. Bring to boil and remove from heat.**
- **Spread clam sauce on Boboli® crust.**
- **Arrange all remaining items on top of sauce and sprinkle with Parmesan. Return to oven 8-10 minutes.**
- **Make a couple green salads.**
- **Remove pizza from oven and cut in 8 wedges while hot. Allow to cool a few minutes before serving.**

Serve with salad on the side.

Barbecued Chicken with Baked Potato Fries

MONDAY

May/Week Four

A little grilling is welcome in any diet.

Preparation time: 40 minutes
Servings: 3-4
Ingredients:

4-5 russet potatoes *(scrubbed and cut into 1/2" strips)*
1 T. olive oil

juice from 1 lemon
1 clove garlic *(smashed and chopped)*

one green bell pepper *(sliced into 1/2" strips)*
one 6" zucchini *(washed and split lengthwise into quarters)*
2 large carrots *(peeled and split into quarters lengthwise)*

6-8 boneless, skinless, chicken breasts
barbecue sauce

- **Place potatoes on oiled cookie sheet in center of 375 degree oven. Bake 10 minutes.**
- **Combine lemon juice and garlic.**
- **Begin grilling vegetables. As they grill, baste them with lemon/garlic mixture. Grill bell pepper about 3 minutes, zucchini about 4 minutes, and carrot about 7 minutes. Turn all vegetables often. When finished set aside on plate.**
- **Turn potatoes. Cook 10 more minutes.**
- **Grill chicken breasts. Do not baste with barbecue sauce until nearly done. Boneless breasts should cook in 12-15 minutes.**
- **At about the 10 minute mark begin basting.** *(Take a second and turn potatoes one more time.)* **Leave basted side down only about 30 seconds at a time, then turn and baste again.**
- **To rewarm vegetables and chicken, place in oven with potatoes for 3 minutes before serving.**

Serve buffet style.

Notes

TUESDAY

May/Week Four

Notes

"Bogus Pork" Medallions

Tonight we revisit one of my favorites. This dinner may take a bit longer, but it is worth it. Yes, I've used canned beets to save a little time.

Preparation time: 40 minutes
Servings: 3
Ingredients:

3 slices medium yellow onion *(quartered)*
2 medium *(unpeeled)* russet potatoes *(sliced in 1/2" slices)*
1 T. olive oil

one 15 oz. can whole beets

1 lb. turkey breast fillets *(sliced)*
1/4 C. flour
1 T. olive oil
2 large cloves garlic *(smashed and chopped)*
or 1 tsp. chopped prepared garlic
1/4 C. chicken broth
fresh-ground black pepper

1/4 C. white wine
1 large tart apple *(peeled, quartered, cored, and sliced in 1/4" slices)*
1 T. brown sugar
1/8 tsp. cinnamon

- **Preheat oven to 400 degrees.**
- **Place onion and potatoes on cookie sheet oiled with 1T. olive oil. Place in oven on center rack for 15 minutes. Turn and return to oven until dinner is ready.**
- **Place beets with juice in medium sauce pan. Cover and set aside.** *Do not turn on burner yet.*
- **Dredge sliced fillets in flour until well coated.**
- **Put remaining 1T. oil and garlic in 10" fry pan over medium-high heat. When garlic begins to sizzle, add floured fillets. Cook until golden brown** *(3-4 minutes per side). If pan gets too dry, add a little chicken broth.* **Season each side with fresh-ground black pepper.**
- **Lift fillets out of fry pan and set in oven with potatoes.**
- **Add wine to fry pan and rub bottom of pan gently with fork to lift up any drippings.**
- **Add apple slices, brown sugar, and cinnamon. Reduce heat to low, cover pan, and cook 5 minutes, stirring occasionally.**
- **While sauce is cooking, turn on burner under beets. Bring to boil, cover and cook 1 minute.**

Serve fillets on individual plates covered with apples and sauce. Serve beets and potatoes on either side of fillets. Delicious!

Lemon/Garlic Chicken and Broccoli Pasta

This is a lovely change-of-pace pasta.

Preparation time: 20 minutes
Servings: 2-3
Ingredients:

8 medium-sized mushrooms *(sliced)*
1/2 lb. broccoli *(cut in 1" pieces)*
two slices medium onion *(quartered)*
1/2 red bell pepper *(cut into 1" long thin strips)*
1 clove garlic *(smashed and chopped)*
1/4 C. white wine

1/2 rind from juiced lemon
1 T. olive oil
one large boneless, skinless chicken breast *(chopped)*
1 clove garlic *(smashed and chopped)*

2 1/2 C. dry spiral multi-colored or penne pasta

juice from one lemon
3/4 C. chicken broth
1 tsp. dry oregano leaves
1 clove garlic *(smashed and chopped)*
2 T. low-sodium soy sauce
2 T. sugar

2 T. corn starch mixed with 1/4 C. water

fixings for a green salad

1/2 C. plain, nonfat yogurt *(stirred smooth)*

4 T. fancy-shred Parmesan

Notes

- **Place pasta water on to boil in large kettle.**
- **Sauté mushrooms, broccoli, onion, red pepper and garlic in wine over medium high heat in large fry pan for 2 minutes. Pour all ingredients into bowl. Set aside.**
- **Chop 1/2 lemon rind into 4 large pieces. Sauté in oil with chicken and garlic in same pan used for vegetables. Sauté 5 minutes. Discard rind.**
- **Place pasta in water to cook.** *Set timer for 8 minutes.*
- **Add juice, broth, oregano, garlic, soy sauce, and sugar to chicken in pan. Drain juice from cooked mushroom mixture into pan.** *Do not add vegetables yet.* **Bring to boil, thicken with corn starch mixture and cook 5 minutes on low heat.**
- **Prepare green salads.**
- **Add vegetables to sauce and return to boil. Remove from heat and stir in yogurt.**
- **Drain and rinse pasta. Spoon sauce over pasta and garnish with Parmesan.**

Serve green salad on the side.

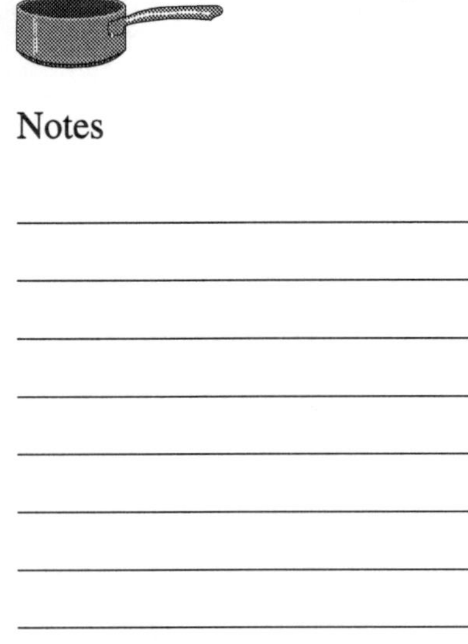

Notes

Pick up a loaf of your favorite crusty bread today.

Pasta Marinara

A repeat of this simple favorite! I've reprinted the Red Sauce recipe from April so you don't have to flip back through the book.

Preparation time: 25 minutes
Servings: 2-3
Ingredients:

Red Sauce
- one 29 oz. can tomato sauce
- 2 cloves garlic *(smashed and chopped)*
- 1 T. dry oregano leaves
- 1 1/2 T. dry basil leaves
- 4 thin slices medium yellow onion *(chopped)*
- a few dashes of Tabasco® sauce *(optional)*

12 oz. dry spinach linguini

fixings for green salad

2-4 T. fancy-shred Parmesan cheese

- **Place large kettle filled 2/3 full of water over high heat.**
- **Place all Red Sauce ingredients in sauce pan. Bring to boil over medium-high heat. Cover, reduce heat to low, and simmer 10 minutes.**
- **Drop pasta into boiling water.** *Set timer for 8 minutes.* **Drain and rinse.**
- **Prepare green salads while pasta cooks.**
- **Divide pasta on two plates.**

Cover each serving with 1/2 to 3/4 C. Red Sauce. Sprinkle 1-2 T. Parmesan cheese over each serving. Add a loaf of your favorite crusty bread. Reserve remainder of Red Sauce for another meal.

Leftover Night

Get that old stuff out of the fridge!

Preparation time: 20 minutes
Servings: 2-3
Ingredients:

leftover Red Sauce
lettuce leaves

- **If you need to cook a little extra pasta, put some water on to boil.**
- **Warm one cup Red Sauce and mix with 1/4 C. stirred, nonfat yogurt. Serve over pasta.** *(Voila! "Creamy" Red Sauce!)*
- **Any leftover Barbecued Chicken? Serve it hot or cold with pasta or chop it up and stir into sauce.**

A refreshing fruit salad *(You bought this stuff on Saturday.)*
Peel one pink and one white grapefruit. Lay sections on a piece of fresh lettuce. Throw a few red seedless grapes on top. Mix 1/2 C. stirred nonfat yogurt with 1 T. honey and drizzle it over the fruit.

Don't skip meals! *It's bad for your health and messes with your metabolism. Each day 9% of Americans don't eat breakfast and 22% skip lunch.*
Are You Normal?, by Bernice Kanner, St. Martin's Press, 1995

"Manly Man Activity!" *Thirty-one percent of men in the U.S. say they enjoy cooking. (Those of us who cook can consider ourselves among the "stud muffins.")*
Men's Health, 33 E. Minor St., Emmaus, PA 18098

FRIDAY

May/Week Four

Notes

SATURDAY

May/June

Notes

SHOPPING DAY

It's shopping day!

There is an unusual pasta dish on Sunday evening. If you have children, or if you don't care for sharp cheeses, you may wish to skip this one. If you're not sure, try it! I find it a wonderful adventure in new flavors.

Why attempt to lower fat intake? *Decreasing daily fat intake from 37% of total calories to 30% can lower your cholesterol by 6% while decreasing your risk of heart attack by up to 24%.*
Research at the University of Arizona, Tucson

Adding three 45-minute exercise programs a week *to a reduced-fat diet might decrease blood cholesterol levels 20 to 50 points.*
Vogue, 350 Madison Avenue, New York, NY 10017

Are you still keeping fresh flowers on hand? *Put a small bouquet of fresh flowers in the refrigerator when you're not at home. It will last longer.*
Esquire Gentleman, 250 West 55th St., New York, NY 10019

GROCERY LIST

Produce

1 6" zucchini
1 medium yellow onion
1/2 lb. fresh asparagus
1/8 lb. broccoli
1 lb. fresh mushrooms
2 green bell peppers
2 red bell peppers
2 tart apples (Granny Smith)
1 bunch fresh parsley
1 head red leaf lettuce
1 head Romaine lettuce
1 large cucumber
3 oz. pine nuts
10 Roma tomatoes
1 fresh lemon
celery

Frozen Foods

one package large, frozen scallops
You may choose to buy fresh scallops later in the week. If so, buy 10 small scallops.
orange juice

Meat/Fish/Poultry

3 boneless, skinless chicken breasts
8-10 oz. snapper *(you may wish to buy fresh fish on Wednesday)*

Canned or Dry Foods

1/2 C. pecan halves
one 29 oz. cans tomato sauce
two 15 oz. cans chicken broth
12 oz. dry spinach spiral pasta
12 oz. dry whole wheat spaghetti
8 oz. fresh egg fettuccine
1 loaf of your favorite hearty bread

Chilled Foods and Dairy

nonfat milk
3 oz. Gorgonzola cheese

Buy if you're out

brown rice
stone ground cornmeal
dried dill weed
dried rosemary
dried basil leaves
balsamic vinegar
sesame oil
corn starch
white cooking wine
red cooking wine
plain, nonfat yogurt
fancy-shred Parmesan

SUNDAY

May/June

A. P. G. Y. Spinach Spirals

What the heck is A.P.G.Y.? It stands for Apples, Pine nuts, Gorgonzola, and Yogurt. This is a slightly exotic pasta. Perhaps more suited for adult tastes (unless your children like very sharp cheeses).

Notes

Preparation time: 25 minutes
Servings: 2
Ingredients:

1 tart green *(Granny Smith)* apple *(cored and chopped)*
2 slices medium yellow onion *(chopped)*
1/4 C. broth

3 oz. Gorgonzola cheese *(crumbled)*
1-2 T. toasted pine nuts *(chopped)*

2 C. dry spinach spirals

1/2 C. broth

2 T. corn starch mixed with 1/4 C. white wine

1/2 C. plain, nonfat yogurt

2 T. fancy-shred Parmesan
2 Roma tomatoes *(chopped)*

- **Place pasta water on to boil in large kettle.**
- **Place apples and onion in a deep sauce pan and sauté 4 minutes in 1/4 C. broth.**
- **Stir Gorgonzola and pine nuts into apple mixture and transfer all to a bowl.**
- **Drop pasta into boiling water.** *Set timer for 10 minutes.* **Drain and rinse pasta.**
- **Pour 1/2 C. broth into pan used to sauté apples. Add any liquid remaining in apple mixture to broth in pan. Bring to boil over medium-high heat.**
- **Thicken with corn starch mixture, reduce heat to low, and cook 5 minutes. Remove from heat.**
- **Stir yogurt until smooth and add to thickened broth over low heat. Do not return to boil. When blended, remove from heat.**
- **Add apple mixture and mix with about 10 gentle stirring strokes.** *As an option you may also add 1/2 C. chopped tofu. It blends beautifully and gives the appearance of lots of cheese.*
- **Divide pasta into two portions and pour sauce over each helping.**

Garnish with Parmesan and tomatoes and serve immediately.

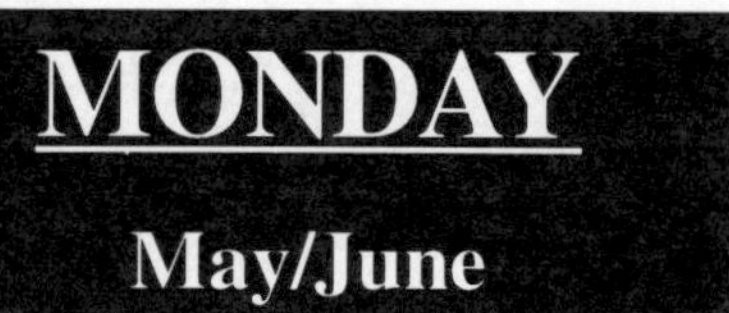

Hot Chicken Salad

This lighter fare will be a nice change as the weather gets warmer. You will be cooking extra chicken breasts to be saved for the cold pasta salad on Sunday.

Notes

Preparation time: 20 minutes
Servings: 2
Ingredients:

a loaf of your favorite hearty bread

3 boneless, skinless chicken breasts
1 T. olive oil
1 clove garlic *(smashed and chopped)*

1/4 C. broth
1/8 lb. broccoli *(chopped in 1" pieces)*

Dressing
1/4 C. orange juice
1 clove garlic *(smashed and chopped)*
1/2 tsp. dry basil leaves
2 T. olive oil
1 T. balsamic vinegar
1/2 tsp. sesame oil

4 leaves Romaine lettuce
4 leaves green or red leaf lettuce
1/2 green pepper *(cut in thin slices)*
2 slices yellow onion *(quartered)*
2-3 Roma tomatoes
1 tart apple *(cored, and chopped into small pieces)*

- **Wrap bread in foil and place in warm oven.**
- **Sauté chicken breast in oil and garlic in non-stick pan over medium-high heat 4 minutes per side.**
- **Add broth and chopped broccoli to pan. Sauté another 2 minutes. Remove pan from heat and set aside.**
- **Combine salad dressing ingredients in glass dish and microwave on high 1 minute or combine in small sauce pan and bring to boil over medium-high heat. Remove from heat. Set aside.**
- **Tear lettuce into large bite-size pieces and arrange on two large serving plates.**
- **Add all cold vegetables and apple.**
- **Thin slice one chicken breast and divide between salads. Arrange hot broccoli on top of each salad.** *Store extra breasts in fridge. One will be used for next Sunday's meal.*

Top with warm salad dressing and serve with warm bread.

Whole Wheat Pasta with Mushroom Sauce

TUESDAY

May/June

Theme and variation on Mushroom Sauce Pasta.

Preparation time: 30 minutes
Servings: 2-3
Ingredients:

12 oz. dry whole wheat spaghetti

1/2 lb. mushrooms *(sliced) Chop 4 mushrooms into tiny pieces.*
1/2 red bell pepper *(thin sliced)*
3 cloves garlic *(smashed and chopped)*
1/4 tsp. crushed rosemary
2 thin slices medium yellow onion *(chopped fine)*
1/4 C. white wine

1/2 C. chicken or vegetable broth

3 T. flour shaken with 1/2 C. nonfat milk

3 T. shredded Parmesan
fresh-ground black pepper

green salad fixings

1/2 C. plain, nonfat yogurt *(stirred smooth)*
dash of Tabasco®

2 T. Parmesan
2 T. fresh chopped parsley *(optional)*

Notes

- **Cook pasta in large heavy-bottomed kettle 8-10 minutes. Drain and rinse.**
- **Use pasta kettle to sauté all mushrooms, red bell pepper, garlic, rosemary, and onion in wine. Sauté 3 minutes and lift mushroom mixture out of pan. Retain liquid.**
- **Add broth and bring to boil.**
- **Mix flour and milk in small container with tight-fitting lid by shaking vigorously 30 seconds until well blended.**
- **Slowly pour flour mixture into boiling liquid, stirring constantly.**
- **Add Parmesan and black pepper. Return mushroom mixture to pan. Cook 5 minutes at low heat.**
- **Prepare green salads.**
- **Remove Mushroom Sauce from heat. Add yogurt and Tabasco®.**
- **Rerinse pasta with hot water. Drain thoroughly.**
- **Gently stir pasta into Mushroom Sauce. Serve immediately.**

Garnish with Parmesan and parsley. Serve with green salad.
Wahoo! Great vitals!

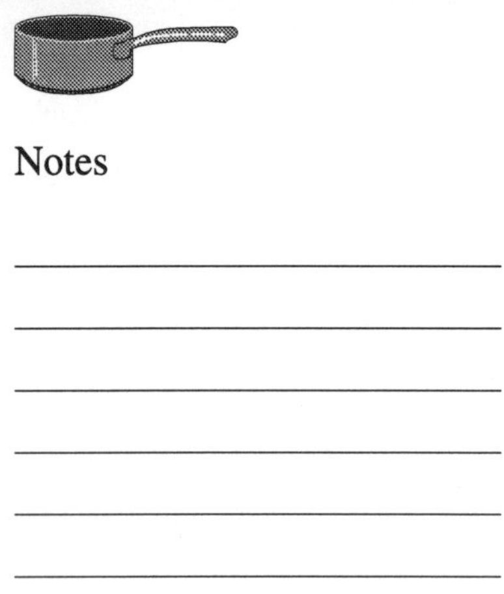

Notes

Poached Snapper

Another quick and delicious fish dinner.

Preparation time: 30 minutes
Servings: 2
Ingredients:

6-7 toasted pecan halves *(chopped)*

2 C. cooked brown rice *(cooked this morning)*
1/4 C. broth
2 slices medium yellow onion *(chopped)*
2 T. chopped parsley *(Save a couple pinches to garnish snapper.)*
fresh-ground black pepper

1/2 lb. baby asparagus

8-10 oz. fresh snapper fillets
1/2 C. white wine
1 clove garlic *(smashed and chopped)*

1/4 tsp. dry dill weed

juice from 1/2 lemon

- **Toast pecans on cookie sheet under broiler.** *Watch them closely! Turn as they begin to brown. Remove from oven and chop.*
- **Mix rice, broth, onion, parsley, and pecans in covered glass bowl. Season with generous amount of fresh-ground pepper and place in microwave. Cook 3 minutes on high. Set aside.**
- **Snap off and discard white bottoms of asparagus. Place tops in steamer basket in large sauce pan. Pour 1/2 C. water into pan.** *Do not turn on heat yet.*
- **Place snapper fillets in sauté pan with wine and garlic. Turn heat on high and cook 2 minutes when wine begins boiling.** *If wine boils away, add another 1/2 C.*
- **Turn snapper with spatula and sprinkle with dry dill weed. Cover, reduce heat to medium, and cook 4 minutes.** *Remove pan from heat.*
- **Turn heat on high under asparagus now. When water boils, cover, and cook for only 2 minutes.**
- **Just before serving, warm Nutty Rice one more minute in microwave.**

Serve snapper in center of individual plates. Sprinkle with a little leftover parsley. Place Nutty Rice on one side, asparagus on the other. Drizzle lemon juice over asparagus.

"Quick cook" rice before work this morning.

"Quick Cooked" rice
Place 1 C. long grain brown rice in a pan with 2 1/4 C. cold water. Cover and bring to boil over high heat. When water boils, turn off heat. Leave pan on burner. Do not lift cover! It will be ready to eat when you get home tonight.

Pasta with Scallops

A return engagement.

Preparation time: 30 minutes
Servings: 2-3
Ingredients:

6 large frozen scallops *(thaw just prior to cooking)* or 10 small, fresh scallops
1 T. olive oil
3 slices medium onion *(quartered)*
1 clove garlic *(smashed and chopped)*
2 stalks celery *(chopped in 1" pieces)*
1/4 C. chicken broth

1 1/2 C. Red Sauce *Use leftovers or whip up a new batch.* *(see page 152)*
dash of Tabasco®
1/4 C. red wine

green salad fixings

8 oz. fresh fettuccine

3 T. fancy-shred Parmesan

Notes

- **Place pasta water on to boil in large kettle.**
- **Place scallops in large fry pan with oil, onion, garlic, celery, and broth. Sauté 3 minutes over medium-high heat.**
- **Add 1 1/2 C. Red Sauce, Tabasco®, and wine. Return to boil. Remove from heat.**
- **Prepare green salads.**
- **Drop pasta into water to cook. Cook 2 1/2 minutes. Drain and rinse.**
- **Serve pasta immediately on individual plates with 3/4 C. Red Sauce per serving.**

Garnish with Parmesan. Serve crisp green salad on the side.

Molti bravi!

FRIDAY

May/June

Notes

Black and White Chili with Corn Bread

Dinner is very easy tonight. Simply make the corn bread and heat up the leftover chili.

Preparation time: 30-35 minutes
Servings: 3-4
Ingredients:

leftover Black and White Chili from freezer
fresh corn bread

- **Place chili in sauce pan over medium-low heat. Cover and warm 15 minutes. Check periodically and give it a stir so it doesn't cook down. If it starts to boil, uncover and reduce heat to low.**

Set frozen Black and White Chili out to thaw before going to work today.

Old-Fashioned Corn Bread

An old Midwest recipe. Oil a 10" cast iron skillet (or similar size baking dish) with 1 T. oil and place on center rack of preheated 400 degree oven. (Remove in 5 minutes or if pan begins to smoke.)

Ingredients:

2 C. cornmeal *(stone ground is best)*
1 to 1 1/4 C. nonfat milk
2 tsp. baking powder
1 egg or 2 egg whites
1 1/2 T. vegetable oil

- **Mix all ingredients in large bowl.**
- **Remove pan from oven.**
- **Pour batter into hot pan and bake for 20-25 minutes.**

This is a dense and flavorful cornbread.
Serve corn bread with molasses, maple syrup, or honey.

SATURDAY

June/Week One

SHOPPING DAY

It's shopping day again! Tonight as the weather warms, a nice Greek salad and some hearty bread might be in order.

Greek Salad

Preparation time: 15 minutes
Servings: 2-3
Ingredients:

a loaf of good bread or 1 package pita bread *(heat in warm oven)*

Dressing
3 T. extra virgin olive oil
2 T. balsamic vinegar
1 large clove garlic *(smashed and chopped)*
1/8 C. vegetable broth

3 oz. feta cheese *(crumbled)*

Salad
4-6 Greek olives *(pitted and halved)*
4-5 Roma or vine ripened tomatoes *(chopped in large pieces)*
1 medium-sized cucumber *(peeled, sliced in 1/2" rounds and quartered)*
1/2 red bell pepper *(chopped in 1" pieces)*
1/2 green bell pepper *(chopped in 1" pieces)*
1/4 of a medium-sized red onion *(cut in 1" pieces)*
a few leaves of Romaine lettuce *(broken into pieces)*

- **Mix dressing ingredients in small bowl and place in microwave. Cook for one minute on high, or place in small sauce pan and bring to boil. Remove from heat. Allow to cool a few minutes before adding to salad.**
- **Toss all salad ingredients in large bowl with crumbled cheese.**

Toss again with dressing and serve in shallow bowls or on large plates with warm bread.

Notes

Go by your favorite bakery and pick up a loaf of crusty olive bread to go with salad.

GROCERY LIST

Produce
10 baby red potatoes
1 medium yellow onion
1 red onion
2 bunches spinach or
1 package prewashed spinach
1 lb. fresh broccoli
1 lb. fresh mushrooms
1 green bell pepper
3 red bell peppers
1 large cucumber
1 head celery
bok choy
one head red leaf lettuce
1 head Romaine lettuce
one head green leaf lettuce
2 large cucumbers
8 Roma tomatoes
2 ripe peaches or nectarines
1 pint fresh strawberries
1 tart apple
2 ripe pears *(if available)*
1 C. fresh blueberries
2 bananas
1 fresh lemon

Frozen Foods
frozen concentrated apple juice

Meat/Fish/Poultry
2 boneless, skinless chicken breasts
6 oz. frozen or fresh scallops

Canned or Dry Foods
1 C. package sliced almonds
one 29 oz. can tomato sauce
two 15 oz. cans chicken broth
one 15 oz. can vegetable broth
one 6 oz. can water chestnuts
one 6 oz. can sliced bamboo shoots
one small can sliced black olives
24 oz. dry spinach spiral pasta
12 oz. dry penne pasta
1 box fortune cookies
a loaf of your favorite hearty bread

Chilled Foods and Dairy
3 oz. feta cheese
1 package pita bread
fresh pesto

Buy if you're out
1 head garlic
1 bunch fresh parsley
balsamic vinegar
Greek olives
caraway seeds
curry powder
powdered nutmeg
sesame oil
corn starch
nonfat mayonnaise
white cooking wine
red cooking wine
plain, nonfat yogurt

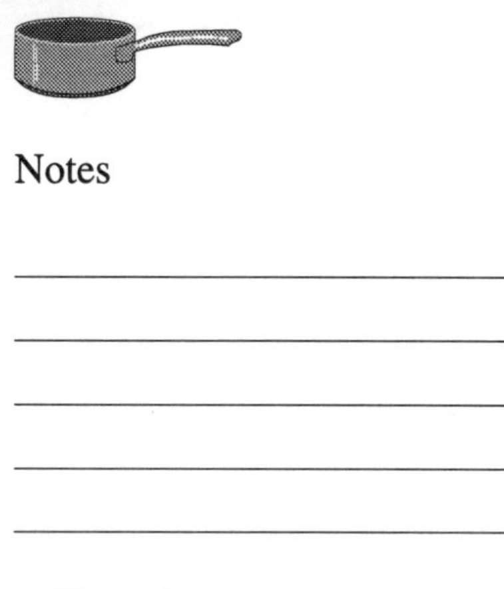

Notes

Chicken Pasta and Fruit Salad Sampler

Another version of chicken pasta salad combined with a seasonal fruit salad. Make a double batch of each salad. They make great leftovers!

Preparation time: 35 minutes

Servings: 2

Ingredients:

1 loaf of your favorite hearty bread

Pasta Salad

2 C. spinach spiral pasta
2 stalks celery *(chopped)*
1/2 cucumber *(peeled, sliced in rounds, and quartered)*
3 slices medium yellow onion *(chopped)*
1/2 red bell pepper *(thin sliced and quartered)*
one chicken breast from Monday night *(chopped)*
1/2 of a 6 oz. can sliced water chestnuts
4 T. sliced almonds *(toasted)*
4 Roma tomatoes

Dressing

4 T. nonfat mayonnaise
1 clove garlic *(smashed and chopped)*
1/4 C. nonfat yogurt or quark
1 tsp. curry powder
fresh-ground black pepper *(to taste)*
1/2 tsp. sesame oil
2 T. concentrated apple juice
2 T. fresh, chopped parsley

Dressing

1/2 C. nonfat yogurt *(stirred smooth)*
1/4 tsp. cinnamon
1/4 C. concentrated apple juice

Fruit Salad

1 blanched peach or nectarine *(chopped)*
1 banana *(sliced in rounds)*
10 strawberries *(topped and cut in half)*
1 pear *(cored and cut in 1/2" pieces)*
1/2 C. blueberries or blackberries

2-3 T. fancy-shred Parmesan

- **Wrap bread in foil and place in warm oven.**
- **Cook pasta. Drain and rinse, and place in a bowl of ice water.**
- **Toss all pasta salad ingredients** *(except pasta)* **in large bowl. Stir dressing ingredients together in separate bowl. Drain pasta and add to salad ingredients. Pour dressing over pasta salad and stir to coat thoroughly. Place in fridge.**
- **In another large bowl, stir yogurt, cinnamon, and apple juice.**
- **Add fruit and gently stir to coat thoroughly. Chill.**
- **Serve salads on large individual plates** *(half fruit salad and half pasta salad)*. **Garnish pasta salad with Parmesan cheese.**

Serve with warm hearty bread.

Make this dinner early in the day and chill it for a few hours before serving.

Leftovers

Come on now! Don't give up on those leftovers. There are probably some memories of great meals in that fridge.

MONDAY

June/Week One

Preparation time: 15-20 minutes
Servings: 3-4
Ingredients:

Do you have leftover....
Hungarian Goulash?
Clam Sauce Pasta?
Red Sauce?

Notes

- **You may need to put some pasta water on to boil if you're short of cooked pasta.**

- **Be careful not to over eat when using up leftovers. If there's more there than you can use up tonight, take some to work for lunch tomorrow.**

If you're concerned about losing weight *simply eat fewer calories than you burn off. Don't crash diet! Exercise regularly. A goal of one or two pounds per week is a safe goal.*
National Exercise for Life Institute, Excelsior, MN

Heavy thoughts! *Obesity accounts for 19% of the $116.9 billion spent annually to treat cardiovascular disease and 57% of the $ 19.8 billion spent to treat diabetes.*
Healthy Weight Journal, 402 S. 14th St., Hettinger, ND 58639

TUESDAY

June/Week One

Notes

Loaded Rice

It's time for the now famous Don Collins "carbo-load!"

Preparation time: 25 minutes
Servings: 2
Ingredients:

8-10 baby red potatoes or 1 large russet potato
1 T. olive oil

1/2 lb. mushrooms *(sliced)*
1/4 red bell pepper *(thin-sliced)*
1 T. olive oil
1 large clove garlic (*smashed and chopped)*
1/4 C. white wine
2 slices medium onion *(quartered)*

3/4 C. chicken or vegetable broth
3 T. corn starch dissolved in 1/8 C. cold water

1 1/2 C. cooked brown rice

1/2 lb. fresh broccoli *(cut into 2" pieces)*

1 C. plain, nonfat yogurt
1 T. pesto
dash of Tabasco®

2 Roma tomatoes *(chopped)*

2 wedges lemon

- **Preheat oven to 400 degrees.**
- **Wash and halve baby red potatoes. If using russet potato, wash and slice** *(unpeeled)* **in 1/2" slices. Place potatoes, flat side down, on oiled cookie sheet.**
- **Sauté sliced mushrooms and bell pepper in oil with garlic, wine, and onion** *(about 4 minutes).* **When done, remove mushroom mixture from pan with perforated spoon. Set aside.**
- **Add broth to pan. Return to boil.**
- **If cooking russet potato slices, turn them now.**
- **Slowly stir corn starch mixture into boiling liquid. Reduce heat to low. Cook 5 minutes, stirring often.** *Set aside 1/2 C. white sauce mixture for Friday's meal.*
- **Add mushrooms to thickened mixture. Return to boil. Remove from heat.**
- **Warm 1 1/2 C. cooked rice 2 minutes on high in microwave on individual serving plates.** *Reserve remaining rice for tomorrow.*
- **Remove potatoes from oven. If using baby reds, push them into rice on individual plates. If using russets, chop into 1" pieces before sprinkling over rice.**
- **Place broccoli in steamer basket in covered sauce pan and turn heat on high. Steam, covered, 2 minutes.**
- **Stir yogurt, pesto, and Tabasco® together until smooth. Microwave 30 seconds on high. Stir again, and add to thickened mushroom sauce.**

Enjoy!

You will need to "quick cook" some rice this morning before work. Make a double batch. (see page 158)

Nested Scallops

This is a wonderfully nutritious meal. It serves as an interesting change of pace and makes a delightful presentation.

Preparation time: 30 minutes
Servings: 2
Ingredients:

1 small yellow onion *(chopped)*
1 clove garlic *(smashed and chopped)*
2 large bunches fresh spinach or 1 package prewashed spinach *(slightly chopped)*
2 T. olive oil
1/2 C. broth

6-8 medium-sized mushrooms *(sliced)*
1/2 red bell pepper *(chopped)*
1/4 C. white wine
1 clove garlic *(smashed and chopped)*

6 oz. frozen or fresh scallops

1 T. pesto

2 T. corn starch dissolved in 1/8 C. water
3/4 C. plain, nonfat yogurt *(stirred smooth)*
1/8 tsp. ground nutmeg

2 Roma tomatoes *(chopped)*

a loaf of your favorite hearty bread

- **Sauté onion, garlic, and spinach in oil and broth 5 minutes over medium-high heat in large fry pan or heavy-bottomed sauce pan.**
- **Pour into a strainer over a bowl and set aside.**
- **Sauté mushrooms and bell pepper in wine and garlic. Sauté 2 minutes and lift out of pan with perforated spoon. Place in strainer with spinach.**
- **Add scallops to pan with leftover wine liquid. Sauté 5 minutes.** *(Add another 1/4 C. wine if pan cooks dry.)*
- **Add pesto and thoroughly coat scallops. Remove from heat and place in separate bowl.** *(If using large scallops, cut them in quarters.)* **Place in 200 degree oven to keep warm.**
- **Return spinach liquid to pan. Bring to boil over medium-high heat. Thicken with corn starch mixture. Reduce heat to medium and cook 2 minutes. Add yogurt, nutmeg and spinach. Heat thoroughly. Remove pan from heat.**
- **Place about 1 C. spinach on center of each serving plate. Using a fork, create a crater or nest shape. Sprinkle red peppers and mushrooms around edges of nest. Top with scallops in center.**

Garnish with fresh, chopped tomato. Serve with hearty bread.

Notes

Pick up a loaf of nutritious whole grain bread today.

THURSDAY

June/Week One

Notes

Broccoli/Chicken Stir Fry

A theme and variation on stir fry.

Preparation time: 30 minutes
Servings: 3-4
Ingredients:

2 boneless, skinless chicken breasts *(chopped into 1/2" cubes)*

1 T. vegetable oil
1/4 tsp. sesame oil

3 slices medium onion *(chopped)*
3 cloves garlic *(smashed and chopped)*

1/2 lb. broccoli *(cut in 2" lengths)*
2 stalks bok choy *(cubed)*
1/2 can sliced water chestnuts *(leftover from Sunday)*
1 T. low-sodium soy sauce
1/4 C. chicken broth

6 mushrooms *(sliced)*
1/4 C. chicken broth

1/2 C. chicken broth
1 T. low-sodium soy sauce

3 T. corn starch mixed with 1/4 C. water

2-3 C. cooked rice *(leftover from Tuesday)*

- **Chop raw chicken and set aside in a bowl. *Important note: Thoroughly wash, rinse, and dry cutting board after chopping chicken before continuing to chop vegetables.***
- **Place oils in large, heavy-bottomed sauce pan or wok over medium-high heat. Sauté onion, garlic and chopped chicken 5 minutes stirring constantly.**
- **Toss in broccoli, bok choy, drained water chestnuts, soy sauce, and 1/4 C. broth. Sauté 2 more minutes.**
- **Add mushrooms and 1/4 C. broth. Sauté another minute.**
- **Remove all ingredients from pan with perforated ladle or spoon and set aside.**
- **Using same pan, mix 1/2 C. broth and 1 T. soy sauce. Bring to boil and thicken with corn starch/water mixture. Reduce heat to low and cook 3-4 minutes.**
- **Add vegetables and meat to sauce and toss until everything is thoroughly coated.**
- **Warm rice 1 1/2 minutes on high in microwave.**

Serve stir fry immediately on individual plates over rice. Eat with chopsticks if you can! Finish the meal with tea and fortune cookies.

Penne Pasta with Red Peppers

Another satisfying pasta entree.

FRIDAY

June/Week One

Preparation time: 30 minutes
Servings: 3
Ingredients:

2 C. dry penne pasta

2 red bell peppers *(cut in 1" strips)*
2 cloves garlic *(smashed and chopped)*
2 slices medium yellow onion *(thin sliced)*
5 black olives *(chopped)*
1 T. olive oil
1/2 C. broth
1/4 C. white wine

2 T. corn starch dissolved into 1/8 C. water

fixings for a green salad
1/2 tart apple *(chopped)*

2-4 T. fancy-shred Parmesan
1 T. fresh chopped parsley

Notes

- **Cook pasta 8 minutes in boiling water. Drain and rinse with warm water.**
- **Sauté bell peppers, garlic, onions, and olives in oil, broth, and wine in same kettle used for pasta. Saute 3 minutes.**
- **Remove all vegetables from kettle with perforated spoon and set aside in large bowl.**
- **Return liquid to boil over high heat and thicken with corn starch/water mixture. Reduce heat to low and continue cooking 2-3 minutes.**
- **Add vegetables and pasta to sauce and stir over high heat 1 minute to reheat. Cover and remove from heat.**
- **Prepare green salads with chopped apple sprinkled over top.**
- **Divide pasta into 3 servings on individual plates** *(or 2 servings with a leftover portion).*
- **Garnish with Parmesan and chopped parsley.**

Serve with fresh green salad. Favoloso!

SATURDAY

June/Week Two

Notes

SHOPPING DAY

It's time once again to prepare for next week. A Sunday barbecue is planned for tomorrow. If you can't find fresh tuna steaks, substitute your meat of choice. I suggest halibut steaks or halibut cheeks if you can get them. You will notice that I suggest you grill a few chicken breasts first. Some will be used Monday night and others come in handy for lunches.

Concerning your health—a small amount of weight loss goes a long way. *Nutritionists say women who lose as little as two pounds can lower their cholesterol, and those who lose seven pounds can lower their blood pressure.*
Nutrition and Health Campaign for Women, Chicago, IL

Handle and store food safely. *Thaw meat and poultry in the fridge; leaving it on the counter to thaw encourages disease-causing bacteria. Clean cutting boards and knives with hot, soapy water after using. (I usually cut all vegetables first and meat last. Then I wash the cutting board.) Cook ground meat of any kind thoroughly until juices run clear. (If you're cooking ground turkey breast it won't produce juice. Cook it until golden brown.) Wrap and store leftovers as soon as possible: the longer they sit on a counter or a cool stove, the greater the possibility of bacterial contamination.*
National Center for Nutrition and Dietetics, Chicago, IL

Fresh strawberries *are available in many parts of the country beginning this month. They are a great addition to breakfast cereal, or a lovely garnish on a plate of food. I even use sliced berries over a green salad. Try 4 or 5 berries sliced over a dish of nonfat frozen vanilla yogurt for dessert. Remember, strawberries are loaded with vitamin C.*

Be sure you aren't going to the store on an empty stomach. *If you have a snack or a meal before you go, it will reduce tendancies toward impulse buying or buying unneccessary snack food.*

GROCERY LIST

Produce

2 large russet potatoes
10 baby red potatoes
one head broccoflower
1/2 lb. baby asparagus
one 8" and one 6" zucchini
one 8" yellow crooked neck squash
one medium yellow onion
1/2 lb. fresh mushrooms
2 green bell peppers
2 red bell peppers
one bunch green onions
one carrot
green salad fixings
one small piece ginger root
2 fresh lemons
one fresh lime
one orange
dried cranberries

Frozen Foods

Meat/Fish/Poultry

3-4 boneless, skinless chicken breasts
turkey bacon
8-12 oz. fresh tuna fillets (4 oz. per person)
If tuna fillets are not available or too expensive, use halibut.
2 Italian turkey sausage links
10 oz. fresh fillet of sole or orange roughy
Buy frozen roughy fillets and keep them frozen.

Canned or Dry Foods

one 29 oz. can tomato sauce
one 29 oz. can "Ready-cut" tomatoes
one 15 oz. can chicken broth
16 oz. dry penne pasta
12 oz. dry spiral pasta (*whole wheat)*
one 6 oz. can sliced black olives
1 large, thin-crust Boboli® shell
1 jar of your favorite jam

Chilled Foods and Dairy

nonfat cream cheese

Buy if you're out

1 head fresh garlic
shelled walnuts or pecans
sliced almonds
old-fashioned rolled oats
dried dill weed
low-salt soy sauce
wheat germ
white cooking wine
red cooking wine
plain, nonfat yogurt
1/2 dozen eggs
pesto

Grilled Tuna and Vegetables

SUNDAY

June/Week Two

You may use halibut fillets or halibut cheeks if fresh tuna is unavailable. Whichever you use, you only need about 3-4 oz. per serving. *I love the taste of the grilled vegetables.*

Preparation time: 30 minutes
Servings: 2-4
Ingredients:

2 large russet potatoes *(cut into strips)*
1 T. olive oil

Lemon/Garlic Baste
2 cloves of garlic
juice of two lemons

3-4 boneless, skinless chicken breasts

1 medium zucchini *(cut into strips)*
1 medium crooked neck squash *(cut into strips)*
1 red bell pepper *(cut into 1/2" wide strips)*
1 green bell pepper *(cut into 1/2" wide strips)*

Ginger/Lime Baste
1 clove garlic *(smashed and chopped)*
1/4 tsp. fresh grated ginger
1 T. low-salt soy sauce
juice from one lime
1/4 C. white wine

three 4 oz. tuna fillets or halibut fillets

- **Preheat oven to 375 degrees. Place potato strips on oiled cookie sheet in oven.** *Set timer for 15 minutes.*
- **Prepare charcoal or stove for grilling.**
- **Mix lemon and garlic.**
- **Grill chicken first. Brush with Lemon/Garlic Baste. When thoroughly browned, remove and cool.** *(Store for later in the week.)*
- **Turn potatoes with spatula.** *Set timer for 15 minutes.*
- **Grill vegetables, brushing them often with Lemon/Garlic Baste. When done, wrap in foil and place at edge of grill to keep warm.**
- **Turn potatoes again.**
- **Mix ingredients for the Ginger/Lime Baste.**
- **Grill tuna or halibut, brushing often with Baste. Grill until meat begins to flake and center of fillet is no longer pink.**

Serve fish in center of plate with vegetables and potatoes on either side.

Notes

MONDAY

June/Week Two

Notes

Penne Pasta with Grilled Chicken

This is a delicious pasta variation that uses chicken breasts you grilled yesterday.

Preparation time: 30 minutes
Servings: 2-3
Ingredients:

1/4 C. white wine
1/2 C. chicken or vegetable stock
1 carrot *(peeled and cut in thin strips 1" long)*
4 slices medium onion *(chopped)*
2 cloves garlic *(smashed and chopped)*
1 small zucchini *(cut in 1/8" rounds)*

2 1/2 C. dry penne pasta

3 T. flour shaken with 1/2 C. nonfat milk

salad fixings

2 T. shredded Parmesan

2 leftover grilled chicken breasts *(thin sliced)*

1/2 C. plain, nonfat yogurt *(stirred smooth)*
2 T. pesto

2 T. Parmesan
2 T. fresh chopped parsley *(optional)*
2 Roma tomatoes *(chopped)*

- **Place pasta water on to boil in heavy-bottomed kettle.**
- **Bring wine and broth to boil in large sauce pan. Drop in carrots, onion, and garlic. Cook 1 minute.**
- **Add zucchini and boil 1 minute.**
- **Remove carrots and zucchini with perforated spoon and set aside.**
- **Pour pasta into boiling pasta water. Set timer for 8 minutes. Drain and rinse.**
- **Return vegetable liquid to boil. Thicken with flour/milk mixture. Reduce heat to low and cook 5 minutes.**
- **Prepare green salads.**
- **Add 2 T. Parmesan to sauce.**
- **Add vegetables and sliced chicken to sauce. Return to boil. Remove from heat.**
- **Mix yogurt and pesto. Microwave 30 seconds on high. Stir into sauce.**
- **Add pasta to sauce.**
- **Serve on individual plates.**
- **Garnish with Parmesan, parsley, and chopped tomato.**

Serve with green salad.

Baby Red Potatoes with Italian Turkey Sausage

TUESDAY

June/Week Two

You'll like this Italianesque potato dish.

Preparation time: 30 minutes
Servings: 3
Ingredients:

Notes

8-10 baby red potatoes *(washed and halved)*
2 T. olive oil

1 link Italian turkey sausage

3/4 C. leftover Red Sauce *(see page 152)*

1 red bell pepper *(cut in 1" strips)*
1/2 green bell pepper *(cut in 1" strips)*
1/4 C. broth
2 slices medium yellow onion *(sliced 1/4" thick and quartered)*
2 cloves garlic *(smashed and chopped) or 1 1/2 tsp. prepared chopped garlic*
5 black olives *(chopped)*

1/2 lb. broccoflower *(cut in 1 1/2" pieces)*

2 T. Parmesan cheese
1 T. fresh chopped parsley

1/2 lemon cut in wedges

- **Place potatoes on oiled cookie sheet in 400 degree oven.**
- **Prick sausage several times with fork, wrap in paper towel and place in covered dish in microwave. Cook three 2-minute cycles, rotating dish after each cycle.**
- **Prepare Red Sauce.** *(Use 3/4 C. tonight and save the rest for leftovers.)*
- **Sauté bell peppers 2 minutes in broth with onion, garlic, and olives in large non-stick fry pan. Remove from pan.**
- **Slice sausage and brown in same pan. Add vegetables and Red Sauce. Bring to boil and remove from heat.**
- **Pour 2 C. water into large sauce pan with 1/2 tsp. salt. Place on high heat and bring to boil.**
- **Drop broccoflower into boiling water. Return to boil and boil 1 minute. Drain in colander.**
- **Remove potatoes from oven.** *(Lift potatoes with metal spatula to preserve crispy bottoms.)* **Stir potatoes into Red Sauce mixture. Serve immediately.**
- **Garnish with Parmesan and chopped parsley.**

Serve potato mixture on one side of plate and broccoflower with lemon wedge on other side.

Poached Sole with "Nutty Rice"

WEDNESDAY

June/Week Two

Notes

Time again for a nice piece of fish. You may use either sole or orange roughy.

Preparation time: 30 minutes
Servings: 2
Ingredients:

2 C. cooked rice
one clove garlic *(smashed and chopped)*
4 chopped green onions
1/4 C. toasted, chopped pecans
1/4 C. broth
fresh-ground black pepper
1/2 lb. baby asparagus
8-10 oz. fresh *(or frozen)* sole or orange roughy fillets
1/2 C. white wine
2 T. toasted sliced almonds
1 T. chopped parsley
juice from 1/2 lemon

- **Mix rice, garlic, onion, pecans, and broth in bowl. Season with a generous amount of fresh-ground black pepper. Cover dish and cook in microwave 2 minutes.**
- **Snap white bottoms off asparagus and place tops in steamer in large sauce pan. Pour 1/2 C. water in pan.** *Do not turn on heat.*
- **Place fillets in sauté pan with wine. Turn heat on high and cook 2 minutes after wine begins boiling.**
- **Turn fillets with spatula and sprinkle with toasted almonds. Cover, reduce heat to medium and cook 4 minutes.** *Remove pan from heat.*
- **Turn heat on high under asparagus now. When water boils, cook for only 2 minutes, covered.**

Serve fish in center of individual plates. Sprinkle with a little chopped parsley. Place rice on one side and asparagus on the other. Pour lemon juice over asparagus. This meal is delicious with a cold glass of Chardonnay.

You will need to "quick cook" some rice this morning before work. *(page 158).*

Pasta "Prosciutto" Americano

Another encore of one of my favoite pastas.

Preparation time: 30 minutes
Servings: 2-3
Ingredients:

a loaf of your favorite crusty bread

Chunky Red Sauce
one 29 oz. can of "Ready-cut" tomatoes
2 cloves garlic *(smashed and chopped)*
1 T. dry oregano leaves
1 1/2 T. dry basil leaves
1/4 C. dry red wine
2 slices medium yellow onion *(chopped)*
a few dashes of Tabasco® sauce *(optional)*
1/2 C. leftover Red Sauce

3 slices cooked turkey bacon *(chopped-use leftover bacon in freezer)*
1 1/2 C. Chunky Red Sauce from above recipe

3 C. dry penne pasta

green salad fixings

2-4 T. fancy-shred Parmesan cheese

Notes

- **Wrap bread in foil and place in warm oven.**
- **Place a large kettle 2/3 full of water on stove. Turn heat on high and cover.**
- **Strain juice from "Ready-cut" tomatoes through colander into sauce pan. Set tomato chunks aside.**
- **Place all Chunky Red Sauce ingredients above** *(except tomato chunks)* **in sauce pan. Bring to boil over medium-high heat and cook, covered, 8 minutes.**
- **Add tomato chunks. Return to boil and remove from heat. Set aside.** *You will have a little over 3 C. sauce. Retain 1 1/2 C. in sauce pan for this recipe. Save the rest for another meal.*
- **Add chopped bacon to 1 1/2 C. Chunky Red Sauce in sauce pan. Return to boil, cover, and remove from heat.**
- **Drop dry pasta into boiling water and cook 8 minutes. Drain and rinse with warm water.**
- **Prepare green salads on individual plates.**
- **Divide pasta on serving plates. Cover each serving with 1/2 to 3/4 C. "Prosciutto" Americano Sauce. Sprinkle 1-2 T. Parmesan cheese over each serving.**

Pick up a loaf of hearty bread today.

Serve with a crisp green salad and crusty bread.

FRIDAY

June/Week Two

Notes

Pizza and Salad

You should have leftover Red Sauce for tonight's dinner. If you've no leftover Red Sauce, see page 152. Feel free to embellish on the ingredients you use for toppings.

Preparation time: 25 minutes
Servings: 2
Ingredients:

1 link Italian turkey sausage *(sliced into 1/8" rounds)*
large Boboli® shell or frozen pizza shell

3/4 C. Red Sauce
1 large clove garlic *(smashed and chopped)*
2 T. fancy-shred Parmesan cheese
1 dash of Tabasco®

2 slices medium yellow onion *(quartered)*
4-6 black olives *(chopped)*
6 medium mushrooms *(sliced in 1/4" slices)*
4 T. fancy-shred Parmesan

fixings for a green salad

- **Preheat oven to 400 degrees.**
- **Prick sausage several times with fork and wrap in paper towel. Place sausage in covered dish and microwave 2 minutes on high. Repeat.**
- **Place Boboli® directly on rack in center of oven and cook 3 minutes.** *(Set a timer so you don't forget.)* **Remove from oven.**
- **Place Red Sauce in small bowl with garlic, 2 T. Parmesan and Tabasco®. Cover bowl. Cook in microwave 2 minutes at full power.** *If you don't have a microwave, put ingredients in a small sauce pan and bring to a boil over medium-high heat. When it boils, cover and remove from heat.*
- **Spread Red Sauce on Boboli® crust.**
- **Arrange onions, olives, and mushrooms on top of Red Sauce and top with Parmesan. Return to oven 8-10 minutes.**
- **Prepare green salads on individual plates while Boboli® is cooking.**
- **Remove pizza from oven and cut in wedges while hot.**

Let Pizza cool 5 minutes before eating. ***It's "Pizza Friday!"***

SHOPPING DAY PLUS MUFFINS

SATURDAY

June/Week Three

A Bonus! Cranberry/Orange Muffins

Makes 1 dozen muffins

- Preheat oven to 375 degrees.
- Mix the following in one bowl: 1 1/2 C. unbleached flour, 1/4 C. wheat germ, 1/2 C. old-fashioned oats, 1/4 C. white sugar, 1 tsp. grated orange rind, 1 tsp. cinnamon, 1 tsp. baking powder, 1 tsp. baking soda, 1/2 C. dried cranberries, 1/4 C. chopped walnuts or pecans.
- In a separate, smaller, bowl mix: 1 egg (beaten), 1 1/4 C. milk, 2 T. white vinegar, 2 T. vegetable oil.
- Stir all ingredients together and place in muffin tins sprayed with vegetable oil spray. (It will make a dozen.)
- Bake 30-35 minutes. *Serve with nonfat cream cheese and your favorite jam.*

Notes

Caution! *These foods often cause choking in toddlers: cherries with pits, hard candy, hot dogs, large meat chunks, nuts, popcorn, raisins, raw apples, pears, carrots, raw celery, and spoonfuls of peanut butter.*
William Sears, MD, San Clemente, CA

More praise for Vitamin C—*Eating foods rich in vitamin C may help prevent bruises by helping build tissue around the skin's blood vessels. Good sources of the vitamin are: citrus fruits, broccoli, cauliflower, and sweet potatoes.*
Prevention's Guide to the Best Home Remedies, 33 East Minor St., Emmaus, PA 18098

Help your children get a handle on weight now! *More than half the overweight children in one study remained overweight into adulthood. Fewer than 1/3 lost weight.*
Research at the University of Iowa, Iowa City

GROCERY LIST

Produce

2 large baking potatoes
1/4 lb. fresh snow peas *(buy frozen peas if fresh snow peas are not available)*
3 medium yellow onions
1/2 lb. fresh broccoli
1 head red cabbage
1 tart apple
1 lb. fresh mushrooms
1 green bell pepper
1 red bell pepper
green salad fixings
one large cucumber
2 slicing tomatoes
1 fresh lemon
1 orange
fresh strawberries

Frozen Foods

frozen corn

Meat/Fish/Poultry

2 boneless, skinless chicken breasts
one Chorizo sausage *(Italian sausage will do)*
4 oz. smoked salmon

Canned or Dry Foods

2 C. dry white beans
one 29 oz. can tomato sauce
two 15 oz. cans chicken broth
8 oz. fresh fettuccine
1 loaf of your favorite hearty bread

Chilled Foods and Dairy

3 oz. sharp cheddar cheese
fresh salsa

Buy if you're out

1 head fresh garlic
powdered cumin
caraway seed
nonfat Italian dressing
plain, nonfat yogurt
shredded Parmesan
1/2 dozen fresh eggs

SUNDAY

June/Week Three

Notes

White Beans and Red Sauce

Another encore dish, and, "oh, so healthful!"

Preparation time: 20 minutes *(after beans are cooked)*
Servings: 2
Ingredients:

Red Sauce
one 29 oz. can tomato sauce
1 T. dry basil
2 tsp. dry oregano
dash of Tabasco® *(to taste)*
4 slices medium onion *(chopped)*
2 cloves garlic *(smashed and chopped)*

1/2 red bell pepper *(chopped)*
1/2 green bell pepper *(chopped)*
3 slices medium yellow onion *(chopped)*

2-3 C. cooked white beans or two 15 oz. cans *(rinsed)*

2-4 T. fancy-shred Parmesan

fresh cucumber, tomato, and sweet onion *(5 slices each per serving)*
low or nonfat salad dressing

- **Use leftover Red Sauce if you have it, or place tomato sauce, spices, onion, and garlic in covered sauce pan. Cook 10 minutes over medium-low heat.** *Measure 2 C. for this recipe and reserve the rest for another meal.*
- **Add peppers and onion to 2 C. Red Sauce. Bring to boil and cook 2 minutes. Remove from heat.**
- **Warm beans in microwave** *(1 minute on high),* **or pour boiling water over beans in large bowl and let stand five minutes. Drain.**

Spoon one cup cooked beans in center of individual plates and cover beans with 1/2-3/4 C. Red Sauce per serving. Garnish with Parmesan. Overlap cucumber, tomato, and onion along edge of plate and dress with lowfat salad dressing.

Cook beans during the day today. *(see page 15)*

Smoked Salmon Pasta

A repeat performance of one of my favorite pasta variations.

MONDAY

June/Week Three

Preparation time: 25 minutes
Servings: 2
Ingredients:

8 mushrooms (*sliced*)
1/2 red bell pepper (*cut into thin 1" long strips*)
2 slices medium yellow onion (*chopped*)
2 cloves garlic (*smashed and chopped*) *or 1/2 tsp. prepared garlic*
1 T. olive oil
1/4 C. dry white wine

1/2 C. chicken or vegetable broth
2 T. corn starch dissolved in about 1/8 C. water

fixings for a green salad

4 oz. smoked salmon (*skin removed and broken into bite-sized pieces*)
1 package frozen snow peas, or 1/8 lb. fresh snow peas

2 T. pesto
3/4 C. plain, nonfat yogurt

8 oz. fresh fettuccine

3 T. fancy-shred Parmesan cheese
3 Roma tomatoes (*chopped*)

Notes

- **Place pasta water on to boil in large kettle.**
- **Sauté mushrooms, red bell pepper, onion, and garlic in oil and wine over medium-high heat 2 minutes. Remove from pan with slotted spoon and set aside.**
- **Add broth to remaining white wine in pan. Bring to boil. Reduce heat to medium.**
- **Stir corn starch mixture into boiling liquid. Reduce heat to low and cook 5 minutes. Stir occasionally.**
- **Make green salads.**
- **Add salmon and snow peas to thickened sauce. Return to boil and cook 1 minute.**
- **Return mushroom mixture to sauce. Cook 1 minute and remove pan from heat.**
- **Mix pesto and yogurt until smooth. Microwave 30 seconds on high to take chill off. Stir again.**
- **Drop pasta into boiling water. When water returns to boil, cook 2 minutes** *(set a timer so you don't forget)*, **drain, and rinse.**
- **In same kettle used to cook pasta, mix salmon mixture and yogurt/pesto over low heat. DO NOT BOIL!**
- **Toss until pasta is well coated.**
- **Serve on individual plates garnished with Parmesan cheese and fresh tomatoes.**

Serve a green salad on the side. Oh yes!!

TUESDAY

June/Week Three

Notes

Spanish Omelet

You will be using some leftover Red Sauce from Sunday.

Preparation time: 20 minutes
Servings: 2
Ingredients:

1 Chorizo sausage link — chopped (*Italian sausage will do*)

1/4 C. Red Sauce *(leftover from Sunday)*
1 clove garlic *(smashed and chopped)*
1/4 tsp. cumin powder
dash of Tabasco®

2 slices of medium onion *(chopped)*
4 fresh mushrooms (*sliced)*
1/4 green bell pepper (*chopped*)
1/4 red bell pepper (*chopped*)

6 eggs
1/4 C. nonfat milk

1 T. olive oil

3 T. fancy-shred Parmesan

2 slices of bread for toast

1 orange (*sliced in 1/4" slices)*

your favorite salsa
1/4 C. plain, nonfat yogurt *(stirred smooth)*

- **Prick Chorizo sausage thoroughly with fork. Wrap in paper towel, place in shallow dish and cook in microwave for three 2-minute bursts at full power.** *(Change paper towel before final 2-minute burst.)* **You may also brown sausage in small pan until thoroughly cooked. Remove from pan and place on paper towel. Discard drippings.**
- **Place leftover Red Sauce, garlic, cumin, and Tabasco® in small sauce pan over medium heat. Bring to boil.**
- **Add vegetables to sauce and cook 2 minutes. Remove from heat.**
- **Break 2 eggs into medium-sized bowl. Separate whites from yolks of remaining eggs. Discard yolks and add whites to bowl. Add milk and beat egg mixture with wire whisk.** *(About 30 seconds.)*
- **Place a 12" non-stick fry pan over medium-high heat and spread olive oil evenly around pan, or spray pan with vegetable oil spray before placing on burner.**
- **Pour egg mixture into pan and cook 1 minute.**
- **Place vegetable sauce, chopped meat, and Parmesan on one side of omelet leaving 1/2 the surface area with nothing on it. Cook 2 more minutes and fold in half.**
- **Loosen bottom of omelet with spatula. Place a serving plate over pan and turn omelet out onto plate. Slide back into pan to finish cooking seamed side.**
- **Lower heat to medium, cover, and cook 2 minutes.**
- **Make toast and garnish side of plate with sliced oranges.**

Serve 1/2 omelet per serving. Garnish with salsa and stirred yogurt.

Baked Potato with Broccoli

Time to revisit the wonder meal!

WEDNESDAY

June/Week Three

Notes

Preparation time: 15-20 minutes
Servings: 2
Ingredients:

- 2 large russet baking potatoes *(washed, rubbed with olive oil, and pricked with a fork)*
- 1/2 lb. fresh broccoli *(cut in 2" lengths)*
- 1/2 C. frozen corn
- 3/4 C. plain, nonfat yogurt *(stirred smooth)*
- sharp cheddar cheese
- salsa
- lemon

- **Prepare potatoes in the morning prior to work and set your oven for "time bake" so that they will have been cooking for 1 hour when you arrive home in the evening.** *(You may also cook them in the microwave. Cook for three 5-minute cycles at full power. Turn the potatoes to a different position after each cycle.)*
- **Place broccoli in steamer basket in sauce pan with a little water. Bring to boil, cover, and cook 3 minutes.** *Set timer so you don't forget.* **Remove pan and uncover when timer goes off.**
- **Measure 1/2 C. frozen corn into glass dish. Cover and thaw in microwave 1 minute at full power.**
- **Stir yogurt, set out cheese (with grater), and salsa while broccoli is cooking.**

If possible, bake potatoes on "time bake" in oven while you're at work.

Split potatoes with a knife and place on serving plates. Top with corn yogurt, and salsa. Garnish with a few gratings of sharp cheddar cheese. Serve broccoli on same plate with a wedge of lemon.

THURSDAY

June/Week Three

Leftovers

Time once again for the leftover adventure!

Preparation time: 15-20 minutes
Servings: 3-4
Ingredients:

Notes

Do you have leftover pastas, white beans or Red Sauce?

Pick up some of your favorite hearty bread on the way home, and plan a green salad to add freshness to leftover night. Chop a few fresh strawberries on top.

- **You may need to put some pasta water on to boil if you're short of cooked pasta.**
- **Try serving separate courses of different pasta leftovers, beans, etc. Eat one course while the next is warming.**

Low fat snack? *Dry-roasted nuts are not significantly lower-in-fat and calories than regular roasted nuts. Nuts are so high in fat to begin with, roasting them in oil hardly makes a difference. Roasted nuts absorb little oil anyway.*
University of California at Berkeley Wellness Letter, P.O. Box 412, Prince Street Station, New York, NY 10012

More on Vitamin C *- taking extra vitamin C may help improve your cholesterol level. One study found people with high levels of the vitamin also had high levels of HDL (good) cholesterol, which helps scour the blood vessels and reduce the risk of heart disease.*
Research by the USDA, Washington, DC, and The National Institutes of Health, Washington, DC

Chicken and Mushrooms over Rice

A theme and variation on chicken and mushrooms.

Preparation time: 30 minutes
Servings: 2-3
Ingredients:

Notes

1/2 lb. fresh white mushrooms
1/2 red bell pepper *(cut in thin 1" strips)*
2 thin slices of a medium yellow onion *(quartered)*
2 cloves garlic *(smashed and chopped)*
1/4 C. chicken broth

2 boneless, skinless chicken breasts
1/4 C. chicken broth

Rot Kohl (Red Cabbage)
1/2 head red cabbage *(chopped)*
1 tart apple *(cored and chopped)*
3 slices yellow onion *(chopped)*
1/2 C. red wine
1 tsp. whole caraway seed

1/4 C. broth
1/4 C. white wine
2 T. corn starch *(dissolved in 1/4 C. water)*

2 C. cooked rice

- **In 12" fry pan, sauté mushrooms, red pepper, onion and garlic in broth - 3 minutes. Remove from pan with perforated spoon and set aside.**
- **Place chicken breasts in same pan. Sauté over medium-high heat 3 minutes, turning once. Add broth and sauté another 3 minutes until lightly browned. Reduce heat to low, add a little water to pan. Cover and cook 5 minutes per side.**
- **Place all cabbage ingredients in large covered sauce pan. Bring to boil and cook 10 minutes over medium-low heat.**
- **Remove chicken from pan. Add broth and wine. Bring to boil and stir to bring up drippings. Thicken with corn starch. Reduce heat. Cook 5 minutes.**
- **Add mushrooms to sauce.**
- **Warm rice 1 1/2 minutes on high in microwave.**
- **Chop chicken and add to mushroom mixture. Bring to boil. Remove from heat.**

"Quick cook" some rice before work today. (see page 158)

Serve chicken/mushroom sauce over a bed of rice. Use a perforated spoon to serve cabbage alongside chicken and rice. Gut Schmecken!

SATURDAY

June/July

Notes

SHOPPING DAY

When planning a birthday, try this version of birthday cake.

- *Buy or bake an angel food cake.*
- *Blend 1/2 C. fresh or frozen raspberries or strawberries (unsweetened) with 1T. sugar.*
- *Spoon 3 T. blended berries onto the center of a dessert plate.*
- *Place a 1" slice of angel food cake on the berries.*
- *Place 1 scoop frozen nonfat yogurt on the cake.*
- *Drizzle 2 tsp. chocolate sauce over the yogurt and sprinkle with a few whole berries.*
- *Place a candle in the serving for the person having a birthday.*

Chocolate anyone? *The average American consumes 11 pounds of chocolate per year compared with 22 pounds by the average Swiss citizen.*
Health, 301 Howard St., Suite 1800, San Francisco, CA 94105

GROCERY LIST

Produce

16 baby red potatoes
2 medium yellow onions
2 large sweet onions
1/2 lb. mushrooms
2 large carrots
1 green bell pepper
2 red bell peppers
1 yellow bell pepper
2 tart apples
1 head red leaf lettuce
1 head green leaf lettuce
green salad fixings
1 large cucumber
8 Roma tomatoes
1 large slicing tomato
1 bunch fresh basil
1 bunch fresh parsley
2 fresh lemons
1 fresh pineapple or
one 8 oz. can chopped pineapple
fresh strawberries and nectarines

Frozen Foods

frozen Bocca Burgers® *(if you wish to eat vegetarian)*
orange juice

Meat/Fish/Poultry

8 boneless, skinless chicken breasts
2 lb. ground turkey breast
turkey bacon

Canned or Dry Foods

1/2 C. package slivered almonds
two 15 oz. cans navy beans
(buy canned beans if you have none in freezer)
one 29 oz. can tomato sauce
one 15 oz. can chicken broth
one 6 oz. can sliced water chestnuts
one 6 oz. can tuna *(packed in water)*
12 oz. dry sea shell pasta
12 oz. bow tie pasta
12 oz. dry whole wheat pasta
hearty burger buns

Chilled Foods and Dairy

3 oz. favorite cheese for burgers

Buy if you're out

1 head garlic
celery
toasted sunflower meats
balsamic vinegar
white vinegar
sesame oil
barbecue sauce
nonfat mayonnaise
Dijon mustard
Worcestershire sauce
dill weed
chili powder
leaf oregano
brown sugar
white cooking wine
Greek olives
capers
plain, nonfat yogurt

Grilled Chicken and Barbecued Beans

SUNDAY

June/July

It's probably a good evening for a barbecue.

Preparation time: 30 minutes
Servings: 4
Ingredients:

8 baby red potatoes washed and halved
1 T. olive oil

Chicken Baste
3 T. balsamic vinegar
1 clove garlic *(smashed and chopped)*
1/8 tsp. sesame oil
1/4 C. white wine

4-8 boneless, skinless chicken breasts

BBQ Sauce
1/3 C. tomato sauce
2 T. Worcestershire
dash Tabasco®
2 T. white vinegar
3 T. brown sugar
1 clove chopped garlic
1 T. chopped onion
1 tsp. dried oregano
2 tsp. chili powder

1/3 C. Barbecue Sauce *(You may use commercial or try recipe above.)*
1 clove garlic *(smashed and chopped) or 1/2 tsp. prepared garlic*
1/2 green bell pepper *(chopped)*
1/2 yellow bell pepper *(chopped)*
2 thin slices medium onion *(chopped)*

1 1/2 C. cooked white beans *(use leftovers in freezer or one 15 oz. can)*
3 Roma tomatoes *(chopped)*

- **Cook halved potatoes on oiled cookie sheet in 400 degree oven for 25 minutes.**
- **Mix Chicken Baste in small bowl.**
- **Cook chicken on grill or Hibachi while basting constantly.** *(Plan at least one extra breast for Wednesday's meal.)* **If you don't have a grill, sauté chicken by adding 2 T. of basting liquid at a time and sautéing until liquid boils away. Chicken will be cooked in 10 minutes.** *Save leftover basting liquid for future use.*
- **Place all Barbecue Sauce ingredients in small sauce pan and bring to boil over medium-high heat. Cover, remove from heat, and let stand 5 minutes.**
- **Put 1/3 C. Barbecue Sauce, garlic, peppers, and onion in sauce pan. Bring to boil. Cook 3 minutes.**
- **Add white beans, tomatoes, and cooked potatoes to sauce and vegetables. Stir until heated through.**

Serve bean mixture in center of plate with chicken breast on the side.

Notes

MONDAY

June/July

Notes

Pasta Putanesca

My family always looks forward to a repeat performance of this classic.

Preparation time: 30 minutes
Servings: 2-3
Ingredients:

Italian Sausage
1 T. olive oil
1 lb. ground turkey breast
2 slices medium yellow onion *(chopped)*
2 tsp. dry basil leaves
1 tsp. dry oregano leaves
1/2 tsp. ground anise
2 large cloves garlic *(smashed and chopped)*
dash of Tabasco® sauce

green salad fixings

1 1/2 C. Red Sauce *Use leftovers or make a new batch.* *(see page 176)*
1/8 C. red wine
2 cloves garlic *(smashed and chopped)*
2 T. green capers *I like the larger capers, they're softer and more flavorful.*
5 Italian or Greek olives *(chopped)*

12 oz. dry whole wheat pasta

3 T. fancy-shred Parmesan
1 T. chopped parsley

- **Place pasta water on to boil in large kettle.**
- **Place all Italian Sausage ingredients in fry pan and cook until browned over medium-high heat** *(about 10 minutes)*. **Remove from heat and set aside.**
- **Prepare green salads on individual plates.**
- **To 1 1/2 C. Red Sauce, add wine, 1/3 of the cooked Italian Sausage, extra 2 cloves garlic, capers, and olives.** *Reserve remainder of sausage for another time.*
- **Cover sauce and place over low heat while finishing dinner preparations.**
- **Drop dry pasta into boiling water. Cook 8 minutes. Drain and rinse.**
- **Divide pasta onto plates and cover with Putanesca Sauce.**

Serve with green salad. Molti Bravi! You're becoming an expert with this dish.

Cold Tuna Pasta Salad

Keeping it cool on summer evenings.

TUESDAY

June/July

Notes

Preparation time: 25 minutes
Servings: 2
Ingredients:

2 C. dry sea shell pasta

Pasta Salad Ingredients
- 1/2 cucumber *(peeled, sliced in 1/4" rounds and quartered)*
- 3 slices medium yellow onion *(chopped)*
- 1/2 red bell pepper *(thin sliced and quartered)*
- 1/4 C. sliced almonds *(toasted)*
- one 6 oz. can tuna *(packed in water, drained)*
- one 6 oz. can sliced water chestnuts *(drained)*
- 4 Roma tomatoes *(chopped)*

Dressing
- 4 T. nonfat mayonnaise
- 1 T. lemon juice
- 1/4 C. plain, nonfat yogurt
- fresh-ground black pepper *(to taste, but be generous)*
- 1 1/2 tsp. Dijon mustard

one nectarine or apple thin sliced or 8 fresh strawberries

1 loaf of your favorite hearty bread

- **Cook pasta in boiling water.**
- **Drain and rinse, and place in bowl of ice water.**
- **Toss Pasta Salad ingredients in large bowl with drained tuna.**
- **Stir all dressing ingredients together in small bowl.**
- **Pour dressing into bowl with all vegetables. Add drained pasta and gently mix with large spoon until pasta is well coated with dressing.**
- **Serve salads on large individual plates. Garnish with sliced fruit.**

Serve with hearty bread.

Pick up a loaf of hearty bread today.

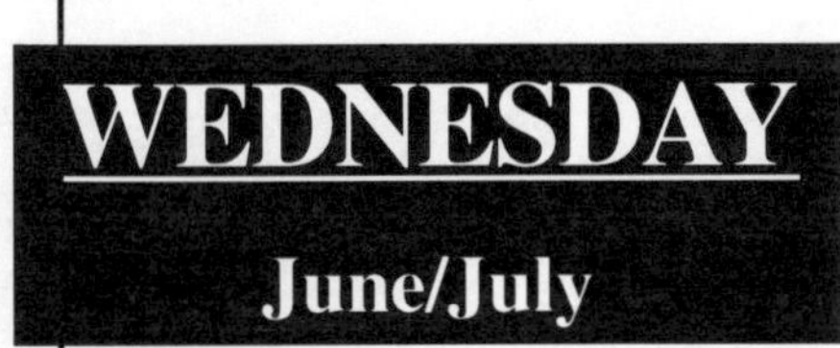

Grilled Chicken Strips on Green Salad

Now you will use the grilled chicken from Sunday's meal.

Notes

Preparation time: 25 minutes
Servings: 2
Ingredients:

5 large leaves red leaf lettuce
5 large leaves green leaf lettuce
1/2 cucumber *(peeled, sliced in 1/4" rounds and quartered)*
3 green onions *(washed and chopped)*
1/2 red bell pepper *(thin sliced and quartered)*
4 Roma tomatoes *(chopped)*

Dressing
2 T. balsamic vinegar
1 clove garlic *(smashed and chopped)*
2 T. orange juice
2 T. white wine
1/2 tsp. dry basil leaves
fresh-ground black pepper *(to taste)*
1/2 tsp. sesame oil

1 leftover grilled chicken breast *(thin sliced)*

4 T. toasted sunflower seeds

1 tart apple *(cored and sliced)*
2-3 T. fancy-shred Parmesan

1 loaf of your favorite hearty bread

Use leftover hearty bread or pick up some today.

- **Break lettuce into large pieces and toss with other vegetables in big bowl.**
- **Prepare dressing by shaking ingredients vigorously in container with tight-fitting lid. Pour over salad and toss.**
- **Divide salad on large individual plates.**
- **Slice chicken breast, lay strips over top of each salad, and sprinkle with sunflower seeds.**
- **Garnish with apple slices and Parmesan cheese.**

Pass the dressing and serve with hearty bread.

Grilled Turkey Burgers, BBQ Beans and German Potato Salad

THURSDAY

June/July

A full-fledged summer Barbecue! Start by cooking some chicken breasts to save for later in the week. You may also use veggie burgers in addition to, or instead of, ground turkey breast.

Preparation time: 1 hr. 30 min.

Servings: 4

Ingredients:

German Potato Salad
- 8 baby red potatoes *(washed and halved)*
- 5 slices medium yellow onion *(chopped)*
- 1 stalk celery *(chopped)*
- 2 T. chopped fresh parsley
- 1/4 C. chicken broth
- 4 T. nonfat mayonnaise
- 1 tsp. Dijon mustard
- 2 T. balsamic vinegar
- 1/4 tsp. dill weed
- 2 slices chopped turkey bacon

BBQ Sauce
- 1/3 C. tom. sauce
- 2 T. Worcestershire
- dash Tabasco®
- 2 T. white vinegar
- 3 T. brown sugar
- 1 T. chopped onion
- 1 tsp. dried oregano
- 2 tsp. chili powder

BBQ Beans
- 1/2 C. BBQ Sauce *(see recipe or use commercial)*
- 1/2 green bell pepper *(chopped)*
- 1/2 fresh pineapple *(chopped in 1/2" pieces)*
- 2 thin slices medium onion *(chopped)*
- 1 1/2 C. cooked white beans *(dried or canned)*
- 3 Roma tomatoes *(chopped)*

Burgers
- burger buns *(whole wheat if possible)*
- 1 lb. ground turkey breast and/or vegetarian burger patties
- condiments for burgers

Notes

Preparation: German Potato Salad
- **Boil halved potatoes.**
- **Sauté onion, celery and parsley in broth** *(2 minutes)*.
- **Combine mayo, mustard, vinegar and dill weed.**
- **Mix ingredients together in bowl with chopped bacon.**
- **Serve warm.**

Preparation: BBQ Beans
- **Make BBQ sauce.**
- **Put 1/2 C. barbecue sauce, green pepper, pineapple and onion in sauce pan. Bring to boil. Cook 3 minutes.**
- **Add white beans and tomatoes. Stir until heated through.**
- **Serve chilled or warm.**

Preparation: Burgers
- **Place buns in shallow pan, cover with damp paper towel and then with foil. Set in warm oven.**
- **Grill burgers.**

Serve Buffet Style with favorite condiments for burgers.

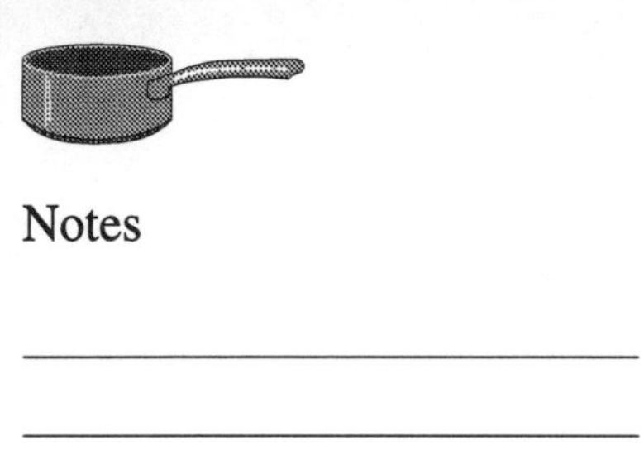

Notes

Bow Tie Pasta with "Creamy" Basil/Tomato Sauce

Another easy sauce. This sauce has the wonderful fresh taste of summer.

Preparation time: 25 minutes
Servings: 2-3
Ingredients:

a fresh loaf of your favorite bakery bread

"Creamy" Basil/Tomato Sauce
3/4 C. broth
1/4 C. white wine
2 cloves garlic *(smashed and chopped)*
2 slices medium yellow onion *(chopped)*
1/4 C. chopped fresh basil leaves

2 T. corn starch *(dissolved in 1/8 C. water)*

4 C. dry bow tie pasta

green salad fixings

8-10 Roma tomatoes *(chopped)*
1/2 C. plain, nonfat yogurt *(stirred smooth)*

2-4 T. fancy-shred Parmesan cheese

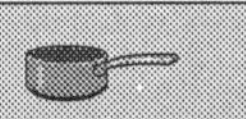

Pick up a loaf of your favorite fresh bakery bread today.

- **Wrap bread in foil and place in warm oven.**
- **Place large kettle on stove filled 2/3 full of water. Cover, turn heat on high.**
- **Place broth, wine, garlic, onion, and chopped basil in sauce pan. Bring to boil.**
- **Thicken with corn starch mixture. Reduce heat to low, cover, and cook 5 minutes.**
- **Drop dry pasta into boiling water and cook 10 minutes.**
- **Prepare green salads while pasta cooks.**
- **Drain pasta and rinse with warm water.**
- **Stir chopped tomatoes into sauce. Return mixture to boil and remove from heat.**
- **Stir yogurt into sauce and serve immediately.**
- **Sprinkle 1-2 T. Parmesan cheese over each serving.**

Serve with crusty bread and crisp green salad on side.

SATURDAY

July/Week One

SHOPPING DAY

***The season for fresh fruits** is coming on strong. This month you may see delicious local berries at a reasonable price. They are great to top nonfat frozen yogurt. Try making a tapioca pudding with fresh berries using juice instead of milk (cherry or the various cranberry styles work well). I use 2 T. tapioca to 1 1/2 C. juice and 1 C. berries. You may need 1/8-1/4 C. sugar to sweeten the pudding.*

***Hooray for garlic!** I use lots of the herb. Not only does it add wonderful zest to a dish, but it appears to have powerful medicinal benefits. "Garlic has been linked to reduction in cholesterol and triglyceride levels, and the lowering of blood pressure. It also appears to increase natural killer-cell activity, which enhances the immune function."**

***And tofu?** I use a fair amount of this wonder food. (It's a staple of Asian cooking.) Made from soybean, tofu is high in protein, rich in calcium, and low in calories. (Some varieties are a little high in fat, but there are many lowfat varieties available.) "Tofu contains photochemicals that may reduce your risk of cancer and heart disease." **

**Vegetarian Times, "Blue-Chip Foods"*, by Winifred Yu, June, 1996

***Looking for value while shopping** may mean looking above and below eye level. The battle for your dollars takes place at eye level. Look for better values on upper and lower shelves. Your willingness to stretch or bend to get a product could stretch your shopping dollar.*

50 Secrets Your Grocer Doesn't Want You to Know, George T. Jacobson, Andante Publishing, P.O. Box 507, Redmond, WA 98073

Notes

____

____

____

____

____

____

____

____

GROCERY LIST

Produce

10 baby red potatoes
one large russet potato
one 6" zucchini
2 medium yellow onions
1 lb. fresh mushrooms
1/2 lb. broccoli
1 green bell pepper
1 red bell pepper
1 head broccoflower
1/2 lb. carrots
1/4 lb. fresh snow peas
2 fresh nectarines or peaches
one bunch fresh parsley
green salad fixings
one large cucumber
3 oz. pine nuts
6 Roma tomatoes
one bunch green onions
1 fresh lemon
firm tofu *(unflavored)*

Frozen Foods

Meat/Fish/Poultry

2 boneless, skinless chicken breasts
1 lb. ground turkey breast
2 small or 1 large orange roughy fillet
(Buy frozen fillets. Do not thaw.)

Canned or Dry Foods

1 C. package shelled pecan halves
two 29 oz. cans tomato sauce
two 15 oz. cans chicken broth
one 6 oz. can chopped black olives
one package 18" *(or standard)* lasagna noodles
12 oz. dry whole wheat pasta
one box bulgar
1 loaf of your favorite Italian bread

Chilled Foods and Dairy

5 oz. part-skim mozzarella cheese
1 pint lowfat Ricotta cheese
1 dozen eggs
fresh salsa
pesto

Buy if you're out

1 head garlic
celery
brown rice
dried rosemary leaves
dried oregano leaves
dried dill weed
ground anise
honey mustard
red cooking wine
white cooking wine
plain, nonfat yogurt
fancy-shred Parmesan

SUNDAY

July/Week One

Notes

Veggie Lasagna

Here is a good weekend recipe. It will take 40 minutes to assemble and about 45 minutes to cook.

Preparation time: 1 1/2 hours

Servings: 4-6

Ingredients:

1 1/2 C. Red Sauce *(see page 176)*

Vegetables and Spices

1/2 small zucchini *(shredded)*
6-8 mushrooms *(chopped)*
6 black olives *(chopped)*
3 slices medium onion *(chopped)*
1 carrot *(grated)*
1 clove garlic *(smashed and chopped)*
1/4 tsp. crushed, dried rosemary
2 tsp. dry basil leaves
1 tsp. dry oregano leaves
1/4 C. broth

five 18" *(extra long)* dry lasagna noodles or 7 standard dry noodles

1/2 C. plain, nonfat yogurt
1/2 C. lowfat Ricotta cheese
1 egg
1 tsp. corn starch

6 oz. part-skim mozzarella *(shredded)*
3 oz. fancy-shred Parmesan

fixings for green salad

a loaf of your favorite Italian bread

- **Prepare Red Sauce.**
- **Place pasta water on to boil and preheat oven to 350 degrees.**
- **Sauté all vegetables and spices in large non-stick fry pan with broth.** *(3 minutes)* **Remove from heat.**
- **Drop noodles into boiling water and set timer for 10 minutes. Drain and rinse.**
- **Blend yogurt, Ricotta cheese, egg, and corn starch in food processor or by stirring vigorously in bowl.**
- **Layer ingredients into oiled 9" X 13" glass baking dish as follows:**
  1 layer of noodles
  1/2 C. vegetable mix
  1/2 C. Red Sauce
  1/3 of the mozzerella and Parmesan
  1/2 C. Ricotta cheese mixture
  Repeat, ending with final layer of noodles, Red Sauce, and remaining mozzarella and Parmesan on top.
- **Cook on center rack of oven 45 minutes at 350 degrees.**
- **Make green salad.** *Serve in a large bowl.*
- **Remove lasagna from oven and let cool 15 minutes before serving.**
- **Wrap bread in foil and place in oven until dinner is served.**

You will have leftovers. It actually freezes nicely for future meals.

Loaded Rice

Back to one of my favorites!

MONDAY

July/Week One

Notes

Preparation time: 25 minutes
Servings: 2
Ingredients:

8-10 baby red potatoes or 1 large russet potato
1 T. olive oil

1/2 lb. mushrooms *(sliced)*
1/4 red bell pepper *(thin-sliced)*
1 T. olive oil
1 large clove garlic *(smashed and chopped)*
1/4 C. white wine
2 slices medium onion *(quartered)*

3/4 C. chicken or vegetable broth
3 T. corn starch dissolved in 1/8 C. cold water

1 1/2 C. cooked brown rice

1 C. plain, nonfat yogurt
1 T. pesto
dash of Tabasco®

2 Roma tomatoes *(chopped)*

- **Preheat oven to 400 degrees.**
- **Wash and halve baby red potatoes. If using russet potato, wash and slice** *(unpeeled)* **in 1/2" slices. Place potatoes, flat side down, on cookie sheet oiled with one tablespoon olive oil.**
- **Sauté sliced mushrooms and bell pepper in oil with garlic, wine, and onion** *(about 4 minutes).* **When done, remove mushroom mixture from pan with perforated spoon. Set aside.**
- **Add broth to pan. Return to boil.**
- **If cooking russet potato slices, turn them now.**
- **Slowly stir corn starch mixture into boiling liquid. Reduce heat to low. Cook 5 minutes, stirring often.**
- **Add mushrooms to thickened mixture. Return to boil. Remove from heat.**
- **Warm 1 1/2 C. cooked rice 2 minutes on high in microwave on individual serving plates.**
- **Remove potatoes from oven. If using baby reds, push them into rice on individual plates. If using russets, chop into 1" pieces before sprinkling over rice.**
- **Stir yogurt, pesto, and Tabasco® together until smooth. Microwave 30 seconds on high. Stir again, and add to thickened mushroom sauce.**

Pour sauce over potato/rice mixture and garnish with fresh chopped tomato. Enjoy!

"Quick cook" rice in morning before work. (see page 158)

TUESDAY

July/Week One

Notes

Leftovers

It's time! Get to it! Eat 'em before they're green!

Preparation time: 15-20 minutes
Servings: 3-4
Ingredients:

Whatever you have!
Lasagna
Tuna Salad
Potato Salad
BBQ Beans

Leftovers can be a hit even with a surprise dinner guest. No need to apologize for these delicious foods. They can be a wonderful adventure for any last minute guest who happens by. Lots of people don't eat this well!

Health Trivia: *One study found that a migraine headache can be caused by a magnesium deficiency. Sources of magnesium are beans, green vegetables, seafood, (particularly halibut, mackerel and shrimp), as well as whole grains.*
The New York Headache Center, New York, NY

Have you ever wondered *about food advertising and promotion budgets? Two popular sugar-laden cereal manufacturers spent $49 million to advertise their products in 1992. By comparison, the National Cancer Institute spent $400,000 to encourage people to eat more fruits and vegetables.*
Health, 301 Howard Street, Suite 1800, San Francisco, CA 94105

Encouraging stats - *most adults say a home-cooked meal is the perfect cure for a long, hard day. That's one reason 80% of Americans prefer to eat at home instead of a restaurant.*
First for Women, 270 Sylvan Ave., Englewood Cliffs, NJ 07632

If you have an ulcer *you may already know to avoid coffee (even decaffeinated). The acids in coffee, not the caffeine, cause pain in ulcer patients.*
Environmental Nutrition, 2112 Broadway, New York, NY 10023

Mustard-Glazed Chicken Breasts

A tasty alternative to the "meat and potatoes" approach.

WEDNESDAY

July/Week One

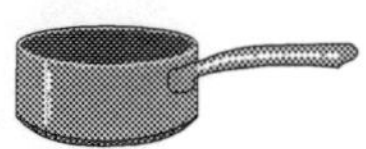

Preparation time: 30 minutes
Servings: 2
Ingredients:

- Bulgar Pilaf
- 2 boneless, skinless chicken breasts
- 1/2 C. chicken broth
- 1 large clove garlic *(smashed and chopped)*
- 1 tsp. honey mustard
- 1/4 C. white wine
- 1/2 lb. fresh broccoli *(cut in 2" lengths)*
- 2 nectarines *(pitted and sliced)*
- 1 lemon *(cut in wedges)*

- **Prepare pilaf if you didn't prepare it this morning.** *If you're preparing the pilaf now, skip the step requiring refrigeration.*
- **Place chicken breasts in small non-stick fry pan over medium-high heat with 1/2 of the broth and chopped garlic. When broth boils, cook 3 minutes before turning. Add remaining broth and cook other side 3 minutes. As broth cooks away, the breast will brown slightly on either side.**
- **Turn breast one more time and spread 1/2 tsp. mustard on each breast. Add 1/4 C. wine to pan, reduce heat to low, cover, and cook an additional 5-10 minutes.**
- **Steam broccoli 2 minutes in medium sauce pan.**
- **Serve chicken breasts flanked by pilaf and broccoli.** *If you made pilaf in the morning, serve it cold.*

Line edge of each plate with sliced nectarine and a lemon wedge for broccoli.

Put on some nice music. Perhaps a glass of white wine is in order.

Notes

Bulgar Pilaf

1 C. bulgar
one 15 oz. can chic. broth
1/2 C. white wine
1 clove garlic (smashed and chopped)
1 carrot (chopped fine)
3-4 green onions (chopped)
1 stalk celery (chopped fine)
juice from 1/2 lemon
2 T. olive oil
3 T. chopped parsley
fresh-ground black pepper
1/4 lb. fresh snow peas
2 large Roma tomatoes

- ***Place all ingredients** (except peas and tomatoes) **in medium sauce pan.***
- ***Bring to boil and cook 5 minutes over medium heat.***
- ***Add peas and tomatoes, turn off heat, cover, and leave on burner for 5 minutes.***

Refrigerate 2-3 hours.

THURSDAY

July/Week One

Notes

Whole Wheat Pasta Bolognese

A return to an old standby. I like the hearty quality of this dish with whole wheat pasta.

Preparation time: 20 minutes
Servings: 2-3
Ingredients:

12 oz. dry whole wheat pasta

Italian Turkey Sausage
1 T. olive oil
1 lb. ground turkey
2 slices medium yellow onion *(chopped)*
2 large cloves garlic *(smashed and chopped)*
2 tsp. dry basil leaves
1 tsp. dry oregano leaves
1/2 tsp. ground anise
dash of Tabasco® sauce
1/8 C. red wine

Red Sauce
one 29 oz. can tomato sauce
2 cloves garlic *(smashed and chopped)*
1/4 C. red wine
1 T. dry oregano
1 1/2 T. dry basil leaves
4 slices medium yellow onion *(chopped)*
a few dashes of Tabasco® sauce *(optional)*

1/3 of the cooked Italian Sausage
1/8 C. red wine
1 1/2 C. Red Sauce

green salad fixings

3 T. fancy-shred Parmesan

- **Place pasta water on to boil in large kettle. Drop pasta into water and cook 8 minutes. Drain and rinse.**
- **Place oil in sauté pan over medium-high heat.**
- **Add ground turkey, onions, garlic, spices, Tabasco® and wine.**
- **Prepare Red Sauce at the same time. Place all ingredients in medium sauce pan and bring to boil. Cover, reduce heat to low, and cook 10 minutes.** *(When Red Sauce is cooked, measure 1 1/2 C. for tonight's recipe and put remainder away in fridge.)*
- **Sauté sausage mix until browned.** *(Reserve 1/3 of the sausage for tonight's recipe and put remainder away in fridge.)*
- **Combine 1/3 of the Italian Sausage, 1/8 C. wine, and 1 1/2 C. Red Sauce in same pan used to cook Red Sauce.** *Bring to boil. Reduce heat to low and cover while finishing dinner preparations.*
- **Prepare green salads.**
- **Divide pasta on two plates and spoon Bolognese Sauce over each serving.**
- **Garnish with Parmesan cheese.**

Encore!

Orange Roughy with Dill

Orange Roughy! What a delicate, versatile fish this is!

FRIDAY

July/Week One

Preparation time: 25 minutes
Servings: 2
Ingredients:

1/4 C. pecans *(chopped – toast in dry fry pan)*
1/4 C. white wine
2 slices medium onion *(chopped)*
3 T. chopped parsley *(fresh or dried)*
2 cups cooked rice

1 large or 2 medium carrots *(peeled and sliced diagonally)*
1 head broccoflower *(cut into 1" pieces)*

1/2 C. white wine
1 clove garlic *(smashed and chopped)*
2 small roughy fillets or 2/3 lb. roughy
fresh-ground black pepper
a couple pinches of dill weed

1/2 fresh lemon *(cut in wedges)*

- **Preheat oven to 400 degrees.**
- **Add nuts, wine, onion, and parsley to rice. Cover and microwave on high 2 1/2 minutes.**
- **Place carrots and broccoflower in steamer basket in medium sauce pan with 3/4 C. water.** *Do not begin cooking yet!*
- **Place wine and garlic in sauté pan and bring to boil.**
- **Slide fish fillets into boiling mixture and season with a few turns fresh-ground black pepper. Cook about 3 minutes per side. Turn fillets and sprinkle dill weed over each fillet.** *Watch liquid in pan. If it cooks away, add another 1/4 C. wine, chicken broth, or water.*
- **Turn heat on under carrot mixture. Bring to boil and steam** *(covered)* **3 minutes. Serve immediately!**

Serve fillets flanked by vegetables and nutty rice on individual serving plates with a wedge of lemon for the broccoflower and carrots.

Notes

"Quick cook" rice before work this morning. *(see page 158)*

SATURDAY

July/Week Two

SHOPPING DAY PLUS BRUNCH

This week you will enjoy some dinner-style salads *that go well with the warmer weather. If you're stuck in a rut with iceberg lettuce you might try the lettuce suggested in the recipes. The variety is refreshing and loose leaf lettuce is much richer in vitamin A and calcium.*

Spice up you life! *A teaspoon of many herbs and spices contains 20 to 50 mg. of potassium. One teaspoon of cayenne pepper, paprika or chili powder packs 750 to 955 IU's of vitamin A.*

Men's Workout, 1115 Broadway, New York, NY 10010

Notes

Tofu Scramble

Don't turn up you nose until you've tried this one!

1 unpeeled russet potato *(chopped)*
3 slices medium onion *(chopped)*
1 clove garlic *(smashed and chopped)*
1 T. olive oil
2 whole eggs and 6 egg whites
1/4 C. nonfat milk
2 tsp. dry oregano leaves
1/2 C. chopped, unflavored tofu
1/2 small zucchini *(chopped)*
4 slices medium onion *(chopped)*
1/2 green bell pepper *(chopped)*
3 mushrooms *(chopped)*
fresh-ground black pepper
salsa
plain, nonfat yogurt *(stirred smooth)*
favorite bread for toast

- **Preheat oven to 400 degrees.**
- **Mix potatoes, onion, and garlic. Place in oiled pan in oven** *(10 minutes).*
- **Turn potatoes with spatula and return to oven** *(10 minutes).*
- **Beat together whole eggs and egg whites, milk, and oregano.**
- **Stir with tofu and vegetables in non-stick 12" fry pan over high heat and season generously with fresh-ground black pepper. Stir egg mixture until cooked.**
- **Spoon salsa and stirred yogurt over top.**

Serve potatoes and toast on the side.

GROCERY LIST

Produce

6-8 baby red potatoes
2 large russet potatoes
one 6" zucchini
1 medium yellow onion
1/2 lb. fresh mushrooms
2 green bell peppers
2 red bell peppers
2 large carrots
celery
1/4 lb. fresh green beans
1/2 lb. fresh asparagus
1 head iceberg lettuce
1 head red leaf lettuce
1 head green leaf lettuce
2 bunches spinach
two large cucumbers
10-12 Roma tomatoes
1 bunch fresh parsley
1 bunch green onions
fresh chives
fresh mint leaves
1 lemon
2 tart apples
unflavored, firm tofu

Frozen Foods

Meat/Fish/Poultry

6 - 8 oz. fresh or frozen crab meat *(if available)*
1/2 lb. ground turkey breast
turkey bacon

Canned or Dry Foods

1 small jar dried chives *(if fresh are unavailable)*
one 15 oz. can vegetable broth
three 15 oz. cans chicken broth
one 29 oz. can tomato sauce
two 6 oz. cans tuna packed in water
one 6 oz. can crab meat *(if fresh is unavailable)*
12 oz. dry spinach spiral pasta
8 oz. fresh cheese tortellini
1/2 lb. bulgar
a loaf of your favorite hearty bread

Chilled Foods and Dairy

4 oz. sharp cheddar cheese
tortillas (wheat or corn)

Buy if you're out

1 head garlic
pine nuts
bulgar
olive oil
Greek olives
capers
balsamic vinegar
Dijon mustard
paprika
white cooking wine
saltine crackers
Tabasco sauce®
plain, nonfat yogurt
nonfat milk
fancy-shred Parmesan
fresh salsa
eggs
fresh pesto

Niçoise

Here is a lowfat version of this classic French salad. The tofu is a substitute for hard boiled egg.

Preparation time: 35 minutes

Servings: 2-3

Ingredients:

6-8 baby red potatoes *(halved)*
1 C. fresh green beans *(snapped)*

Dressing
1/2 tsp. grated or zested lemon rind
1/4 tsp. fresh-ground black pepper
1 tsp. Dijon mustard
2 finely chopped green onions
2 T. olive oil
2 T. white wine
2 T. lemon juice
1/4 C. vegetable broth
Put all ingredients together in container with tight-fitting lid and shake vigorously

three 1/4" slices firm, plain tofu *(chopped)*
1/4 tsp. Dijon mustard
1/4 C. white wine
8 leaves green leaf lettuce *(keep 2 leaves whole and tear 6 into pieces)*
two 6 oz. cans tuna *(drained)*
4 Roma tomatoes *(quartered lengthwise)*
6-8 Italian or Greek olives

1/4 C. dry white wine
juice from 1 lemon
2 green onions *(chopped)*
fresh-ground black pepper

3 T. capers
2 T. chopped parsley

2 tart apples *(cored and thin sliced)*

1 loaf of your favorite hearty bread

- **Boil potatoes in 3 C. water 15 minutes. Lift out with perforated spoon and drop washed, snapped beans into water. Reduce heat and boil 3-4 minutes. Drain in colander. Place potatoes and beans in bowl of ice water. Drain before adding to salad.**
- **Mix dressing.**
- **Sauté tofu with mustard and wine until wine boils away. Remove from heat.**
- **Toss broken lettuce leaves, tofu, and green beans in large bowl with 1/2 the dressing.**
- **Arrange whole lettuce leaves on large platter. Sprinkle tuna chunks, green beans, tofu, tomatoes, and olives around edge of platter.**
- **Toss potatoes with wine, 1 T. lemon juice, 1/2 the chopped onions and pepper.**
- **Place potatoes in center of platter.**
- **Sprinkle capers and parsley around platter and drizzle with remaining dressing.**
- **Prepare sliced apple and fan out 1/2 apple per person as side serving.**

Serve large platter in center of table with your favorite hearty bread.

SUNDAY

July/Week Two

Notes

You are making the Tabbouleh for Monday to be served with Crab Cakes. Tomorrow's dinner is half finished!

- *In large bowl mix 1 C. bulgar, 2 cloves garlic, and 2 C. boiling water. Cover. Let stand 25 minutes.*
- *Add 1/2 chopped cucumber, 2 stalks chopped celery, 4 T. chopped parsley, 4-5 chopped green onions, 1/4 C. white wine, 2 dashes Tabasco® sauce, 1/4 C. balsamic vinegar, juice from 1/2 lemon, 1/2 C. chopped fresh tomato, and 2 T. chopped fresh mint leaves.*
- *Stir ingredients together. Cover with plastic wrap and chill overnight.*

MONDAY

July/Week Two

Notes

Crab Cakes

More delicious summer fare. You may use fresh, frozen, canned, or "mock" crab in the preparation. If using canned crab, be sure to drain it well.

Preparation time: 30 minutes
Servings: 2-3
Ingredients:

Tabbouleh Salad made on Sunday

Crab Cakes

6-8 oz. crab meat
4 thin slices medium onion *(chopped fine)*
one stalk celery *(chopped fine)*
2 T. fresh chopped parsley
1 egg and 1 egg white *(slightly beaten)*
1 1/4 C. crushed saltine crackers
1/4 red bell pepper *(chopped fine)*
1/4 tsp. fresh-ground black pepper
1/2 tsp. Dijon mustard
1/2 tsp. paprika

White Sauce

3/4 C. chicken broth
1/4 C. white wine
1 thin slice onion *(chopped)*
1 clove garlic *(smashed and chopped)*
2 T. flour shaken with 1/3 C. nonfat milk

2 bunches spinach
1/4 C. broth

1/2 tsp. Dijon mustard
1 tsp. lemon juice

1/4 tsp. nutmeg
1/4 C. plain, nonfat yogurt *(stirred smooth)*

- **Preheat 9" X 13" baking dish in 400 degree oven.**
- **Combine ingredients for crab cakes in large bowl. Mix well with hands and form into patties. Set aside on plate.**
- **Remove baking dish from oven and spread with 1 T. oil. Place patties in hot dish and return to oven for 15 minutes.**
- **Mix first four ingredients of White Sauce in sauce pan. Bring to boil.**
- **Thicken with flour mixture. Cook 10 minutes over low heat. Stir often.**
- **Turn crab cakes and return to oven.**
- **Place large heavy-bottomed kettle or fry pan on medium-high heat. Sauté spinach in 1/4 C. broth until thoroughly wilted** *(about 5 minutes)*.
- **Place half the white sauce in small bowl and add mustard and lemon juice.**
- **Add nutmeg and yogurt to sauce left in pan and stir into spinach over medium heat. Remove from heat when well blended.**

Serve Crab Cakes with Mustard Sauce flanked by Tabbouleh Salad and Creamed Spinach.

Taco Salad

You've done this one before. Another quick meal to keep your kitchen cool. (The only cooking involves the ground turkey.)

TUESDAY

July/Week Two

Preparation time: 15-20 minutes
Servings: 3-4
Ingredients:

1/4 C. Red Sauce *(see page 194)*

1/2 lb. ground turkey breast
1 T. olive oil
2 slices medium yellow onion *(chopped)*
1 clove garlic *(smashed and chopped)*
1 tsp. oregano leaves
1/2 tsp. ground cumin
1 T. mild chili powder
dash of Tabasco®

1/2 green pepper *(cut in 1" cubes)*
1 clove garlic *(smashed and chopped)*
2 slices yellow onion *(quartered)*
1 T. chili powder
1/4 C. broth or water

6-8 leaves washed red leaf lettuce
1/2 head chopped iceberg lettuce

sharp cheddar cheese
2-3 Roma tomatoes *(chopped)*

flour or corn tortillas

1/2 C. plain, nonfat yogurt *(stirred smooth)*
salsa

Notes

- **Make a fresh batch of Red Sauce.** *(Use 1/4 C. for this meal and reserve the rest.)*
- **Sauté ground turkey in olive oil along with onion, garlic, and spices in large non-stick fry pan over medium-high heat. Sauté 5 minutes stirring constantly. Add 1/4 C. Red Sauce. Cover, reduce heat to low, and cook an additional 5 minutes.**
- **When meat is done, remove from pan, place in bowl and set aside.**
- **Using same fry pan, sauté green pepper, garlic, and onions with chili powder and broth. Sauté 2 minutes over high heat. Remove from pan and set aside.**
- **Place 2 washed leaves red leaf lettuce on each plate as bed for salad. Top with chopped iceberg lettuce.**
- **Divide meat and sautéed vegetables onto beds of lettuce.**
- **Garnish with a grating of sharp cheese and chopped tomato.** *Go easy on the cheese! Only two or three draws across the grater per salad are needed.*
- **Warm tortillas by setting them, one at a time, in large fry pan for about 30 seconds per side over medium-high heat.**
- **Spoon yogurt and salsa over salad to suit your taste.**

Serve with tortillas on the side.

"Creamy" Spinach Spirals Prima Vera

WEDNESDAY

July/Week Two

Notes

Another return engagement that will keep the kitchen cool.

Preparation time: 25 minutes
Servings: 3
Ingredients:

2 T. toasted pine nuts *(chopped)*

1 carrot *(peeled and sliced)*
1 C. vegetable broth or chicken broth

6 medium mushrooms *(sliced)*
2 slices medium yellow onion *(quartered)*
1 large clove garlic *(smashed and chopped)*
fresh-ground black pepper

1/2 green pepper *(chopped in 1" squares)*
1/2 red bell pepper *(chopped in 1" squares)*
one 6" long zucchini *(cut in 1/4" rounds)*

2 C. dry spinach spirals pasta

1/2 C. white wine
3 T. corn starch *(dissolved in 1/8 C. water)*
2 dashes of Tabasco®

3/4 C. plain, nonfat yogurt
2 T. pesto

3 T. fancy-shred Parmesan
1 large Roma tomato *(chopped, use for garnish)*

- **Place pasta water on to boil in large kettle.**
- **Toast pine nuts in dry shallow pan on stove top. It will take only a few minutes, so stay with them.** *(Toast extra! They store, unrefrigerated, in any container with tight-fitting lid.)*
- **Sauté carrot in 1/4 C. broth 2 minutes. Remove from pan.**
- **Sauté mushrooms, onions, and garlic 2 minutes in same pan. Season to taste with fresh-ground pepper. Remove from pan and set aside with carrots.**
- **Sauté peppers and zucchini using another 1/8 C. broth if needed. Sauté 1 minute. Remove from pan and set aside with other veggies.**
- **Drop pasta into boiling water and cook 8 minutes. Drain and rinse.**
- **Pour white wine, leftover broth from sauté pan, and any remaining broth into pasta kettle and bring to boil. Reduce heat and gradually stir in corn starch mixture. It will thicken. Add Tabasco® and cook over low heat 5 minutes.**
- **Stir yogurt and pesto together until smooth. Microwave 20 seconds on high to take chill off, and stir once more.**
- **Add veggies and pasta to thickened sauce. Return to boil and remove from heat.**
- **Blend yogurt mixture into vegetable sauce.**
- **Spoon onto individual serving plates in generous portions.**

Favoloso!

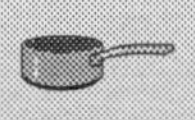

Quark for Tomorrow

Tonight you will make quark. It is ridiculously simple and is great as a snack spread on crackers, a base for dips, or as sour cream substitute on baked potatoes.

- *Place a large coffee filter in a strainer.*
- *Set strainer over a bowl.*
- *Fill filter with nonfat, plain yogurt.*
- *Place in fridge until just before dinner tomorrow evening.*

(Save the liquid and use it in your sauce Friday evening. Substitute for equal amount broth.)

Baked Potato with Fresh Asparagus

THURSDAY

July/Week Two

Asparagus may be in season in your part of the world now. It will compliment this variation on the baked potato theme.

Preparation time: 15-20 minutes
Servings: 2
Ingredients:

- 2 large russet baking potatoes *(washed, rubbed with olive oil, and pricked with a fork)*
- 2 T. chopped fresh or dry chives
- 3/4 C. quark or plain, nonfat yogurt *(stirred smooth)*
- 1/2 lb. fresh asparagus
- 2 slices cooked turkey bacon *(chopped) You should have leftovers in freezer.*
- 2 lemon wedges

- **Prepare potatoes in the morning prior to work and set your oven for "time bake" so that they have been cooking 1 hour when you arrive home in the evening.** *(You may also cook them in the microwave. Cook for three 5-minute cycles at full power. Turn the potatoes to a different position after each cycle.)*
- **Stir chives into quark** *(or yogurt)* **and set aside in bowl.**
- **Wash asparagus and snap off white ends. Place tops in steamer basket in sauce pan with 1/2 C. water over high heat. When water boils, cover, and steam 2 minutes.**

Split potatoes and place on serving plates. Top with bacon and quark or yogurt. Serve asparagus on same plate with a wedge of lemon.

Notes

If you have "time bake" on your oven, you may wish to wash potatoes, prick them with a fork, rub them with olive oil, and place them in a shallow pan in the oven before work today. Set the oven temperature at 400 degrees so that it turns on 1 hour before you are to arrive home.

FRIDAY
July/Week Two

Notes

Tortellini with Pesto "Cream" Sauce

We revisit this old friend. It goes together with little effort.

Preparation time: 25 minutes
Servings: 2-3
Ingredients:

8 oz. fresh tortellini or 1 1/2 C. dry

1 C. broth
1 slice onion *(chopped)*
2 cloves garlic *(smashed and chopped)*
3 T. corn starch dissolved in 1/4 C. water
2 T. Parmesan cheese
dash of Tabasco®

green salad fixings

1/2 C. plain, nonfat yogurt *(stirred smooth)*
1 1/2 T. pesto

3 Roma tomatoes *(chopped)*
3-4 T. fancy-shred Parmesan cheese

- **Place pasta water on to boil in large kettle.**
- **Drop tortellini into boiling water.** *Cook fresh tortellini 10-12 minutes, dry 20 minutes. Set a timer so you don't overcook it.*
  Note: If you're using fresh tortellini, make sauce before cooking tortellini. If using dry, cook before preparing sauce.
- **Place broth, onion, and garlic in small sauce pan and bring to boil. Reduce heat to low and cook 5 minutes. Thicken with corn starch/water mixture. Add Parmesan and Tabasco®. Cook, uncovered, an additional 5 minutes. Remove from heat.**
- **Make green salads while sauce and pasta cook.**
- **Drain and rinse pasta.**
- **Stir yogurt and pesto until smooth and add to thickened broth. Do not return to heat.**
- **Serve on individual plates with white sauce spooned over top of tortellini.**

Garnish with tomatoes and Parmesan and serve with a crisp green salad.

SHOPPING DAY

SATURDAY

July/Week Three

There are more main course salads in store this week. *You will begin to have a pretty healthy repertoire of salads by the time you've completed this week of "dining in."*

Notes about some of the most important nutrients in your diet:

Calcium - *Most women consume less than the recommended dietary allowance (RDA) of 800 milligrams (mg.) per day. Moreover, many experts say post menopausal women should consume 1,500 mg. of calcium a day. Calcium helps fight bone loss. Good sources include milk (nonfat is fine), seafood, broccoli, and green leafy vegetables.*

Zinc - *A deficiency delays wound healing and impairs immune function. Good sources include meat, eggs, and seafood.*

Vitamin C - *As an antioxidant, vitamin C may protect against cataracts, heart disease, and cancer. Citrus fruits, melon, berries and broccoli are good sources.*

Fiber - *Fiber helps prevent constipation and intestinal problems. It also improves glucose tolerance and may protect against colon cancer. Vegetables, fruits and whole grains are excellent sources.*

Lifetime Health Letter, The University of Texas Health Science Center at Houston, Houston, TX

Notes

GROCERY LIST

Produce

one 6" zucchini
1 medium red onion
2 medium yellow onions
1/2 lb. fresh mushrooms
1/2 lb. fresh broccoli
2 green bell peppers
2 red bell peppers
2 large carrots
1 head cabbage
1 head Romaine lettuce
1 head green leaf lettuce
2 large cucumbers
10-12 Roma tomatoes
2 medium tomatoes
1 bunch fresh cilantro
1 bunch green onions
fresh ginger root
1 lemon and 1 lime
1/2 C. toasted sunflower meats
1 fresh nectarine or peach
1 tart apple

Frozen Foods

one can frozen orange juice

Meat/Fish/Poultry

6 - 8 oz. fresh or frozen baby shrimp *(if available)*
4-5 boneless, skinless chicken breasts

Canned or Dry Foods

1/2 C. package sliced almonds
1 small jar dried chives *(if fresh are unavailable)*
three 15 oz. cans chicken broth
one 29 oz. can tomato sauce
two 6 oz. cans sliced water chestnuts
two 6 oz. cans chopped clams
one 6 oz. can baby shrimp *(if fresh is unavailable)*
12 oz. dry spiral pasta
8 oz. fresh angel hair pasta
16 oz. dry sea shell pasta

Chilled Foods and Dairy

4 oz. feta cheese
pita bread
fresh hummus

Buy if you're out

1 head garlic
1 bunch fresh parsley
frozen peas
low-sodium soy sauce
sesame oil
brown sugar
Dijon mustard
nonfat mayonnaise
1 small bottle Greek olives
white cooking wine
sliced almonds
brown rice
Tabasco® sauce
plain, nonfat yogurt

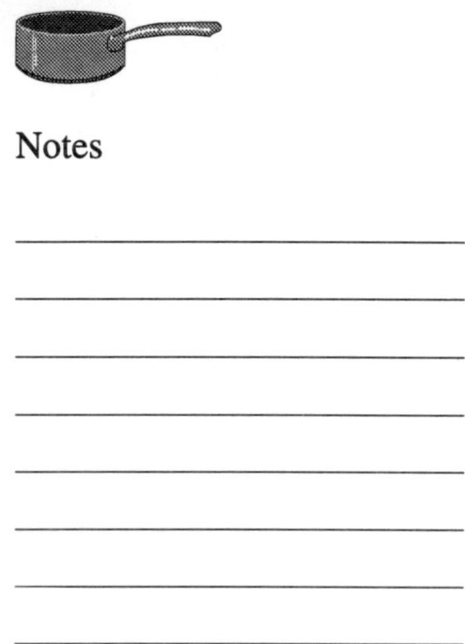

Notes

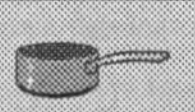

"Quick cook" rice before work this morning. *(see page 158)*

Teriyaki Chicken

Prepare this Teriyaki Chicken over a barbecue for a taste of summer.

Preparation time: 30 minutes
Servings: 2-3
Ingredients:

Teriyaki Sauce
- 1/2 C. white wine
- 1/2 C. orange juice
- 4 cloves garlic *(smashed and chopped)*
- 2 thin slices onion *(chopped very fine)*
- 6 T. low-sodium soy sauce
- 1 tsp. sesame oil
- 1/2 tsp. freshly grated ginger
- 2 T. brown sugar

- 4-5 boneless, skinless chicken breasts
- 1 T. vegetable oil

- 1/2 head cabbage *(cored and chopped)*
- 2 large carrots *(peeled and sliced diagonally)*
- 2 slices medium onion *(quartered)*
- 1/4 C. orange juice

- 2-3 C. cooked brown rice *("quick cooked" this morning)*

- **Mix all teriyaki sauce ingredients in small sauce pan over medium-high heat. Bring to boil. Reduce heat to low and cook, covered, 5 minutes.** *(Set 1/2 C. aside in dish to dress rice and vegetables.)*
- **Grill breasts and baste with Teriyaki Sauce. Cook about 8 minutes per side.** *You will have at least one leftover breast. Save it for the salad Tuesday evening.*
- **Place vegetables in medium-sized sauce pan with 1/4 C. orange juice. Bring to boil. Add 1/4 C. Teriyaki Sauce. Stir to coat all vegetables with sauce. Reduce heat and cook, uncovered, 5 minutes stirring often.**
- **Measure 1 C. rice per serving into bowl. Mix with remaining 1/4 C. teriyaki sauce. Microwave 2 minutes on high.**

Serve on individual plates with rice in center and chicken and vegetables on either side.

Angel Hair Pasta with Clam Sauce

MONDAY
July/Week Three

A repeat performance! Remember this tasty yet lowfat version of a classic clam sauce pasta?

Preparation time: 30 minutes
Servings: 3
Ingredients:

Notes

12 medium-sized mushrooms *(sliced and chopped)*
1 small 6" zucchini *(split down the middle and sliced)*
1 clove garlic *(smashed and chopped)*
2/3 C. white wine

4 slices medium onion *(chopped)*
1 clove garlic *(smashed and chopped)*
1/2 C. broth
2 tsp. dry oregano
1 tsp. dry basil

two 6 oz. cans chopped clams *(with juice)*
3 dashes Tabasco®

4 T. flour
1/2 C. nonfat milk

4 T. Parmesan cheese

fixings for a green salad

8 oz. fresh angel hair pasta

3/4 C. plain, nonfat yogurt *(stirred smooth)*

2 T. fancy-shred Parmesan cheese
1 T. chopped fresh parsley

- **Place pasta water on to boil in large kettle.**
- **In bottom of heavy sauce pan sauté mushrooms, zucchini and garlic in white wine. Sauté 2 minutes. Remove veggies from pan with perforated spoon.**
- **Place onion, garlic, broth, oregano, and basil in sauce pan and bring to boil.**
- **Add clams** *(with juice)* **and Tabasco®. Return to boil.**
- **Shake flour and 1/2 C. milk in container with tight-fitting lid until mixture is smooth.**
- **When liquid returns to boil, slowly stir in flour mixture.**
- **Add 4 T. Parmesan. Reduce heat and cook, uncovered, 5 minutes.**
- **Prepare green salads.**
- **Slide pasta into boiling water.** *Cook no more than two minutes.* **Drain and rinse.**
- **Stir yogurt into Clam Sauce and serve immediately over pasta.**

Garnish with shredded Parmesan and chopped parsley. Heavenly!

TUESDAY

July/Week Three

Notes

Pick up some hearty bread today.

Cold Teriyaki Chicken Pasta Salad

More light fare for hot summer days.

Preparation time: 25 minutes
Servings: 2
Ingredients:

2 C. dry spiral pasta

1/2 lb. fresh broccoli *(chopped in 1" pieces and lightly steamed)*

1/2 cucumber *(peeled, sliced in 1/4" rounds and quartered)*
3 slices medium yellow onion *(chopped)*
1/2 red bell pepper *(thin sliced and quartered)*
4 Roma tomatoes *(chopped)*
1/2 of a 6 oz. can sliced water chestnuts *(drained)*

Dressing
4 T. nonfat mayonnaise
1 clove garlic *(smashed and chopped)*
1/4 C. nonfat yogurt or quark
2 T. orange juice
fresh-ground black pepper *(to taste)*
1/2 tsp. sesame oil

1 Teriyaki Chicken Breast from Sunday night *(chopped)*

1 loaf of your favorite hearty bread

- **Cook pasta in boiling water.**
- **Place broccoli in steamer basket in sauce pan and steam 2 minutes. Remove from heat and place in bowl of ice water.**
- **Drain and rinse pasta and place in bowl of ice water with broccoli.**
- **Toss vegetables and water chestnuts in large bowl.**
- **Prepare dressing.**
- **Drain pasta and broccoli.**
- **Pour dressing into large bowl with vegetables. Add pasta, broccoli, and chopped chicken. Gently mix with large spoon until pasta is well coated with dressing.**
- **Serve salads on large individual plates.**

Serve with hearty bread.

Leftovers

WEDNESDAY

July/Week Three

You probably have salads among your leftovers. This should be a very easy meal. Call it "Salad Sampler Night."

Preparation time: 15-20 minutes
Servings: 3-4
Ingredients:

Notes

Cold Teriyaki Chicken Pasta Salad
Taco Salad
Pasta and Clam Sauce

Very Interesting! *44% of US women ages 18-30 said they worked out to compensate for poor eating habits.*
The Gallup Organization, Princeton, NJ

"He's a Big Boy!" *The heavier a man is in his 20's the more likely he is to develop asteoarthritis in the knees and hips in later life. Being 20 lb. overweight can double the risk.*
Research at Johns Hopkins University, Baltimore, MD

Shelf Life of Milk. *It should last up to a week past its sell date if stored properly.*
Buy it Fresh, Keep it Fresh, by Joe Elder, Fawcett Books, 1991

THURSDAY

July/Week Three

Notes

Cold Shrimp Pasta Salad

Keeping it cool on summer evenings.

Preparation time: 25 minutes
Servings: 2
Ingredients:

1/4 C. sliced almonds *(toasted)*

2 C. dry shell pasta

1/2 cucumber *(peeled, sliced in 1/4" rounds, and quartered)*
3 slices medium yellow onion *(chopped)*
1/2 red bell pepper *(thin sliced and quartered)*
1/2 green bell pepper *(thin sliced and quartered)*
1/4 C. frozen peas *(thawed)*
1/4 C. chopped fresh cabbage
4 Roma tomatoes *(chopped)*
one 6 oz. can baby shrimp *(drained)* or 6 oz. frozen baby shrimp

Dressing
4 T. of nonfat mayonnaise
1 clove garlic *(smashed and chopped)*
1/4 C. nonfat yogurt
2 T. lime juice
1/2 tsp. fresh grated ginger
3 T. chopped cilantro
fresh-ground black pepper *(to taste)*
1 tsp. Dijon mustard

one nectarine or apple *(thin sliced)*

1 loaf of your favorite hearty bread

- **Toast almonds under broiler.** *(Stay with them so they don't burn.)*
- **Cook pasta 10 minutes. Drain and rinse and place in bowl of ice water.**
- **Toss vegetables in large bowl with drained shrimp.**
- **Stir dressing ingredients together and pour into bowl with vegetables.**
- **Add drained pasta and gently toss to coat all ingredients.**
- **Serve salads on large individual plates. Garnish with sliced fruit.**

Serve with hearty bread.

Pick up a fresh loaf of your favorite bakery bread on the way home from work tonight.

Greek Salad

FRIDAY

July/Week Three

This is a nice relaxing meal to linger over on a Friday evening.

Preparation time: 25 minutes
Servings: 2
Ingredients:

Notes

1 package pita bread

1 cucumber *(peeled, cubed)*
1/2 red onion *(chopped in 1" pieces)*
1 red bell pepper *(chopped in 1" pieces)*
1 green bell pepper *(chopped in 1" pieces)*
6-8 Greek olives
6 Roma tomatoes *(chopped in 1" pieces) or 4 slicing tomatoes*
4 oz. feta cheese

Dressing
2 T. olive oil
1 clove garlic *(smashed and chopped)*
2 T. lemon juice
2 T. balsamic vinegar
1/8 C. vegetable broth
fresh-ground black pepper *(to taste)*
2 T. chopped fresh parsley

6 large leaves green leaf lettuce or Romaine lettuce
(washed and patted dry)
hummus

- **Warm pita bread in 200 degree oven.**
- **Toss vegetables in large bowl with feta cheese.**
- **Stir dressing ingredients together and pour into bowl with vegetables. Gently toss until well coated.**
- **Lay whole lettuce leaves on large serving plate as bed for salad.**
- **Arrange vegetables on platter over lettuce.**
- **Serve in center of table with small plates at each place setting.**

Serve with warm pita bread and hummus.

SATURDAY
July/August

Notes

SHOPPING DAY

Grab your checkbook and head for the grocery store. There are so many wonderful fresh foods available this time of year!

About vitamin B6: *Particularly in older people, a deficiency in this vitamin may lead to mental changes and decreased sensitivity to insulin. Good sources include: herring, salmon, nuts, and brown rice. (Three of these items are in your menus next week.)*
Lifetime Health Letter, The University of Texas Health Science Center at Houston, PO Box 420342, Palm Coast, FL 32142

These fish contain less than 5% fat: *black sea bass, catfish, cod, flounder, grouper, haddock, halibut, orange roughy, pollock, red snapper, sea trout, shark, sole, striped bass, swordfish, tiilapia and whiting. They dry out easily when baked, broiled, or grilled, so cook them quickly.*
US Department of Agriculture, Washington, DC

"Milking" the fat notes: *Switching to 2% milk may not be enough of a fat reduction. One cup of whole milk has 8 gm. of fat; 2% milk, 5 gm.; and 1%, 3 gm. Skim milk has only .5 gm.*
McCall's, 110 5th Ave. New York, NY 10011

Peach season is coming. *Follow these easy directions to remove peach skins. Cover peaches with boiling water and let stand 2 minutes. Lift peaches out with perforated spoon and submerge in second bowl filled with ice water. Let stand 2 minutes. Skins should lift off easily. Slice and serve.*

GROCERY LIST

Produce

one 6" zucchini
4 large russet potatoes
1 medium yellow onion
1 large sweet onion
1/2 lb. fresh mushrooms
1 green bell pepper
1 red bell pepper
3 large carrots
1 butternut squash
1/2 lb. fresh broccoli
1 head Romaine lettuce
1 head green leaf lettuce
green salad fixings
1 bunch green onions
1 large cucumber
6-8 Roma tomatoes
3 fresh peaches or nectarines
1/2 pint fresh raspberries
1 fresh lemon

Frozen Foods

orange juice
frozen raspberries *(if fresh unavailable)*

Meat/Fish/Poultry

1 lb. fresh salmon fillets
3 boneless, skinless chicken breasts

Canned or Dry Foods

chopped black olives
one 29 oz. can tomato sauce
three 15 oz. cans chicken broth
one 15 oz. can vegetable broth
one small can artichoke hearts
one 6 oz. can sliced water chestnuts
one 6 oz. can sliced bamboo shoots
16 oz. dry whole wheat spiral pasta
16 oz. dry radiatore pasta
8 oz. fresh cheese tortellini
1/4 lb. roasted cashews
fortune cookies

Chilled Foods and Dairy

1 dozen eggs

Buy if you're out

1 head garlic
frozen corn
sesame oil
low-sodium soy sauce
brown rice
Italian or Greek olives
corn starch
red wine vinegar
plain, nonfat yogurt

Grilled Salmon

Another natural for hot summer evenings. Fire up the barbecue!

SUNDAY

July/August

Preparation time: 45 minutes
Servings: 2-3
Ingredients

Basting Sauce
1/4 C. white wine
1/4 C. orange juice
2 cloves garlic *(smashed and chopped)*
1 thin slice onion *(chopped very fine)*
2 T. Worcestershire sauce
1 T. brown sugar

Pilaf mix
1 medium carrot *(peeled and chopped)*
1/4 C. frozen peas
1/4 C. frozen corn
1 T. chopped parsley
3 T. lemon juice
1/4 C. broth
1 clove garlic *(smashed and chopped)*
3 slices medium onion *(chopped)*
1 T. low-salt soy sauce

3-4 fresh salmon fillets *(3 to 4 oz. per serving) You're cooking an extra for Tuesday's meal.*

2-3 C. cooked brown rice *("quick cooked" this morning)*

Notes

"Quick cook" rice before work this morning. Make a double batch. *(see page 158)*

- **Put all Basting Sauce ingredients in small sauce pan over medium-high heat. Bring to boil. Reduce heat to low and cook, covered, 5 minutes.** *(Set 1/4 C. aside in small dish to dress rice.)*
- **Boil 1/4 C. water in a sauce pan. Add chopped carrot and cook 1 minute. Add all other Pilaf ingredients. Cook 1 minute. Remove from heat.**
- **Place salmon fillets on grill** *(skin side down)*. **Baste with sauce. Cook 3 minutes and turn. Cook another 3 minutes. Turn skin side back down, baste again, and set timer for 5 minutes. Turn once more and cook another 3 minutes. Turn skin side back down and move to edge of grill until ready to serve.** *Meat should begin to flake.*
- **To Pilaf mixture, add 2 C. rice and 1/4 C. basting liquid. Return to high heat until liquid boils. Reduce heat and fluff with a fork while cooking 2 minutes.** *Put extra rice in fridge for tomorrow. You have cooked at least one extra fillet which will be used in the salad on Tuesday evening. When cool, wrap it in foil and place in fridge.*

Serve on individual plates with 1 C. rice per serving in center and salmon fillet to the side.

MONDAY

July/August

Notes

Broccoli/Cashew Stir Fry

A stir fry loaded with nutrients. This is a most rewarding meatless meal. You should have some rice left over in the fridge.

Preparation time: 30 minutes
Servings: 2-3
Ingredients:

1 T. olive oil
1/4 tsp. sesame oil
1/4 C. vegetable broth *(open one 15 oz. can)*
3 slices medium onion *(chopped)*
2 cloves garlic *(smashed and chopped)*
1/2 lb. broccoli *(cut in 1" pieces)*

6 mushrooms *(sliced)*
1/2 C. roasted cashews
1/2 red bell pepper *(cubed)*
1/2 C. sliced, peeled water chestnuts
1/2 C. sliced bamboo shoots
2 T. low-sodium soy sauce

1 1/4 C. vegetable broth *(remainder of can)*
2 T. corn starch mixed with 1/4 C. water

1 medium tomato *(chopped)*

1 1/2 - 2 1/2 C. cooked rice *(leftover)*

- **Place oils and broth in large heavy-bottomed sauce pan or wok over high heat. Sauté onion, garlic, and broccoli 2 minutes stirring constantly.**
- **Add mushrooms, cashews, red pepper, water chestnuts, bamboo shoots, and soy sauce. Sauté an additional 2 minutes.**
- **Remove all ingredients from pan with perforated ladle or spoon and set aside on large plate.**
- **Using same pan, add remaining broth and bring to boil.**
- **Thicken with corn starch, water mixture. Reduce heat and cook 3-4 minutes.**
- **Return vegetables to pan and add tomatoes. Stir to coat with sauce and remove from heat.**
- **Warm 3/4 cup rice per serving in microwave 2 minutes. If you don't have a microwave, warm rice over medium-high heat in shallow sauce pan with 1/8 C. water. Keep an eye on it so it doesn't cook down.**
- **Spoon stir fry over rice on individual plates and serve immediately.**

Finish the meal with a cup of tea and a fortune cookie.

Caesar Salad with Grilled Salmon

More delicious light, summer fare. You should have one salmon fillet leftover from Sunday evening.

Preparation time: 25 minutes
Servings: 2
Ingredients:

Salad
- 7 large leaves Romaine lettuce *(broken)*
- 3 large leaves green leaf lettuce *(broken)*
- 1/2 cucumber *(peeled, sliced in 1/4" rounds and quartered)*
- 3 green onions *(chopped)*
- 1/2 red bell pepper *(thin sliced and quartered)*
- 4 Roma tomatoes *(chopped)*
- 4 mushrooms *(thin-sliced)*

Dressing
- 1/2 tsp. fresh-ground black pepper
- 3 T. vegetable broth
- 1 T. balsamic vinegar
- 2 cloves garlic *(smashed and chopped)*
- 1 tsp. Dijon mustard
- 5 T. lemon juice
- 1 1/2 tsp.Worcestershire sauce

- 1 grilled salmon fillet *(broken into pieces)*
- 2-3 T. fancy-shred Parmesan
- 1 loaf of your favorite hearty bread
- fresh nectarine or peach *(served on side)*

Notes

- **Toss vegetables in large bowl with broken lettuce leaves.**
- **Whisk dressing ingredients together.**
- **Pour dressing into bowl with vegetables and toss.**
- **Serve salads on large individual plates. Sprinkle with broken pieces of salmon.**
- **Garnish with Parmesan cheese.**

Serve with your favorite hearty bread and sliced peach or nectarine.

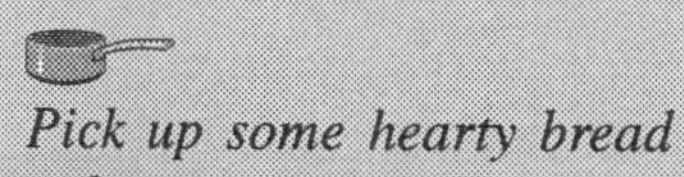

Pick up some hearty bread today.

WEDNESDAY

July/August

Notes

Pasta Prima Vera

A great time to revisit Pasta Prima Vera. Make fresh Red Sauce. (see page 194)

Preparation Time: 30 minutes
Servings: 2
Ingredients:

2 1/2 C. dry spiral pasta

1 1/2 C. Red Sauce

1 T. olive oil
1/2 tsp. crushed garlic
1 large carrot *(peeled and sliced)*
2 slices medium onion *(quartered)*

1/4 C. broth *(use vegetable if you are cooking vegetarian)*
1/2 medium green pepper *(cubed in 1" chunks)*
1 small zucchini 6" long *(cut in 1/8" rounds)*
6 medium mushrooms *(sliced in 1/4" slices)*

2 Roma tomatoes *(cut in 1" chunks)*

2-4 T. fancy-shred Parmesan cheese
4 T. chopped black olives

- **Place pasta water on to boil in large sauce pan.**
- **Drop dry pasta into boiling water and cook 8 minutes.** *(Set a timer so you don't forget.)* **Drain and rinse.**
- **Make Red Sauce.**
- **Measure olive oil and garlic into sauté pan over medium-high heat. Start with carrot and onion. Sauté 1 minute.**
- **Add broth, green pepper, zucchini, and mushrooms and sauté 2 minutes. Remove veggies from pan and set aside.**
- **Pour 1 1/2 C. Red Sauce into same pan used to cook pasta. Bring to boil.**
- **Add all vegetables** *(including Roma tomatoes)* **to sauce and remove from heat.**
- **If pasta is cold, microwave 1 minute on high to reheat, or measure 1 to 1 1/2 C. per serving and place in bowl with boiling water for 1 minute prior to serving. Drain and rinse in colander.**
- **Divide pasta onto separate plates and ladle veggie sauce over it.**

Garnish with Parmesan and chopped olives and serve immediately.

Chicken Breasts with Caramelized Onions

THURSDAY

July/August

A meal worth heating up the kitchen for.

Preparation time: 30 minutes
Servings: 2
Ingredients:

Garlic Potatoes
4 large russet potatoes *(peeled and cubed)*
1 clove garlic *(peeled)*
3/4 C. water

Marinated Butternut Squash
1 T. olive oil
1/4 C. broth
6 large fresh basil leaves *(cut in thin strips)*
1 clove garlic *(smashed and chopped)*
3 dashes Tabasco®
1 butternut squash *(sliced in 1/2" rounds)*

Caramelized Onions
1/2 large sweet onion *(sliced and quartered) finely chop 2 slices*
1 clove garlic *(smashed and chopped)*
1/4 C. chicken broth

3 boneless, skinless chicken breasts
1/2 C. chicken broth
1 clove garlic *(smashed and chopped)*

1/4 C. broth
1/4 C. white wine
2 T. corn starch *(dissolved in 1/4 C. water)*

1 tsp. butter
fresh-ground black pepper
1/8 C. nonfat milk

Notes

Reserve 1 1/2 - 2 C. mashed potatoes for potato patties on Tuesday, page 220.

- **Place potatoes and peeled garlic in medium sauce pan with 3/4 C. water. Bring to boil, reduce heat to low and cook 15 minutes. Remove from heat. Leave covered.**
- **Mix oil, broth, basil, garlic and Tabasco® in large flat baking dish. Lay squash in dish. Turn often until ready to cook.**
- **In large fry pan, sauté onion and garlic in broth. Sauté until onions are browned. Remove from pan and set aside.**
- **Place chicken breasts in same pan used to cook onions with 1/4 C. of the chicken broth and garlic. Sauté over medium-high heat 3 minutes turning once. Add remaining 1/4 C. broth and sauté another 3 minutes until lightly browned. Reduce heat to low, add a little water to pan, cover and cook 5 minutes per side.** *(Use a timer if necessary so you don't forget.) You have cooked an extra breast. Save it for tomorrow night's meal.*
- **In separate oiled, medium-sized fry pan, sauté squash rounds over medium-high heat until each side is golden brown. Spoon basting liquid over rounds as they cook. When both sides are browned, turn off heat. Pour all remaining basting liquid and herbs over them, and cover.**
- **Remove chicken from pan. Add broth and wine. Bring to boil and stir gently to bring up drippings. Thicken with corn starch mixture. Reduce heat. Cook 5 minutes. Return onions and chicken to sauce.**
- **Mash potatoes and garlic in pan with any leftover cooking water and 1 tsp. butter.** *Do not add more butter. One tsp. will add the flavor-any more will add the fat.* **Season with fresh-ground black pepper. Add nonfat milk as you finish mashing.**

Serve chicken breast covered with onion sauce. Place potatoes and squash on either side. Lay cooked strips of basil over squash rounds. Bravo!

FRIDAY

July/August

Notes

Pick up a loaf of your favorite hearty bread today.

Cold Chicken/Peach Salad

No need to heat up the kitchen with this delicious salad.

Preparation time: 25 minutes
Servings: 2
Ingredients:

Salad Fixings

3-4 leaves Romaine lettuce *(broken)*
8-10 inside leaves from red leaf lettuce head *(broken)*
1/2 cucumber *(peeled, sliced in 1/4" rounds)*
3 green onions *(chopped)*
1/2 red bell pepper *(thin sliced)*
4 Roma tomatoes *(chopped)*
4-6 canned artichoke hearts *(rinsed)*
1 grilled chicken breast *(thin sliced) leftover from last night*
1 fresh peach *(skinned and sliced) a nectarine will do*

Dressing

1/4 C. fresh or frozen raspberries *(puréed)*
2 T. olive oil
1/4 C. vegetable broth
2 T. red wine vinegar
2 cloves garlic *(smashed and chopped)*
1/2 tsp. dry basil leaves
1/2 tsp. chopped garlic
fresh-ground black pepper

2-3 T. fancy-shred Parmesan
1 loaf of your favorite hearty bread

- **Toss vegetables in large bowl with broken lettuce leaves.** *(Save chicken and peaches to lay over top of greens.)*
- **Place dressing ingredients in container with tight-fitting lid and shake vigorously.**
- **Pour dressing into serving bowl and set on table with salads.**
- **Serve salads on large individual plates. Sprinkle with thin slices of chicken breast and arrange peach slices around edge of salad.**
- **Garnish with Parmesan cheese.**

Serve with your favorite hearty bread.

SATURDAY
August/Week One

SHOPPING DAY

It's not your imagination! The recipes in this book do use less meat than you may be accustomed to, especially red meat. When eating meat, skinless chicken breasts, turkey breast, and fish cut considerable fat from your diet.

Concerned about your cholesterol level? *You may be able to decrease your cholesterol level 50 points by exercising three times a week for 45 minutes and eating a healthful lowfat diet.*
Vogue, 350 Madison Ave., New York, NY 10017

We make a considerable investment in groceries over a lifetime - all the more reason to be organized. *The average American makes 8,958 trips to the supermarket in a lifetime - and spends $288,215.*
In An Average Lifetime, by Tom Heymann, Fawcett Columbine, 1991

Rich in Beta Carotene - *The following vegetables are excellent sources for beta carotene: sweet potatoes, broccoli, cantaloupe, carrot, kale, spinach, and winter squash. Beta carotene acts as an antioxidant which can help the body fight against cancer and heart disease.*
Eating Well, "Nutrition Sense," by Elizabeth Hiser, M.S., R.D.

When you need lots of chicken breasts, *buy the large bags of frozen boneless, skinless breasts. Most stores carry them.*

Notes

GROCERY LIST

Produce

2 medium yellow onions
1 large sweet onion
8-10 baby red potatoes
2 green bell peppers
2 red bell peppers
1/2 lb. carrots
1 head iceberg lettuce
1 head red leaf lettuce
1 head green leaf lettuce
1 head Romaine lettuce
1 bunch fresh parsley
1 bunch green onions
celery
one red cabbage
1/2 lb. fresh mushrooms
1/2 lb. fresh asparagus
green salad fixings
one large cucumber
6-8 Roma tomatoes
1 ripe cantaloupe
4 fresh lemons

Frozen Foods

Meat/Fish/Poultry

5 boneless, skinless chicken breasts
6-8 large, cooked, shelled shrimp
1/2 lb. true cod fillet *(You may wish to buy the cod fillets on Tuesday.)*
turkey bacon

Canned or Dry Foods

one 29 oz. can tomato sauce
two 15 oz. cans black beans
1 small can sliced black olives
three 15 oz. cans chicken broth
one 6 oz. can sliced water chestnuts
one 6 oz. can sliced bamboo shoots
16 oz. dry penne pasta

Chilled Foods and Dairy

4 oz. sharp cheddar cheese
4 oz. mozzarella cheese
whole wheat tortillas
salsa

Buy if you're out

1 head garlic
toasted sunflower meats
frozen corn
turkey bacon
sesame oil
white cooking wine
low or nonfat salad dressing
1 dozen eggs

SUNDAY

August/Week One

Notes

Make a batch of quark this morning. Place strainer over bowl. Line with coffee filter and fill with 2 C. nonfat yogurt. Place in fridge. Let stand all day.

Fajita Pollo and Black Bean Salad

This adds a new twist to Fajitas. Prepare the bean salad earlier in the day and chill for the evening meal.

Preparation time: 30 minutes
Servings: 2-4
Ingredients:

2-3 boneless, skinless chicken breasts
1 T. olive oil
2 cloves garlic *(smashed and chopped)*
1 tsp. chili powder
1/4 tsp. ground cumin

1/4 C. broth
1 green bell pepper *(cut in 1" chunks)*
1 red bell pepper *(cut in 1" chunks)*
3 slices of a medium sweet onion *(quartered)*
1 tsp. chili powder
1/4 tsp. ground cumin

4-8 whole wheat flour tortillas

4 ripe Roma tomatoes *(chopped)*
1/2 head chopped iceberg lettuce
6 oz. grated cheddar cheese
salsa
1 C. plain, nonfat yogurt or quark *(stirred smooth)*

- **Slice 2-3 chicken breasts into thin (1/8") slices.**
- **Place sliced chicken in shallow 10" non-stick fry pan with oil, garlic, 1 tsp. chili powder and 1/4 tsp. ground cumin. Sauté 5 minutes over medium-high heat.**
- **Remove meat from pan. Set aside.**
- **Using same pan, combine broth, peppers, onion, and remaining spices and sauté 3 minutes. Set aside on another plate or dish.**
- **Warm 2 tortillas per person in microwave by placing all tortillas between two serving plates and cooking for two 40 second cycles. Or warm them in oven at 350 degrees for 10 minutes in a shallow, covered pan.**
- **Set chopped tomatoes, lettuce, grated cheese, salsa, and yogurt out in individual bowls.**
- **Allow diners to build their own fajitas.**
- **Don't forget the black bean salad.**

Buenos!

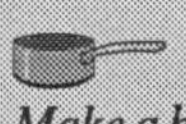

Black Bean Salad

1 C. cooked rice
1 T. chili powder
1/4 tsp. powdered cumin
1/4 C. broth
2 T. chopped, fresh cilantro
1 clove garlic *(smashed and chopped)*
4 slices medium yellow onion *(chopped)*
3 T. balsamic vinegar
3 dashes Tabasco®
1/4 green bell pepper *(chopped)*
1/4 red bell pepper *(chopped)*
1/2 C. frozen corn
two 15 oz. cans black beans
(save 1/2 C. beans in fridge)

- **Cook rice.**
- **Place first 8 ingredients in bowl. Microwave, covered, 3 minutes on high.**
- **Add all remaining ingredients. Stir thoroughly.**
- **Chill 2 hours.**

Pasta "Donaldo"

MONDAY

August/Week One

Here's a repeat of a favorite recipe in my household!

Preparation Time: 30 minutes
Servings: 4
Ingredients:

2 slices turkey bacon *(cooked crispy and chopped)*
You may substitute 5 T. chopped, toasted pine nuts if you are cooking vegetarian.
16 oz. dry penne pasta *(you may also use mostaciolli or rigatoni)*
1/2 lb. mushrooms *(sliced)*
3 cloves garlic *(smashed and chopped)*
1/4 C. white wine
3/4 C. chicken or vegetable broth
1 T. butter
3 T. flour *(shaken with 1/3 C. nonfat milk)*
1/4 tsp. ground nutmeg
1/4 C. shredded part-skim mozzarella
1/4 C. fancy-shred Parmesan
fixings for green salad
1 C. plain, nonfat yogurt *(stirred smooth)*
1 T. fresh parsley *(chopped)*

Notes

- **Place pasta water in large kettle over high heat.**
- **Cook bacon as indicated.** *(see box)*
- **Place pasta in boiling water and cook 8 minutes.** *Set a timer so you don't forget.* **Drain and rinse.**
- **Sauté mushrooms in garlic and wine. Cook 2 minutes. Remove from pan. Set aside.**
- **Add broth to pan. Bring to boil. Add butter. Drain excess liquid from mushroom mixture into pan.**
- **Mix flour and milk in container with tight-fitting lid. Shake vigorously 30 seconds.**
- **Pour flour paste into boiling liquid, stirring constantly. Return to boil. Turn heat to low. Add bacon, nutmeg, and cheeses** *(reserve 4 T. Parmesan for garnish)*, **and continue cooking 10 minutes. Stir occasionally.**
- **Prepare green salads.**
- **Stir yogurt until smooth. Microwave 20 seconds on high to bring to room temperature.**
- **Gently stir yogurt mixture into the cheese sauce.**
- **Rerinse pasta with warm water to make sure it doesn't stick together. Drain thoroughly and stir into sauce.**

Serve on 4 individual plates and garnish with remaining Parmesan and chopped parsley. Serve green salad on the side.

Cooking bacon

Wrap bacon slices in paper towel, set on plate and microwave two 2-minute cycles at high setting until crispy but not burned. If you don't have a microwave, put bacon in shallow pan covered with foil and bake 20 minutes in 400 degree oven. Lay bacon on fresh paper towel after cooking.

True Cod with Black Bean Sauce

Time again for this delicious fish dinner. The bean sauce, made from Sunday's beans, is a nice compliment to the flavor. The potatoes were saved from Thursday, page 215.

Preparation time: 35 minutes
Servings: 2
Ingredients:

1-2 C. leftover mashed potatoes
4-6 green onions *(chopped)*
1 egg white *(beaten)*
1 T. olive oil

Black Bean Sauce
1/2 C. black beans *(held over from Sunday evening)*
1 clove garlic *(smashed and chopped)*
1 slice medium yellow onion *(slice 1/8" thick and chop)*
1 T. Worcestershire sauce
1/4 C. broth

1/2 lb. fresh asparagus

1/2 lb. true cod fillets
1/2 C. white wine

lemon wedges

Notes

You may need to buy fresh fish today.

- **Mix all potato ingredients** *(except oil)* **and form into patties. Sauté in large non-stick fry pan in oil over medium-high heat until browned on both sides. Remove from heat, cover, and set aside.**
- **Place all black bean sauce ingredients in blender or food processor. Blend thoroughly. Pour into small oven-safe dish, cover and place in oven next to potatoes.** *If you don't have a blender or food processor, mash beans with a fork, then add all other wet ingredients and spices and place in oven.*
- **Wash asparagus and snap off white bottoms. Place tops in steamer with water in covered sauce pan.** *Do not begin cooking yet.*
- **Place fish fillets in sauté pan with white wine. Bring to boil over high heat. Season with black pepper and cook 2 minutes. Turn fillets and cook another 2 minutes.** *If fillets are more than 1/2" thick, you may have to cook 3-4 minutes per side.* **Cover pan and remove from heat.**
- **Just prior to serving, turn heat on under asparagus. When water boils, cover and cook 1 minute**. *If using larger, thicker stalks you will need to cook 3 minutes.* **Remove from heat and leave covered until ready to serve.**
- **Arrange fish on individual serving plates. Spoon 2 T. black bean sauce over each fillet. Place asparagus and potato patties on either side.**

Set a wedge of lemon on each plate for squeezing over the asparagus.

Lemon Chicken with Rice

Here comes a delicious rerun! Enjoy!

Preparation time: 30 minutes
Servings: 2
Ingredients:

Notes

1/4 C. chicken broth
1/2 tsp. sesame oil
1 T. low-sodium soy sauce
1 1/2 C. cooked rice
3 green onions *(chopped)*
1 stalk celery *(finely chopped)*
1/2 red bell pepper *(chopped)*

2 boneless, skinless chicken breasts
1 T. olive oil
2 cloves garlic *(smashed and chopped)*
1/2 C. chicken broth

2 medium carrots *(peeled and sliced in 1/8" rounds)*

1/4 C. white wine
juice from 1 lemon
2 T. white sugar

3 T. corn starch mixed with 1/3 C. water

"Quick cook" rice before work this morning. *(see page 158)*

- **Preheat oven to 350 degrees.**
- **In an oven-safe bowl, mix 1/4 C. chicken broth, sesame oil, and soy sauce.**
- **Add rice, onions, celery, and red bell pepper. Stir thoroughly, cover, and place in preheated oven on center rack. Set timer for 20 minutes.**
- **Brown chicken breasts over medium-high heat in oil and garlic. Add broth, cover, and cook 5 minutes.**
- **Place carrots in steamer basket over a little water in medium sauce pan with tight-fitting lid.** *Do not turn on heat under carrots yet.*
- **Remove chicken from pan and set aside.**
- **Add wine, lemon, any remaining broth, and sugar to sauté pan. Stir until boiling and all drippings have come up from bottom of pan.**
- **Quickly stir in corn starch mixture and cook 2 minutes over medium-high heat.**
- **Return chicken breasts to pan with sauce, reduce heat to low, and cover.**
- **Turn heat on high under carrots. When water boils, reduce heat and cook, covered, 2 minutes.**

Serve meal on individual plates, spooning lemon sauce over chicken. If you wish, spoon sauce over rice and carrots as well.

THURSDAY

August/Week One

Notes

Green Salad with Shrimp

Cool it with a no cook meal!

Preparation time: 25 minutes
Servings: 2
Ingredients:

2 bunches fresh leaf lettuce
(one red, one green) washed carefully and patted dry
1/2 cucumber *(peeled, sliced in 1/4" rounds and quartered)*
3 green onions *(chopped)*
1/2 C. red cabbage *(thin sliced, chopped)*
1/2 red bell pepper *(thin sliced and quartered)*
4 Roma tomatoes *(chopped)*

6-8 large, cooked, chilled and deveined shrimp
or one 6 oz. can drained, baby shrimp

4 T. toasted sunflower seeds

2-3 T. fancy-shred Parmesan

1 loaf of your favorite hearty bread

1/2 chilled cantaloupe *(sliced in wedges and rind removed)*
low or nonfat Italian dressing

- **Toss first 6 ingredients together in large bowl.**
- **Divide salad on large individual plates.**
- **Place shrimp around top of salad.**
- **Sprinkle salad with sunflower seeds.**
- **Garnish salads with Parmesan cheese.**

Serve with hearty bread and chilled cantaloupe slices.

Pick up a loaf of fresh bakery bread on your way home tonight.

Leftover Night

It's been two weeks! Time to salvage leftovers.

Preparation time: 20 minutes
Servings: 2-3
Ingredients:

Whatever you have in the fridge.
leftover Red Sauce
leftover pasta
leftover Black Bean Salad

Notes

Lower your risk of heart attack *by consuming more folic acid and vitamin B6. Good sources of folic acid are leafy green vegetables, beans, and yeast. Good sources of B6 are fish, lean pork, peanuts and whole grains.*
The Journal of the American Medical Association, 515 N. State St., Chicago, IL, 60610

New mothers? *Babies who breast-feed for at least three months are less likely to need braces when they're older.*
McCall's Good Health, 110 Fifth Ave., New York, NY 10011

Take a walk! *Walking before or after a meal speeds up your metabolism, boosts your energy and eases your stress. Walking with someone you care about encourages closeness and allows uninterrupted conversation.*
The Balancing Act, Nutrition and Weight Guide, by Georgia G. Kostas, Cooper Clinic, 1993

It's true! *Skinless chicken is much less fattening! A 3.5 ounce piece of roasted white-meat chicken with the skin has 222 calories and 11g of fat; a skinless piece, 173 calories and 5g of fat.*
Self, 350 Madison Ave., New York, NY 10017

SATURDAY
August/Week Two

Notes

SHOPPING DAY

Buy carrots that are *slender, firm and smooth. Avoid carrots that have cracks or those that have begun to wither. Remove greens if they're still attached, it makes the carrots look fresh, but it robs them of moisture and vitamins.*
The Food Lover's Tiptionary, by Sharon Tyler Herbst, Hearst Books

Don't buy diet soda in large quantities. *Most are made with aspartame, an artificial sweetener that has a shelf life of about three months. The soda will taste bitter after the sweetener goes stale.*
Tufts University Diet and Nutrition Letter, 203 Harrison Ave., Boston, MA

The price is right! *Purchase a portable water filter system and keep a reservoir of filtered water in your fridge at all times. It's far less expensive than buying soda or bottled water, and water is the most effective thirst quencher.*

Comparing the numbers:

A leading 2 gallon portable water filtration system:	*Reservoir -*	*$ 40*
filters last about 2 months	*6 filters -*	*$ 36*
Total annual cost of filter system		***$ 76***
(Second year will be $36-$54)		
Buying six-packs of soda *at a cost of $2 per six-pack*		***$104***
(Calculated at one six-pack per week over 1 year.)		
Buying bottled water *at $1.50 per gallon*		***$ 78***
(Calculated at 1 gallon per week over 1 year.)		

We won't talk about the plastic sent to the landfills!

GROCERY LIST

Produce
3 medium russet potatoes
or 8-10 baby red potatoes
1 medium yellow onion
1 lb. fresh mushrooms
2 green bell peppers
2 red bell peppers
3 large carrots
1/2 lb. fresh broccoli
one head green leaf lettuce
green salad fixings
1 head iceberg lettuce
fresh cucumber
10-12 Roma tomatoes
one bunch fresh basil
one bunch fresh parsley
1 fresh lemon

Frozen Foods

Meat/Fish/Poultry
2 boneless, skinless chicken breasts
1/2 lb. ground turkey breast
one Italian turkey or chicken sausage link

Canned or Dry Foods
one 29 oz. can tomato sauce
one 15 oz. can black beans
1 small can chopped black olives
two 15 oz. cans chicken broth
one 15 oz. can vegetable broth
12-16 oz. dry penne pasta
8 oz. fresh fettuccine
one large, thin-crust Boboli®

Chilled Foods and Dairy
salsa
3 oz. sharp cheddar cheese

Buy if you're out
1 head garlic
frozen corn
powdered cumin
chili powder
cornmeal
brown rice
white cooking wine
pesto
tortillas
Parmesan cheese
plain, nonfat yogurt

Mexican Chicken Breasts

Tickle your taste buds with a repeat of this spicy meal.

Preparation time: 30 minutes
Servings: 2
Ingredients:

1/4 C. Red Sauce *(see page 194)*
1 T. chili powder
1/2 tsp. cumin
1 tsp. oregano

Coating for Chicken
5 T. flour
2 T. cornmeal
1 T. chili powder
1 tsp. oregano
1/2 tsp. cumin
1/8 tsp. black pepper

2 boneless, skinless chicken breasts
1 T. olive oil
2 cloves garlic *(smashed and chopped)*
3 slices medium yellow onion *(chopped)*

1/4 red bell pepper *(chopped)*
1/4 green bell pepper *(chopped)*
1 thin slice onion *(chopped)*
1 T. chili powder
1/2 C. broth
1/2 C. frozen corn
1/2 C. cooked rice

one 15 oz. can black beans *(drained and rinsed)*
1/4 C. salsa

2 thin slices extra-sharp cheddar cheese
flour tortillas

- **Mix Red Sauce, 1 T. chili powder, 1/2 tsp. cumin, and 1 tsp. oregano in small bowl and microwave on high 1 1/2 minutes, or bring to boil in small sauce pan over medium-high heat. Remove from heat. Set aside.**
- **In a plastic bag, mix flour, cornmeal, 1 T. chili powder, 1 tsp. oregano, 1/2 tsp. cumin, and black pepper. Shake to mix thoroughly.**
- **Drop chicken breasts into bag and shake until coated.**
- **Preheat sauté pan with oil over medium-high heat. Place coated breasts, garlic, and all but 1 T. onion in pan and cook until breasts are golden brown on both sides. Reduce heat to low, cover, and cook 5 minutes. Turn again if necessary.**
- **While breasts are cooking, put red and green pepper, onion, chili powder, and broth in shallow sauce pan. Bring to boil and cook 1 minute. Add corn, boil 2 more minutes** *(stirring occasionally)*, **and stir in cooked rice. Reduce heat to low and continue cooking 2 minutes** *(again, stirring occasionally).*
- **Turn breasts and cover with Red Sauce. Place cheese slice over each breast. Cover, reduce heat to low, and cook 5 minutes.**
- **Place rinsed beans and salsa in sauce pan over low heat.**

Serve on individual plates with the breast in the center flanked by black beans and rice mixture. Serve a warm, rolled tortilla on the side.

SUNDAY
August/Week Two

Notes

"Quick cook" rice in the morning before work. (see page 158)

MONDAY
August/Week Two

Notes

Plan to pick up a loaf of hearty bread today.

Pasta Marinara

Use leftover Red Sauce from last night. (If possible, reserve 1/4 C. for tomorrow's meal.) Your overall preparation time will be about 15 minutes.

Preparation time: 15-20 minutes
Servings: 2
Ingredients:

1 1/2 C. Red Sauce *(leftover from last night)*
8 oz. fresh fettuccine
fixings for green salad
2-4 T. fancy-shred Parmesan
1 T. chopped fresh parsley
a loaf of hearty bread

- **Place large kettle filled 2/3 full of water over high heat.**
- **Warm Red Sauce 2 minutes on high in microwave or in small sauce pan over medium heat.**
- **Drop pasta into boiling water.** *Set timer for 3 minutes.*
- **Prepare green salads.**
- **When pasta is cooked, drain and rinse with warm water.**
- **Divide pasta on two plates.**
- **Cover each serving with 1/2 to 3/4 C. Red Sauce. Sprinkle 1-2 T. Parmesan and chopped parsley over each serving.**

Serve with green salad and hearty bread.

Taco Salad

TUESDAY
August/Week Two

A warm weather winner! We'll repeat it with a twist. What's different? Look and see! (The only cooking involves the ground turkey.)

Preparation time: 15-20 minutes
Servings: 3-4
Ingredients:

1/2 lb. ground turkey breast
1 T. olive oil
2 slices medium yellow onion *(chopped)*
1 clove garlic *(smashed and chopped)*
1 tsp. oregano leaves
1/2 tsp. ground cumin
1 T. mild chili powder
dash of Tabasco®
1/4 C. Red Sauce *(use leftovers)*

1/2 green pepper *(cut in 1" cubes)*
1 clove garlic *(smashed and chopped)*
2 slices yellow onion *(quartered)*
1 T. chili powder
1/4 C. broth or water

6-8 leaves washed red leaf lettuce
1/2 head chopped iceberg lettuce

sharp cheddar cheese
4-T. sliced black olives
2-3 Roma tomatoes *(chopped)*

whole wheat tortillas

1/2 C. plain, nonfat yogurt *(stirred smooth)*
salsa

Notes

- **Sauté ground turkey in olive oil along with onion, garlic, and spices in large non-stick fry pan over medium-high heat. Sauté 5 minutes stirring constantly. Add 1/4 C. Red Sauce. Cover, reduce heat to low, and cook an additional 5 minutes.**
- **When meat is done, remove from pan, place in bowl and set aside.**
- **Using same fry pan, sauté green pepper, garlic, and onions with chili powder and broth. Sauté 2 minutes over high heat. Remove from pan and set aside.**
- **Place 2 washed leaves red leaf lettuce on each plate as bed for salad. Top with chopped iceberg lettuce.**
- **Divide meat and sautéed vegetables onto beds of lettuce.**
- **Garnish with a grating of sharp cheese, black olives and chopped tomato.**
- **Warm tortillas by setting them, one at a time, in large fry pan for about 30 seconds per side over medium-high heat.**
- **Spoon yogurt and salsa over salad to suit your taste.**

Serve with tortillas on the side.

Pasta with Tomato/Basil "Cream" Sauce

Similar to marinara, but using fresh basil and fresh tomato. Most refreshing!

Preparation time: 25 minutes
Servings: 2-3
Ingredients:

Sauce
1 C. vegetable broth
2 cloves garlic *(smashed and chopped)*
1 T. dry oregano
1/4 C. fresh basil leaves *(chopped fine)*
2 slices medium yellow onion *(chopped)*
a few dashes of Tabasco® sauce *(optional)*

2 T. corn starch dissolved in 1/3 C. water

2 C. dry penne pasta

green salad fixings

6-8 Roma tomatoes or slicing tomatoes *(chopped)*

1/2 C. plain, nonfat yogurt *(stirred smooth)*

2-4 T. fancy-shred Parmesan cheese
2 T. fresh parsley

a loaf of crusty bread

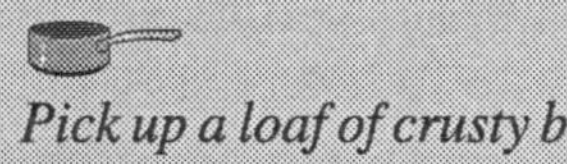

Pick up a loaf of crusty bread on your way home from work.

- **Place large kettle filled 2/3 full of water over high heat.**
- **Place all sauce ingredients in sauce pan. Bring to boil over medium-high heat.**
- **Reduce heat to medium. Thicken with corn starch mixture. Cook 5 minutes.**
- **Cook dry pasta.** *Set timer for 8 minutes.*
- **Prepare green salads.**
- **Stir chopped tomatoes into sauce.**
- **Stir yogurt until creamy smooth. Add to sauce. Stir to blend thoroughly and remove from heat. *<u>Do not boil.</u>***
- **When pasta is cooked, drain and rinse with warm water.**
- **Divide pasta on two** *(or three)* **plates.**

Cover each serving with 1/2 to 3/4 cup sauce. Sprinkle 1-2 T. Parmesan cheese and fresh, chopped parsley over each serving. Serve with crisp green salad and crusty bread.

Loaded Rice

Back to one of my favorites.

Preparation time: 25 minutes
Servings: 2
Ingredients:

Notes

8-10 baby red potatoes or 1 large russet potato
1 T. olive oil

1/2 lb. mushrooms *(sliced)*
1/4 red bell pepper *(thin-sliced)*
1 T. olive oil
1 large clove garlic *(smashed and chopped)*
1/4 C. white wine
2 slices medium onion *(quartered)*

3/4 C. chicken or vegetable broth
3 T. corn starch dissolved in 1/8 C. cold water

1 1/2 C. cooked brown rice

1 C. plain, nonfat yogurt
1 T. pesto
dash of Tabasco®

2 Roma tomatoes *(chopped)*

- **Preheat oven to 400 degrees.**
- **Wash and halve baby red potatoes. If using russet potato, wash and slice** *(unpeeled)* **in 1/2" slices. Place potatoes, flat side down, on cookie sheet oiled with one tablespoon olive oil.**
- **Sauté sliced mushrooms and bell pepper in oil with garlic, wine, and onion** *(about 4 minutes).* **When done, remove mushroom mixture from pan with perforated spoon. Set aside.**
- **Add broth to pan. Return to boil.**
- **If cooking russet potato slices, turn them now.**
- **Slowly stir corn starch mixture into boiling liquid. Reduce heat to low. Cook 5 minutes, stirring often.**
- **Add mushrooms to thickened mixture. Return to boil. Remove from heat.**
- **Warm 1 1/2 C. cooked rice 2 minutes on high in microwave on individual serving plates.**
- **Remove potatoes from oven. If using baby reds, push them into rice on individual plates. If using russets, chop into 1" pieces before sprinkling over rice.**
- **Stir yogurt, pesto, and Tabasco® together until smooth. Microwave 30 seconds on high. Stir again, and add to thickened mushroom sauce.**

Pour sauce over potato/rice mixture and garnish with fresh chopped tomato. Enjoy!

"Quick cook" rice before work this morning. *(see page 158)*

FRIDAY

August/Week Two

Notes

Pizza and Salad

Make Red Sauce and enjoy a Pizza Friday.

Preparation time: 25 minutes
Servings: 2
Ingredients:

1 link Italian turkey or chicken sausage *(see page 194)*
large Boboli® shell or frozen pizza shell

3/4 C. Red Sauce *(leftover from Monday)*
1 large clove garlic *(smashed and chopped)*
2 T. fancy-shred Parmesan cheese
1 dash of Tabasco®

2 slices medium yellow onion *(quartered)*
4-6 black olives *(chopped)*
6 medium mushrooms *(sliced in 1/4" slices)*
4 T. fancy-shred Parmesan

fixings for a green salad

- **Preheat oven to 400 degrees.**
- **Prick sausage several times with fork and wrap in paper towel. Place sausage in covered dish and microwave 2 minutes on high. Repeat.**
- **Place Boboli® directly on rack in center of oven and cook 3 minutes.** *(Set a timer so you don't forget.)* **Remove from oven.**
- **Prepare Red Sauce.**
- **Place 3/4 C. Red Sauce in small bowl with garlic, 2 T. Parmesan, and Tabasco®. Cover bowl. Cook in microwave 2 minutes at full power.** *If you don't have a microwave, put ingredients in a small sauce pan and bring to a boil over medium-high heat. When it boils, cover and remove from heat.*
- **Spread Red Sauce on Boboli® crust.**
- **Press sausage firmly with flat side of a fork to force out excess fat. Slice in rounds.**
- **Arrange onions, olives, mushrooms, and sausage slices on top of Red Sauce and top with Parmesan. Return to oven 8-10 minutes.**
- **Prepare green salads on individual plates while Boboli® is cooking.**
- **Remove pizza from oven and cut in wedges while hot.**

Let Pizza cool 5 minutes before eating. Serve green salad on the side. Light a candle and treat yourself to a glass of beer or wine.

SATURDAY

August/Week Three

SHOPPING DAY

Safety tip: *Always cook meat or poultry immediately if you thaw it in the microwave. It may get slightly cooked while defrosting, which encourages bacteria to multiply if it isn't thoroughly cooked right away.*
Mayo Clinic Health Letter, 200 First St. SW, Rochester, MN 55905

Getting your fiber? *The average American eats only 11g of fiber daily: 20-35g are recommended.*
Eating on the Run, by Evelyn Tribole, M.S., R.D., Leisure Press, 1992

Wonderful grapefruit! *One study found that grapefruit helps reduce cholesterol levels. For four weeks, participants took capsules of grapefruit pectin that were the equivalent of two grapefruits. Their cholesterol dropped an average of 8%.*
Research at University of Florida, Gainesville, FL

Trouble with headaches? *These foods can trigger headaches: monosodium glutamate (MSG), sodium nitrates, (which are food additives found in bacon, cold cuts, hot dogs, and smoked foods); and tyramine, (which is found in aged cheese, chicken liver, fava beans, overripe bananas, and avocados).*
Environmental Nutrition, 2112 Broadway, New York, NY 10023

Buy fruit *for next Saturday which is slightly green. It will continue to ripen as the week progresses. Refrigerate grapes and berries. Leave other fruit out on counter top.*

Notes

____

____

____

____

____

____

____

____

GROCERY LIST

Produce

one 6" zucchini
10-12 small baby red potatoes
3 medium russet potatoes
2 medium yellow onions
1 lb. fresh mushrooms
1 green bell pepper
1 red bell pepper
3 large carrots
1 lb. fresh broccoli
green salad fixings
1 bunch green onions
1 package prewashed spinach
  or 2 bunches fresh spinach
1 large cucumber
8-10 Roma tomatoes
2 fresh lemons
1 tart apple
3/4 C. dried apricots
banana, strawberries, nectarine,
  seedless grapes, and blueberries *(for Sat. brunch)*
firm, unflavored tofu

Frozen Foods

concentrated apple juice

Meat/Fish/Poultry

12 oz. fresh or frozen halibut fillets
6-8 large cooked, shelled shrimp *(frozen is OK)*
2 boneless, skinless chicken breasts

Canned or Dry Foods

three 15 oz. cans chicken broth
one 6 oz. can sliced water chestnuts
one 6 oz. can sliced bamboo shoots
12 oz. dry whole wheat spiral pasta
apricot jam
a loaf of your favorite hearty bread

Chilled Foods and Dairy

plain, nonfat cream cheese
butter

Buy if you're out

one head garlic
pine nuts
frozen peas
turkey bacon
1/2 C. package pecan halves
1/2 C. package shelled walnuts
shredded coconut
brown rice
old-fashioned oats
white cooking wine
Dijon mustard
Worcestershire sauce
sesame oil
low-sodium soy sauce
bran flakes
pesto
plain, nonfat yogurt
nonfat milk

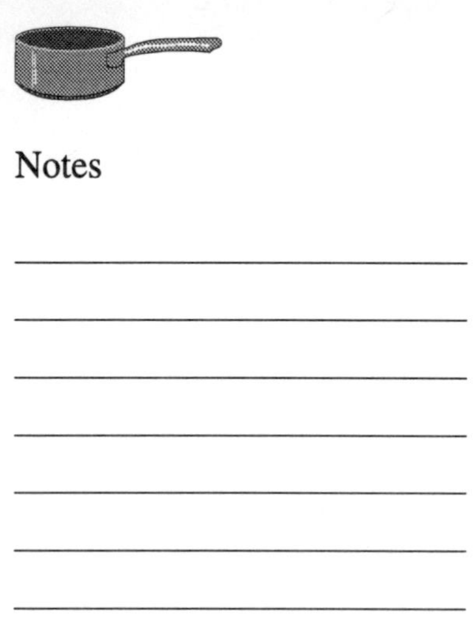

Notes

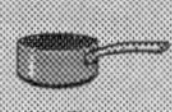

"Quick cook" rice before work this morning. (see page 158)

Grilled Halibut with Nutty Rice

You may use halibut fillets or halibut steaks. Cook them over an outdoor grill.

Preparation time: 30 minutes *(if rice is cooked)*
Servings: 2
Ingredients:

2 C. cooked rice
3 T. chopped pecans *(toasted under broiler)*
2 chopped green onions
fresh-ground black pepper

three 4 oz. halibut fillets or three medium halibut steaks
1 small clove garlic *(smashed and chopped)*
1/2 C. broth or white wine
3 T. Worcestershire sauce

1 1/2 C. frozen peas
1 tsp. butter *(melted)*
2 tsp. lemon juice

- **Place rice and toasted pecans in bowl with chopped green onions. Season with black pepper and cook in microwave 3 minutes, or place in covered baking dish with 1/4 C. water in a 300 degree oven for 15 minutes.**
- *Stove top method:* **Place halibut in sauté pan with garlic and 1/2 of the broth** *(or wine)*. **Cook over high heat 2 minutes. Turn and add remaining broth. Spread Worcestershire sauce over each fillet. Cover, lower heat to medium, cook 3 minutes.** *Grilling method:* **Mix garlic, broth** *(or wine),* **and Worcestershire in small bowl. Use as baste.**
- **Place fillets on grill. Grill 2 minutes per side, basting after each turn. Repeat process twice. Total cooking time will be 10-12 minutes.**
- **Place peas in shallow pan with 1/4 C. water and bring to boil over medium-high heat.**
- **Add 1 tsp. butter and lemon juice. Cook 1 minute.**

Serve halibut flanked with nutty rice and peas.

Spinach Salad with Turkey Bacon

MONDAY
August/Week Three

Good summertime fare. Tonight we'll enjoy some of those wonderful leafy green vegetables.

Preparation time: 25 minutes
Servings: 2
Ingredients:

2 bunches fresh spinach *(washed carefully and patted dry)*
You may also substitute one bag of prewashed spinach if your store carries it.
1/2 cucumber *(peeled, sliced in 1/4" rounds and quartered)*
3 green onions *(washed and chopped)*
1/2 red bell pepper *(thin sliced and quartered)*
4 Roma tomatoes *(chopped)*

1/2 C. tofu *(chopped)*
1 tsp. Dijon mustard
1/4 C. broth

Dressing
2 strips cooked turkey bacon *(chopped - use cooked bacon in freezer)*
2 T. balsamic vinegar
1 clove garlic *(smashed and chopped)*
2 tsp. Dijon mustard
6 T. chicken or vegetable broth
2 T. olive oil
2 T. white wine
fresh-ground black pepper *(to taste)*
1/2 tsp. sesame oil

1 tart apple *(cored and sliced)*

2-3 T. fancy-shred Parmesan

a loaf of your favorite hearty bread

Notes

- **Toss vegetables in large bowl.**
- **Sauté tofu with mustard and broth in small non-stick fry pan over medium-high heat. Sauté 2 minutes. Remove from pan with perforated spoon and place in bowl with vegetables. Toss.**
- **Combine dressing ingredients in same pan used to sauté tofu. Cook over medium-high heat 2 minutes. Let cool 5 minutes.**
- **Pour warm dressing into bowl with vegetables and toss again.**
- **Serve 1/2 sliced apple on small plate to the side of each salad.**
- **Serve salads on large individual plates topped with Parmesan.**

Pass the hearty bread! Enjoy!

TUESDAY

August/Week Three

Notes

Chicken Breasts with Mushroom Sauce

Go ahead, heat up the kitchen! You'll be glad you did!

Preparation time: 30 minutes

Servings: 2

Ingredients:

2-3 medium russet potatoes *(peeled and quartered)*
1 clove garlic (peeled)

1/2 lb. fresh white mushrooms
1/4 C. white wine
2 thin slices of a medium yellow onion *(quartered)*
1 clove garlic *(smashed and chopped)*

2 boneless, skinless chicken breasts
1/4 C. chicken broth
1 clove garlic *(smashed and chopped)*

1/2 lb. fresh broccoli *(cut into 2" lengths)*
1 carrot *(cut in ribbon-thin strips)*

1/4 C. broth
1/4 C. white wine
2 T. corn starch *(dissolved in 1/4 C. water)*

1 tsp. butter
fresh-ground black pepper
1/8 C. nonfat milk

lemon wedges

- **Peel and quarter potatoes. Place potatoes and peeled garlic in medium sauce pan with 1/2 C. water. Bring to boil, reduce heat to low and cook 15 minutes.**
- **In 12" fry pan, sauté mushrooms 3 minutes in wine, onion and garlic. Remove from pan.**
- **Place chicken breasts in same pan with half of chicken broth and garlic. Sauté over medium-high heat 3 minutes turning once. Add remaining broth and sauté another 3 minutes until lightly browned. Reduce heat to low, add a little water to pan, cover and cook 5 minutes per side. Check often to be sure they don't get too dark.**
- **Place broccoli and carrot in steamer basket in sauce pan with 3/4 C. water.** *Don't begin cooking until just before you serve.*
- **Remove chicken from pan. Add 1/4 C. broth and wine. Bring to boil and stir gently to bring up drippings. Thicken with corn starch mixture. Reduce heat. Cook 5 minutes. Return mushrooms to sauce.**
- **Mash potatoes and garlic in pan with any leftover water and 1 tsp. butter.** *(One teaspoon of butter is sufficient to add flavor.)* **Season with fresh-ground black pepper. Add nonfat milk as you finish mashing.**
- **Turn burner on high under broccoli and carrots. When water boils, cover and cook 2 minutes.**

Serve chicken breasts covered with mushroom sauce. Place potatoes and vegetables on either side. Garnish with fresh lemon wedges.

Leftover Night

It's been two weeks again. If you have leftovers, tonight is "their night out!"

Preparation time: 20 minutes
Servings: 2-3
Ingredients:

Whatever you have in the fridge!
Garlic Mashed Potatoes and Mushroom Sauce
leftover pasta
leftover Red Sauce

Notes

__Pizza trivia:__ last year pizza accounted for 1 of every 20 lunches and dinners eaten at home. The typical meal of 3 slices of commercially prepared pizza can have as much as 27g of fat and 750 calories. It's important to note that Domino's and Little Caesar's, among others, now offer a "half cheese" or reduced-fat option.
Prevention Magazine, "Taking Fat Out of Pizza", Holly McCord, R.D., Nutrition Editor

__Bedtime Snack?__ Be careful about fattening snacks just before bed. According to the International Association of Ice Cream Manufacturers, most ice cream in the US is eaten between 9 P.M. and 11 P.M. If these are your hours of weakness, try nonfat frozen yogurt or several graham crackers and a glass of nonfat milk.

__More milk trivia:__ 38% of the calories in 2% milk are from fat.
Nutrition Action Health Letter, Center for Science in the Public Interest, 1875 Connecticut Ave. N.W., Washington, DC

__Sweet corn is in season!__ There are few things more refreshing than an ear of freshly picked sweet corn. Don't spoil the tenderness by adding salt to the cooking water; that toughens the kernels.
The Food Lover's Tiptionary, by Sharon Tyler, Herbst, Hearst Books, 1994

__Cut the cheese -__ literally that is! The average American eats 28 pounds of cheese a year, more than twice the amount we ate in the late 1960's. This is partially due to the popularity of cheesy foods like pizza and nachos. Be careful about the amount you consume since it is high in fat.
Good Housekeeping, 959 Eighth Ave., New York, NY 10019

THURSDAY
August/Week Three

"Creamy" Pasta Prima Vera

It's so easy! This is the second or third time. You should be right at 25 minutes in preparation time!

Preparation time: 30 minutes
Servings: 2-3
Ingredients:

2 C. dry spiral pasta

1 carrot *(peeled and sliced)*
1 C. chicken broth
6 medium mushrooms *(sliced)*
2 slices medium yellow onion *(quartered)*
1/2 green bell pepper *(cut into 1" chunks)*
1 clove garlic *(smashed and chopped) or 1 tsp. prepared chopped garlic*
fresh-ground black pepper
one 6"- 8" long zucchini *(cut into 1/4" rounds)*

plain, nonfat yogurt *(stirred smooth)*
2 T. pesto
dash of Tabasco® *(optional)*

2 T. corn starch dissolved into 1/8 C. water

2-4 T. fancy-shred Parmesan
2 T. toasted pine nuts *(chopped)*
1 large Roma tomato *(chopped into 1" chunks)*

- **Place pasta water on to boil in large, heavy-bottomed kettle. When water boils, add dry pasta and cook.** *Set timer for 8 minutes.* **Drain and rinse.**
- **In same kettle you used for pasta, sauté carrot in 1/4 C. broth 2 minutes.**
- **Add mushrooms, onions, green pepper, and garlic. Sauté 2 minutes. Season with about 4 turns of fresh-ground pepper.**
- **Add zucchini and sauté another 2 minutes.** *If pan cooks dry, add another 1/4 cup broth.*
- **Remove all vegetables from kettle with perforated spoon and set aside. Add remaining broth to kettle and bring to boil over high heat.**
- **Mix yogurt, pesto and** *(optional)* **Tabasco® in small bowl.**
- **Thicken liquid in kettle with corn starch/water mixture, reduce heat to low, and cook 2-3 minutes. Remove from heat and add pesto/yogurt mixture.**
- **Add all vegetables and cooked pasta to thickened sauce and gently stir over medium-high heat until coated. Cover and remove from heat. *Do not boil.***
- **Divide into 2-3 servings on individual plates.**

Garnish with Parmesan, chopped pine nuts, and tomato.
Favoloso!

Notes

Shrimp/Broccoli Stir Fry

Another loaded stir-fry.

Preparation time: 30 minutes
Servings: 2-3
Ingredients:

1 T. olive oil
1/4 tsp. sesame oil
1/4 C. vegetable broth
3 slices medium onion *(chopped)*
2 cloves garlic *(smashed and chopped)*
1/2 lb. broccoli *(cut in 1" pieces)*

6 mushrooms *(sliced)*
1/2 of a 6 oz. can sliced bamboo shoots
1/2 red bell pepper *(cubed)*
1/2 C. sliced, peeled water chestnuts
2 T. low-sodium soy sauce

1 C. vegetable broth
2 T. corn starch mixed with 1/4 C. water

6-8 large, cooked and shelled shrimp
1 medium tomato *(chopped)*

1 1/2 C. cooked rice

- **Place oils and broth in large heavy-bottomed sauce pan or wok over high heat. Sauté onion, garlic, and broccoli 2 minutes stirring constantly.**
- **Add mushrooms, sliced bamboo shoots, red pepper, water chestnuts, and soy sauce. Sauté an additional 2 minutes.**
- **Remove all ingredients from pan with perforated ladle or spoon and set aside.**
- **Using same pan, add 1 C. broth and bring to boil.**
- **Thicken with corn starch and water mixture. Reduce heat and cook 3-4 minutes.**
- **Add shrimp and chopped tomato and return vegetables to pan. Stir to coat with sauce** *(2 minutes)* **and remove from heat.**
- **Serve immediately over warmed rice on individual plates.**

You must know how by now! Eat with chopsticks! Have a fortune cookie and tea to finish the meal.

FRIDAY

August/Week Three

Notes

"Quick cook" some rice before work this morning.

Quick Cooked Rice

Place 1 C. long grain brown rice in a pan with 2 1/4 C. cold water. Cover and bring to boil over high heat. When water boils turn off heat. Leave pan on burner. Do not lift cover! It will be ready to eat when you get home tonight.

SATURDAY

August/Week Four

Notes

SHOPPING DAY PLUS BRUNCH

I Can't Believe They're Healthful Muffins!

1 3/4 C. barley flour, rye flour, or unbleached white flour
1 T. baking powder
1/3 C. crushed bran flakes
1/4 C. chopped walnuts
1/3 C. coconut
1/2 smashed ripe banana
1 C. nonfat milk with 1 tsp. vanilla added
1/4 C. unsweetened concentrated apple juice
1/2 C. cooked oats
3/4 C. chopped dried apricots

- **Preheat oven to 350 degrees.**
- **Mix dry ingredients** *(first 5 items)* **in large bowl.**
- **Mix wet ingredients in another bowl and add dried apricots.**
- **Stir all ingredients together** *(wet to dry).*
- **Spray muffin tins with vegetable oil spray.**
- **Pour batter into tins** *(makes 1 dozen).*
- **Bake at 350 degrees approximately 35 minutes, or until tops brown and spring back to the touch.** *(Makes 1 dozen.)*

Serve with nonfat cream cheese (or quark) and apricot jam.

Fresh Fruit Cup

1/2 C. plain, nonfat yogurt *(stirred smooth)*
4 T. brown sugar
1 banana *(sliced in rounds)*
1 nectarine *(thin sliced)*
8-10 strawberries *(tops removed /sliced in half)*
10 seedless grapes
1/4 C. blueberries *(washed/stems removed)*

- **Stir yogurt and brown sugar together.**
- **Combine fruit and place in small bowls.**
- **Spoon yogurt mixture over fruit.**

GROCERY LIST

Produce

one 6" zucchini
10-12 baby white potatoes
2 medium yellow onions
1/2 lb. fresh mushrooms
2 green bell peppers
2 red bell peppers
1 yellow bell pepper
celery
1 bunch collard or other greens
8-10 ears fresh sweet corn
1/2 lb. fresh broccoli
1 head Romaine lettuce
1 head green leaf lettuce
green salad fixings
1 bunch green onions
one large cucumber
8-10 Roma tomatoes
one pear and 1/2 pt. berries
2 fresh lemons
1 lb. fresh peas *(in the pod)*
plain, firm tofu
1 fresh peach or nectarine

Frozen Foods

2 frozen snapper fillets *(if you are unable to buy fresh fish)*
frozen peas *(if fresh unavailable)*

Meat/Fish/Poultry

8-10 boneless, skinless chicken breasts
6-9 large, cooked, shelled shrimp
2 fresh snapper fillets *(You may wish to purchase fresh fish on Wednesday.)*

Canned or Dry Foods

one 29 oz. can tomato sauce
one 29 oz. can "Ready-cut" tomatoes
one 15 oz. can chicken broth
one 15 oz. can vegetable broth
one 6 oz. can sliced water chestnuts
16 oz. bowtie pasta
16 oz. whole wheat spiral pasta
one 1/2 C. package slivered almonds
a loaf of your favorite hearty bread

Chilled Foods and Dairy

flour tortillas

Buy if you're out

1 head garlic
1 bunch fresh parsley
brown rice
brown sugar
sesame oil
Dijon mustard
red cooking wine
Tabasco®
fancy-shred Parmesan
1 dozen eggs

Barbecued Chicken and Sweet Corn with "Creamed" Peas and Potatoes

SUNDAY

August/Week Four

Prepare chicken over a barbecue or grill. Cook extras! You'll use them for two very different meals on Monday and Tuesday.

Preparation time: 30 minutes
Servings: 2-3
Ingredients:

Notes

Barbecue Sauce
- 1/2 C. tomato sauce
- 1/4 C. red wine
- 2 T. balsamic vinegar
- 2 cloves garlic *(smashed and chopped)*
- 1 thin slice onion *(chopped very fine)*
- 2 T. Worcestershire sauce
- 1/4 tsp. sesame oil
- 1/8 C. brown sugar
- 2 T. chili powder
- 1 tsp. crushed oregano leaves

Place all ingredients in bowl. Mix well. Cover and cook in microwave 2 minutes.

White Sauce for Peas and Potatoes
- 1/2 C. chicken or vegetable broth
- 2 slices medium onion *(sliced thin and chopped)*
- 1 small clove garlic *(smashed and chopped)*
- 1/4 tsp. fresh-ground black pepper
- 1 tsp. butter
- 2 T. flour shaken with 1/3 C. nonfat milk

- 10-12 new white baby potatoes
- 8-10 ears fresh corn on the cob
- 8-10 boneless, skinless chicken breasts
- 1 lb. fresh peas in the pod *(shelled)*
- 1/8 C. plain, nonfat yogurt *(stirred smooth)*

- **Prepare and cook Barbecue Sauce as directed above.**
- **Mix white sauce ingredients** *(first 5 ingredients)* **in small sauce pan. Bring to boil. Thicken with flour mixture.** *(Be sure to shake flour and milk thoroughly to blend out lumps.)* **Cook over low heat 10 minutes. Remove from heat and set aside.**
- **Wash potatoes and place in large sauce pan with 1/2 C. water. Bring to boil and cook 15 minutes. Drain in colander.**
- **Husk corn. Place large kettle filled 2/3 full of water on high heat. Reduce heat to low when water boils.** *Do not put corn in until you are ready to serve dinner.*
- **Barbecue chicken over hot coals or grill. Before you baste with barbecue sauce, cook each side 6 minutes, turning twice.** *Cook three breasts without sauce.* **Baste remaining breasts and cook all chicken an additional 6 minutes per side.** *Save unbasted breasts for tomorrow, Tuesday, and freeze one.*
- **Place white sauce back over medium heat. When it begins to boil, add peas and potatoes. Return to boil, cook one minute, and remove from heat. Stir in yogurt.**
- **Return corn water to boil and drop in corn. Boil 1 minute. Remove and drain in colander.**

Serve family style in large bowls at table.

MONDAY
August/Week Four

Caesar Salad with Grilled Chicken

More delicious light, summer fare. You'll use one grilled chicken breast left over from Sunday evening.

Preparation time: 25 minutes
Servings: 2
Ingredients:

1 loaf of your favorite hearty bread

Romaine lettuce and green leaf lettuce
(Use about 4 leaves Romaine and 2 green leaf per person.)
1/2 cucumber *(peeled, sliced in 1/4" rounds and quartered)*
3 green onions *(washed and chopped)*
1/2 red bell pepper *(thin sliced and quartered)*
one leftover grilled chicken breast *(thin sliced)*
4 Roma tomatoes *(chopped)*
4 mushrooms *(thin-sliced)*

1/4 C. chopped firm tofu
1/2 tsp. Dijon mustard
1/8 C. white wine or broth

Dressing
1/2 tsp. fresh-ground black pepper
3 T. vegetable broth
1 T. balsamic vinegar
2 cloves garlic *(smashed and chopped)*
1 tsp. Dijon mustard
5 T. lemon juice
one slice cooked turkey bacon *(chopped – from freezer)*
1 1/2 tsp. Worcestershire sauce

1/2 fresh nectarine or peach *(sliced)*
2-3 T. fancy-shred Parmesan

- **Toss vegetables in large bowl with broken lettuce leaves.**
- **Sauté tofu in liquid mixed with mustard** *(2 minutes)*. **Pour into salad mixture.**
- **Stir dressing ingredients together, microwave covered 2 minutes on high. Let cool 5 minutes and toss with salad.**
- **Serve salads on large individual plates. Sprinkle with pieces of sliced chicken.**
- **Serve sliced nectarine on the side.**
- **Garnish with Parmesan cheese.**

Serve with your favorite hearty bread.

Notes

Chicken Cacciatore

Perfect for the summer season with all the fresh vegetables that are available. Make Red Sauce and reserve the rest for another meal.

Preparation time: 20 minutes
Servings: 2-3
Ingredients:

Notes

Red Sauce
- one 29 oz. can tomato sauce
- 2 cloves garlic *(smashed and chopped)*
- 1 T. dry oregano
- 1 1/2 T. dry basil leaves
- 4 thin slices medium yellow onion *(chopped)*
- a few dashes of Tabasco® sauce *(optional)*

2 C. dry whole wheat spiral pasta

1 1/2 C. Red Sauce

one clove garlic *(smashed and chopped)*
2 dashes of Tabasco®

1 carrot *(peeled and sliced in rounds)*
4 slices medium onion *(quartered)*
1/2 green bell pepper *(cubed)*
1/2 red bell pepper *(cubed)*
6-8 medium-sized mushrooms *(sliced)*
one 6" zucchini *(sliced in rounds and halved)*

1 plain chicken breast from Sunday evening's dinner *(chopped)*

2-4 T. fancy-shred Parmesan and 2 T. chopped fresh parsley

- **Prepare Red Sauce.**
- **Cook pasta 8 minutes in large heavy-bottomed kettle. Drain and rinse.**
- **To 1 1/2 C. Red Sauce, add garlic and Tabasco®. Bring to boil and add vegetables in the order given, cooking 1 minute after each addition: carrots, onion, peppers, mushrooms, and zucchini.**
- **Stir in chicken breast and cook 2 minutes at medium heat.**
- **Rinse pasta with warm water and toss with sauce in large pasta kettle. Serve immediately.**

Garnish with Parmesan and fresh chopped parsley.

Notes

Red Snapper with Red Sauce

Quick and easy. You have leftover Red Sauce from last night.

Preparation time: 25 minutes
Servings: 2
Ingredients:

4 green onions *(chopped)*
1 stalk celery *(chopped fine)*
2 T. fresh parsley *(chopped)*
1/2 C. broth
fresh-ground black pepper
2 C. cooked brown rice

juice from 1/2 of a lemon
1/2 C. water

3 slices of red bell pepper *(chop)*
2 slices green bell pepper *(chop)*
1 slice medium yellow onion *(chop)*
1/8 C. leftover Red Sauce

1/2 lb. fresh broccoli *(cut into 2" pieces)*

1/2 lb. fresh snapper fillets

1/2 a fresh lemon *(cut in wedges)*

- **Mix onion, celery, parsley, broth, fresh-ground pepper, and rice. Cover and microwave 3 minutes on high. Leave covered.**
- **Mix lemon juice with 1/2 C. water and set aside.**
- **Place peppers and onion in small sauce pan with Red Sauce. Bring to a boil. Reduce heat to low.**
- **Place broccoli in steamer basket in saucepan with 3/4 C. water.** *Do not turn on heat yet.*
- **Saute fish in lemon juice and water over high heat. When liquid boils, reduce heat to medium and cook 3 minutes per side. After turning final time, spoon Red Sauce and vegetables over fillets and cover. Reduce heat to medium** *(add 1/2 C. water if pan is dry)* **and cook an additional 3 minutes.** *Remove from heat and leave covered until served.*
- **Turn burner on high under broccoli. When water boils, cover, and cook 3 minutes.**
- **Arrange fish on individual serving plates flanked by broccoli on one side and rice on the other. Garnish with lemon wedges.**

Light a candle and take your time with this dinner.

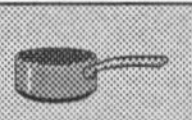

"Quick cook" some rice this morning before work. Cook a double recipe. You'll use it up before the end of the week. *(see page 237)*

You may need to pick up fresh fish on the way home from work if you opted not to purchase it on Saturday.

Bow Tie Pasta with Chunky Red Sauce

THURSDAY
August/Week Four

A return to one of my simple favorites. Save 3/4 C. Red Sauce for tomorrow.

Preparation time: 25 minutes
Servings: 2-3
Ingredients:

Notes

Chunky Red Sauce
- one 29 oz. can "Ready-cut" tomatoes
- 1/4 C. red wine
- 2 cloves garlic *(smashed and chopped)*
- 2 slices medium yellow onion *(chopped)*
- 1 1/2 T. dry basil leaves
- 1 T. dry oregano leaves
- dash of Tabasco®
- 1/2 C. Red Sauce *(left over from Tuesday)*

- 4 C. dry bow tie pasta
- green salad fixings
- 2-4 T. fancy-shred Parmesan
- a loaf of your favorite hearty bread

- **Place large kettle on stove filled 2/3 full of water. Turn heat on high and cover.**
- **Set colander over sauce pan. Pour chopped tomatoes into colander and drain liquid into sauce pan. Set tomato chunks aside.**
- **Add all Chunky Red Sauce ingredients** *(except tomato chunks)* **to tomato juice in sauce pan. Bring to boil. Reduce heat to low. Cover and cook 5 minutes.**
- **Pour dry pasta into boiling water. Cook 10 minutes. Drain and rinse.**
- **Make green salads while pasta cooks.**
- **Add tomato chunks to Red Sauce and bring to boil. Remove from heat.**
- **Spoon sauce over pasta on individual serving plates.**

Sprinkle with 1-2 T. Parmesan cheese. Serve with bread and salad on side.

Pick up a loaf of hearty bread today.

FRIDAY
August/Week Four

Notes

Cajun Shrimp and Rice

A delicious way to use up leftover rice.

Preparation time: 30 minutes
Servings: 3-4
Ingredients:

1/2 green bell pepper *(chopped)*
8 medium mushrooms *(sliced)*
2 thin slices medium onion *(chopped)*
1 clove garlic *(smashed and chopped)*
1 T. olive oil *(optional)*
1/4 C. broth

3/4 C. Chunky Red Sauce *(left over from last night)*
1 T. chili powder
1 T. dry oregano leaves
1 tsp. cumin
a couple dashes of Tabasco®

6-9 large frozen, deveined, shelled, cooked shrimp

1/2 C. broth
1 bunch collard greens or other seasonal greens *(stems removed)*

2 T. olive oil
3 T. balsamic vinegar
fresh-ground black pepper

2-4 tortillas

2 C. cooked brown rice *(leftover from Wednesday)*

1/2 C. plain, nonfat yogurt *(stirred smooth)*

- **Sauté vegetables 3 minutes in large sauce pan with garlic, oil and broth. Remove vegetables from pan and set aside.**
- **Place Chunky Red Sauce and spices in same sauce pan. Cook 10 minutes over medium heat.**
- **Add shrimp and remove from heat.**
- **Measure broth into large kettle. Bring to boil. Add greens and toss over high heat until wilted. Reduce heat to medium, cover, and cook 5 minutes. Combine oil and vinegar and toss with greens. Remove from heat. Season with fresh-ground black pepper.**
- **Place tortillas between two serving plates and microwave 30 seconds on high.**
- **Add rice to shrimp, vegetable, Red Sauce mixture. Mix thoroughly and reheat over medium-high heat stirring constantly. Serve immediately flanked by greens.**

Add a dollop of yogurt to each serving and enjoy warm tortillas on the side.

SATURDAY
August/September

SHOPPING DAY

Back problems? *There is a direct correlation between lack of fitness and back problems. Strong leg, back, and abdominal muscles provide primary stability for the spine and can prevent development of back problems.*
Hold it! You're Exercising Wrong! by Edward J. Jackowski, Fireside, 1995

Debunking myths **-** *saltwater fish is no higher in sodium than freshwater fish. An internal regulatory system in fish prevents the flesh from taking up sodium from the water. However, when fish is canned, smoked, or pickled, sodium is artificially added so the sodium content increases dramatically.*
University of California at Berkeley Wellness Letter, Volume 12, November, 1995

Notes

GROCERY LIST

Produce

2 large sweet onions
1/2 lb. fresh broccoli
3/4 lb. fresh mushrooms
2 green bell peppers
2 red bell peppers
8-10 baby red potatoes
1 bunch fresh parsley
1/4 lb. fresh snow peas
1 head iceberg lettuce
1 head leaf lettuce
green salad fixings
1 large cucumber
4 Roma tomatoes
fresh peaches, pears, strawberries, blueberries and bananas

Frozen Foods

frozen concentrated apple juice
frozen snow peas *(if fresh unavailable)*

Meat/Fish/Poultry

1 lb. ground turkey breast
2 boneless, skinless chicken breasts
3-5 oz. smoked salmon

Canned or Dry Foods

1/2 C. package sliced almonds
one 29 oz. can tomato sauce
two 15 oz. cans chicken broth
one 6 oz can sliced water chestnuts
12 oz. dry multi-colored spiral pasta
12 oz. dry whole wheat spiral pasta
12 oz. dry sea shell pasta
8 oz. fresh fettuccine
loaf of hearty bread

Chilled Foods and Dairy

3 oz. sharp cheddar cheese

Buy if you're out

one head garlic
celery
nonfat mayonnaise
ground anise
white cooking wine
red cooking wine
whole wheat tortillas
fresh salsa
pesto

SUNDAY
August/September

Notes

Chicken Pasta and Fruit Salad Sampler

Observance of the Labor Day weekend will also celebrate some of the bounties of harvest time —fresh vegetables in the pasta salad plus delicious "in season" fruits.

Preparation time: 35 minutes
Servings: 2
Ingredients:

Pasta Salad
- 2 C. dry spiral pasta
- 2 stalks celery *(chopped)*
- 1/2 cucumber *(peeled, sliced in 1/4" rounds and quartered)*
- 3 slices medium yellow onion *(chopped)*
- 1/2 red bell pepper *(thin sliced and quartered)*
- one cooked chicken breast from freezer *(chopped)*
- 1/2 of a 6 oz. can sliced water chestnuts
- 4 T. sliced almonds *(toasted)*
- 4 Roma tomatoes *(chopped)*

Pasta Salad Dressing
- 4 T. nonfat mayonnaise
- 1 clove garlic *(smashed and chopped)*
- 1/4 C. nonfat yogurt or quark
- 1 tsp. curry powder
- fresh-ground black pepper *(to taste)*
- 1/2 tsp. sesame oil
- 2 T. concentrated apple juice
- 2 T. fresh, chopped parsley

Stir all ingredients together.

Fruit Salad Dressing
- 1/2 C. nonfat yogurt *(stirred smooth)*
- 1/4 C. concentrated apple juice
- 1/4 tsp. cinnamon

Fruit Salad
- 1 blanched peach *(cut in 1/2" pieces)*
- 1 banana *(sliced in rounds)*
- 10 strawberries *(topped and cut in half)*
- 1 pear *(cored and cut in 1/2" pieces)*
- 1/2 C. blueberries or blackberries

- 2-3 T. fancy-shred Parmesan
- 1 loaf of your favorite hearty bread

- **Cook pasta 10 minutes in boiling water. Drain and rinse and place in bowl of ice water while you prepare the rest of the salad.**
- **Toss remaining pasta salad ingredients in large bowl.**
- **Combine pasta dressing ingredients and toss with pasta salad.**
- **Drain pasta** *(remove any pieces of ice)* **and add to salad mix. Gently stir to thoroughly coat all ingredients. Cover and refrigerate until mealtime.**
- **Combine fruit salad dressing in another large bowl.**
- **Add fruit and gently stir to coat. Cover and refrigerate.**
- **Serve salads on same plate.**

Garnish pasta salad with Parmesan and pass the bread.

Smoked Salmon Pasta

Time to revisit this Northwest favorite.

Preparation time: 25 minutes
Servings: 2
Ingredients:

8 mushrooms (*sliced*)
1/2 red bell pepper (*cut into thin 1" long strips*)
2 slices medium yellow onion (*chopped*)
2 cloves garlic (*smashed and chopped*)
or 1/2 tsp. prepared chopped garlic
1 T. olive oil
1/4 C. dry white wine

1/2 C. chicken or vegetable broth
2 T. corn starch dissolved in about 1/8 C. water

fixings for a green salad

4 oz. smoked salmon (*skin removed and broken into bite-sized pieces*)
1 package frozen snow peas, or 1/8 lb. fresh snow peas

2 T. pesto
3/4 C. plain, nonfat yogurt

8 oz. fresh fettuccine

3 T. fancy-shred Parmesan cheese
3 Roma tomatoes (*chopped*)

- **Place pasta water on to boil in large kettle.**
- **Sauté mushrooms, red bell pepper, onion, and garlic in oil and wine over medium-high heat 2 minutes. Remove from pan with slotted spoon and set aside.**
- **Add broth to remaining white wine in pan. Bring to boil. Reduce heat to medium.**
- **Stir corn starch mixture into boiling liquid. Reduce heat to low and cook 5 minutes. Stir occasionally.**
- **Make green salads.**
- **Add salmon and snow peas to thickened sauce. Return to boil and cook 1 minute.**
- **Return mushroom mixture to sauce. Cook 1 minute and remove pan from heat.**
- **Mix pesto and yogurt until smooth. Microwave 30 seconds on high to take chill off. Stir again.**
- **Drop pasta into boiling water. When water returns to boil, cook 2 minutes** *(set a timer so you don't forget),* **drain, and rinse.**
- **In same kettle used to cook pasta, mix salmon mixture and yogurt/pesto over low heat. *Do Not Boil!***
- **Toss until pasta is well coated.**
- **Serve on individual plates garnished with Parmesan cheese and fresh tomatoes.**

Serve a green salad on the side.
Oh yes!! Yes!!!

MONDAY
August/September

Notes

LABOR DAY

TUESDAY
August/September

Notes

Pasta Bolognese

Tonight this favorite will be made from scratch. It still goes quickly, even cooking your own Italian Sausage. Try cooking the turkey and Red Sauce simultaneously, it will go faster.

Preparation time: 20 minutes
Servings: 2-3
Ingredients:

2 1/2 C. dry spiral pasta

Italian Turkey Sausage
1 T. olive oil
1 lb. ground turkey breast
2 slices medium yellow onion *(chopped)*
2 large cloves garlic *(smashed and chopped)*
2 tsp. dry basil leaves
1 tsp. dry oregano leaves
1/2 tsp. ground anise
dash of Tabasco® sauce
1/8 C. red wine

Red Sauce
one 29 oz. can tomato sauce
2 cloves garlic *(smashed and chopped)*
1/4 C. red wine
1 T. dry oregano
1 1/2 T. dry basil leaves
4 slices medium yellow onion *(chopped)*
a few dashes of Tabasco® sauce *(optional)*

1/3 of the cooked Italian Sausage
1/8 C. red wine
1 1/2 C. Red Sauce

green salad fixings

3 T. fancy-shred Parmesan

- **Place pasta water on to boil in large kettle. Drop pasta into water and cook 8 minutes. Drain and rinse.**
- **Begin preparing Italian Sausage by placing oil in sauté pan over medium-high heat.**
- **Add ground turkey, onions, garlic, spices, Tabasco® and wine.**
- **Prepare Red Sauce at the same time. Place all ingredients in medium sauce pan and bring to boil. Cover, reduce heat to low, and cook 10 minutes.** *(When Red Sauce is cooked, measure 1 1/2 C. for tonight's recipe and put remainder away in fridge.)*
- **Sauté sausage mixture until browned.** *(Reserve 1/3 of the sausage for tonight's recipe and put remainder away in fridge.)*
- **Combine 1/3 of the Italian Sausage, 1/8 C. wine, and 1 1/2 C. Red Sauce in same pan used to cook Red Sauce.** *Bring to boil. Reduce heat to low and cover while finishing dinner preparations.*
- **Prepare green salads.**
- **Divide pasta on plates and spoon Bolognese Sauce over each serving.**
- **Garnish with Parmesan cheese.**

Serve with a crisp green salad.
Presto! (Not to be confused with Pesto.)

Loaded Rice

WEDNESDAY

August/September

Time for a "carbo-load!"

Preparation time: 25 minutes
Servings: 2
Ingredients:

8-10 baby red potatoes or 1 large russet potato
1 T. olive oil

1/2 lb. mushrooms *(sliced)*
1/4 red bell pepper *(thin-sliced)*
1 T. olive oil
1 large clove garlic *(smashed and chopped)*
1/4 C. white wine
2 slices medium onion *(quartered)*

3/4 C. chicken or vegetable broth
3 T. corn starch dissolved in 1/8 C. cold water

1 1/2 C. cooked brown rice

1 C. plain, nonfat yogurt
1 T. pesto
dash of Tabasco®

2 Roma tomatoes *(chopped)*

Notes

"Quick cook" some rice before work this morning. *(see page 237)*

- **Preheat oven to 400 degrees.**
- **Wash and halve baby red potatoes. If using russet potato, wash and slice** *(unpeeled)* **in 1/2" slices. Place potatoes, flat side down, on cookie sheet oiled with one tablespoon olive oil.**
- **Sauté sliced mushrooms and bell pepper in oil with garlic, wine, and onion** *(about 4 minutes).* **When done, remove mushroom mixture from pan with perforated spoon. Set aside.**
- **Add broth to pan. Return to boil.**
- **If cooking russet potato slices, turn them now.**
- **Slowly stir corn starch mixture into boiling liquid. Reduce heat to low. Cook 5 minutes, stirring often.**
- **Add mushrooms to thickened mixture. Return to boil. Remove from heat.**
- **Warm 1 1/2 C. cooked rice 2 minutes on high in microwave on individual serving plates.**
- **Remove potatoes from oven. If using baby reds, push them into rice on individual plates. If using russets, chop into 1" pieces before sprinkling over rice.**
- **Stir yogurt, pesto, and Tabasco® together until smooth. Microwave 30 seconds on high. Stir again, and add to thickened mushroom sauce.**

Pour sauce over potato/rice mixture and garnish with fresh chopped tomato. Enjoy!

THURSDAY

August/September

Notes

Soft Shell Tacos

It won't take long to prepare supper this evening. You should have left-over turkey sausage from Tuesday evening.

Preparation time: 15-20 minutes
Servings: 3-4
Ingredients:

1/2 lb. cooked turkey sausage *(leftover from Tuesday night)*
1 clove garlic *(smashed and chopped)*
1/2 tsp. ground cumin
1 T. mild chili powder
dash of Tabasco®
1/4 C. leftover Red Sauce *(leftover from Tuesday night)*

1/2 green pepper *(cut in 1" cubes)*
1 clove garlic *(smashed and chopped)*
2 slices yellow onion *(chopped)*
1 T. chili powder
1/4 C. broth or water

flour or corn Tortillas

1/2 C. plain, nonfat yogurt *(stirred smooth)*
salsa
1/2 head iceberg lettuce *(chopped)*
sharp cheddar cheese *(grated)*
2-3 Roma tomatoes *(chopped)*

- **Place cooked sausage, garlic, spices and Red Sauce in sauté pan. Simmer over low heat 10 minutes. Remove from pan and set aside.**
- **Using same fry pan, sauté green pepper, garlic, onions, and chili powder in broth 2 minutes over high heat. Remove from pan and place in another small bowl.**
- **Place 4 tortillas between two dinner plates and microwave 45 seconds.**
- **On individual plates, spoon yogurt and salsa onto center of each tortilla, add meat, veggies, and lettuce, and garnish with a grating of sharp cheese and chopped tomato.**

Fold the tortillas around the ingredients and enjoy.

Leftovers

FRIDAY

August/September

Before too many days of the month go by, clean out the fridge. Leftovers like fruit salad and cold pasta salad should be eaten within a few days.

Preparation time: 15-20 minutes
Servings: 3-4
Ingredients:

leftover Fruit Salad
leftover Chicken Pasta Salad
leftover Red Sauce

Notes

If you're making a green salad, *don't throw away the outside leaves of the lettuce. They are loaded with vitamin A. Wash them well and toss them into the salad.*

If you're having a loaf of hearty bread, *try eating it without any spread. The bread actually tastes quite wonderful plain. If you want something on it, spread it with some quark.*

Margarine may actually be more harmful than butter. *A recent USDA study established a link between trans-fatty acids found in margarine and heart disease. Butter and margarine have the same amount of fat grams per serving. It appears that the altered molecules (trans-fatty acids) of the processed margarine are more difficult for the body to break down.*
The Wall Street Journal, 420 Lexington Ave., New York, NY 10070-0180

Is red wine beneficial to health? *A report a few years ago stated that the French cut their risk of heart disease by consuming red wine with meals. New research suggests that it is the antioxidants in the wine, not the wine itself, that is beneficial to health. The same antioxidants can be found in fresh fruits and vegetables.*
The Lancet, 428 E. Preston St., Baltimore, MD 21202

Check out these lowfat snacks: *10 thin pretzel sticks (110 calories, 1 gm. fat). Two fig bars (105 calories, 2 gm. fat).*
University of Texas Lifeline Health Letter, 1100 Holcombe Blvd., Houston, TX

Diabetes is linked to heart disease. *In many diabetics, the liver makes more fat than the body can use. Burning 500 calories a day through exercise can help reduce the risk of heart problems.*
Harvey L. Katzeff, MD, director of *The Diabetes Program*, North Shore Hospital, Manhasset, NY

SATURDAY

September/Week One

Notes

SHOPPING DAY

Kiwi anyone? *This odd little fruit is fat-free, low in calories, and high in fiber. It's also a good source for vitamin C and potassium. Store the fruit at room temperature for 3-5 days. It's ripe when it's easy to squeeze.*
Jenny Craig's Body Health, 1633 Broadway, New York, NY 10018

Vitamin supplements *will not compensate for bad eating habits. Get proper nourishment through good diet and take vitamin supplements if you wish.*
William Castelli, M.D., director of *The Framingham Heart Study*, Framingham, Massachusetts

Storing vegetables in the fridge *saves nutrients. When stored in the fridge, vegetables lose only 1/4 to 1/3 the vitamin C they'd lose being stored at room temperature. Be sure to use the hydrator in the bottom of the fridge. The drawers preserve moisture while not letting vegetables get too cold. Store vegetables in plastic bags when possible.*

Be sure to check spices *when checking on staples before shopping. Keep chili powder, leaf basil, leaf oregano, and powdered cumin on hand at all times. When adding leaf herbs like oregano and basil, I measure the amount into the palm of my hand and briskly rub my hands together to break up the leaves. This releases a little more flavor.*

GROCERY LIST

Produce

4-5 large russet potatoes
3-4 oz. fresh snow peas
one 6" zucchini
1 medium yellow onion
1/2 lb. fresh mushrooms
2 green bell peppers
2 red bell peppers
2 jalapeno peppers
5 medium carrots
1/2 lb. fresh broccoli
1 head iceberg lettuce
1 head red leaf lettuce
1 bunch fresh parsley
1 cucumber
green salad fixings
10-12 Roma tomatoes
1 ripe cantaloupe
2 ripe kiwis
1 fresh lime
1 ginger root
6-8 ears corn *(You may wish to pick up fresh corn on the way home from work Tuesday evening.)*

Frozen Foods

Meat/Fish/Poultry

6 boneless, skinless chicken breasts
1 lb. ground turkey breast
8-10 large, cooked, shelled shrimp *(frozen shrimp are OK)*
1 lb. turkey breast fillets

Canned or Dry Foods

one 29 oz. can tomato sauce
one 29 oz. can chopped tomatoes
one 15 oz. can tomato sauce
oat bran or bran flake cereal
1/2 lb. dry kidney beans or three 15 oz. cans kidney beans
two 15 oz. cans vegetable broth
two 15 oz. cans chicken broth
12 oz. dry whole wheat spaghetti
a loaf of hearty bread

Chilled Foods and Dairy

plain, nonfat yogurt
whole wheat tortillas

Buy if you're out

garlic
celery
toasted sunflower meats
pine nuts
cornmeal
ground anise
ground cloves
ground sage
paprika
cayenne pepper
capers
Greek olives
Dijon mustard
red cooking wine
eggs
salsa

Vegetarian Chili and Corn Bread

SUNDAY

September/Week One

This is a purely vegetarian chili. Very satisfying! The preparation time assumes one is starting with cooked beans. Prepare the chili in the early afternoon. Remove from heat and let stand for a few hours before serving.

Preparation time: 50 minutes *(20 to assemble, 30 to cook)*
Servings: 4-6
Ingredients:

2 cloves garlic *(smashed and chopped)*
1 medium onion *(chopped)*
2 stalks celery *(chopped)*
2 jalapeno peppers *(chopped fine)*
one 24 oz. can chopped tomatoes
one 15 oz. can tomato sauce
one 15 oz. can vegetable broth
2 carrots *(shredded)*
1 green bell pepper *(chopped)*
1 red bell pepper *(chopped)*
4 cups cooked kidney beans or
three 15 oz. cans beans *(rinsed)*
3 T. chili powder
1/2 tsp. ground cloves
1 tsp. ground cumin
1 C. plain, nonfat yogurt *(stirred smooth)*

- **Combine all ingredients** *(except yogurt)* **in 8 quart sauce pan.**
- **Cover and simmer 30 minutes. Remove from heat, cover and let stand 2-3 hours.**
- **Make corn bread** *(see box)* **1/2 hour before serving dinner.**
- **Swirl 2 T. smooth yogurt into each serving.**

Old-Fashioned Corn Bread
An old family favorite!

Preheat oven to 400 degrees. Place oiled 10" cast iron skillet *(or similar size baking pan)* in hot oven while mixing batter. (Leave no more than 5 minutes or when pan begins to smoke.)

2 C. cornmeal *(preferably stone-ground)*
1 1/4 C. nonfat milk
2 tsp. baking powder
1 egg or 2 egg whites
1 1/2 T. vegetable oil

Mix all ingredients. Remove pan from oven and pour batter into hot pan. Bake 20-25 minutes, until cracks begin to open on top.

Makes a dense corn bread with a robust corn flavor!

Notes

Cook beans during the day today. (see page 113) If not, be sure you have canned beans on hand.

MONDAY
September/Week One

Notes

Garlic/Lime Sautéed Shrimp

Remember how this lovely dish spiced up your life? You'll have leftover rice. Save it for tomorrow night.

Preparation time: 30 minutes
Servings: 2
Ingredients:

1/4 C. white wine
8-10 cooked and deveined cocktail shrimp
juice from one lime
1 clove garlic *(smashed and chopped) or 1 tsp. prepared garlic*
1/4 tsp. fresh ginger

4 slices medium onion *(chopped)*
1 clove garlic *(smashed and chopped) or 1 tsp. prepared chopped garlic*
1/2 C. broth
1 large carrot *(cut in thin strips 1" long)*

3 dashes cayenne pepper
4 oz. fresh or frozen snow peas

2 T. corn starch dissolved in 1/4 C. water

2 C. cooked rice

2 fresh kiwi fruits *(peeled and sliced in rounds)*
2 Roma tomatoes *(chopped)*

- **Place wine, shrimp, lime juice, garlic, and ginger in large fry pan. Sauté 2 minutes. Remove from pan with perforated spoon and place in bowl. Leave juice in pan.**
- **Place onion, 1 clove garlic, broth, and carrot strips in same pan and sauté 1 minute.**
- **Add cayenne pepper and snow peas and sauté 2 minutes.**
- **Use perforated spoon to lift vegetables out of pan. Leave juice. Return to boil.**
- **Thicken by slowly stirring corn starch mixture into liquid.**
- **Reduce heat and cook, uncovered, 5 minutes.**
- **Warm rice in microwave on individual plates.**
- **Peel and slice kiwi. Overlay slices along edge of two serving plates.**
- **Return shrimp and vegetables to sauce.**

Serve over a bed of warmed rice with sliced kiwi overlapped along edge of plate.

"Quick cook" a double batch of rice this morning. *(see page 237)*

Fried Chicken and Sweet Corn

TUESDAY

September/Week One

Here's a lowfat version of fried chicken. It's the season for sweet corn! If possible, buy the corn the day you are to cook it.

Preparation time: 60 minutes, but worth the wait!
Servings: 3-4
Ingredients:

Spiced Potatoes
1 T. chili powder
1 tsp. cumin powder
1 clove garlic *(smashed and chopped)*
one thin slice onion *(chopped)*
2 T. balsamic vinegar
1/4 C. broth
4-5 russet potatoes *(scrubbed and cut into 1/2" slices)*

Oven Fried Chicken
1/2 C. flour
1/4 C. cornmeal
1/2 tsp. ground sage
1/4 tsp. nutmeg
1/2 tsp. ground black pepper
1 tsp. dry basil leaves
1 tsp. dry oregano leaves
1 tsp. paprika
1 clove garlic *(smashed and chopped)*
2 thin slices onion *(chopped fine)*
2 egg whites *(beaten stiff)*
1/2 C. nonfat milk
6-8 boneless, skinless chicken breasts

3 T. olive oil *(used for oiling 2 cookie sheets)*

6-8 ears fresh sweet corn *(husked)*

1/2 cantaloupe *(sliced thin, rind removed)*

Notes

- **Preheat oven to 400 degrees.**
- **Mix potato spices, garlic, onion, vinegar, and broth in large bowl. Place potatoes in liquid and stir to coat thoroughly. Leave in liquid while preparing chicken.** *(Place potatoes on cookie sheet oiled with 1 T. olive oil. Wait and place potatoes in oven with the chicken.)*
- **Prepare Oven Fried Chicken coating by mixing flour, cornmeal, spices, garlic, and onion in shallow bowl.**
- **Beat egg whites until stiff and fold into milk. Dip chicken first in milk mixture and then dredge in flour/cornmeal mixture. Place on cookie sheet oiled with 2 T. oil.**
- **Put chicken and potatoes into oven for 20 minutes. Turn. Cook an additional 20 minutes.**
- **Place large kettle on high heat filled with 3 quarts water.**
- **Drop corn in boiling water just before serving. Cook 1 minute after water returns to boil. Remove from water and drain.**

Serve chicken, potatoes and corn together on individual plates. Fan out cantaloupe and serve on plate in center of table.

WEDNESDAY

September/Week One

Notes

You may need to pick up fresh bread at the bakery today.

Hot Vegetable Nest

Tonight we revisit an interesting meal you sampled last March.

Preparation time: 25 minutes
Servings: 2
Ingredients:

1 loaf of your favorite hearty bread

1 large carrot *(sliced in rounds)*
1 T. olive oil
1/4 C. vegetable broth
1 clove garlic *(smashed and chopped)*

two 1/4" slices medium onion *(quartered)*
1 1/2 C. broccoli *(chopped)*

6 medium mushrooms *(sliced)*

1/4 head iceberg lettuce *(shredded)*

1 tsp. Dijon mustard
1/2 C. plain, nonfat yogurt *(stirred smooth)*

2 Roma tomatoes *(chopped)*

1 T. toasted pine nuts *(chopped)*
Use previously stored nuts, or toast fresh under broiler.

- **Wrap bread in foil and place in warm oven.**
- **Start by placing carrots, oil, broth, and garlic in sauté pan over medium-high heat. Sauté 2 minutes.**
- **Add onion and broccoli. Sauté 1 minute.**
- **Add mushrooms. Sauté 1 minute. Remove from heat and set aside.**
- **Arrange shredded lettuce in nest shape on individual serving plates.**
- **Combine mustard and yogurt and microwave 20 seconds on high.**
- **Return sauté pan with vegetables to heat and add yogurt sauce. Blend thoroughly and remove from heat. *Do not boil.***
- **Add tomatoes, and spoon vegetable mixture over lettuce. Serve immediately.**

Top with pine nuts. Serve with warmed bread.

Hot Fajita Salad

Here it is again! A most satisfying salad entrée.

Preparation time: 30 minutes
Servings: 2-4
Ingredients:

1 lb. turkey breast fillets *(cut in 1/8" strips)*
1 T. olive oil
2 cloves garlic *(smashed and chopped)*
or 1 tsp. commercially prepared chopped garlic
1 tsp. chili powder
1/4 tsp. ground cumin

1/4 C. broth
1 green bell pepper *(cut in 1" chunks)*
1 red bell pepper *(cut in 1" chunks)*
3 slices of a medium sweet onion *(quartered)*
1 tsp. chili powder
1/4 tsp. ground cumin

several leaves red leaf lettuce *(broken)*
1/2 head chopped iceberg lettuce
4 ripe Roma tomatoes *(chopped)*
8 slices peeled cucumber *(chopped)*

1 C. quark *(prepared this morning) stir before serving*
salsa

2 T. toasted sunflower seeds

4 whole wheat flour tortillas

- **Slice turkey breast fillets in thin (1/8") slices.**
- **Place poultry in shallow 10" non-stick fry pan with oil, garlic, 1 tsp. chili powder, and 1/4 tsp. ground cumin over medium-high heat and sauté 5 minutes.**
- **Remove meat from pan and set aside.**
- **Add broth, peppers, onion and remaining spices to same pan and sauté 3 minutes. Lift vegetables out with perforated spoon and set aside.**
- **Lay broken leaf lettuce on plates and top with chopped iceberg lettuce. Sprinkle with tomato and cucumber.**
- **Spoon fajita mixture over lettuce and sprinkle with tomato and cucumber.**
- **Top with quark and salsa to taste and garnish with a few toasted sunflower seeds.**
- **Warm tortillas in microwave by placing them between two serving plates and cooking 20 seconds on high, or warm in oven at 350 degrees in shallow, covered pan 5 minutes.**

Roll warmed tortillas and serve on side.

THURSDAY
September/Week One

Notes

Prepare quark this morning.

Line a strainer with a large coffee filter. Measure 2 C. yogurt into filter. Place over bowl and set in fridge.

FRIDAY

September/Week One

Notes

Pasta Putanesca

Spicy pasta night. This is one of my wife's favorites.

Preparation time: 30 minutes
Servings: 2-3
Ingredients:

Italian Turkey Sausage
1 T. olive oil
1 lb. ground turkey breast
2 slices medium yellow onion *(chopped)*
2 tsp. dry basil leaves
1 tsp. dry oregano leaves
1/2 tsp. ground anise
2 large cloves garlic *(smashed and chopped)*
dash of Tabasco® sauce

green salad fixings

1 1/2 C. Red Sauce *use leftovers or make a new batch (see page 248)*
1/8 C. red wine
2 cloves garlic *(smashed and chopped)*
2 T. green capers
5 Italian or Greek olives *(chopped)*

12 oz. dry whole wheat spaghetti

3 T. fancy-shred Parmesan
1 T. chopped parsley

- **Place pasta water on to boil in large kettle.**
- **Place all Italian Sausage ingredients in fry pan and cook until browned over medium-high heat** *(about 10 minutes)*. **Remove from heat and set aside.** *Use 1/3 of the Italian Sausage in tonight's recipe and save remainder for another time.*
- **Prepare Red Sauce.** *Reserve 1 1/2 C. for tonight's meal and save the rest for a future meal.*
- **Prepare green salads on individual plates.**
- **To 1 1/2 C. Red Sauce, add wine, 1/3 of the cooked Italian Sausage, extra 2 cloves garlic, capers, and olives.**
- **Cover sauce and place over low heat while finishing dinner preparations.**
- **Drop dry pasta into boiling water. Cook 8 minutes. Drain and rinse.**
- **Divide pasta onto plates and cover with Putanesca Sauce.**

Garnish with Parmesan and parsley.
Serve with green salad. You've done it again!

SHOPPING DAY

SATURDAY

September/Week Two

Check the cupboard and the fridge, add to the list as needed, and go "stock up!"

Why cook with nonfat yogurt? *A cup of yogurt provides about a third of a person's daily calcium and at least 20% of recommended protein intake. It also adds a nice flavor "ping" without adding fat.*
University of Texas Lifeline Health Letter, 1100 Holcombe Blvd., Houston, TX

Put some change in your own pocket. *Eat dinner at home and brown bag your lunch. There are over 160,000 fast food restaurants in the US; over $70,000,000,000 (that's right, ten zeros) is spent at them each year.*
The American Journal of Cardiology, Vol. 70

The most nutritious wheat bread *is made from 100% whole wheat flour. Check the ingredients. Many commercially prepared "wheat breads" are made with white flour and darkened with caramel coloring.*
Kathy Kapica, Ph.D., R.D., Chicago, IL

Notes

GROCERY LIST

Produce

6 medium russet potatoes
8-10 baby red potatoes
2 medium yellow onions
1/4 lb. fresh mushrooms
1 green bell pepper
2 red bell peppers
1/2 lb. fresh broccoli
green salad fixings
1/4 lb. pistachios
4-5 Roma tomatoes
one bunch green onions
2 fresh peaches or nectarines
3-4 tart apples
one bunch fresh cilantro
one bunch fresh parsley
1 fresh lemon
1 fresh lime

Frozen Foods

one package frozen spinach

Meat/Fish/Poultry

2 boneless, skinless chicken breasts
1 lb. thin sliced turkey breast fillets *(or buy unsliced fillets)*
1 1/2 lb. ground turkey breast

Canned or Dry Foods

one 29 oz. can tomato sauce
two 15 oz. cans chicken broth
12 oz. dry bow tie pasta
one 15 oz. can sliced beets *(not pickled)*

Chilled Foods and Dairy

1 dozen eggs

Buy if you're out

one head garlic
celery
frozen corn
frozen peas
dried rosemary
dried fennel seed
brown sugar
sesame oil
brown rice
saltine crackers
white cooking wine
plain, nonfat yogurt

SUNDAY
September/Week Two

Notes

Take a few minutes to make some quark this morning. Line a strainer with a large coffee filter. Measure 2 C. nonfat yogurt into filter. Place over a bowl and set in fridge.

Turkey Meat Loaf

One has to have a little Old World comfort food. This version of meat loaf has a fraction of the fat found in the traditional ground beef variety.

Preparation time: 1 hour and 30 minutes
Servings: 3-4
Ingredients:

Meat Loaf
1 lb. ground turkey breast
1 C. crushed saltine crackers
1 clove garlic *(smashed and chopped)*
2 thin slices onion *(chopped very fine)*
two egg whites *(slightly beaten)*
1 tsp. dry oregano leaves
2 tsp. dry basil leaves
1/2 tsp. ground black pepper
1/3 C. chicken broth
1/4 tsp. crushed rosemary leaves

Tomato Glaze
1/2 C. leftover Red Sauce
1 T. brown sugar
1 T. Worcestershire sauce

2-4 medium-sized baking potatoes *(one per person)*

2 green onions *(chopped fine)*
1 C. quark

1/2 red bell pepper *(chopped)*
2 cups frozen whole kernel corn
1/4 C. chicken broth

2 tart apples *(sliced in thin slices)*

- **Preheat oven to 375 degrees.**
- **In large bowl mix all Meat Loaf ingredients. Mix with hands until will blended. Pack Meat Loaf into medium-size loaf pan.**
- **Prepare Tomato Glaze by mixing Red Sauce, brown sugar, and Worcestershire in small bowl. Cover top of the Meat Loaf with Tomato Glaze.**
- **Wash potatoes and prick with fork. Rub with a little olive oil and place in shallow pan.**
- **Place Meat Loaf and potatoes in 375 degree oven. Cook 1 hour. Remove from pan while hot. Cool 10 minutes before serving.**
- **Stir green onions and quark together.**
- **Mix red bell pepper, corn and broth in small sauce pan. Bring to boil and cook 1 minute. Remove from heat.**
- **Core and slice apple.**
- **Slice Meat Loaf. Place on individual plates with corn, split baked potato and apple slices.**
- **Set onion/quark mixture on table to dress potatoes.**

A dinner just like Grandma used to make!

Mustard-Glazed Chicken Breasts

MONDAY
September/Week Two

This simple meal bears repeating.

Preparation time: 30 minutes
Servings: 2
Ingredients:

10 small baby red potatoes *(halved)*
1 T. olive oil

2 boneless, skinless chicken breasts
1/2 C. chicken broth
1 large clove garlic *(smashed and chopped)*
1 tsp. honey or Dijon mustard
1/4 C. white wine

1/2 lb. fresh broccoli *(cut in 2" lengths)*

1-2 fresh peaches *(peeled, pitted and thinly sliced)*
2 lemon wedges

Notes

- **Preheat oven to 400 degrees.**
- **Place potatoes face down on oiled cookie sheet on center rack of oven. Cook 25 minutes.**
- **Place chicken breasts in small non-stick fry pan over medium-high heat with 1/4 C. of the broth and chopped garlic. When broth boils, cook 3 minutes before turning. Add remaining broth and cook other side 3 minutes.** *(As broth cooks away, breast will brown slightly on either side.)* **Reduce heat to low, turn breasts final time, and spread with mustard. Add 1/4 C. wine to pan, cover, and cook an additional 5-10 minutes.** *(If breasts are thin, cook five minutes. If they're large, cook 10 minutes.)*
- **Place broccoli in steamer basket in large, covered sauce pan with a little water. When chicken is nearly done, turn burner on high under broccoli and cook, covered, 3 minutes after water boils.**

Serve on individual plates. Flank chicken breast with potatoes and broccoli. Line plate with peach slices and garnish broccoli with lemon wedge.

TUESDAY

September/Week Two

Notes

Leftover Night

It's time once again to go after the free food.

Preparation time: 20 minutes
Servings: 2-3
Ingredients:

Anything you have there!

Have you tried making an adventure of leftover night? Try it tonight. Enjoy reheating each course just before serving, making each small entrée feel like an elegant multi-course meal.

Don't overcook leftovers! *Remember, the longer food is exposed to high heat, the more the nutritional loss. Besides, who likes wimpy, limp vegetables?*

Cook some green peas *to go with leftovers tonight. Simply place 1 C. frozen peas in a medium sauce pan with 1/4 C. water. Bring to boil and cook 1 minute. Serve immediately. What? You don't like peas? Learn to like them! Peas have 40% more fiber and more iron than green beans. They also have 25 % more vitamin A and C.*

Calories burned at home *are every bit as effective as calories burned at the gym or by playing sports. We burn 205 calories an hour laying bricks, 315 calories an hour painting the exterior of a home, and 375 calories an hour gardening.*
Fitness Without Exercise, by Bryant A. Stamford, Ph.D and Porter Shimer, Warner Books, 1992

Men, get your exercise! *Healthy men who are sedentary, especially those who are over age 55, have a significantly higher risk of stroke than healthy men who are physically active.*
American Journal of Epidemiology, Vol. 139, No. 9

Bow Tie Pasta with "Creamy" Red Sauce

WEDNESDAY

September/Week Two

I'm really fond of this simple variation on Red Sauce pasta.

Preparation time: 25 minutes
Servings: 2-3
Ingredients:

"Creamy" R*ed Sauce*
1 C. Red Sauce *(see page 248)*
1/2 C. plain, nonfat yogurt *(stirred smooth)*

12 oz. bow tie pasta

green salad fixings

2-4 T. fancy-shred Parmesan cheese
2 T. fresh chopped parsley

Notes

- **Place large kettle on stove filled 2/3 full of water. Turn heat on high and cover.**
- **Make Red Sauce.** *Use 1 C. in this recipe and reserve remainder for another meal.*
- **Stir 1 C. Red Sauce and 1/2 C. yogurt together.** *(Do not boil!)*
- **Pour dry pasta into boiling water and cook 10 minutes. Drain and rinse.**
- **Prepare green salads.**
- **Divide pasta on two plates and cover with sauce.**

Sprinkle 1-2 T. Parmesan cheese and a little chopped parsley over each serving. A glass of Merlot would taste good with this meal.

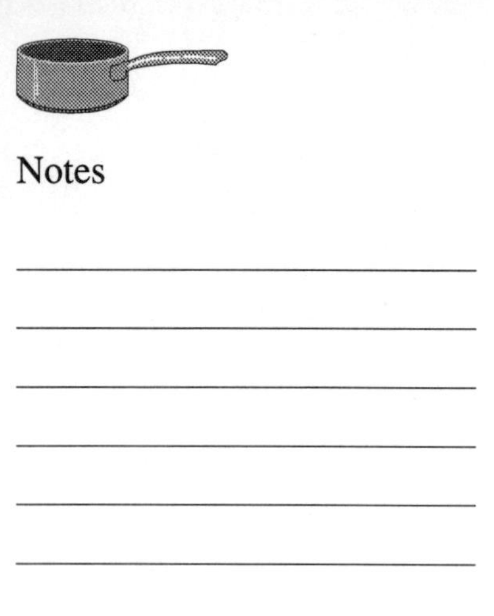

Notes

"Quick cook" rice this morning. (see p. 237)

Thai Lime Fry

Time to renew this delicious recipe!

Preparation time: 30 minutes
Servings: 2
Ingredients:

1/2-3/4 C. turkey breast fillets *(chopped fine)*
1 clove garlic *(smashed and chopped)*
1 T. vegetable oil

2 stalks celery *(chopped)*
2 slices medium onion *(chopped)*
1 large clove garlic *(smashed and chopped)*
1/2 C. broth
1/2 tsp. sesame oil

1/4 green pepper *(cut into cubes)*
1/4 red pepper *(cut into cubes)*
6 medium mushrooms *(sliced)*

1/4 C. cilantro *(chopped)*
juice from 1/2 lime
2 dozen pistachios *(shelled and chopped)*
1 package frozen spinach *(thawed and drained)*
a dash of cayenne pepper *(more if you like it hotter)*

2 C. cooked brown rice

2 Roma tomatoes *(chopped)*

- **Sauté chopped meat and garlic in oil 5 minutes over medium-high heat in large fry pan or wok until brown.**
- **Add celery, onion, garlic, broth, and sesame oil. Sauté 1 minute.**
- **Add peppers and mushrooms and sauté another 2 minutes. Remove from pan with perforated spoon and set aside.**
- **Add cilantro, lime juice, pistachios, spinach and cayenne to liquid in pan. Sauté 3 minutes.**
- **Prior to serving, warm rice on serving plates in microwave 1 minute on high.**
- **Return all ingredients to pan. Toss thoroughly.**
- **Add tomato just before serving.**

Serve over rice.

"Bogus Pork" Medallions

FRIDAY

September/Week Two

With the fall season upon us, these old-fashioned "meat and potatoes" style dinners are most appealing.

Preparation time: 40 minutes
Servings: 3
Ingredients:

3 slices medium yellow onion *(quartered)*
2 medium *(unpeeled)* russet potatoes *(sliced in 1/2" slices)*
1 T. olive oil

one 12 oz. package frozen corn
4 thin slices red bell pepper *(chopped)*
1/4 C. water

1 lb. turkey breast fillets *(sliced)*
1/4 C. flour
1 T. olive oil
2 large cloves garlic *(smashed and chopped)*
or 1 tsp. chopped prepared garlic
1/4 C. chicken broth
fresh-ground black pepper

1/4 C. white wine
1 large tart apple *(peeled, quartered, cored, and sliced in 1/4" slices)*
1 T. brown sugar
1/8 tsp. cinnamon

Notes

- **Preheat oven to 400 degrees.**
- **Place onions and potatoes on cookie sheet oiled with 1T. olive oil. Place in oven on center rack for 15 minutes. Turn and return to oven until dinner is ready.**
- **Place corn, red pepper, and water in sauce pan and set aside.**
- **Dredge sliced fillets in flour until well coated.**
- **Put remaining 1 T. oil and garlic in 10" fry pan over medium-high heat. When garlic begins to sizzle, add floured fillets. Cook until golden brown** *(3-4 minutes per side)*. *If pan gets too dry, add a little chicken broth.* **Season each side with fresh-ground black pepper.**
- **Lift fillets out of fry pan and set in oven with potatoes.**
- **Add wine to fry pan and rub bottom of pan gently with fork to lift up any drippings.**
- **Add apple slices, brown sugar, and cinnamon. Reduce heat to low, cover pan, and cook 5 minutes, stirring occasionally.**
- **While sauce is cooking, turn on burner under corn. When water boils, cover and cook 3 minutes.**

Serve fillets on individual plates covered with apples and sauce. Serve corn and potatoes on either side of fillets. Delicious!

SATURDAY
September/Week Three

Notes

SHOPPING DAY

Buy fresh ginger that is firm and plump. *It will last in the fridge for up to a month if wrapped in a paper towel and stored in a loosely closed plastic bag. It will keep up to 6 months if it is peeled, sliced, placed in a small jar, and covered with rice wine. Simply pat it dry when you're ready to use it. It can also be frozen (unpeeled). Simply grate a little with a lemon zester when you wish to use it.*
Family Circle, 110 Fifth Avenue, New York, NY 10011

Lighter salads? *Some of the items we add to green salads are quite fattening. For example: a handful of fried-in-oil croutons adds 143 calories and 7 grams of fat; 4 cheddar cheese chunks adds 9.5 grams of fat; a few spoonfuls of crumbled feta cheese adds only 3 grams of fat.*
Men's Health, 33 East Minor Street, Emmaus, PA 18098

Still smoking? *Smoking can contribute to stomach ulcers. Nicotine inhibits the production of the fatty acid prostaglandin, which is vital to protecting you stomach's lining.*
Department of Veterans Affairs Medical Center, Dallas, TX

Use green pepper in your green salad. *Just 1/2 of a green pepper provides 100% of the RDA for vitamin C.*
Nancy Clark, RD, a nutritionist with Sports Medicine, Brookline, MA

GROCERY LIST

Produce

3 white potatoes
20 baby red potatoes
2 medium red potatoes
2 medium yellow onions
1/2 lb. fresh mushrooms
2 green bell peppers
2 red bell peppers
one head bok choy
one acorn squash
1 bunch spinach
1 bunch Swiss chard
1/8 lb. fresh broccoli
green salad fixings
one large cucumber
8-10 Roma tomatoes
2 tart apples
1 fresh lemon
fresh ginger root
8 oz. dried cranberries
one orange
firm tofu
dried cranberries

Frozen Foods

3 frozen halibut fillets
If unable to purchase fresh fish or if frozen is easier for you.

Meat/Fish/Poultry

3 fresh halibut fillets *(if available) or purchase on Wednesday*
2 Italian turkey sausage links
1 lb. ground turkey breast
6-8 large, cooked, shelled shrimp
1 boneless, skinless chicken breast

Canned or Dry Foods

one 29 oz. can tomato sauce
two 15 oz. cans navy beans
two 15 oz. cans chicken broth
one 6 oz. can sliced water chestnuts
one 6 oz. can sliced bamboo shoots
12 oz. dry whole wheat spaghetti
12 oz. dry whole wheat spiral pasta
wheat germ
1/2 C. package chopped pecans or walnuts
1/2 C. package sliced almonds

Chilled Foods and Dairy

nonfat cream cheese

Buy if you're out

garlic
celery
fresh parsley
dried fennel seed
nutmeg
saltine crackers
brown rice
sesame oil
sliced almonds
fortune cookies
fresh pesto
fancy-shred Parmesan
plain, nonfat yogurt

Apple Sausage and Red Potatoes

Remember this interesting variation for ground turkey?

Preparation time: 40-45 minutes
Servings: 3
Ingredients:

8-10 baby red potatoes
1 T. olive oil

1 acorn squash

Apple Sausage Mixture

1 lb. ground turkey breast	1 clove garlic *(smashed and chopped)*
1/2 tsp. dry basil leaves	3 slices medium onion *(chopped fine)*
1/2 T. cinnamon	1 egg *(beaten)*
dash of nutmeg	3/4 C. low-salt soda crackers *(crushed)*

1 large apple *(cored and chopped into very small pieces)*

1 T. olive oil

1/4 tsp. cinnamon
1 tsp. lemon juice
2 T. brown sugar

1/2 C. white wine
1/2 C. chicken broth
2 T. flour mixed with 1/4 C. nonfat milk
4-5 turns fresh-ground black pepper
2 dashes ground nutmeg

1/2 C. plain, nonfat yogurt *(stirred smooth)*

SUNDAY

September/Week Three

Notes

- **Place potatoes , flat side down, on oiled cookie sheet in preheated 400 degree oven for 30 minutes.**
- **Cook whole squash 2 minutes on high in microwave. Remove and prick several times with fork. Cook another 5 minutes on high. Remove and cool a few minutes.**
- **In large bowl, mix turkey, spices, apple, garlic, onion, egg, and cracker crumbs.** *You may mix thoroughly with hands or use food processor.*
- **Shape mixture into tubular lengths approximately 1" by 3" in size.** *(Don't expect the shaped sausages to be perfect in appearance, as the mixture will be a bit soft and sticky.)*
- **Place shaped sausages on large plate and microwave for 3 minutes. This will bind them so that they won't fall apart while browning.** *(If you don't have a microwave, set the shaped sausages in a shallow pan and bake them in the oven for 10 minutes with potatoes.)*
- **Brown sausages in shallow fry pan with 1 T. oil over medium-high heat.** *Be sure to turn them often.*
- **When thoroughly browned** *(5 minutes)*, **lift out of pan and place in oven with potatoes.**
- **Halve squash, remove seeds, sprinkle with cinnamon, lemon juice, and brown sugar. Put in oven with potatoes and sausages.**
- **Add wine and chicken broth to fry pan and bring up any drippings over medium-high heat** *(gently rub bottom of pan with fork when wine comes to boil).*
- **Shake flour and milk vigorously in container with tight-fitting lid until will blended. Slowly stir into broth mixture. It will thicken. Season with black pepper and nutmeg. Reduce heat and cook 5 minutes stirring often.**
- **Remove white sauce from heat and stir in yogurt.**

Serve on individual plates with 2 sausages and 1/2 the potatoes on each plate. Spoon White Sauce over each sausage. Cut squash into quarters and place next to sausages.

MONDAY

September/Week Three

Notes

White Beans and Red Sauce

Hopefully you have beans in the freezer. If not, use two 15 oz. cans white beans.

Preparation time: 20 minutes *(after beans are cooked)*
Servings: 2
Ingredients:

2-3 C. cooked white beans or two 15 oz. cans *(rinsed)*

Red Sauce
one 29 oz. can tomato sauce
2 cloves garlic *(smashed and chopped)*
4 slices medium onion *(chopped)*
1 T. dry basil
2 tsp. dry oregano
cayenne pepper to taste *(optional)*

2-4 T. fancy-shred Parmesan
fresh cucumber, tomato and sweet onion *(5 slices each per serving)*
low or nonfat salad dressing

- **If using canned beans, rinse thoroughly in colander.**
- **Use leftover Red Sauce if you have it, or place tomato sauce, garlic, onion and spices in covered sauce pan. Cook 10 minutes over medium heat.**
- **Warm beans in microwave** *(set for 2 minutes).* **If you don't have a microwave, pour boiling water over beans in large bowl, let stand five minutes and drain.**

Spoon one cup cooked beans per serving in center of individual plates. Cover beans with 1/2-3/4 C. Red Sauce per serving. Garnish with Parmesan. Overlap onion, tomato, and cucumber along edge of plate and dress with lowfat salad dressing.

Hot and Sour Stir Fry

Quick and easy. Just the ticket for these cooler evenings.

TUESDAY
September/Week Three

Notes

Preparation time: 30 minutes
Servings: 3-4
Ingredients:

1 T. olive oil
1/4 tsp. sesame oil
3 thin slices medium onion *(chopped)*
2 cloves garlic *(smashed and chopped)*
1 boneless, skinless chicken breast *(chopped into 1/2" cubes)*
1/8 lb. broccoli *(cut in 2" lengths)*
2 T. low-sodium soy sauce
1/4 C. chicken broth
6 mushrooms *(sliced)*

1 1/4 C. chicken broth
1/8 tsp. cayenne pepper
1 T. white sugar
5 T. white vinegar
3 T. corn starch mixed with 1/4 C. water

5-6 deveined, cooked shrimp *(thawed)*

2-3 C. cooked rice

1 medium tomato *(chopped)*

- **Place oils in large heavy-bottomed sauce pan over high heat. Sauté onion, garlic, and chicken 5 minutes, stirring constantly.**
- **Toss in broccoli, soy sauce, and 1/4 C. broth. Sauté 2 more minutes.**
- **Add mushrooms. Sauté another minute.**
- **Remove all ingredients from pan with perforated ladle or spoon and set aside.**
- **Using same pan, mix remaining broth, cayenne, sugar, and vinegar and return to heat. Bring to boil and stir in corn starch/ water mixture. Reduce heat to low, add shrimp, and cook 3-4 minutes. Stir occasionally.**
- **Warm 3/4 C. rice per serving in microwave for 2 minutes on high, or warm rice over medium-high heat in shallow sauce pan with about 1/8 C. of water.** *Keep an eye on it so it doesn't cook down.*
- **Return vegetables and chicken to broth and add tomatoes. Toss over medium heat until everything is thoroughly coated. Serve immediately over warm rice.**

"Quick cook" some rice before work this morning. (see page 237)

Plan to eat with chopsticks, it tastes so much better that way!
Have a fortune cookie and tea to finish the meal.

Gingered Halibut

WEDNESDAY

September/Week Three

Notes

Pick up fresh halibut fillets on the way home from work this evening. If you can't find them, frozen halibut steaks will do.

We revisit another wonderful fish dinner!

Preparation time: 30 minutes
Servings: 2
Ingredients:

3 medium white potatoes *(peeled and quartered)*
1/8 tsp. dry fennel
3/4 C. water

1/4 red bell pepper *(thin sliced)*
1/2 C. white wine

15 oz. fresh halibut or 3 small halibut fillets
fresh-ground pepper

2-3 gratings fresh ginger
2 T. plain, nonfat yogurt *(stirred smooth with ginger)*

1 bunch Swiss chard *(discard stems and slice leaves in thin strips)*
1/2 C. broth
1/4 C. dried cranberries
2 T. balsamic vinegar

fresh-ground black pepper
2 T. toasted, sliced almonds *(toast under broiler)*

- **Place potatoes, fennel seed, and water in medium sauce pan and bring to boil. Reduce heat, cover, and cook 15 minutes. Remove from heat. Leave covered.**
- **Sauté 1/2 the red pepper slices in wine 1 minute. Remove peppers from pan and set aside.**
- **Place fillets in wine left over from sautéing peppers. Season with fresh-ground black pepper and poach over medium-high heat 4 minutes per side.**
- **Turn halibut in pan and spread ginger/yogurt mixture over two fillets. Top with cooked red pepper strips. If pan is dry, add 1/2 C. water or white wine. Cover and cook 4 minutes.**
- **Place chard, broth, cranberries, vinegar, and remaining red pepper in large kettle. Sauté until wilted** *(about 3 minutes).* **Reduce heat to low and cook another 4 minutes. Toss frequently.**
- **Serve on individual plates with potatoes and chard on either side of fish. Garnish chard with black pepper and toasted almonds.**

Enjoy a nice glass of chilled fumé blanc with this meal.

"Cossack" Red Potatoes and Sausage

THURSDAY

September/Week Three

A return engagement of an international favorite.

Preparation time: 30 minutes
Servings: 2-3
Ingredients:

10 baby red potatoes
1 T. olive oil

2 links Italian chicken or turkey sausage
2 T. broth

1/4 C. chicken broth with 2 dashes Tabasco® sauce
1 clove garlic *(smashed and chopped)*
1 large carrot *(peeled and sliced in 1/8" slices)*

1/2 green bell pepper *(chopped in 1" pieces)*
1/2 red bell pepper *(chopped in 1" pieces)*
one slice medium yellow onion *(quartered)*

2 T. pesto
3 T. broth
dash of Tabasco®

4 Roma tomatoes *(chopped in large pieces)*
4-6 T. fancy-shred Parmesan cheese

Notes

- **Preheat oven to 400 degrees.**
- **Wash potatoes, cut in half and place face down on oiled cookie sheet in oven.**
- **Prick sausage several times with fork. Wrap in paper towel, place in covered dish and microwave 2 minutes on high. Repeat process twice. Cool slightly and slice in 1/8" rounds.**
- **Place sausage in large fry pan and sauté with 2 T. broth 3 minutes.**
- **Add remaining broth** *(with Tabasco®)*, **garlic, and carrots. Sauté 2 minutes.**
- **Add peppers and onion and sauté an additional 3 minutes.**
- **Remove potatoes from oven and add to sausage/vegetable mixture.**
- **Mix pesto, broth, and Tabasco®.**
- **Stir chopped tomatoes and pesto mixture into sausage/vegetable/potato mixture.**

Serve immediately on individual plates and garnish with Parmesan cheese.

FRIDAY

September/Week Three

Notes

Whole Wheat Pasta with Halibut

A return engagement of this delicious seafood pasta. This time you'll vary it by adding a cup of fresh chopped spinach.

Preparation time: 25 minutes

Servings: 2-3

Ingredients:

1 1/2 C. leftover Red Sauce
or make fresh batch *(see page 248)*

2 thin slices medium yellow onion *(quartered)*
1 clove garlic *(smashed and chopped)*
1 stalk celery *(chopped in 1/2" pieces)*
1 C. fresh spinach *(chopped)*
1 T. olive oil
1/4 C. broth

12 oz. dry whole wheat spaghetti

green salad fixings

6 medium mushrooms *(sliced)*
1 cooked halibut fillet or steak
(broken into pieces with bones and skin removed)

2 T. Parmesan
2 T. fresh chopped parsley *(optional)*

- **Place pasta water on stove over high heat in large heavy-bottomed kettle.**
- **Prepare Red Sauce** *(if you don't have leftovers).*
- **Sauté onions, garlic, celery, and spinach in oil and broth 3 minutes over medium-high heat in large fry pan.**
- **Add Red Sauce and bring to boil. Cover, and remove from heat.**
- **Drop pasta into boiling water and cook 7-9 minutes.**
- **Prepare green salads.**
- **Add mushrooms and broken halibut to Red Sauce. Return to boil, cover and reduce heat to low.**
- **Drain and rinse pasta when cooked.**
- **Serve immediately on individual plates covered with Halibut Sauce.**

Garnish with Parmesan and parsley and serve with green salad. Molti bravi!

SHOPPING DAY PLUS MUFFINS

SATURDAY

September/October

The culmination of the growing season is here! Time to reap the harvest at the grocery store!

Buying sweets and snack food. *You pay the price for these items in more ways than one. Here's what it takes to work off* ***6 Hershey's Kisses:***
Do intermediate-level aerobics for 25 minutes.
Play full-court basketball for 14 minutes.
Train with weights for 25 minutes.
Play racquetball for 14 minutes.
Ride a stationary bike at 13 mph for 17 minutes.
Race walk for 9 minutes.
Swim the side stroke for 17 minutes.
Play a hard game of squash for 9 minutes.
Vitality, 8080 North Central, LB 78, Dallas, TX 75206

Grocery store trivia! *At grocery stores, men usually like to have their groceries put in paper bags; women usually choose plastic.*
Men's Health, 33 East Minor Street, Emmaus, PA 18098

Notes

Cranberry/Orange Muffins

Makes 1 dozen muffins

- Preheat oven to 375 degrees.
- Mix the following in large bowl: 1 1/2 C. unbleached flour, 1/4 C. wheat germ, 1/2 C. old-fashioned oats, 1/4 C. white sugar, 1 tsp. grated orange rind, 1 tsp. cinnamon, 1 tsp. baking powder, 1 tsp. baking soda, 1/2 C. dried cranberries, 1/4 C. chopped walnuts or pecans.
- In a separate, smaller bowl mix: 1 egg (beaten), 1 1/4 C. milk, 2 T. white vinegar, 2 T. vegetable oil.
- Stir all ingredients together (wet to dry) and place in muffin tins which have been sprayed with vegetable oil spray.
- Bake 30-35 minutes.

Serve with nonfat cream cheese or quark and your favorite jam.

GROCERY LIST

Produce

8-10 baby red potatoes
2 medium yellow onions
1 lb. fresh mushrooms
2 green bell peppers
2 red bell peppers
2 large carrots
1/8 lb. fresh broccoli
green salad fixings
one head iceberg lettuce
6-8 Roma tomatoes
1 fresh lemon

Frozen Foods

Meat/Fish/Poultry

1/2 lb. turkey breast fillets
2 boneless, skinless chicken breasts
1 lb. ground turkey breast

Canned or Dry Foods

one 29 oz. can "Ready-cut" tomatoes
three 15 oz. cans chicken broth
one 6 oz. can sliced water chestnuts
one 6 oz. can sliced bamboo shoots
16 oz. dry penne pasta
1/2 C. package whole blanched almonds
12 oz. package large egg noodles
1 loaf fresh rye bread

Chilled Foods and Dairy

3 oz. sharp cheddar cheese
whole wheat tortillas
1 bottle of beer

Buy if you're out

1 head garlic
bok choy
turkey bacon
brown rice
corn starch
paprika
cayenne pepper
dry mustard
beer
red cooking wine
pesto
salsa

SUNDAY

September/October

Jaegersnitzel

Once again, that delicious Old World meal for Sunday dinner. This version features egg noodles instead of rice.

Preparation time: 40 minutes
Servings: 2-3
Ingredients:

Notes

1 loaf fresh rye bread

2-3 C. cooked egg noodles

1 turkey breast fillet *(cut into 1" cubes)*
1 T. olive oil
2 cloves garlic *(smashed and chopped)*

1/2 medium onion *(sliced and quartered)*

one 15 oz. can chicken broth
1 large carrot *(peeled and sliced in 1/8" rounds)*
8-10 mushrooms *(thick sliced)*

1 T. paprika
1/4 tsp. white pepper
1/8 tsp. cayenne pepper
1/4 tsp. crushed rosemary leaves
1/4 tsp. dry mustard

3 T. corn starch mixed with 1/4 C. broth

1/4 C. beer

3/4 C. plain, nonfat yogurt *(stirred smooth)*

- **Wrap bread in foil and place in warm oven.**
- **Set large kettle 2/3 full of water on high heat. When water boils, add noodles and cook 7 minutes. Drain and rinse.**
- **In large, heavy-bottomed sauce pan, sauté cubed turkey with oil and garlic. Sauté over medium high heat 5 minutes, until golden brown.**
- **Add onions and sauté another 3 minutes. Remove ingredients from pan and set aside.**
- **Add broth, carrots, and mushrooms. Bring to boil and cook 3 minutes. Remove carrots and mushrooms and set aside with meat.**
- **Add all spices to broth and boil 2 minutes. Thicken with corn starch which has been mixed with 1/4 C. water.**
- **Add beer and all meat and vegetables to broth mixture. Cook 5 minutes, stirring occasionally.**
- **Remove from heat. Stir in yogurt.**

Serve over cooked noodles on individual plates with warmed rye bread.

Pasta "Prosciutto" Americano

A family favorite to start off the week.

Preparation time: 30 minutes
Servings: 2-3
Ingredients:

Chunky Red Sauce
one 29 oz. can "Ready-cut" tomatoes
2 cloves garlic *(smashed and chopped)*
1 T. dry oregano leaves
1 1/2 T. dry basil leaves
1/4 C. dry red wine
2 slices medium yellow onion *(chopped)*
a few dashes of Tabasco® sauce *(optional)*
1/2 C. leftover Red Sauce

a loaf of your favorite crusty bread

3 slices cooked turkey bacon *(cooked)*
1 1/2 C. Chunky Red Sauce

2 1/2 C. dry penne pasta *(whole wheat if you can find it)*

green salad fixings

2-4 T. fancy-shred Parmesan cheese

- **Place a large kettle 2/3 full of water on stove. Turn heat on high and cover.**
- **Strain juice from "Ready-cut" tomatoes through colander into sauce pan. Set tomato chunks aside on plate.**
- **Place all Chunky Red Sauce ingredients** *(except tomato chunks)* **in sauce pan. Bring to boil over medium-high heat and cook, covered, 8 minutes.**
- **Wrap bread in foil and place in warm oven.**
- **Add tomato chunks. Return to boil and remove from heat. Set aside.** *You will have a little over 3 C. sauce. Retain 1 1/2 C. in sauce pan for this recipe. Reserve the rest for another meal.*
- **Cook bacon and add to 1 1/2 C. Chunky Red Sauce retained in sauce pan. Return to boil, cover, and remove from heat.**
- **Drop dry pasta into boiling water and cook 8 minutes. Drain and rinse with warm water.** *Set 1/2 C. cooked pasta aside for tomorrow's recipe.*
- **Prepare green salads on individual plates.**
- **Divide remaining pasta between two plates. Cover each serving with 1/2 to 3/4 C. "Prosciutto" Americano Sauce. Sprinkle 1-2 T. Parmesan cheese over each serving.**

Serve with a crisp green salad and crusty bread.

MONDAY
September/October

Notes

Pick up a fresh loaf of crusty Italian bread today.

Cooking bacon

Wrap bacon slices in paper towel, set on plate and microwave two 2-minute cycles at high setting until crispy but not burned. If you don't have a microwave, put bacon in shallow pan covered with foil and bake 20 minutes in 400 degree oven. Lay bacon on fresh paper towel after cooking.

TUESDAY
September/October

Notes

Leftovers

What a way to start off the month! Free food! Keep up the good habits and eat your leftovers.

Preparation time: 15-20 minutes
Servings: 3-4
Ingredients:

leftover Jaegersnitzel
leftover White Beans and Red Sauce
leftover Red Sauce

Tonight your food is fast food. It's cheaper and better for you. *The average American spends $250 a year on fast food.*
The American Journal of Cardiology, Vol. 70

Remember how high in vitamin C bell peppers are? *Although green peppers are high in vitamin C, red bell peppers have nearly twice as much. Yellow and orange are even higher in vitamin C than red.*
University of California Berkeley Wellness Letter, PO Box 420148, Palm Coast, Florida, 32142

Hooray for the tomato! *A recent study found that people who ate 7 or more servings of tomato per week had a 50% to 60% lower risk of developing cancer of the mouth, esophagus, stomach, colon and rectum. Cooking does not reduce the good health effects.*
Environmental Nutrition, 52 Riverside Drive, Suite 15-A, New York, NY 10024

Trouble with canker sores? *Rinsing out the mouth with carbamide peroxide can help the healing process; it simply helps keep the sore clean.*
Family Circle, 110 Fifth Avenue, New York, NY 10011-5601

Consume whole foods. *Focus your eating habits on whole foods such as whole grains, vegetables, legumes, and fruit. Choose an apple instead of apple juice; brown rice instead of white rice, a whole baked potato instead of french fries. Less processed foods contain more fiber, which fills you up, so you feel more satisfied on fewer calories.*
Prevention's 101 Tips to Banish That Potbelly, Rodale Press, Inc., Emmaus, PA 19098

An American phenomena? *Some 8% of all meals are eaten in the car.*
American Dietetic Association, Chicago, IL

Add exercise to your daily regimen. *Americans are eating 10% fewer calories now than in 1970, but we still weigh more. The reason? We're less active.*
Self, 350 Madison Avenue, New York, NY 10017

Loaded Rice

WEDNESDAY
September/October

Time for the best meatless meal ever!

Preparation time: 25 minutes
Servings: 2
Ingredients:

8-10 baby red potatoes or 1 large russet potato
1 T. olive oil

1/2 lb. mushrooms *(sliced)*
1/4 red bell pepper *(thin-sliced)*
1 T. olive oil
1 large clove garlic *(smashed and chopped)*
1/4 C. white wine
2 slices medium onion *(quartered)*

3/4 C. chicken or vegetable broth
3 T. corn starch dissolved in 1/8 C. cold water

1 1/2 C. cooked brown rice

1 C. plain, nonfat yogurt
1 T. pesto
dash of Tabasco®

2 Roma tomatoes *(chopped)*

- **Preheat oven to 400 degrees.**
- **Wash and halve baby red potatoes. If using russet potato, wash and slice** *(unpeeled)* **in 1/2" slices. Place potatoes, flat side down, on cookie sheet oiled with one tablespoon olive oil.**
- **Sauté sliced mushrooms and bell pepper in oil with garlic, wine, and onion** *(about 4 minutes).* **When done, remove mushroom mixture from pan with perforated spoon. Set aside.**
- **Add broth to pan. Return to boil.**
- **If cooking russet potato slices, turn them now.**
- **Slowly stir corn starch mixture into boiling liquid. Reduce heat to low. Cook 5 minutes, stirring often.**
- **Add mushrooms to thickened mixture. Return to boil. Remove from heat.**
- **Warm 1 1/2 C. cooked rice 2 minutes on high in microwave on individual serving plates.**
- **Remove potatoes from oven. If using baby reds, push them into rice on individual plates. If using russets, chop into 1" pieces before sprinkling over rice.**
- **Stir yogurt, pesto, and Tabasco® together until smooth. Microwave 30 seconds on high. Stir again, and add to thickened mushroom sauce.**

Pour sauce over potato/rice mixture and garnish with fresh chopped tomato. Encore!

Notes

"Quick cook" some rice this morning before work. Cook a double batch. You'll use the other half tomorrow night. *(see page 237)*

THURSDAY
September/October

Notes

Chicken Almond Stir Fry

A repeat of that most satisfying stir fry! You'll be using "quick cooked" rice from yesterday.

Preparation time: 30 minutes
Servings: 3-4
Ingredients:

2 boneless, skinless chicken breast *(chopped into 1/2" cubes)*
1 T. vegetable oil
1/4 tsp. sesame oil
3 slices medium onion *(sliced in 1/8" thick slices and chopped)*
2 cloves garlic *(smashed and chopped)*

1/8 lb. broccoli *(cut in 2" lengths)*
2 stalks bok choy *(cubed)*
one 6 oz. can sliced water chestnuts *(drained)*
2 T. low-sodium soy sauce
one 6 oz. can sliced bamboo shoots *(drained)*
one 15 oz. can low-sodium chicken broth

6 mushrooms *(sliced)*

1/4 C. whole almonds *(toasted)*

5 T. corn starch mixed with 1/4 C. water

2-3 C. cooked rice

- **Chop raw chicken and set aside in bowl. *Important note: thoroughly wash, rinse and dry cutting board after chopping chicken before continuing to chop vegetables. I usually pour boiling water over the board after chopping raw meat.***
- **Place oils in large heavy-bottomed sauce pan or wok over high heat. Sauté onion, garlic and chopped chicken** *(about 5 minutes)* **stirring constantly.**
- **Toss in broccoli, bok choy, drained water chestnuts, 1 T. soy sauce, bamboo shoots, and 1/4 C. broth. Sauté 2 more minutes.**
- **Add mushrooms and a little more broth. Sauté another minute.**
- **Remove all ingredients from pan with perforated ladle or spoon and set aside.**
- **Toast almonds under broiler.** *(Watch carefully! It goes quickly.)*
- **Using same pan, mix remaining broth and 1 T. soy sauce. Bring to boil and thicken with corn starch/water mixture. Reduce heat and cook 3-4 minutes.**
- **Add vegetables, meat and almonds to sauce and toss until everything is thoroughly coated. Serve immediately over warmed rice on individual plates.**

Remember! Stir fry tastes better with chopsticks!

Soft Shell Tacos

FRIDAY

September/October

A delicious old favorite. (The only cooking involves the ground turkey and Red Sauce.)

Preparation time: 15-20 minutes
Servings: 3-4
Ingredients:

1 lb. cooked turkey sausage *(see page 258) Use 1/2 of the Sausage tonight, and save the rest.*
1/4 C. Red Sauce *(see page 248)*
1 clove garlic *(smashed and chopped)*
1/2 tsp. ground cumin
1 T. mild chili powder
dash of Tabasco®

1/2 green pepper *(cut in 1" cubes)*
1 clove garlic *(smashed and chopped)*
2 slices yellow onion *(chopped)*
1 T. chili powder
1/4 C. broth or water

flour or corn Tortillas

1/2 C. plain, nonfat yogurt *(stirred smooth)*
salsa
1/2 head iceberg lettuce *(chopped)*
sharp cheddar cheese *(grated)*
2-3 Roma tomatoes *(chopped)*

- **Prepare Sausage.**
- **Prepare Red Sauce.**
- **Place 1/2 of cooked sausage, Red Sauce, garlic, and spices in sauté pan. Simmer over low heat 10 minutes. Remove from pan and set aside.**
- **Using same fry pan, sauté green pepper, garlic, onions, and chili powder in broth 2 minutes over high heat. Remove from pan and place in another small bowl.**
- **Place 4 tortillas between two dinner plates and microwave 45 seconds.**
- **On individual plates, spoon yogurt and salsa onto center of each tortilla, add meat, veggies, and lettuce, and garnish with a grating of sharp cheese and chopped tomato.**

Go easy on the cheese! Only two or three draws across the grater per salad are needed.

Notes

SATURDAY

October/Week One

Notes

SHOPPING DAY

It's shopping day!

Good eating habits will cost less. *In a recent study where people with high cholesterol levels went on low fat diets, they were asked to keep track of food expenditures. Participants saved an average $1.67 per day ($610 annually) when they planned their meals with less meat and lower fat, avoided vending machines, brown-bagged lunches, and ate healthful snacks like fresh fruit. Their cholesterol levels decreased as well.*
Research at I.M. Bassett Research Institute, Cooperstown, NY; and Pennsylvania State University, University Park.

The 80-20 Rule. *If you are generally healthy, you don't need to worry about maintaining a perfect diet. If you make healthy eating choices 80% of the time, occasional high-fat or high-calorie foods the other 20% of the time won't be a problem.*
Healthwise Handbook, Healthwise Incorporated, P.O. Box 1989, Boise, ID 83701

A common misunderstanding. *Some chicken and turkey sausages may be lower-in-fat than pork or beef sausages, but the fat content is still high. Read labels. Don't be fooled by percentages. Look for grams per serving. I always use the microwave to render as much fat as possible out of any sausage before I use it in a recipe.*

GROCERY LIST

Produce

2 large baking potatoes
one 6" zucchini
2 medium yellow onions
1 lb. fresh mushrooms
1 green bell pepper
1 red bell pepper
2 large carrots
celery
1 head broccoflower
1 head Romaine lettuce
green salad fixings
1 bunch green onions
2 cucumbers
8 Roma tomatoes
1 orange
1 fresh lemon

Frozen Foods

one package frozen spinach
2 frozen sole or roughy fillets *(If you don't have time to buy fresh fish during the week)*

Meat/Fish/Poultry

2 boneless, skinless chicken breasts

Canned or Dry Foods

curry powder
ground cloves
ground coriander
powdered ginger
raisins
one 29 oz. can tomato sauce
one 15 oz. can chicken broth
one 15 oz. can cooked pumpkin
one 6 oz. can chopped black olives
one 15 oz. can whole beets *(don't buy pickled)*
16 oz. dry whole wheat penne pasta
white rice
1 C. package chopped pecans
one large, thin-crust Boboli®
1 package pita bread

Chilled Foods and Dairy

one dozen eggs
3 oz. sharp cheddar cheese
1% buttermilk *(1 quart)*

Buy if you're out

1 head garlic
1 bunch fresh parsley
pine nuts
frozen corn
frozen peas
ground anise
dry dill weed
old-fashioned rolled oats
molasses
white cooking wine
red cooking wine
part-skim mozzarella
plain, nonfat yogurt
salsa
butter

Chicken Curry

SUNDAY

October/Week One

I love a good curry! Mix the spices to your personal taste. A true curry isn't restricted to commercially prepared curry powder, it's whatever combination from a basic group of spices that seems to work best for your pallet.

Preparation time: 45 minutes
Servings: 2-4
Ingredients:

pita bread *(6-8 pieces)*

1/2 C. frozen peas
2-3 cups cooked white rice

Cucumber Relish
1 cucumber *(sliced in very thin slices)*
2 thin slices medium yellow onion *(quartered)*
1/4 cup plain, nonfat yogurt *(stirred smooth)*
1 tsp. lemon juice
2 T. fresh parsley *(chopped)*

1/4 lb. fresh white mushrooms *(sliced)*
2 thin slices of a medium yellow onion *(quartered)*
1 carrot *(cut in ribbon thin strips about 1/2" long)*
2 cloves garlic *(smashed and chopped)*
1/4 C. white wine

2 boneless, skinless chicken breasts
1/2 C. broth
1 clove garlic *(smashed and chopped)*
1/4 tsp. ground cumin
2 tsp. curry powder
1 tsp. chili powder
1/8 tsp. ground coriander
1/8 tsp. ground cloves

1/4 C. white wine
1/2 C. tomato sauce

- **Wrap pita bread in foil and place in warm oven.**
- **Add frozen peas to cooked rice in medium sized bowl. Stir well, cover, and place in microwave. Cook 2 minutes.**
- **Stir Cucumber Relish ingredients together. Refrigerate.**
- **Sauté mushrooms, onion, carrot, and garlic in wine 3 minutes. Remove from pan.**
- **Place chicken breasts in same pan with half of chicken broth and garlic. Sauté over high heat 3 minutes turning constantly. Add remaining broth and spices. Sauté another 3 minutes until lightly browned. Reduce heat to low, add a little water to pan. Cover and cook 5 minutes.**
- **Remove chicken from pan. Let chicken cool slightly and chop into bite-sized pieces.**
- **Add wine to pan. Bring to boil and stir to bring up drippings.**
- **Add tomato sauce plus any liquid left in mushroom mixture.**
- **Return chicken to pan, cover and cook over low heat 15 minutes.**
- **Add veggie mixture 10 minutes before serving.**
- **Rewarm rice in microwave prior to serving.**

Place Chicken Curry, rice, and Cucumber Relish on table in serving dishes. Let people help themselves. Serve with warm pita bread.

Notes

"Quick cook white rice during the day today. It will speed up preparations tonight. (see page 237)

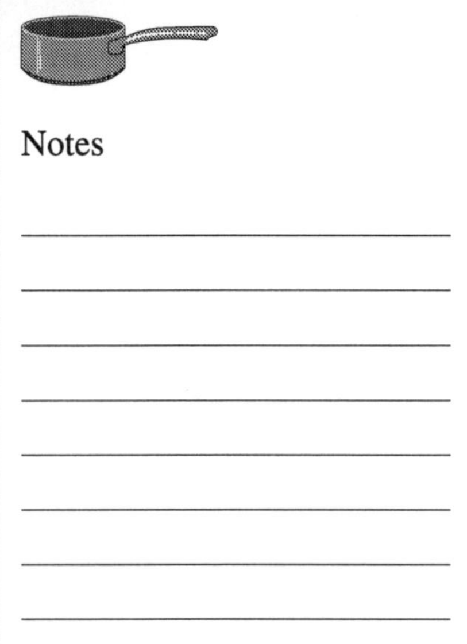

Omelet with Italian Turkey Sausage and Spinach

This omelet goes fast. You'll use leftover Red Sauce and Italian Sausage. Save 1/2 C. Italian Sausage and 3/4 C. Red Sauce for this Friday.

Preparation time: 20 minutes
Servings: 2
Ingredients:

6 eggs *(2 whole eggs and 4 whites)*
1/4 C. plain, nonfat yogurt or quark
black pepper
several dashes of nutmeg

1/2 C. Red Sauce *(use leftovers from Friday)*

1/2 C. cooked Italian Sausage *(leftovers from Friday)*

1 package frozen spinach *(thawed and drained)*
2 slices of a medium onion *(chopped)*
4 fresh mushrooms *(sliced)*
1 clove garlic *(smashed and chopped)*
1/4 C. broth
1 T. olive oil

2 T. fancy-shred Parmesan

2 T. Parmesan

2 slices of bread for toast
one orange *(sliced in thin rounds)*

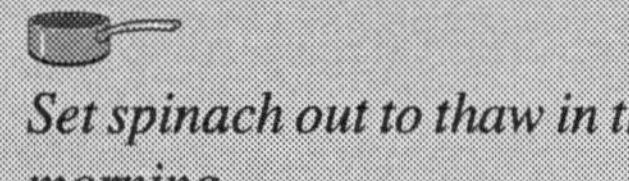

Set spinach out to thaw in the morning.

- **Break 2 eggs into medium-sized bowl. Separate whites from yolks of remaining eggs. Discard yolks and add whites to bowl with whole eggs. Beat 30 seconds with wire whisk.**
- **Stir yogurt or quark smooth and beat into eggs. Season with black pepper and nutmeg** *(set aside)*.
- **Press spinach to side of strainer with large spoon to force liquid out.**
- **Place vegetables, garlic and broth in large fry pan oiled with 1 T. olive oil and sauté 3 minutes.**
- **Remove veggies and liquid from pan and set aside.**
- ***Wash the pan before reusing or the omelet will stick down.* Recoat pan with vegetable oil spray or oil.**
- **Drain excess liquid from veggies and add to egg mixture. Beat again and pour egg mixture into pan.**
- **Cook 3 minutes over medium-high heat lifting edges and letting liquid run underneath until running egg is cooked.**
- **Place filling** *(1/2 C. Italian Sausage, vegetable mixture and Parmesan)* **down center of omelet. Fold edges over filling and cook 2 more minutes.**
- **Place a dinner plate over omelet pan and turn pan upside down while holding plate over top. You have now turned omelet out onto plate. Slide omelet back into pan so that folded seam of omelet is now on the hot surface. Cook another 3 minutes.**
- **Halve omelet and remove from pan to two serving plates. Spread 1/4 C. Red Sauce over each half and garnish with Parmesan.**

Serve with hot toast and a sliced orange for garnish.

Penne Pasta with Mushroom Sauce

TUESDAY

October/Week One

Encore! Penne Pasta with a slightly wild flavor.

Preparation time: 30 minutes
Servings: 2-3
Ingredients:

3 C. dry penne pasta

1/2 lb. mushrooms *(sliced) chop 4 mushrooms into tiny pieces*
1/2 red bell pepper *(thin sliced)*
3 cloves garlic *(smashed and chopped)*
1/4 tsp. crushed rosemary
2 thin slices medium yellow onion (*chopped fine)*
1/4 C. white wine

1/2 C. chicken or vegetable broth

3 T. flour shaken with 1/2 C. nonfat milk

3 T. shredded Parmesan
fresh-ground black pepper

green salad fixings

1/2 C. plain, nonfat yogurt *(stirred smooth)*
dash of Tabasco®

2 T. Parmesan
2 T. fresh chopped parsley *(optional)*

Notes

- **Cook pasta in large heavy-bottomed kettle 8-10 minutes. Drain and rinse.**
- **Use pasta kettle to sauté all mushrooms, red bell pepper, garlic, rosemary, and onion in wine. Sauté 3 minutes and lift mushroom mixture out of pan. Retain liquid.**
- **Add broth and bring to boil.**
- **Mix flour and milk in small container with tight-fitting lid by shaking vigorously 30 seconds until well blended.**
- **Slowly pour flour mixture into boiling liquid, stirring constantly.**
- **Add Parmesan and black pepper. Return mushroom mixture to pan. Cook 5 minutes at low heat.**
- **Prepare green salads.**
- **Remove Mushroom Sauce from heat. Add yogurt and Tabasco®.**
- **Rerinse pasta with hot water. Drain thoroughly.**
- **Gently stir pasta into Mushroom Sauce. Serve immediately.**

You've done it again!

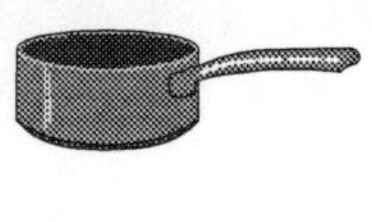

WEDNESDAY

October/Week One

Notes

"Quick cook" some rice before work this morning. *(see page 237)*

Pick up 1/2 lb. fresh sole on the way home from work tonight. You may use orange roughy if you can't get fresh sole.

Poached Sole with Nutty Rice

Time again for a nice piece of fish. You may use either sole or orange roughy.

Preparation time: 30 minutes
Servings: 2
Ingredients:

2 C. cooked rice
one clove garlic *(smashed and chopped)*
4 green onions *(chopped)*
1/4 C. toasted, chopped pecans *(toast under broiler)*
1/4 C. broth
fresh-ground black pepper

one 15 oz. can whole beets
1 tsp. butter

8-10 oz. fresh *(or frozen)* sole or orange roughy fillets
1/2 C. white wine
1 clove garlic *(smashed and chopped)*
1/4 tsp. dry dill weed

1 T. chopped parsley

- **Mix rice, garlic, onion, pecans, and broth in bowl. Season with a generous amount of fresh-ground black pepper. Cover dish and cook in microwave 2 minutes.**
- **Place beets and butter in medium sauce pan. Cover, bring to boil, and remove from heat.**
- **Slide fillets into sauté pan with wine and garlic. Turn heat on high and cook 2 minutes after wine begins boiling.**
- **Turn fillets with spatula and sprinkle with dill weed. Cover, reduce heat to medium and cook 4 minutes. If pan cooks dry, add 1/2 C. water.** *Remove pan from heat.*

Serve fish in center of individual plates. Sprinkle with a little chopped parsley. Place rice on one side. Lift beets from pan with perforated spoon and place on other side.

Baked Potato with Broccoflower

Returning to a wonder meal!

Preparation time: 15-20 minutes
Servings: 2
Ingredients:

2 large russet baking potatoes
(washed, rubbed with olive oil, and pricked with a fork)

1 head broccoflower *(cut in 2" lengths)*

1/2 C. frozen corn
1/2 C. frozen peas

3/4 C. plain, nonfat yogurt *(stirred smooth)*
sharp cheddar cheese
salsa

lemon wedges

- **Prepare potatoes in the morning prior to work.** *(You may also cook them in the microwave. Cook for three 5-minute cycles at full power. Turn the potatoes to a different position after each cycle.)*
- **Place broccoflower in steamer basket in sauce pan with a little water. Bring to boil, cover, and cook 3 minutes.** *Set timer so you don't forget.* **Remove pan and uncover when timer goes off.**
- **Measure corn and peas into separate dishes. Cover and thaw in microwave 1 minute at full power.**
- **Stir yogurt, set out cheese** *(with grater)*, **and salsa while broccoflower is cooking.**

Split potatoes and place on serving plates. Top with corn, peas, yogurt, and salsa. Garnish with a few gratings of sharp cheddar cheese. Serve broccoflower on same plate with a wedge of lemon.

THURSDAY
October/Week One

Notes

Before work this morning, wash and prick potatoes and place in oven. Set your oven for "time bake" so that they will have been cooking 1 hour when you arrive home in the evening.

FRIDAY

October/Week One

Notes

Pizza and Salad

This should be easy. You'll use leftover Red Sauce and Italian Sausage from earlier this week.

Preparation time: 25 minutes
Servings: 2
Ingredients:

1 Boboli® shell or frozen pizza shell

3/4 C. Red Sauce *(leftover from Monday)*
1 large clove garlic *(smashed and chopped)*
2 T. fancy-shred Parmesan cheese
1 dash of Tabasco®

1/2 C. Italian Sausage *(leftover)*
2 slices medium yellow onion *(quartered)*
4-6 black olives *(chopped)*
6 medium mushrooms *(sliced in 1/4" slices)*
4 T. fancy-shred Parmesan

fixings for a green salad

- **Preheat oven to 400 degrees.**
- **Place Boboli® directly on oven rack in center of oven and cook 3 minutes.** *Remove from oven.*
- **Place Red Sauce in small bowl with garlic, 2 T. Parmesan and Tabasco®. Cover bowl. Cook in microwave 2 minutes at full power, or bring to boil over medium-high heat in small sauce pan. Remove from heat.**
- **Spread Red Sauce on Boboli® crust and arrange Italian Sausage, onions, olives, and mushrooms over top. Sprinkle with remaining Parmesan and return to oven 8-10 minutes.**
- **Prepare green salads while pizza cooks.**
- **Remove pizza from oven and cut in wedges while hot.**

Let Pizza cool 5 minutes before eating.
Serve Pizza on large serving plate in center of table. Light a candle and treat yourself to a glass of beer or wine. ***It's "Pizza Friday!"***

SHOPPING DAY PLUS MUFFINS

SATURDAY

October/Week Two

Notes

Fill up, not out. *Complex carbohydrates, which come from grain foods, have less than half the calories found in fatty foods. You will get full, not fat, from eating complex carbohydrates. Good sources are whole grain breads, cereals (eat your breakfast), and pasta. US dietary guidelines suggest eating twice as many foods from the grain group than any other food group.*
The American Dietetic Association, Chicago, IL

After all that good information about diet, *I've included a special "Oktoberfest" meal this week. True, the sausages suggested are loaded with fat. I suggest rendering a good portion of the fat, but you'll still consume a heavier dose than you're used to. It's OK once in a while! You eat carefully most of the time - remember the "80-20" rule!*

Pumpkin Spice Muffins

Combine dry and wet ingredients in separate bowls. Beat wet ingredients thoroughly. Stir wet and dry ingredients together. Spoon into oiled muffin tins and cook 35 minutes at 375 degrees.

Dry

1 3/4 C. white flour
1/2 C. oats
1 tsp. baking powder
1 tsp. baking soda
1 tsp. cinnamon
1/4 tsp. nutmeg
1/4 tsp. powdered ginger
1/8 tsp., ground cloves
1/3 C. chopped pecans
1/2 C. raisins
1/4 C. white sugar

Wet

1 egg plus 2 egg whites
1 C. buttermilk
1/4 C. molasses
3 T. vegetable oil
3/4 C. cooked pumpkin
(use canned)
1 tsp. vanilla

Makes 1 dozen.

GROCERY LIST

Produce

1 lb. large red potatoes
2 medium yellow onions
1 white onion
celery
1/2 lb. fresh mushrooms
1 green bell pepper
2 red bell peppers
2 heads red cabbage
1/8 lb. fresh broccoli
1 bunch fresh parsley
1 head Romaine lettuce
green salad fixings
green or red leaf lettuce
6-8 Roma tomatoes
1 fresh slicing tomato
1 large fresh cucumber
3 tart apples
2 fresh Bartlett pears
1 fresh lime
1 fresh lemon
8-10 dried apricots

Frozen Foods

one package frozen raspberries
frozen concentrated
orange juice
5 large frozen scallops
frozen nonfat vanilla yogurt

Meat/Fish/Poultry

1 lb. assorted German-style sausages
(knockwurst, bratwurst etc.)
2 chorizo sausages
5 boneless, skinless chicken breasts
6 large, shelled, raw shrimp

Canned or Dry Foods

one 29 oz. can tomato sauce
four 15 oz. cans chicken broth
one 6 oz. can apricot nectar
grainy mustard
1/2 C package pecan halves
12 oz. dry whole wheat spaghetti
1 small box wild rice
chocolate sauce
a loaf of hearty bread

Chilled Foods and Dairy

plain, nonfat yogurt

Buy if you're out

1 head garlic
toasted sunflower meats
frozen peas
turkey bacon
garlic dill pickles
red and white
cooking wine
caraway seed
saffron threads
sesame oil
brown rice
white rice

SUNDAY

October/Week Two

Bavarian Sausage Feast

This meal is in honor of "Oktoberfest." It's one of the few times you eat such things in the course of the year, so enjoy!

Preparation time: 1 hour 30 minutes

Servings: 3-6 *(or as many as you buy for)*

Ingredients:

Notes

Hot German Potato Salad

4 slices cooked turkey bacon *(in freezer)*
1 lb. red potatoes *(cut into bite-sized pieces)*
1/2 large yellow onion *(chopped)*
1 clove garlic *(smashed and chopped)*
2 stalks celery *(chopped)*
1/4 C. white wine

1/2 C. plain, nonfat yogurt or quark *(stirred smooth)*
1 1/2 tsp. Dijon mustard
3 T. balsamic vinegar

3-4 large dill pickles *(chopped)*
fresh-ground black pepper

Rot Kohl (Red Cabbage)

1/2 - 1 head red cabbage *(chopped)*
1/2 medium yellow onion *(coarsely chopped)*
1-2 tart apples *(peeled, cored and chopped)*
3/4 C. red wine
2 tsp. caraway seeds

bratwurst	*Any combination of your favorite*
knackwurst	*Bavarian style sausages will do.*
Polish sausage	*Plan on 2 sausages per person.*

A loaf of hearty bread

grainy mustard

- **Chop 4 slices cooked turkey bacon and drop into large bowl.**
- **Boil bite-sized potato pieces 15 minutes in 1 C. water with a little salt. Drain.**
- **Sauté onion, garlic, and celery 2 minutes in white wine. Add to bowl with bacon.**
- **Mix yogurt, mustard, and vinegar together and stir into above mixture.**
- **Add pickles and cooked potatoes. Gently stir. Season with generous amount of fresh-ground black pepper. Set aside.**
- **Place all red cabbage ingredients in large sauce pan. Bring to boil. Stir occasionally. Reduce heat to low. Cook, covered, 20 minutes.**
- **Grill sausages until golden brown. Prick skins with fork while cooking to help fat escape.**
- **Rewarm potato salad in microwave just before serving.**
- **Set out bowls of potato salad and cabbage and a platter of cooked sausages. Serve cafeteria style.**

Serve with hearty bread or rolls and some grainy mustard. An icy cold glass of German beer or wine would be perfect with this meal.

Hot Chicken Salad

MONDAY

October/Week Two

We'll lighten up a bit after yesterday's "pork out."

Preparation time: 20 minutes
Servings: 2
Ingredients:

1 boneless, skinless chicken breast
1 T. olive oil
1 clove garlic *(smashed and chopped)*
1/4 C. broth
1/8 lb. broccoli *(chopped in 1" pieces)*

leftover hearty bread

Dressing
1/4 C. orange juice
1 clove garlic *(smashed and chopped)*
1/2 tsp. basil leaves
2 T. olive oil
1 T. balsamic vinegar
1/2 tsp. sesame oil

4 leaves Romaine lettuce
4 leaves green or red leaf lettuce
1/2 green pepper *(cut in thin slices)*
2 slices yellow onion *(quartered)*
2-3 Roma tomatoes *(chopped)*
1 tart apple *(cored, and chopped in small pieces)*

Notes

- **Sauté chicken breast in oil and garlic in a non-stick pan over medium-high heat 4 minutes per side.**
- **Add broth and chopped broccoli to pan and sauté another 2 minutes. Remove pan from heat and set aside.**
- **Wrap leftover bread in foil and place in warm oven.** *(If bread is hard, sprinkle few drops of water on foil.)*
- **Combine dressing ingredients and warm in small sauce pan over medium heat.**
- **Tear lettuce into large bite-size pieces and place on two large serving plates.**
- **Arrange all cold vegetables and apple on top.**
- **Slice chicken into thin slices and lay over top of salads with hot broccoli.**

Top with warm dressing and serve with a warm slice of your favorite hearty bread.

TUESDAY
October/Week Two

Notes

Pick up a loaf of hearty bread for tonight's meal.

Paella

A return to this staple in Spanish cooking. Paella originated as a peasant dish and was prepared with whatever was available. The "classic" Paella may have sausage, shrimp, various shellfish, scallops, and squid as well as a fair amount of oil. The seafood items are placed over the top just prior to cooking in the oven. This recipe is slightly scaled down with fewer seafood items and much less oil.

Preparation time: 1 hour
Servings: 2-4
Ingredients:

6-8 raw, shelled shrimp
2 chopped, spicy sausage links *(chorizo if you can find them)*
2 T. olive oil
3 cloves garlic *(smashed and chopped)*
1 medium yellow onion *(chopped)*
1/2 red and 1/2 green bell pepper *(chopped)*
1/2 C. white wine
1 1/2 C. uncooked white rice
2 C. vegetable or chicken broth
dash of cayenne pepper
2 tsp. saffron threads *(crumbled)*
6 medium white mushrooms *(sliced)*
1/2 C. frozen peas
juice from one lime
a loaf of hearty bread
2 oranges *(sliced)*
4 Roma tomatoes *(chopped)*

- **Preheat oven to 400 degrees.**
- **Clean and devein shrimp by making a slice along the back to remove vein. Rinse well to remove all shell and eggs.**
- **If using uncooked sausage, prick thoroughly with fork, wrap in paper towel and cook at full power in microwave for two 2 minute bursts. Cool and chop.**
- **Place oil and garlic in large oven-safe pan.** *A cast-iron skillet will work if you have a tight-fitting lid.* **Sauté shrimp lightly in garlic and oil. Lift out of pan. Sauté chorizo sausage in oil** *(about 2 minutes)*. **Add onions, bell peppers, and wine. Sauté 2 minutes.**
- **Add rice, broth, cayenne pepper, and saffron. Bring to boil over high heat. Reduce heat to medium. Cook, uncovered, 15 minutes stirring often.**
- **After rice has cooked 15 minutes, distribute mushrooms, shrimp, and peas around top of rice. Sprinkle with lime juice, cover, and cook 20 minutes in oven.**
- **Wrap bread in foil. Place in oven with Paella for the final 5 minutes of cooking.**
- **Slice oranges to serve on side.**
- **Remove pan from oven and sprinkle with tomatoes. Return to oven and cook another 5 minutes - uncovered.**

Set pan in middle of table and let people help themselves. Serve with warm bread and sliced oranges.

Whole Wheat Spaghetti Marinara

WEDNESDAY

October/Week Two

Pasta Marinara with a "granola" touch.

Preparation time: 25 minutes
Serves: 2-3
Ingredients:

Red Sauce
one 29 oz. can tomato sauce
2 cloves garlic *(smashed and chopped)*
or 1 tsp. commercially prepared chopped garlic
1 T. dry oregano leaves
1 1/2 T. dry basil leaves
4 thin slices medium yellow onion *(chopped)*
a few dashes of Tabasco® sauce *(optional)*

12 oz. dry whole wheat spaghetti

fixings for green salad

2-4 T. fancy-shred Parmesan cheese

Notes

- **Place large kettle filled 2/3 full of water over high heat.**
- **Place all Red Sauce ingredients in sauce pan. Bring to boil over medium-high heat. Cover, reduce heat to low, and simmer 10 minutes.**
- **Drop pasta into boiling water.** *Set timer for 8 minutes.* **Drain and rinse.**
- **Prepare green salads while pasta cooks.**
- **Divide pasta on two plates.**

Cover with 1/2 to 3/4 C. Red Sauce per serving. Sprinkle 1-2 T. Parmesan cheese over each serving. (You will have extra Red Sauce. Use it for tomorrow's leftovers or for White Beans with Red Sauce and Peppers next week).

THURSDAY
October/Week Two

Notes

Leftovers

Time once again for clean up. Be sure to eat your free food!

Preparation time: 15-20 minutes
Servings: 3-4
Ingredients:

leftover pasta
leftover Paella
leftover Red Sauce

Americans spent 46% of their food expenditures on restaurant meals, *and other food eaten away from home in 1993. This was up from 39% in 1980 and 34% in 1970.*
University of California Berkeley Wellness Letter, PO Box 420148, Palm Coast, Florida, 32142

Exercise pays long term dividends. *Regardless of your age, regular exercise pays off in a longer and healthier life. A recent 10 year study of men between the ages of 20 and 82 found that just 30 minutes of brisk daily exercise can reduce one's chances of dying prematurely up to 50%.*
Journal of the American Medical Association, Vol. 273, No. 14

Meat eaters' trivia. *Americans consumed an average of 67.3 pounds of beef in 1991. That figure is down from 77.2 pounds in 1981. During the same time frame, chicken consumption was up 23%.*
R B Magazine, 633 Third Ave., New York, NY 10017

Are you eating breakfast? *A recent study found that overweight people who started eating a morning meal lost an average of 17 pounds in 12 weeks. They also managed to maintain their weight loss better than people who skipped breakfast.*
Research at Vanderbilt University, Nashville, TN

Storing fish in the fridge? *First of all, store fish no more than 2 days. When you bring fresh fish home, wrap it loosely (so air will circulate) in moisture-proof and vapor-proof paper, and place it in the coldest part of the fridge.*
Exercise for Men Only, 350 Fifth Avenue, New York, NY 10118

Just eat nutritiously! *The number of Americans currently dieting is somewhere in the neighborhood of 48 million.*
CARE, the relief and development organization, New York, NY

Chicken Breasts with Apricot Sauce

FRIDAY

October/Week Two

Perhaps you would like to entertain tonight? Try this elegant dinner on friends.

Preparation time: 30 minutes
Servings: 4
Ingredients:

4 C. cooked rice
6 toasted pecan halves *(chopped – toast under broiler)*
1/4 C. broth
3 T. chopped parsley

8 dried apricots *(cut in half and placed in 1/4 C. water)*

4 boneless, skinless chicken breasts
2 cloves garlic *(smashed and chopped)*
1 T. olive oil
1/4 C. water or white wine

3/4 head red cabbage
6 slices medium onion

1/2 C. dry white wine
one small can apricot nectar
3 T. corn starch dissolved in 1/8 C. water

2 fresh, chilled pears *(halved and cored)*
3/4 C. frozen or fresh raspberries *(pureed)*
2 T. chocolate sauce

Notes

- **Preheat oven to 350 degrees.**
- **Mix rice, pecans, broth, and chopped parsley in bowl. Microwave 3 minutes on high. Set aside.**
- **Place chopped apricots and water in dish. Microwave 2 minutes. Set aside.**
- **Sauté chicken breasts in garlic and oil in non-stick fry pan over medium-high heat about 5 minutes per side or until golden brown. If pan gets dry, add about 1/4 C. water or white wine. When browned, place in oven for 10 minutes.** *Set fry pan aside, you will use it later as is.*
- **Place cabbage and onion in medium sauce pan with 1/2 C. water. Bring to boil, cover, and cook 10 minutes over medium heat.**
- **Mix cabbage dressing in small bowl.** *(see box)* **Pour over cabbage and blend thoroughly.** *Set aside until dinner is served.*
- **Pour wine into pan in which chicken was cooked. Rub bottom gently with fork over medium-high heat until wine boils. Add nectar and return to boil.**
- **Thicken with corn starch mixture and reduce heat to low.**
- **Add apricots with liquid and cook 5 minutes.**
- **Serve breasts on individual plates. Spoon generous amounts of apricot sauce over breasts and flank breasts with warmed rice and cabbage.**

Finish meal with chilled, fresh pear halves drenched in pureed raspberries with a drizzle of chocolate sauce. Mmmmmmmm!

"Quick cook" rice in the morning before work. Use 1 1/2 C. brown rice, 1/2 C. wild rice and 4 C. water. Bring to boil over high heat. Turn off heat and leave it for the day. Do not lift lid!

Dressing for cabbage

1 T. olive oil
2 T. balsamic vinegar
1/4 tsp. Dijon mustard
4 T. broth
2 T. orange juice
2 strips cooked turkey bacon *(chopped fine)*

SATURDAY

October/Week Three

Notes

SHOPPING DAY

Find time today to get out to the grocery store!

Shocking? *The average American consumes the fat equivalent of six sticks of butter each week. (That's a whopping 1 1/2 lb. of fat.)*
National Center for Health Statistics, Hyatville, MD

Lowfat or 2% milk *still contains 5 grams of fat per 8 oz. serving. Use 1% (2.5 grams per serving) or nonfat milk. Keep this in mind particularly if you have a daily latte.*
Runner's World, 33 East Minor Street, Emmaus, PA 18098

Undertaking a major health-related lifestyle change, *such as exercising more or eating a lower-fat diet, is hard work. It may take as long as two years before the change is second nature to you.*
David Schlundt, Ph.D. assistant professor of psychology, Vanderbilt University, Nashville, TN

Old habits die hard. *Men are more likely to call themselves "meat and potatoes" eaters (55%). Only 30% of women think of themselves in that way.*
Family Circle, 110 Fifth Ave., New York, NY, 10011

Here's to "good times!" *Over the past 10 years, heavy alcohol consumption among college students increased from 41.7% to 43%. Alcohol consumption accounts for 5% - 7% of the total calorie consumption among men.*
Healthy Weight Journal, 402 S. 14th St. , Hettinger, ND, 58639

GROCERY LIST

Produce

one 6" zucchini
3/4 lb. fresh broccoli
1/2 head green cabbage
2 medium yellow onions
1 1/2 lb. fresh mushrooms
2 green bell peppers
2 red bell peppers
1 yellow or orange bell pepper
4 large carrots
one head bok choy
green salad fixings
one large cucumber
5-6 Roma tomatoes
fresh ginger root
1 fresh lemon
1 fresh lime

Frozen Foods

frozen, concentrated orange juice
8 oz. frozen snapper *(if no access to fresh fish)*

Meat/Fish/Poultry

2-3 boneless, skinless chicken breasts
5-6 cooked, deveined shrimp
8 oz. fresh snapper *(you may wish to pick up fresh fish the day you cook it)*

Canned or Dry Foods

one 29 oz. can tomato sauce
two 15 oz. cans chicken broth
one 6 oz. can sliced water chestnuts
one 6 oz. can sliced bamboo shoots
1 small can chopped black olives
1/2 lb. dry navy beans or two 15 oz. cans beans
12-16 oz. dry whole wheat spiral pasta
8 oz. fresh cheese ravioli
fortune cookies

Chilled Foods and Dairy

Buy if you're out

one head garlic
fresh parsley
celery
frozen peas
low-sodium soy sauce
cayenne pepper
sesame oil
brown rice
brown sugar
fresh pesto
fancy-shred Parmesan

White Beans, Red Sauce & Peppers

SUNDAY

October/Week Three

Peppers are in! Try this variation on Beans and Red Sauce.

Preparation time: 20 minutes *(after beans are cooked)*
Servings: 2
Ingredients:

2 C. cooked white beans
1 1/2 C. Red Sauce *(see page 291)*
green salad fixings
1/2 red bell pepper *(cubed)* 1/2 green bell pepper *(cubed)* 4 slices medium yellow onion *(quartered)* cayenne pepper to taste *(optional)*
2-4 T. fancy-shred Parmesan

Notes

- **Prepare a batch of Red Sauce.** *Use 1 1/2 C. for tonight's meal and store the rest.*
- **Prepare green salads.**
- **Add peppers, onions, and optional cayenne pepper to 1 1/2 C. of the Red Sauce and bring to boil. Cover pan, reduce heat to low and cook 2 minutes.**

Spoon one cup cooked beans per serving in center of individual plates. Cover with Red Sauce and Peppers. Garnish with Parmesan. Serve with fresh green salad.

Cook dry navy beans during the day today. Cook extra and freeze some.

- *Start beans in morning. Wash and sort 2 cups navy beans and place in large kettle filled 2/3 full of water. Bring to boil and turn off heat. Let stand (covered) 3-4 hr.*
- *Drain water from beans. Add 8 cups fresh water and bring to boil. (Leave uncovered to prevent pan from boiling over.) Once boiling, reduce heat to low. After about 10 minutes, cover. Cook over low heat 2 hours or until tender. Remove from heat. Drain and rinse before serving.*

MONDAY
October/Week Three

Notes

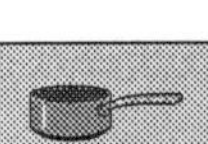

"Quick cook" rice this morning. (see page 237) Make a double batch.

You may need to pick up fresh snapper today.

Red Snapper and Pesto with Pilaf

Hopefully you'll have cooked some rice before work this morning. If not, put rice on as soon as you get home and take a break while it cooks.

Preparation time: 25 minutes
Servings: 2
Ingredients:

Rice Pilaf
3 slices medium yellow onion *(chopped)*
1 carrot *(peeled and chopped)*
1 stalk celery *(chopped)*
1/2 C. frozen peas
2 T. fresh parsley
1 clove garlic *(smashed and chopped)*
1/2 C. chicken broth mixed with 2 T. low-salt soy sauce
1 1/2 C. rice *(cooked this morning)*
fresh-ground black pepper to taste

1/2 lb. fresh broccoli *(cut in 2" pieces)*

1 large clove garlic *(smashed and chopped)*
6 thin slices of a red bell pepper
1/4 C. white wine
1 large or 2 small red snapper (or Pacific snapper) fillets

1 tsp. fresh pesto

1/2 a fresh lemon *(cut in wedges)*

- **Stir pilaf ingredients together in medium-size bowl and cook, covered, in microwave 3 minutes.**
- **Place broccoli in saucepan with 3/4 C. water in preparation for steaming.** *Don't turn on burner yet.*
- **Place garlic, bell pepper, and wine in non-stick fry pan over high heat and sauté 2 minutes. Lift red pepper out and set aside on plate.**
- **Slide fish into wine and garlic mixture over high heat. When wine boils, cook 3 minutes per side. If wine boils away, add another 1/3 C. liquid** *(wine, water, or broth)***.**
- **Turn burner on high under broccoli. When water boils, cover and cook 2 minutes.**
- **Turn fish, spread with pesto, and lay pepper strips over fish fillets.**
- **Fish and broccoli should be done at the same time.**
- **Arrange fish on individual serving plates flanked by broccoli on one side and rice on the other. Garnish with lemon wedges.**

Light a candle and enjoy a lovely dinner.

Hot and Sour Stir Fry

TUESDAY

October/Week Three

Time to spice it up with this old favorite.

Preparation time: 30 minutes
Servings: 3-4
Ingredients:

1 T. olive oil
1/4 tsp. sesame oil
3 thin slices medium onion *(chopped)*
2 cloves garlic *(smashed and chopped)*
1 boneless, skinless chicken breast *(chopped into 1/2" cubes)*

1/8 lb. broccoli *(cut in 2" lengths)*
2 T. low-sodium soy sauce
1/4 C. chicken broth
6 mushrooms *(sliced)*

1 1/4 C. chicken broth
1/8 tsp. cayenne pepper
1 T. white sugar
5 T. white vinegar
3 T. corn starch mixed with 1/4 C. water

5-6 deveined, cooked shrimp *(thawed)*

1 1/2 C. leftover cooked rice

1 medium tomato *(chopped)*

- **Place oils in large heavy-bottomed sauce pan over high heat. Sauté onion, garlic, and chicken 5 minutes, stirring constantly.**
- **Toss in broccoli, soy sauce, and 1/4 C. broth. Sauté 2 more minutes.**
- **Add mushrooms. Sauté another minute.**
- **Remove all ingredients from pan with perforated ladle or spoon and set aside.**
- **Using same pan, mix remaining broth, cayenne, sugar, and vinegar and return to heat. Bring to boil and stir in corn starch/water mixture.**
- **Reduce heat to low, add shrimp, and cook 3-4 minutes. Stir occasionally.**
- **Warm 3/4 C. rice per serving in microwave for 2 minutes on high, or warm rice over medium-high heat in shallow sauce pan with about 1/8 C. of water.** *Keep an eye on it so it doesn't cook down.*
- **Return vegetables and chicken to broth and add tomatoes. Toss over medium heat until everything is thoroughly coated. Serve immediately over warm rice.**

I love a cold beer with this meal. Eat with chopsticks! Finish with tea and a fortune cookie.

Notes

WEDNESDAY

October/Week Three

Notes

Ravioli with Red Sauce

A wonderful standby!

Preparation time: 20 minutes
Servings: 2 *(or more)*
Ingredients:

1/2 lb. fresh mushrooms
1 thin slice medium yellow onion
1 clove garlic *(smashed and chopped)*
1 T. olive oil
1/4 C. white wine

1 1/2 C. leftover Red Sauce or freshly made Red Sauce
(see page 291)

8 oz. fresh ravioli

green salad fixings

1/2 tsp. pesto
1/2 tsp. butter
2 slices bread for toast

3-4 T. fancy-shred Parmesan cheese
2 T. fresh parsley *(chopped)*

- **Put pasta water on to boil in large kettle.**
- **Sauté mushrooms, onion, and garlic 3 minutes in oil and white wine. Remove from heat.**
- **Make Red Sauce if you have no leftovers.**
- **Drop ravioli into boiling water.** *Fresh ravioli will cook in 10-12 minutes. Set a timer so you don't overcook it.* **Drain and rinse.**
- **Prepare green salads.**
- **Warm 1 1/2 C. Red Sauce if using leftovers.**
- **Mix pesto and butter together and spread on toast.**
- **Serve on individual plates. Line outside of plate with ravioli leaving a circular space in center of plate. Spoon mushrooms into center of plate with perforated spoon.** *Reserve juice.*
- **Stir juice from mushrooms into 1 1/2 C. Red Sauce. Spoon Red Sauce over ravioli and mushrooms.**

Garnish with Parmesan and parsley. Serve with green salad and Pesto Toast.

"Creamy" Pasta Prima Vera

THURSDAY
October/Week Three

Use whole wheat spirals for variation on this dish. Feel free to embellish upon the vegetable combinations to suit your own tastes.

Preparation time: 25 minutes
Servings: 3
Ingredients:

1 carrot *(peeled and sliced)*
1 C. vegetable broth or chicken broth

6 medium mushrooms *(sliced)*
2 slices medium yellow onion *(quartered)*
1 large clove garlic *(smashed and chopped)*
fresh-ground black pepper

1/2 green pepper *(chopped in 1" squares)*
1/2 red bell pepper *(chopped in 1" squares)*
one 6" long zucchini *(cut in 1/4" rounds)*
3 T. chopped black olives

2 1/2 C. dry whole wheat spiral pasta

1/2 C. white wine
3 T. corn starch *(dissolved in 1/8 C. water)*
2 dashes of Tabasco®

3/4 C. plain, nonfat yogurt
2 T. pesto

3 T. fancy-shred Parmesan
1 large Roma tomato *(chopped, use for garnish)*

Notes

- **Place pasta water on to boil in large kettle.**
- **Sauté carrot in 1/4 C. broth 2 minutes. Remove from pan.**
- **Sauté mushrooms, onions, and garlic 2 minutes in same pan. Season to taste with fresh-ground pepper. Remove from pan and set aside with carrots.**
- **Sauté peppers, zucchini, and olives using another 1/8 C. broth if needed. Sauté 1 minute. Remove from pan and set aside with other veggies.**
- **Drop pasta into boiling water and cook 8 minutes. Drain and rinse.**
- **Pour white wine, leftover broth from sauté pan, and any remaining broth into pasta kettle and bring to boil. Reduce heat and gradually stir in corn starch mixture. It will thicken. Add Tabasco® and cook over low heat 5 minutes.**
- **Stir yogurt and pesto together until smooth. Microwave 20 seconds on high to take chill off, and stir once more.**
- **Add veggies to thickened sauce. Return to boil and remove from heat.**
- **Blend yogurt mixture into vegetable sauce.**
- **Spoon over pasta onto individual serving plates in generous portions.**

Favoloso!

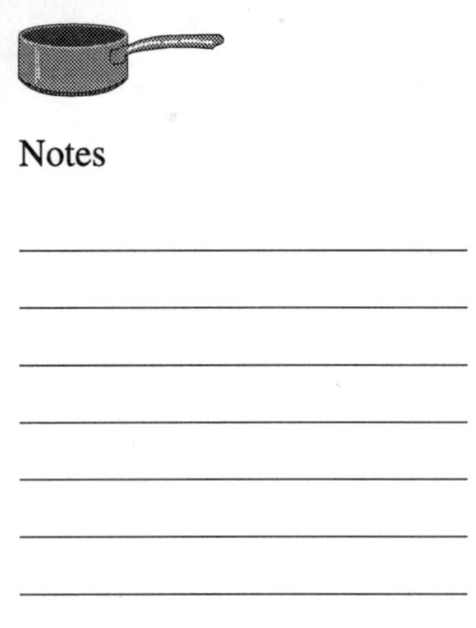

Notes

"Quick cook" some rice before work this morning. (see page 237)

Teriyaki Chicken

A light version of Teriyaki that's worth repeating.

Preparation time: 30 minutes
Servings: 2-3
Ingredients:

Teriyaki Sauce
1/2 C. white wine
1/4 C. orange juice
2 cloves garlic *(smashed and chopped)*
2 thin slices onion *(chopped very fine)*
6 T. low-sodium soy sauce
1 tsp. sesame oil
1/2 tsp. freshly grated ginger
2 T. brown sugar

2-3 C. cooked brown rice *("quick cooked" this morning)*
1/8 C. water

2-3 boneless, skinless chicken breasts
1 T. vegetable oil
1/2 C. water

1/2 head cabbage *(cored and chopped)*
2 large carrots *(peeled and sliced diagonally)*
1/8 lb. broccoli *(cut in 2" pieces)*
2 slices medium onion *(quartered)*
1/4 C. orange juice
1/4 C. Teriyaki Sauce *(from recipe above)*

1 T. fresh parsley *(chopped)*

- **Measure all Teriyaki Sauce ingredients into small sauce pan. Place over medium-high heat and bring to boil. Reduce heat to low and cook, covered, 5 minutes.** *Set aside 1/4 C. to dress vegetables.*
- **Place cooked rice plus 1/8 C. water in covered, oven-safe, bowl in 250 degree oven.**
- **Place chicken breasts in sauté pan with vegetable oil over medium-high heat. Baste chicken with teriyaki sauce. Cook 3 minutes and turn breasts. Reduce heat to medium and baste again. Add 1/2 C. water to pan, cover, and set timer for 5 minutes.**
- **Place vegetables in medium-size sauce pan with 1/4 C. orange juice. Bring to boil. Add 1/4 C. teriyaki sauce. Stir to coat all vegetables with sauce. Reduce heat and cook, uncovered, 5 minutes - stirring often.**
- **Turn chicken breasts and baste again with teriyaki sauce. Cook 2 minutes. Repeat.**

Serve on individual plates with 1 C. rice per serving in center and chicken and vegetables on either side. Sprinkle fresh parsley over rice.

SHOPPING DAY

SATURDAY
October/Week Four

Fruit makes fat-free snacks. *Check out these suggestions for healthful fat-free snacks. One medium peach (48 calories), one cup watermelon cubes (50 calories), one cup cantaloupe cubes (57 calories), one cup honeydew cubes (60 calories), one medium nectarine (60 calories).*
Good Housekeeping, 959 Eighth Ave., New York, NY 10019

Slightly cooking carrots makes them easier to digest. *One minute of cooking in boiling water helps break down the tough fibrous walls so that the body more easily accesses the nutrients. Be careful that you don't overcook since that will decrease the beta carotene.*
Runner's World, 33 E. Minor St., Emmaus, PA 18008

Storing carrots in the fridge vegetable bin *will help preserve nutrients. However, don't store them next to apples. The ethylene gas emitted by apples will give carrots a bitter flavor.*
The Food Lover's Tiptionary, by Sharon Tyler Herbst, Hearst Books, 1994

A recomended chew. *A recent study at Indiana University showed a significant reduction in cavities among young people who chewed a stick of sugarless gum for 20 minutes following a meal.*
Prevention Magazine , "Your Healthy Smile", Yun Lee, August 1996

Notes

GROCERY LIST

Produce
2 large russet baking potatoes
2 medium potatoes
4-5 baby red potatoes
one 6" zucchini
2 small turnips
3 medium yellow onions
3/4 lb. fresh mushrooms
one head broccoflower
2 green bell peppers
2 red bell peppers
3 large carrots
1/2 head green cabbage
green salad fixings
1 tart apple
6-8 Roma tomatoes
1 bunch fresh parsley
2 fresh lemons

Frozen Foods

Meat/Fish/Poultry
1 lb. turkey breast fillets
2 boneless, skinless chicken breasts
1/2 lb. ground turkey breast

Canned or Dry Foods
one 29 oz. can tomato sauce
one 29 oz. can "Ready-cut" tomatoes
one 15 oz. can "Ready-cut" tomatoes
one 15 oz. can tomato sauce
one 15 oz. can kidney beans
two 15 oz. cans chicken broth
two 6 oz. cans minced clams
8 oz. fresh angel hair pasta
12 oz. dry egg noodles
a loaf of your favorite hearty bread

Chilled Foods and Dairy
nonfat milk
3 oz. sharp cheddar cheese

Buy if you're out
one head garlic
frozen corn
dry dill weed
paprika
chili powder
powdered cumin
nonfat mayonnaise
Dijon mustard
dill pickles
honey
red and white cooking wine
plain nonfat yogurt

SUNDAY

October/Week Four

Notes

Hungarian Goulash

Great cool weather fare.

Preparation time: 40 minutes
Servings: 3-4
Ingredients:

a loaf of your favorite hearty bread

4-5 baby red potatoes *(scrubbed and cut into quarters)*
2 small turnips *(peeled and cut into pieces the same size as potatoes)*
1/4 C. water
1/4 C. red wine

1/2 lb. turkey breast fillets *(cut into 1" pieces)*
Reserve other 1/2 lb. uncooked breast for Wednesday.
1 T. olive oil
1 clove garlic *(smashed and chopped)*

one 29 oz. can "Ready-cut" tomatoes
2 large carrots *(peeled and sliced into 1/2" rounds)*
2 cloves garlic *(smashed and chopped)*
1/2 medium onion *(chopped in large pieces)*
2 T. paprika
1 tsp. oregano leaves
1 bay leaf

1 green bell pepper *(chopped into 1" chunks)*

- **Wrap bread in foil and place in warm oven.**
- **Place potatoes and turnips in medium sauce pan over high heat with 1/4 C. water and 1/4 C. red wine. When liquid boils, reduce heat to medium and cook, covered, 15 minutes.**
- **Sauté turkey pieces over medium-high heat with oil and garlic until brown.** *Wrap rest of fillets and store for Wednesday evening's meal.*
- **Drain juice from tomatoes into large sauce pan.** *(Set tomatoes aside in bowl.)* **Add carrots, garlic, onion, and spices. Bring to boil and cook 4 minutes.**
- **Add cooked turkey and bell pepper. Cook 3 minutes.**
- **Add potatoes, turnips, and tomatoes. Reduce heat to low and cook, uncovered, 3-4 minutes. Stir occasionally.**

Serve in bowls with warm bread on the side.

Angel Hair Pasta with Clam Sauce

MONDAY

October/Week Four

Remember this tasty yet lowfat version of a classic-style clam sauce pasta?

Preparation time: 30 minutes
Servings: 3
Ingredients:

12 medium-sized mushrooms *(sliced and chopped)*
1 small (6") zucchini *(split down the middle and sliced)*
1 clove garlic *(smashed and chopped)*
2/3 C. white wine

4 slices medium onion *(chopped)*
1 clove garlic *(smashed and chopped)*
1/2 C. broth
2 tsp. dry oregano
1 tsp. dry basil

two 6 oz. cans chopped clams *(with juice)*
3 dashes Tabasco®

4 T. flour
1/2 C. nonfat milk

4 T. Parmesan cheese

green salad fixings

8-12 oz. fresh angel hair pasta

3/4 C. plain, nonfat yogurt *(stirred smooth)*

2 T. fancy-shred Parmesan cheese
1 T. chopped fresh parsley

Notes

- **Place pasta water on to boil in large kettle.**
- **In heavy sauce pan, sauté mushrooms, zucchini and garlic in white wine. Sauté 2 minutes. Remove veggies from pan with perforated spoon.**
- **Place onion, garlic, broth, oregano, and basil in sauce pan and bring to boil.**
- **Add clams** *(with juice)* **and Tabasco®. Return to boil.**
- **Shake flour and 1/2 C. milk in container with tight-fitting lid until mixture is smooth.**
- **When liquid returns to boil, slowly stir in flour mixture.**
- **Add 4 T. Parmesan. Reduce heat and cook, uncovered, 5 minutes.**
- **Prepare green salads.**
- **Slide pasta into boiling water.** *Cook angel hair pasta no more than 2 minutes.* **Drain and rinse with warm water.**
- **Stir yogurt into clam sauce and serve immediately over pasta.**

Garnish with Parmesan and parsley and serve with green salad. Heavenly! Pasta della mare!

TUESDAY

October/Week Four

Notes

Leftovers

Wrap up the month by unwrapping the leftovers.

Preparation time: 15-20 minutes
Servings: 3-4
Ingredients:

Hungarian Goulash
pasta
Teriyaki Chicken
leftover Red Sauce

Tips on weight loss. *When losing weight, focus on monthly goals, not daily or weekly goals. This is helpful particularly if you have a considerable amount to lose. Never starve yourself! Eat regular meals, but concentrate on reducing fat intake. Finally, you must exercise! Walks will do.*
New Body, 1700 Broadway, New York, NY 10019

Bar none. *Candy bars will truly round out your day. If you must have a candy bar snack, try a lower fat treat like Nature's Plus Calcium Almond Bar (150 calories, 2 gm. fat) or Kellogg's Nutri-grain Cereal Bar (140 calories, 3 gm. fat). A Snickers bar has 280 calories and 14 gm. fat.*
University of California Berkeley Wellness Letter, PO Box 420148, Palm Coast, Florida, 32142

Trouble sleeping? *Eat something starchy or sweet just before bed. This will stimulate production of serotonin in the brain. The chemical has a calming effect.*
Judith Wurtman, Ph.D., Nutritionist and Researcher, Massachusetts Institute of Technology, Cambridge, MA

Bone up *on foods that are good sources of calcium. On average, Americans don't eat recommended amounts of calcium, which is important for bone density, blood clotting, muscle contraction, and enzyme activity. Good sources include nonfat milk or yogurt, calcium-fortified juices, leafy greens, and raw or lightly cooked broccoli.*
International Food Information Council Foundation, Washington, DC

Stroganoff

Here is a repeat performance of an Old World "meat and potatoes" style dinner. Don't tell people it's lowfat and they won't know. If you don't like dill pickle, the recipe provides an option.

WEDNESDAY

October/Week Four

Preparation time: 30 minutes
Servings: 2-3
Ingredients:

1/2 lb. turkey breast fillet *(thin sliced)*
1 small yellow onion *(chopped)*
2 cloves garlic *(smashed and chopped)*
1 T. olive oil

1/4 lb. mushrooms *(sliced)*

1/2 head green cabbage *(choppped)*
4 slices medium onion *(chopped)*
1 large carrot *(grated)*

1/2 C. chicken broth *(Substitute 1/2 C. wine if not using dill pickles.)*
3/4 C. nonfat milk
3 T. flour shaken with 1/4 C. nonfat milk
1 1/2 T. paprika
2 large or 3 small dill pickles *(chopped) - optional*

2 1/2 C. egg noodles

1 T. lemon juice

1/2 C. plain, nonfat yogurt *(stirred smooth)*

Notes

- **Put water for noodles on to boil.**
- **In large fry pan or cast iron skillet, sauté turkey, onion, and garlic in oil 5 minutes over medium-high heat.**
- **Add mushrooms. Sauté another 2 minutes.**
- **Remove mixture from pan and set aside. Set pan on cool burner.**
- **Place chopped cabbage, onion and grated carrot in bowl. Mix dressing** *(see box)* **and stir into cabbage mixture. Set aside.**
- **Pour broth in same fry pan over medium-high heat and swirl with fork to bring up drippings.**
- **Add 3/4 C. milk and bring to boil. Reduce heat to medium and remove pan from burner while you shake flour and milk mixture.**
- **Return pan to heat, return to boil, and slowly stir in flour mixture.**
- **Add paprika and pickle. Reduce heat to low and cook 5 minutes. Stir occasionally.**
- **Cook noodles now.** *Set timer for 8 minutes.* **Drain and rinse.**
- **Add meat mixture and lemon juice to sauce. Cook 3 minutes. Stir occasionally.**
- **Stir yogurt into meat sauce just before serving.**

Serve over noodles on individual plates with cabbage slaw on the side.

Dressing for Slaw
2 T. nonfat mayonnaise
1 T. honey
1/2 tsp. Dijon mustard
2 T. nonfat yogurt

THURSDAY

October/Week Four

Notes

Place potatoes in oven on "time bake" before work this morning.

Set Chili out of freezer to thaw in morning. If you have no Chili in freezer, use Quick Chili recipe.

Baked Potato with Chili

A return to the wonder meal! The chili makes it feel like a different meal.

Preparation time: 15-20 minutes
Servings: 2
Ingredients:

2 large russet baking potatoes
(washed, rubbed with olive oil and poked with a fork)
2 C. frozen chili from freezer or see recipe for Quick Chili on this page
fixings for green salad
3/4 C. plain, nonfat yogurt *(stirred smooth)*
sharp cheddar cheese

- **Prepare potatoes in the morning.** *(You may also cook them in the microwave. Cook three 5-minute cycles at full power. Turn the potatoes to a different position after each cycle.)*
- **Place Chili in small pan over medium heat, or in covered glass bowl in microwave.** *Warm thoroughly. Or follow the recipe for Quick Chili below.*
- **Make green salads.**
- **Stir yogurt, set out cheese and grater.**

Split potatoes and place on serving plates. Top with Chili and yogurt. Garnish with a few gratings of sharp cheddar cheese. Have a crisp salad to complete this meal.

Quick Chili

Ingredients:

1/2 lb. ground turkey breast
1/2 medium onion *(chopped)*
1 clove garlic *(smashed and chopped)*
1/2 green bell pepper *(chopped)*
1/2 red bell pepper *(chopped)*
1/2 C. broth
2 T. chili powder
1 tsp. powdered cumin
1 tsp. dried oregano leaves
1/2 C. red wine
one 1 oz. can tomato sauce
one 15 oz. can kidney beans *(rinsed)*
one 15 oz. can "Ready cut" tomatoes

- **In large fry pan, sauté first 5 ingredients in broth 5 minutes over high heat.**
- **Add spices, wine and tomato sauce. Reduce heat to medium and cook 5 minutes.**
- **Add beans and "Ready-cut" tomatoes, bring to boil. Serve.**

Dilled Chicken Breasts

Another delicious theme and variation on chicken breasts.

FRIDAY

October/Week Four

Preparation time: 30 minutes
Servings: 2
Ingredients:

2 medium russet potatoes *(sliced in 1/4" slices - skins on)*
1 T. olive oil
3 slices medium yellow onion *(quartered)*
fresh-ground black pepper

2 boneless, skinless chicken breasts
1 T. olive oil
1 large clove garlic *(smashed and chopped)*
1/2 C. white wine
1/4 tsp. dill weed

1/2 lb. fresh broccoflower *(cut in 1" pieces)*

1/2 lemon *(cut in wedges)*
1 tart apple *(thin sliced)*

Notes

- **Preheat oven to 400 degrees.**
- **Place potatoes flat side down on oiled cookie sheet. Sprinkle with onions and season with fresh-ground black pepper. Slide into oven and bake 15 minutes.**
- **Place chicken breasts in small non-stick fry pan with oil and garlic. Brown each side over medium-high heat. Add wine and sprinkle with dill. Reduce heat to low and cook 5 minutes per side.**
- **Turn potatoes to brown other side.**
- **Place broccoflower in steamer basket in saucepan with 3/4 cup water. Turn burner on high just before dinner is served. When water boils, cover and steam 3 minutes.**

Serve chicken breasts flanked by potatoes and broccoflower. Spoon a little juice from pan over breasts. Place a wedge of lemon on each plate. Don't forget the apple! Divide it between plates and fan out slices as garnish.

SATURDAY
November/Week One

Notes

SHOPPING DAY

Do you have everything you need for the coming week? Grab your shopping bags and sashay off to the store!

***A recent conference on calcium intake sponsored by The National Institutes of Health** offered some suggestions concerning natural calcium intake. Good sources:*

- *Dairy products are among the best sources.*
- *Acidophilus milk, yogurt, and hard cheeses are most easily tolerated if you are sensitive to dairy products.*
- *Calcium fortified fruit juices are a good source.*
- *Broccoli is rich in calcium.*

Your daily calcium intake goal:

All women 25 to 50 and men 23 to 65 - 1,000 mg.
All young adults under 25 - 1,200 to 1,500 mg.
All women over 50 and men over 65 - 1,500 mg.

(Nonfat frozen yogurt is an excellent source. One of my favorite desserts or snacks is nonfat frozen yogurt with fresh fruit.)

You've probably decided who you will be having over for Thanksgiving dinner. Suggest that the guest who loves baking bring pies for dessert. (You supply the nonfat frozen yogurt for topping.)

GROCERY LIST

Produce

one 6" zucchini
8-10 baby red potatoes
3 medium russet potatoes
2 large beets
2 medium yellow onions
1 lb. fresh mushrooms
1 green bell pepper
1 red bell pepper
3 large carrots
1 lb. fresh broccoli
green salad fixings
8 Roma tomatoes
1 tart apple
1 fresh lemon

Frozen Foods

3 frozen halibut fillets or steaks
(if you don't have access to good fresh fish)

Meat/Fish/Poultry

1 lb. ground turkey breast
1 boneless, skinless chicken breast
3 fresh halibut fillets *(You may wish to buy fresh fish on Thursday.)*

Canned or Dry Foods

one 29 oz. can tomato sauce
one 29 oz. can "Ready-cut" tomatoes
two 15 oz. cans chicken broth
12 oz. dry multi-colored spiral pasta
1 package spinach lasagna noodles
1 package egg lasagna noodles
one 6 oz. can chopped black olives
one large, thin-crust Boboli®
loaf of hearty Italian bread

Chilled Foods and Dairy

4 oz. part-skim mozzarella
one dozen eggs
plain, nonfat yogurt
lowfat Ricotta cheese

Buy if you're out

1 head garlic
1 bunch fresh parsley
brown rice
fancy-shred Parmesan
rubber gloves *(You'll need them to handle beets this week.)*

Lasagna

SUNDAY
November/Week One

Lasagna with a slightly different twist. Use a combination of egg and spinach noodles. Save all leftover Red Sauce for Tuesday's dinner.

Preparation time: 40 minutes *(45 minutes cooking time)*

Servings: 4-6

Ingredients:

Italian Turkey Sausage
- 1 T. olive oil
- 1 lb. ground turkey breast
- 2 slices medium yellow onion *(chopped)*
- 2 tsp. dry basil leaves
- 1 tsp. dry oregano leaves
- 1/2 tsp. ground anise
- 2 large cloves garlic *(smashed and chopped)*
- dash of Tabasco® sauce

- 1 C. cooked Italian Turkey Sausage *(see above)*

- 1 1/2 C. Red Sauce *(see page 291)*

- 4 spinach lasagna noodles and 4 egg lasagna noodles

- 1/2 C. plain, nonfat yogurt
- 1/2 C. part-skim or lowfat Ricotta cheese
- 1 egg
- 1 tsp. corn starch

- 1 T. olive oil
- 8 sliced fresh mushrooms
- 6 oz. part-skim mozzarella
- 3 oz. shredded Parmesan

- fixings for a green salad

- a loaf of your favorite Italian bread

Notes

- **Place pasta water on to boil. Preheat oven to 350 degrees.**
- **Cook Italian Sausage while you wait for water to boil.**
- **Assemble Red Sauce.**
- **Slide noodles into boiling water and set timer for 10 minutes.**
- **Remove sausage from heat when cooked and set aside.**
- **Blend yogurt, Ricotta cheese, egg, and corn starch with electric mixer, or in food processor.**
- **Rub a 9" X 13" glass baking dish with 1 T. olive oil and layer ingredients as follows:**
  - **1 layer of noodles**
  - **1/2 C. Italian Sausage**
  - **1/2 C. Red Sauce**
  - **1/2 C. Ricotta cheese mixture**
  - **all mushrooms**
  - **another layer of noodles**
  - **5 oz. of the mozzarella**
  - **1/2 C. sausage**
  - **1/2 C. Red Sauce**
  - **1/2 C. Ricotta cheese mixture**
  - **another layer of noodles**
  - **1/2 C. Red Sauce**
  - **Remaining mozzarella and Parmesan**
- **Cook on center rack of oven, uncovered, 40 minutes.**
- **Make green salads while lasagna is cooking.**
- **Remove lasagna from oven and cool for 15 minutes before serving.**
- **Wrap bread in foil and place in oven while lasagna cools.**

Light some candles and have a nice glass of red wine.

MONDAY

November/Week One

Notes

"Quick cook" some rice before work this morning. *(see page 237)*

Loaded Rice

This miracle meal will start off the week.

Preparation time: 25 minutes
Servings: 2
Ingredients:

8-10 baby red potatoes or 1 large russet potato
1 T. olive oil

1/2 lb. mushrooms *(sliced)*
1/4 red bell pepper *(thin-sliced)*
1 T. olive oil
1 large clove garlic *(smashed and chopped)*
1/4 C. white wine
2 slices medium onion *(quartered)*

3/4 C. chicken or vegetable broth
3 T. corn starch dissolved in 1/8 C. cold water

1 1/2 C. cooked brown rice

1 C. plain, nonfat yogurt
1 T. pesto
dash of Tabasco®

2 Roma tomatoes *(chopped)*

- **Preheat oven to 400 degrees.**
- **Wash and halve baby red potatoes. If using russet potato, wash and slice** *(unpeeled)* **in 1/2" slices. Place potatoes, flat side down, on cookie sheet oiled with one tablespoon olive oil.**
- **Sauté sliced mushrooms and bell pepper in oil with garlic, wine, and onion** *(about 4 minutes).* **When done, remove mushroom mixture from pan with perforated spoon. Set aside.**
- **Add broth to pan. Return to boil.**
- **If cooking russet potato slices, turn them now.**
- **Slowly stir corn starch mixture into boiling liquid. Reduce heat to low. Cook 5 minutes, stirring often.**
- **Add mushrooms to thickened mixture. Return to boil. Remove from heat.**
- **Warm 1 1/2 C. cooked rice 2 minutes on high in microwave on individual serving plates.**
- **Remove potatoes from oven. If using baby reds, push them into rice on individual plates. If using russets, chop into 1" pieces before sprinkling over rice.**
- **Stir yogurt, pesto, and Tabasco® together until smooth. Microwave 30 seconds on high. Stir again, and add to thickened mushroom sauce.**

Pour sauce over potato/rice mixture and garnish with fresh chopped tomato. Enjoy!

Pasta Prima Vera

TUESDAY

November/Week One

Tonight it's Red Sauce prima vera. You should have leftover Red Sauce from making Lasagna last Sunday.

Preparation Time: 30 minutes
Servings: 2
Ingredients:

2 1/2 C. dry spiral pasta

1 T. olive oil
1/2 tsp. crushed garlic
1 large carrot *(peeled and sliced)*
2 slices medium onion *(quartered)*

1/4 C. broth *(use vegetable if you are cooking vegetarian)*
1/2 medium green pepper *(cubed in 1" chunks)*
1 small zucchini 6" long *(cut in 1/8" rounds)*
6 medium mushrooms *(sliced in 1/4" slices)*

1 1/2 C. Red Sauce *(leftover from last Sunday)*

2 Roma tomatoes *(cut in 1" chunks)*

2-4 T. fancy-shred Parmesan cheese
4 T. chopped black olives

Notes

- **Place pasta water on to boil in large sauce pan.**
- **Drop dry pasta into boiling water and cook 8 minutes.** *(Set a timer so you don't forget.)* **Drain and rinse.**
- **Measure olive oil and garlic into sauté pan over medium-high heat. Start with carrot and onion. Sauté 1 minute.**
- **Add broth, green pepper, zucchini, and mushrooms. Sauté 2 minutes. Remove veggies from pan and set aside.**
- **Pour 1 1/2 C. Red Sauce into same pan used to cook pasta. Bring to boil.**
- **Add all vegetables** *(including Roma tomatoes)* **to sauce and remove from heat.**
- **If pasta is cold, microwave 1 minute on high to reheat, or measure 1 to 1 1/2 C. per serving and place in bowl with boiling water for 1 minute prior to serving. Drain and rinse in colander.**
- **Divide pasta onto separate plates and ladle veggie sauce over it.**

Garnish with Parmesan and chopped olives and serve immediately.

WEDNESDAY

November/Week One

Notes

Leftovers

It's been awhile since we last met with our old friends in the back of the fridge. Time to renew old acquaintances!

Preparation time: 15-20 minutes
Servings: 3-4
Ingredients:

leftover Stroganoff
leftover Hungarian Goulash
leftover lasagna

Make a green salad to freshen up the leftovers tonight. *Throw some chopped, tart apple on top.*

Another reason to watch your fat intake and exercise regularly. *36% of American women and 31% of American men over age 20 are overweight. On average, we weigh 8 lb. more than a decade ago. The definition of "overweight" is 20% above desirable weight. How does that translate into actual pounds? A woman 5'4" would be packing an additional 25 lb.; a man 5' 10" an additional 30 lb.*
Journal of the American Medical Association, Volume 272, No. 3

Mushrooms are mushrooming! *You're using lots of mushrooms in my recipes. They're an excellent source of vitamins: a serving (1.5 cups) provides 25% of the daily requirement of niacin, lots of B vitamins, 10% of daily iron needs, and lots of potassium. They're low in calories and have no fat or sodium. It's best to cook mushrooms, since some can contain toxic substances in their raw state.*

Baked Halibut

You may use fresh or frozen halibut fillets or halibut steaks. Whichever you use, you only need about 4 oz. per serving. I often buy the bags of frozen halibut steaks at the local warehouse store (your supermarket may have them), and keep them in the freezer. Tonight you will cook one extra and freeze it. It will be used next week.

THURSDAY

November/Week One

Notes

Preparation time: 30 minutes
Servings: 2
Ingredients:

2 whole cooked beets

3 medium white potatoes *(unpeeled, washed, and quartered)*
1 clove garlic *(peeled)*
3/4 C. water

1 small clove garlic *(smashed and chopped)*
1/4 tsp. grated ginger
1/8 C. plain, nonfat yogurt

three 4-6 oz. fresh or frozen halibut fillets *(if frozen, thaw before cooking)*
1 T. olive oil
fresh-ground black pepper

2 tsp. lemon juice
1/2 tsp. butter

1/8 C. nonfat milk
2 tsp. butter

dash of paprika

- **If you were unable to cook beets on "time bake" today, use microwave method. Place beets in shallow bowl. Cook two 5-minute cycles. Prick with fork. If beets are still too firm, cook one more 3-minute cycle. Remove to cool.**
- **Or – remove cooked beets from oven.** *Adjust "time bake" controls to manual operation and temperature to 450 degrees.*
- **Place potatoes, garlic, and water in medium sauce pan over medium-high heat. When water boils, reduce heat to low and cook, covered, 15 minutes.**
- **Mix garlic and ginger with yogurt.**
- **Place halibut in oiled pan or oven-proof dish. Grind fresh pepper over halibut.**
- **Spread yogurt mixture over two of the halibut fillets, cover dish with foil, and place on center rack of 450 degree oven.** *(Set timer for 20 minutes.)*
- **Wearing rubber gloves, rub beets briskly under cold running water. Skins will come off easily. Slice in 1/8" slices. Set aside.**
- **Measure lemon juice and butter in small dish and microwave 15 seconds on high.**
- **Mash potatoes with leftover water and garlic.**
- **Add 1/8 C. milk and 2 tsp. butter and continue mashing.**
- **Serve halibut on two plates, flanking fish with mashed potatoes and beets. Drizzle lemon/butter mixture over beets. Sprinkle a dash of paprika over potatoes.**

Wrap extra fillet and store in freezer. This meal is excellent with a cold glass of Fumé Blanc.

In the morning before work, wash beets and cut off greens. Wrap in foil and place in oven on "time bake" for 1 hour at 400 degrees. Set timer to complete cooking just as you're arriving home.

You may need to stop and pick up 2/3 lb. fresh halibut after work today.

FRIDAY

November/Week One

Notes

White Pizza and Salad

Don's White Pizza!

Preparation Time: 25 minutes
Servings: 2
Ingredients:

White Sauce
1/2 C. broth
1/4 C. white wine
1 clove garlic *(smashed and chopped)*
3 slices medium onion *(chopped fine)*
2 tsp. dry oregano leaves
2 T. corn starch dissolved in 1/8 C. water
3 T. fancy-shred Parmesan
Bring broth, wine, garlic, onion, and oregano to boil.
Thicken with corn starch mixture and add Parmesan.
Reduce heat to low. Cook 5 minute. Remove from heat.

1 cooked boneless, skinless chicken breast *(sliced in thin slices)*
1 T. olive oil
1 large clove garlic *(smashed and chopped)*

1 Boboli® shell or frozen pizza shell

1 dash of Tabasco®
1/8 C. plain, nonfat yogurt *(stirred smooth)*

2 slices medium yellow onion *(quartered)*
1/2 red bell pepper *(chopped)*
6 medium mushrooms *(sliced)*

4 T. fancy-shred Parmesan cheese

fixings for a green salad

- **Preheat oven to 400 degrees.**
- **Prepare White Sauce.** *Follow directions in box.*
- **Sauté chicken breast in oil and garlic over medium-high heat in small sauté pan. Cook about 5 minutes per side turning every 2 minutes. If it starts to get too dark, add 1/4 C. water to pan and reduce heat. When cooked, slice into thin strips.**
- **Place Boboli® directly on oven rack in center of oven and cook 3 minutes.**
- **Stir Tabasco® and yogurt into 3/4 C. white sauce.**
- **Spread white sauce on Boboli® crust and arrange onions, peppers, and mushrooms over sauce. Arrange sliced chicken over veggies and top with remaining Parmesan. Return to oven 8-10 minutes.**
- **Prepare green salads while pizza cooks.**
- **Remove pizza from oven and cut in 8 wedges while hot.**

Serve the Pizza on individual serving plates a few slices at a time with fresh green salad.

SATURDAY
November/Week Two

SHOPPING DAY

More bad news about soda pop. *Most sodas are high in phosphorous, which inhibits calcium absorption. If you or a family member drink 3-4 cans of soda per day (with up to 12 tsp. sugar per can), you may wish to consider cutting back. Teenagers, who consume large amounts of soda, should be concerned about loss in bone density and excessive weight gain.*

Fresh grapes are great, healthful snacks. *Expensive? Perhaps a little. However, we think nothing of spending $2-$3 per week on snack items! Grapes keep best if stored in an open container in the fridge. Fruit and vegetable prices vary a great deal throughout the year, but the nutritional value for the money is still a good bargain.*

Perish the thought! *The average American eats 6,991 hot dogs and 8,389 hamburgers in a lifetime. (If that's the average, some of us are eating more than our share!)*
In An Average Lifetime, by Tom Heymann, Fawcett Columbine, 1994

Insomnia? *Try eating a fresh bagel before retiring for the night. (Spread it with a little quark. Wash it down with a glass of nonfat milk.) The carbohydrates in bagels stimulate insulin production. This, in turn, helps the brain absorb tryptophan, a sleep inducing enzyme.*
Sleep, the Gentle Tyrant, by Wilse B. Webb, Anker Publishing, 1994

Notes

GROCERY LIST

Produce

- one 6" zucchini
- 8-10 baby red potatoes
- 2 medium yellow onions
- 1 lb. fresh mushrooms
- 2 green bell peppers
- 2 red bell peppers
- celery
- one bunch collard greens or kale
- 3 large carrots
- 1/2 lb. fresh broccoli
- bok choy
- 1/8 lb. fresh green beans
- one head iceberg lettuce
- red leaf lettuce
- green salad fixings
- one head green cabbage
- 7-9 Roma tomatoes
- 1 cucumber
- 3 oz. fresh green beans
- 1 fresh lemon
- 1 fresh lime
- 2 crisp apples
- fresh ginger root
- toasted sunflower meats

Frozen Foods

- orange juice
- 1 frozen halibut fillet *(if you don't have a leftover fillet in freezer)*

Meat/Fish/Poultry

- 5 boneless, skinless chicken breasts
- 2 links hot Italian sausage
- 1 lb. turkey breast fillets

Canned or Dry Foods

- one 29 oz. can tomato sauce
- one 29 oz. can chopped tomatoes
- two 15 oz. cans chicken broth
- three 15 oz. cans vegetable broth
- one 15 oz. can kidney beans
- one 15 oz. can garbanzo beans
- 12 oz. dry penne pasta
- 12 oz. dry whole wheat spiral pasta
- a loaf of your favorite hearty bread *(olive or seed bread if you can find it)*

Chilled Foods and Dairy

- whole wheat tortillas
- 3 oz. sharp cheddar cheese
- fresh salsa

Buy if you're out

- 1 head garlic
- 1 bunch parsley
- frozen corn
- frozen peas
- ground cumin
- dried rosemary
- chili powder
- honey mustard
- sesame oil
- brown rice
- capers
- white cooking wine
- plain, nonfat yogurt

SUNDAY

November/Week Two

Notes

Minestrone Soup

What a wonderful cold weather staple. I've added a couple Italian sausages to give it a more robust quality. The secret to a great soup meal is a loaf of excellent bread. I like an olive bread or Italian seed bread with Minestrone.

Preparation time: 25 minutes
Servings: 2
Ingredients:

1 loaf of your favorite hearty bread

one 29 oz. can chopped tomatoes
three 15 oz. cans vegetable broth
1/2 medium yellow onion *(chopped)*
2 cloves garlic *(smashed and chopped)*
1 stalk celery *(chopped)*
dash of Tabasco®
3 T. dry sweet basil leaves
1 T. dry oregano leaves
1/8 lb. fresh green beans *(cut in 1" lengths) - frozen will do*
1/2 green bell pepper *(chopped)*
1 medium carrot *(sliced)*
1 small zucchini *(chopped)*
5-6 mushrooms *(sliced)*
one 15 oz. can garbanzo beans *(drain and use 1/2 can)*
1 small can red kidney beans *(drain and use 1/2 can)*
1/2 C. frozen corn

1/2 C. dry cooked pasta

fixings for a green salad

shredded Parmesan cheese

- **Wrap bread in foil and place in 200 degree oven.**
- **Place large kettle on burner over high heat. In order listed, add all ingredients in large box above. Bring to boil. Cover and cook 10 minutes.**
- **Cook a handful of any dry pasta in the cupboard. Drain and rinse.**
- **Remove soup from heat, add cooked pasta, cover, and let stand 5-10 minutes.**
- **Prepare green salads.** *Sprinkle a few leftover garbanzo and kidney beans over salads.*
- **Garnish each bowl of soup with 2 T. shredded Parmesan.**

Serve with warm bread and green salad.

Hot Fajita Salad

MONDAY

November/Week Two

Notes

A return to this light dinner. This is a favorite with my 20-something kids!

Preparation time: 30 minutes

Servings: 2-4

Ingredients:

1 lb. turkey breast fillets *(cut in 1/8" strips)*
1 T. olive oil
2 cloves garlic *(smashed and chopped) or 1 tsp. commercially prepared chopped garlic*
1 tsp. chili powder
1/4 tsp. ground cumin

1/4 C. broth
1 green bell pepper *(cut in 1" chunks)*
1 red bell pepper *(cut in 1" chunks)*
3 slices of a medium sweet onion *(quartered)*
1 tsp. chili powder
1/4 tsp. ground cumin

several leaves red leaf lettuce *(broken)*
1/2 head chopped iceberg lettuce
4 ripe Roma tomatoes *(chopped)*
8 slices peeled cucumber *(chopped)*

1 C. quark *(prepared this morning) stir before serving*
salsa

2 T. toasted sunflower seeds

4 whole wheat flour tortillas

- **Slice turkey breast fillets.**
- **Place poultry in shallow 10" non-stick fry pan with oil, garlic, 1 tsp. chili powder, and 1/4 tsp. ground cumin over medium-high heat and sauté 5 minutes.**
- **Remove meat from pan and set aside.**
- **Add broth, peppers, onions, and remaining spices to same pan and sauté 3 minutes. Lift vegetables out with perforated spoon and set aside.**
- **Lay broken leaf lettuce on plates and top with chopped iceberg lettuce. Sprinkle with tomato and cucumber.**
- **Spoon fajita mixture over lettuce and sprinkle with tomato and cucumber.**
- **Top with quark and salsa to taste and garnish with a few toasted sunflower seeds.**
- **Warm tortillas in microwave by placing them between two serving plates and cooking 20 seconds on high, or warm in oven at 350 degrees 5 minutes in shallow, covered pan.**

Roll warmed tortillas and serve on side.

Make some quark this morning before work.

Quark

Line a strainer with a large coffee filter. Measure 2 C. nonfat yogurt into filter. Place over a bowl and set in fridge for the day.

TUESDAY

November/Week Two

Notes

Penne Pasta with Mushroom Sauce

Ah, the wonders of mushrooms! Here's a great vitamin-laden pasta with both mushrooms and red bell pepper.

Preparation time: 30 minutes
Servings: 2-3
Ingredients:

1/2 lb. dry penne pasta

1/2 lb. mushrooms *(sliced - chop 4 mushrooms into tiny pieces)*
3 cloves garlic *(smashed and chopped)*
1/2 red bell pepper *(slice in 1/4" slices about 1" long)*
2 thin slices medium yellow onion *(chopped fine)*
1/4 C. white wine

1 C. chicken or vegetable stock
3 T. flour *(shaken with 1/2 C. nonfat milk)*
fresh-ground black pepper

green salad fixings

3 T. shredded Parmesan

1/2 C. plain, nonfat yogurt
dash of Tabasco®

2 T. Parmesan
1 T. fresh parsley *(chopped)*

- **Cook pasta in large heavy-bottomed kettle 8-10 minutes. Drain and rinse.**
- **Use pasta kettle to sauté all mushrooms, garlic, pepper, and onion in wine. Sauté 3 minutes and lift mushroom mixture out of pan.**
- **Add broth and bring to boil.**
- **Place flour and milk in small container with tight-fitting lid and shake vigorously for 30 seconds until well blended.**
- **Slowly pour flour mixture into boiling liquid, stirring constantly. Season with a few turns black pepper. Cook 5 minutes.**
- **Prepare green salads on individual plates.**
- **Add Parmesan and mushrooms to White Sauce. Return to boil.**
- **Remove White Sauce from heat. Add pre-stirred yogurt and Tabasco®.**

Gently stir pasta into White Sauce and serve immediatly. Garnish with Parmesan and parsley.

Mustard-Glazed Chicken Breasts

WEDNESDAY

November/Week Two

Good, hearty, meat-and-potatoes-style cooking for cooler weather.

Preparation time: 30 minutes
Servings: 2
Ingredients:

10 small baby red potatoes
1 T. olive oil

2 boneless, skinless chicken breasts
1/2 C. chicken broth
1 large clove garlic *(smashed and chopped)*
1 tsp. honey mustard
1/4 C. white wine

1 bunch collard greens, mustard greens or kale *(leaves broken and stems discarded)*
2 tsp. olive oil
1/4 C. broth
juice from 1 lemon
1 clove garlic *(smashed and chopped)*
1/4 red bell pepper *(sliced very thin)*

2 apples *(cored and thinly sliced)*

Notes

- **Preheat oven to 400 degrees.**
- **Place potatoes face down on oiled cookie sheet. Place in hot oven.**
- **Place chicken breasts in small non-stick fry pan over medium-high heat with 1/2 of the broth and chopped garlic. When broth boils, cook 3 minutes before turning. Add remaining broth and cook other side 3 minutes.** *(As broth cooks away, breast will brown slightly on either side.)*
- **Spread mustard on each breast and turn final time. Add 1/4 C. wine to pan, reduce heat to medium, cover, and cook an additional 5-10 minutes.** *(If breasts are thin, cook 5 minutes. If they're large, cook 10 minutes.)*
- **Wash greens thoroughly and place in strainer. Heat oil, broth, lemon juice, and garlic in large heavy-bottomed kettle over medium-high heat. Add greens and pepper slices. Toss until leaves are thoroughly wilted. Cover, reduce heat to low and cook 7 minutes. Lift out with tongs and serve immediately.**
- **Surround chicken breasts with potatoes, greens, and sliced apple.**

Light a candle. Put on some music and have a nice glass of chardonnay with this meal.

THURSDAY

November/Week Two

Whole Wheat Pasta with Halibut

Were returning to this theme and variation on marinara sauce. Use whole wheat spaghetti or spirals if you can find them, and the halibut you froze last week.

Preparation time: 25 minutes
Servings: 2-3
Ingredients:

Red Sauce
one 29 oz. can tomato sauce
2 cloves garlic *(smashed and chopped)*
1 T. dry oregano leaves
1 1/2 T. dry basil leaves
4 thin slices medium yellow onion *(chopped)*
a few dashes of Tabasco® sauce *(optional)*

2 thin slices medium yellow onion *(quartered)*
1 clove garlic *(smashed and chopped)*
1 stalk celery *(chopped in 1/2" pieces)*
1 T. olive oil

1 1/2 C. Red Sauce *(see above)*

2 1/2 C. dry whole wheat pasta

green salad fixings

6 medium mushrooms *(sliced)*
1 cooked halibut fillet or steak *(broken into pieces with bones and skin removed)*

2 T. Parmesan
2 T. fresh chopped parsley *(optional)*

Notes

- **Place pasta water on stove over high heat in large heavy-bottomed kettle.**
- **Prepare a new batch of Red Sauce.**
- **Sauté onions, garlic, and celery in oil 3 minutes over medium-high heat in large fry pan.**
- **Add 1 1/2 C. Red Sauce and bring to boil. Cover, and remove from heat.**
- **Drop pasta into boiling water and cook 7-9 minutes.**
- **Prepare green salads.**
- **Add mushrooms and broken halibut to Red Sauce. Return to boil, cover, and reduce heat to low.**
- **Drain and rinse pasta when cooked.**
- **Serve immediately on individual plates covered with Halibut Sauce.**

Garnish with Parmesan and parsley and serve with green salad.

Molti bravi!

Teriyaki Chicken

One last time this year! "Don's Teriyaki Dinner" with additions.

Preparation time: 30 minutes

Servings: 2-3

Ingredients:

Teriyaki Sauce
1/2 C. white wine
1/4 C. orange juice
2 cloves garlic *(smashed and chopped)*
2 thin slices onion *(chopped very fine)*
6 T. low-sodium soy sauce
1 tsp. sesame oil
1/2 tsp. freshly grated ginger
2 T. brown sugar

2-3 C. cooked brown rice *("quick cooked" this morning)*
1/8 C. water

2-3 boneless, skinless chicken breasts
1 T. vegetable oil
1/2 C. water

1/2 head cabbage *(cored and chopped)*
1 C. bok choy *(chopped)*
2 large carrots *(peeled and sliced diagonally)*
1/8 lb. broccoli *(cut in 2" pieces)*
2 slices medium onion *(quartered)*
1/4 C. orange juice
1/4 C. Teriyaki Sauce *(from recipe above)*

3 Roma tomatoes *(chopped)*

1 T. fresh parsley *(chopped)*

- **Measure all Teriyaki Sauce ingredients into small sauce pan. Place over medium-high heat and bring to boil. Reduce heat to low and cook, covered, 5 minutes.** *Set aside 1/4 C. to dress vegetables.*
- **Place cooked rice plus 1/8 C. water in covered, oven-safe, bowl in 250 degree oven.**
- **Place chicken breasts in sauté pan with vegetable oil over medium-high heat. Baste chicken with Teriyaki Sauce. Cook 3 minutes and turn breasts. Reduce heat to medium and baste again. Add 1/2 C. water to pan, cover, and set timer for 5 minutes.**
- **Place vegetables in medium-size sauce pan with 1/4 C. orange juice. Bring to boil. Add 1/4 C. Teriyaki Sauce. Stir to coat all vegetables with sauce. Reduce heat and cook, uncovered, 5 minutes - stirring often.**
- **Turn chicken breasts and baste again with Teriyaki Sauce. Cook 2 minutes. Repeat.**
- **Add chopped tomatoes to vegetable mixture and stir to coat with sauce just prior to serving.**

Serve on individual plates with 1 C. rice per serving in center and chicken and vegetables on either side. Sprinkle fresh parsley over rice.

FRIDAY

November/Week Two

Notes

"Quick cook" some rice before work this morning. *(page 237)*

SATURDAY
November/Week Three

Notes

SHOPPING DAY

When I go to the supermarket *I always start in the produce section and fill my cart with produce first. I'm less likely to buy things I don't need when the cart is full of fresh fruits and vegetables.*

I usually read the label on breakfast cereal before making a purchase. *Cereals should be low in sugar but high in fiber (3-5g or more) to provide the best nutritional value. Chopping a little fresh fruit (bananas or berries) over the top of your cereal adds additional fiber.*

When buying fresh broccoli, look for broccoli with a deep green color and crisp leaves. *Buds should be tightly closed. When you get home, store it in an airtight plastic bag in the vegetable drawer.*
The Food Lover's Tiptionary, by Sharon Tyler Herbst, Hearst Books, 1994

GROCERY LIST

Produce

6-8 medium russet potatoes
8-10 baby red potatoes
1 medium yellow onion
1 bunch green onions
1 1/2 lb. fresh mushrooms
1 acorn squash
1 green bell pepper
1 red bell pepper
1 lb. fresh broccoli
green salad fixings
4 Roma tomatoes
1 mediium tomato
2-4 tart apples
one bunch fresh parsley
1 fresh lemon

Frozen Foods

Meat/Fish/Poultry

1 lb. ground turkey breast
2 boneless, skinless chicken breasts
10 oz. orange roughy fillets *(keep frozen)*

Canned or Dry Foods

one 29 oz. can tomato sauce
two 15 oz. cans chicken broth
one 15 oz. can vegetable broth
one 6 oz. can sliced water chestnuts
one 6 oz. can sliced bamboo shoots
12 oz. dry bow tie pasta
1/2 C. package pecan halves
1/2 C. package roasted cashews
raisins

Chilled Foods and Dairy

3 oz. sharp cheddar cheese
plain, nonfat yogurt
eggs
shredded Parmesan

Buy if you're out

1 head garlic
frozen corn
frozen peas
saltine crackers
brown rice
low-sodium soy sauce
sesame oil
Worcestershire sauce
brown sugar
cinnamon
dried rosemary leaves
white cooking wine
pesto

Turkey Meat Loaf

SUNDAY
November/Week Three

Ah yes! Old World comfort food on a cold evening.

Notes

Preparation time: 1 hour and 30 minutes
Servings: 3-4
Ingredients:

Meat Loaf
- 1 lb. ground turkey breast
- 1 C. crushed saltine crackers
- 1 clove garlic *(smashed and chopped)*
- 2 thin slices onion *(chopped very fine)*
- two egg whites *(slightly beaten)*
- 1 tsp. dry oregano leaves
- 2 tsp. dry basil leaves
- 1/2 tsp. ground black pepper
- 1/3 C. chicken broth
- 1/4 tsp. crushed rosemary leaves

Tomato Glaze
- 1/2 C. leftover Red Sauce
- 1 T. brown sugar
- 1 T. Worcestershire sauce

- 2-4 medium-sized baking potatoes *(one per person)*

- 2 green onions *(chopped fine)*
- 1 C. quark

- 1/4 red bell pepper *(chopped)*
- 2 cups frozen whole kernel corn
- 1/4 C. chicken broth

- 2 tart apples *(sliced in thin slices)*

- **Preheat oven to 375 degrees.**
- **In large bowl mix all Meat Loaf ingredients. Mix with hands until will blended.**
- **Prepare Tomato Glaze by mixing Red Sauce, brown sugar, and Worcestershire in small bowl.**
- **Pack Meat Loaf into medium-sized loaf pan and cover top with Tomato Glaze.**
- **Wash potatoes and prick with fork. Rub with a little olive oil and place in shallow pan.**
- **Place Meat Loaf and potatoes in 375 degree oven. Cook 1 hour. Remove Loaf from pan while hot. Cool 10 minutes before serving.**
- **Stir green onions and quark together.**
- **Mix red bell pepper, corn and broth in small sauce pan. Bring to boil and cook 1 minute. Remove from heat.**
- **Core and slice apple.**
- **Slice Meat Loaf. Place on individual plates with corn, split baked potato and apple slices.**
- **Set onion/quark mixture on table to dress potatoes.**

Make some quark this morning.

Quark
Line a strainer with a large coffee filter. Measure 2 C. nonfat yogurt into filter. Place over a bowl and set in fridge today.

Yahoo! Great home cookin'!

MONDAY

November/Week Three

Bow Tie Pasta with Mushroom Red Sauce

This will feel like a totally different dish with bow tie pasta.

Preparation time: 25 minutes
Servings: 2-3
Ingredients:

Notes

12 oz. bow tie pasta

3/4 lb. mushrooms *(sliced - chop 4 mushrooms in tiny pieces)*
1/2 red bell pepper *(chopped)*
1 clove garlic *(smashed and chopped)*
2 thin slices medium yellow onion *(chopped fine)*
1/8 C. white wine

1 1/2 C. Red Sauce *(If no leftovers, see page 320)*

green salad fixings

1 clove garlic *(smashed and chopped)*

2 T. Parmesan
2 T. fresh chopped parsley *(optional)*

- **Cook pasta in large heavy-bottomed kettle 8-10 minutes. Drain and rinse.**
- **Use pasta kettle to sauté all mushrooms, bell pepper, garlic, and onion in wine. Sauté 3 minutes and lift veggies out of pan with perforated spoon.**
- **Prepare a new batch of Red Sauce if necessary.**
- **Prepare green salads.**
- **Pour 1 1/2 C. Red Sauce into kettle used to cook pasta and mushrooms. Add additional garlic and bring to boil.**
- **Return mushrooms to kettle with Red Sauce and garlic. Bring to boil and remove from heat.**
- **Gently stir pasta into Mushroom Red Sauce.**
- **Serve immediately on individual plates. Garnish with Parmesan and parsley.**

Serve with crunchy green salad.

Bravo!

Orange Roughy with Pesto

Roughy is so versatile! This fish lends itself to many variations.

TUESDAY

November/Week Three

Preparation time: 25 minutes
Servings: 2
Ingredients:

8 pecan halves - *toasted under the broiler (chopped)*
3 slices medium yellow onion *(chopped)*
1 1/2 C. rice *("quick cooked" this morning)*
1/2 C. chicken broth
fresh-ground black pepper

1/2 lb. fresh broccoli *(cut in 2" lengths)*

1 large clove garlic *(smashed and chopped)*
6 thin slices of a red bell pepper
1/4 C. white wine

1 large or 2 small roughy fillets

2 tsp. fresh pesto

1/2 fresh lemon *(cut in wedges)*

- **Place pecans, onions, and rice in bowl with broth. Season with fresh-ground black pepper. Cook, covered, in microwave 3 minutes on high.**
- **Place broccoli and 1/2 C. water in covered sauce pan.** *Wait to turn on burner.*
- **Place garlic, bell pepper, and wine in non-stick fry pan over high heat and sauté 2 minutes. Remove red pepper and onion with perforated spoon and set aside.**
- **Slide fish into wine and garlic mixture over high heat. When wine boils, cook 3 minutes per side.** *Set timer so you don't forget.* **If wine boils away add another 1/3 C. liquid** *(wine, water or broth)*.
- **Turn fish, spread with pesto and lay sautéed pepper strips over fish fillets.**
- **Turn burner on high under broccoli. When water boils, cover and cook 2 minutes.**
- **Arrange fish on individual serving plates flanked by broccoli on one side and rice on the other. Garnish with lemon wedge.**

Light a candle and enjoy a lovely dinner.

Notes

"Quick cook" some rice before work this morning. (see page 237) Make a double batch. You'll use the rest on Friday.

Notes

Chicken Breasts with Mushroom Sauce

Winter squash makes a delightful addition to this recipe.

Preparation Time: 30 minutes

Servings: 2

Ingredients:

1 acorn squash

3-4 medium potatoes *(peeled and quartered)*
3/4 C. water
1 clove garlic *(peeled)*

Topping for Squash
1/2 apple *(cored and chopped)*
juice from 1/2 lemon
1 tsp. butter
2 T. raisins
1/4 medium onion *(chopped)*
cinnamon

1/2 lb. fresh white mushrooms *(sliced - chop 4 mushrooms into tiny pieces)*
2 thin slices of a medium yellow onion *(quartered)*
1 clove garlic *(smashed and chopped)*
1/4 C. white wine

2 boneless, skinless chicken breasts
1/4 C. chicken broth
1 clove garlic *(smashed and chopped)*

1/2 C. broth
1/4 C. white wine
3 T. corn starch *(dissolved in 1/4 C. water)*

1/8 C. nonfat milk
1 tsp. butter

- **Preheat oven to 400 degrees.**
- **Microwave whole squash 2 minutes on high. Remove and prick several times with fork. Continue microwaving 6 minutes on high.** *Let cool 5 minutes.*
- **Place potatoes in medium sauce pan with water and garlic. Bring to boil, cover, and reduce heat.** *Peek at them in about 5 minutes to be sure the water hasn't boiled away.*
- **In 12" fry pan, sauté all squash topping ingredients 2 minutes. Set aside in dish.** *Rinse pan and reuse for next step.*
- **In same 12" fry pan, sauté mushrooms, onion and garlic in wine 3 minutes. Remove veggies from pan with perforated spoon. Set aside.**
- **Cut squash in half, remove seeds and pulp, and spoon apple mixture into each half.**
- **Bake, uncovered, in preheated oven until dinner is served.**
- **Place chicken breasts in same pan used for mushrooms with half of the chicken broth and garlic. Sauté over medium-high heat 3 minutes turning once. Add remaining broth and sauté another 3 minutes until lightly browned. Reduce heat to low, add a little water to pan. Cover and cook 5 minutes per side.**
- **Remove chicken from pan. Add broth and wine. Bring to boil and stir to bring up drippings. Thicken with corn starch mixture. Reduce heat. Cook 5 minutes. Add mushrooms to sauce.**
- **Mash potatoes with garlic. Add nonfat milk and butter as you finish mashing.**

Serve chicken breast and a scoop of potatoes covered with mushroom sauce. Place squash along side.

Leftovers

THURSDAY

November/Week Three

This month we'll keep the fridge cleaned out since we'll need the space next week. Round 'em up! Clean 'em out!

Preparation time: 15-20 minutes
Servings: 3-4
Ingredients:

leftover Minestrone Soup
leftover Meat Loaf
leftover pasta
leftover squash

Notes

More on equality! *A recent Yale University study has debunked the theory that men carry less body fat than women. The study found that men and women both average about 23% body fat.*
Research at Yale University School of Medicine, New Haven, CT

Are you getting any exercise? *The average American woman spends 30 hours per week watching TV. If she were to spend half that time walking, she could walk the distance from San Francisco to New York in one year.*
Self, 350 Madison Avenue, New York, NY 10017

A word about "lite" or "low calorie" frozen dinners. *Those that are low in fat, salt, and calories are "lite" because the portions are very small. If you must eat one, add some fresh fruit or salad to the meal.*
Center for Science in the Public Interest, Washington, DC

Sad but true! *Only 35% of American families eat dinner together every night.*
US Department of Agriculture Survey, Washington, DC

The price is right! *The US Department of Agriculture recommends that in maintaining good nutrition one should drink at least eight 8 oz. glasses of water per day.*

FRIDAY

November/Week Three

Notes

Broccoli/Cashew Stir Fry

It's been a long time since you had this delicious meal.

Preparation time: 30 minutes
Servings: 2-3
Ingredients:

1 T. olive oil
1/4 tsp. sesame oil
1/4 C. vegetable broth *(open one 15 oz. can)*
3 slices medium onion *(chopped)*
2 cloves garlic *(smashed and chopped)*
1/2 lb. broccoli *(cut in 1" pieces)*

6 mushrooms *(sliced)*
1/2 C. roasted cashews
1/2 red bell pepper *(cubed)*
1/2 C. sliced, peeled water chestnuts
1/2 C. sliced bamboo shoots
2 T. low-sodium soy sauce

1 1/4 C. vegetable broth *(remainder of can)*
2 T. corn starch mixed with 1/4 C. water

1 medium tomato *(chopped)*

3/4 C. leftover cooked rice *(per person)*

- **Place oils and broth in large heavy-bottomed sauce pan or wok over high heat. Sauté onion, garlic, and broccoli 2 minutes stirring constantly.**
- **Add mushrooms, cashews, red pepper, water chestnuts, bamboo shoots, and soy sauce. Sauté an additional 2 minutes.**
- **Remove all ingredients from pan with perforated ladle or spoon and set aside on large plate.**
- **Using same pan, add remaining broth and bring to boil.**
- **Thicken with corn starch water mixture. Reduce heat and cook 3-4 minutes.**
- **Return vegetables to pan and add tomatoes. Stir to coat with sauce and remove from heat.**
- **Warm 3/4 cup rice per serving in microwave 2 minutes. If you don't have a microwave, warm rice over medium-high heat in shallow sauce pan with 1/8 C. water. Keep an eye on it so it doesn't cook down.**
- **Spoon stir fry over rice on individual plates and serve immediately.**

Chopsticks anyone?

SHOPPING DAY

SATURDAY

November/Week Four

Today you'll stock up for the Thanksgiving feast. *I usually buy everything early, except the turkey. I order a fresh bird and pick it up the day before Thanksgiving. To feed the masses and provide adequate leftovers, I figure about 2 lb. per person, i.e., a 12 lb. bird for 6 people. You may not be able to get fresh turkey conveniently, so frozen will do just fine. Keep it frozen until approximately 48 hours prior to cooking.*

You should use leftover turkey gravy *within 2 days of Thanksgiving. Gravy will jell when refrigerated but thins nicely when rewarmed. Add a few tablespoons of water as you warm it. It is suggested that leftover gravy be brought to a rolling boil before being reused.*
Parents, 685 Third Ave., New York, NY 10017

The grocery list today is extensive. *Get your supplies early and avoid the rush at the grocery store. It's easier to find needed ingredients like unseasoned, unbuttered stuffing mix, canned cranberries, etc., when you shop early.*

Stressing out over the thought of cooking Thanksgiving dinner? *Turn the dinner into a potluck. Invite family or friends to bring one of the dishes that make up the meal. You can orchestrate what people bring even to the point of supplying them with a recipe suggestion. If they don't cook, assign them a relish tray, canned cranberries, or good rolls from your favorite bakery. This can also reduce your costs if money is tight. Everyone sharing in the meal is more in the spirit of the holiday.*

I have planned groceries to feed 4-8 people on Thanksgiving.

Notes

GROCERY LIST

Produce

- 5 lb. russet potatoes
- 3 sweet potatoes or yams
- 3 large yellow onions
- celery
- 1/2 lb. fresh mushrooms
- 1 green bell pepper
- 2 red bell peppers
- 1 lb. carrots
- 1 lb. fresh broccoli
- 4-6 tart apples
- green salad fixings
- red leaf lettuce
- green leaf lettuce
- one large cucumber
- 4 Roma tomatoes
- 1/4 lb. dried cranberries
- 1 fresh lemon

Frozen Foods

- frozen corn

Meat/Fish/Poultry

- 1 frozen turkey *(if not ordering a fresh bird)*
- 1/2 lb. turkey breast fillet
- 2 lb. ground turkey breast *or 1 lb. ground turkey breast and 1 lb. lean ground pork*
- turkey bacon
- 2 boneless, skinless chicken breasts

Canned or Dry Foods

- one 29 oz. can tomato sauce
- 2 bags or boxes dried bread for stuffing *about 32 oz. (buy unseasoned and unbuttered)*
- 1 C. package slivered almonds
- one 15 oz. can pickled beets
- one 15 oz. can pitted black olives
- six 15 oz. cans chicken broth
- two 15 oz. cans whole cranberries
- two 6 oz. cans sliced water chestnuts
- 12 oz. dry spinach spiral pasta
- 8 oz. fresh fettuccine
- a loaf of hearty bread
- dinner rolls *you may wish to pick them up fresh on Wed.*

Chilled Foods and Dairy

- nonfat milk

Buy if you're out

- 1 head garlic
- dried thyme
- dried bay leaf
- dried sage
- dried rosemary
- butter-flavor cooking spray
- gravy separator
- eggs

SUNDAY

November/Week Four

Notes

Potato Soup

Great cold weather fare!

Preparation time: 30 minutes
Servings: 3-4
Ingredients:

hearty bread
2 pieces cooked turkey bacon
3 large russet potatoes *(peeled and cut in 1" chunks)*
1 clove garlic *(smashed and chopped)*
1 medium yellow onion *(chopped)*
1 large carrot *(chopped)*
2 stalks celery *(chopped)*
1/2 red bell pepper *(chopped)*
1 bay leaf
3 dashes Tabasco® sauce
1/4 C. frozen corn
two 15 oz. cans chicken or vegetable broth
1 C. nonfat milk
1 T. butter
5 T. flour mixed with 1/4 C. milk *(shaken until smooth)*
fresh-ground black pepper
2 T. fresh parsley *(chopped fine)*
3/4 C. plain, nonfat yogurt *(stirred smooth)*

- **Wrap bread in foil and place in warm oven.**
- **Layer bacon in glass dish 4 strips to a layer. Separate with a layer of paper towel.** *(Cook no more than 3 layers at once.)* **Microwave two 2-minute cycles at high setting until crispy but not burned. Repeat if necessary. If you don't have a microwave, put bacon in shallow pan covered with foil and bake 20 minutes in 400 degree oven. Lay bacon on fresh paper towel after cooking.** *(Freeze leftovers.)*
- **Place turkey bacon, potatoes and all other items in shaded area in large heavy-bottomed sauce pan. Bring to boil over high heat. Reduce heat to low, cover, and cook 20 minutes.**
- **Add milk and butter - return to boil. Slowly pour flour/milk mixture into soup to thicken. Continue stirring.**
- **Add pepper and parsley. Reduce heat and cook 5 minutes.**
- **Stir yogurt in just prior to serving.**

Serve with hearty bread.

Pasta Marinara

It's so easy it almost seems like a break from cooking.

MONDAY

November/Week Four

Preparation time: 25 minutes
Servings: 2-3
Ingredients:

a loaf of hearty Italian seed bread

Red Sauce
one 29 oz. can tomato sauce
1 T. olive oil *(optional)*
2 cloves garlic *(smashed and chopped)*
1 T. dry oregano
1 1/2 T. dry basil leaves
4 thin slices medium yellow onion *(chopped)*
a few dashes of Tabasco® sauce *(optional)*

8 oz. fresh egg fettuccine

green salad fixings

2-4 T. fancy-shred Parmesan cheese

Notes

- **Place large kettle filled 2/3 full of water over high heat.**
- **Place all Red Sauce ingredients in sauce pan. Bring to boil over medium-high heat. Cover. Reduce heat to low. Simmer 10 minutes.**
- **Drop pasta into boiling water.** *Set timer for 3 minutes.* **Drain and rinse.**
- **Make green salad while pasta is cooking.**
- **Divide pasta on two plates.**
- **Cover each serving with 1/2 to 3/4 C. Red Sauce. Sprinkle 1-2 T. Parmesan cheese over each serving.**

Serve with green salad and hearty bread.

TUESDAY

November/Week Four

Notes

If you are cooking a frozen Turkey on Thanksgiving, you should set the frozen bird on a platter in the fridge to begin thawing this morning.

Tyrolean Stew

Time to warm your bones on a cold winter night.

Preparation time: 30 minutes
Servings: 3-4
Ingredients:

2 medium russet potatoes *(unpeeled and quartered)*
1 T. olive oil

1/2 lb. turkey breast fillet *(cubed)*
1 T. olive oil
1 clove garlic *(smashed and chopped)*

1 C. leftover Red Sauce
1/8 teaspoon dried rosemary leaves *(crushed)*
1 large carrot *(peeled and sliced diagonally in 1/8"slices)*
2 slices medium yellow onion *(quartered)*
1/2 green bell pepper *(cut in 1" cubes)*
1/2 red bell pepper *(cut in 1" cubes)*

- **Place potatoes on oiled cookie sheet in 400 degree oven.** *Set timer for 10 minutes.*
- **In large, heavy-bottomed sauce pan, sauté cubed, raw turkey with oil and garlic over medium-high heat 5 minutes or until browned. Remove from pan and set aside to cool.**
- **Turn potatoes to another flat side and continue cooking.**
- **Measure Red Sauce into same pan used to cook turkey and add crushed rosemary leaves.**
- **Add carrot, bring to boil and cook 2 minutes, stirring occasionally.**
- **Add onion and boil 1 minute.**
- **Add peppers and boil 1 minute.**
- **Add cooked turkey and potatoes, cook 1 more minute.**

Serve in bowls with toasted leftover bread.

Leftovers

Tonight you'll have leftovers. You'll need the extra time to make dressing.

WEDNESDAY

November/Week Four

Notes

Preparation time: 15-20 minutes
Servings: 3-4
Ingredients:

leftover Potato Soup
leftover Tyrolean Stew

Make a green salad to go with leftovers - *chop a tart apple over the top. Finish the salad with a sprinkle of toasted sunflower seeds.*

If thawing a frozen turkey, *it's unwise to leave it on the counter to thaw overnight. Turkey should be thawed slowly (over the course of a day or two) in the fridge.*

Do not stuff the turkey with warm stuffing before going to bed! *Once again, this is very dangerous. Store the stuffing and turkey separately in the fridge. Stuff it in the morning just before putting it into the oven.*

You will probably have extra stuffing after filling turkey cavities. *Place extra stuffing in an oiled, covered casserole dish and store in the fridge. Cook about 1 hour before dinner.*

About preparing a turkey! *Run water through the carcass and use your fingers to remove any excess fat or blood along the back bone inside the cavity. Pull off any large fat deposits around neck and tail. If you've never cooked a turkey before, be sure to look in the flap of skin by the neck. There will probably be a paper bag filled with giblets (heart, liver, gizzard, etc.). I cook the giblets and neck separately in a 2 quart sauce pan with 1 quart water. Cook over medium heat 1-2 hours. When the water boils reduce to low. Freeze broth. If you like giblets, save them to serve on the turkey platter. (Some people chop them into the stuffing.) If no one eats them, discard after making broth.*

Assembly of Turkey Dressing

- **Brown sausage ingredients in large frying pan.** *(Step 1.)*
- **Add broth and cook 5 minutes.** *(Step 2.)*
- **Add celery, onion, and red bell pepper. Sauté 5 minutes.** *(Step 3)*
- **Pour above mixture into roaster pan, or very large bowl, and toss with remaining ingredients.** *(Step 4.)*
- **Cover and chill over night.**

Dressing for turkey

1.
1 lb. ground turkey breast, or 1/2 lb. each ground turkey breast and ground pork
1/4 tsp. sage
1/8 tsp. crushed rosemary
1 tsp. dry basil leaves
1 tsp. dry oregano leaves
2 cloves garlic (smashed and chopped)
3 slices medium onion (chopped)
1 T. olive oil

2.
1/4 C. broth

3.
1 1/2 C. chopped celery
1 1/2 C. chopped onion
1/2 chopped red bell pepper

4.
1 large (32 oz.) bag unseasoned bread cubes (If there is a season packet, throw it away!)
2 chopped tart apples
1 can sliced water chestnuts
1 C. toasted almond slivers
1 C. dried cranberries
three 15 oz. cans chicken broth
1 tsp. fresh-ground black pepper
1 T. dry oregano leaves
3 tsp. dry basil leaves
1/2 tsp. sage
1 tsp. thyme
2 eggs plus 2 egg whites (beaten)

THURSDAY
November/Week Four

Notes

Thanksgiving Dinner

The dressing was made last night, and the bird was stuffed this morning. ***Be sure to allow enough time to cook the turkey.*** ***You should cook a large (over 15 lbs.) stuffed turkey 20-25 minutes per pound.*** *Before placing turkey in oven, wrap tips of legs and wings in foil. Cook the bird at 350 degrees in a covered roaster pan. Check the turkey about 2/3 of the way through the cooking cycle. If using a thermometer, insert into inner thigh muscle. The internal temperature should be 185 degrees when the bird is cooked. Remove cover during the final hour of cooking to allow the bird to brown. Prepare potatoes and sweet potatoesearly but don't start cooking them until about 40 minutes before you're ready to serve dinner. Now we can concentrate on the rest of the meal. Oh yes, take time to set the table right after breakfast.*

Preparation time: 1-2 hours *(not counting turkey cooking time)*

Servings: 4-8

Ingredients:

mashed potatoes
sweet potatoes
cranberries
fresh broccoli
your favorite fresh rolls
relish tray
gravy
broccoli

Sweet Potatoes

butter-flavored cooking spray
1 tart apple *(peeled, cored, and thin sliced)*
3-4 sweet potatoes *(peeled and cut into 2" pieces)*
2 T. brown sugar
1/4 C. chicken broth

- **Spray 9" X 9" pan with butter-flavored spray.**
- **Arrange apples in bottom of pan.**
- **Sprinkle with cinnamon.**
- **Layer in sweet potatoes.**
- **Sprinkle with brown sugar.**
- **Pour broth over top.**
- **Cover with foil. Place in 350 degree oven for 30 minutes.**

Mashed Potatoes

10-12 medium-sized potatoes *(peeled and quartered)*
4 large cloves garlic *(peeled)*
2 C. water

- **Prepare potatoes and cover with water until ready to cook.**
- **Pour off all but 2 C. water before cooking.**
- **Boil potatoes and garlic in water 20-25 minutes.**
- **Pour excess water into bowl.** *(You'll use it when you make gravy.)*
- **Add 2 T. butter.**
- **Mash potatoes, garlic, and butter thoroughly until no lumps appear.**
- **Slowly add 1/4 C milk and continue mashing until potatoes are light and fluffy.**

Thanksgiving Dinner

(continued)

Cranberries

one or two 15 oz. cans cranberries

- **Empty cranberries into small glass serving dish.**
- **Chop with spoon to get rid of any sign of can imprint.**

Relish Tray *(optional)*

clean 2 stalks celery *(cut into sticks)*
peel 2 large carrots *(cut into sticks)*
use sliced pickled beets *(canned)*
black olives *(pitted)*

Arrange in divided serving dish, tray, or plate.

Gravy

liquid from cooking turkey *(fat separated and discarded)*
excess water from cooking potatoes
1/2 C. flour mixed with 1 C. nonfat milk
fresh-ground black pepper

- **Use bottom of roaster to make gravy. Begin by pouring all liquid in large pan or bowl.**
- **Using a gravy separator, pour juice back into roaster. Discard fat** *(in an empty can).*
- **Add cooking water from potatoes and bring liquid to boil.**
- **Thicken with 1/2 C. flour shaken with 1 C. milk. Shake about 50 seconds to remove all lumps.**
- **Stir constantly. Season with black pepper. When liquid boils, reduce heat to low and cook 10 minutes.**

Broccoli

1 lb. fresh broccoli *(cut into 2" pieces)*

- **Place in steamer basket with 1/2 C. water in large sauce pan.**
- **Begin cooking 5 minutes before serving the meal.**
- **Cook 2 minutes when water boils.**

Order for Final Preparations

- **Take turkey out of oven. Leave in roaster pan 20-30 minutes before removing.**
- **Cook potatoes** *(prepared earlier). Cook 25 minutes over medium heat until potatoes are tender. Remove from heat.*
- **Place sweet potatoes in oven.** *Cook 35 minutes at 350 degrees.*
- **Lift turkey out of pan and place on platter.** *(Have a helper begin to remove dressing from carcass about 5 minutes before sitting down to eat.)*
- **Prepare cranberries and relish tray.**
- **Make gravy.**
- **Wrap rolls in foil and place in oven to warm.**
- **Mash potatoes.**
- **Pour gravy into gravy server.**
- **Turn heat on under broccoli.**
- **Set out food in serving bowls and carve turkey.**

Gather everyone at the table and give thanks!

FRIDAY

November/Week Four

Notes

Leftovers

Now the fun begins! Haul out the leftovers and enjoy the meal one more time.

After dinner tonight, remove all remaining meat from turkey carcass. *Place some meat in fridge. Separate 1 C. dark meat and freeze. Also freeze any additional meat you can't eat within 2 days.*

Break up carcass and place in roaster pan on stove top with 2 quarts water. *Bring to boil and cook 1 1/2 hours. Let cool, remove bones and skin, and pour liquid into large pan or bowl. Refrigerate overnight. (Discard bones and skin.) In the morning, skim off and discard fat. Reheat and strain broth. Pour into container with tight fitting lid and store until Sunday.*

If you have leftover mashed potatoes, dressing, turkey, and gravy try this:

- **Spray 9" X 9" pan with cooking spray.**
- **Spread 1" layer of dressing in bottom. Cover with gravy.** *Add layer of sliced carrot rounds and 1 stalk chopped celery.*
- **Use leftover celery from relish tray.**
- **Add layer of white meat turkey. Spread with gravy.**
- **Place a 1" layer of mashed potatoes on top.**
- **Save about 1/2 C. gravy to pour over servings.**
- **Cover with foil. Refrigerate overnight.**
- **Cook 45 minutes at 350 degrees tomorrow evening for dinner. Let cool 15 minutes before serving. Serve in bowls with a few spoons of warm gravy over each serving.**

Make a green salad to go with it, and don't forget the cranberries.

SATURDAY

December/Week One

SHOPPING DAY

You will have a slightly smaller list this week as you will be making good use of leftover turkey meat and turkey carcass.

GROCERY LIST

Produce

2 medium yellow onions
one 8" zucchini
2 medium white potatoes
4-5 baby red potatoes
1 lb. fresh mushrooms
1 green bell pepper
1 red bell pepper
4 large carrots
1 lb. fresh broccoli
green salad fixings
4-5 Roma tomatoes
4 oranges
1 fresh lemon
pine nuts

Frozen Foods

8 oz. package snow peas

Meat/Fish/Poultry

Canned or Dry Foods

one 29 oz. can tomato sauce
seven 15 oz. cans chicken broth
12 oz. dry whole wheat spiral pasta
8 oz. fresh cheese tortellini
12 oz. package egg noodles
loaf of hearty bread

Chilled Foods and Dairy

1/2 dozen eggs
fresh pesto
plain, nonfat yogurt

Buy if you're out

1 head garlic
fresh parsley
celery
frozen corn
frozen peas
brown rice
sesame oil
chopped black olives
Worcestershire sauce
white wine vinegar
white cooking wine

Turkey Noodle Soup

You'll be using the broth from the turkey and a little leftover meat.

Preparation time: 30 minutes
Servings: 3-4
Ingredients:

hearty bread

Soup Ingredients

2 quarts broth *(You may add canned chicken broth if you run short.)*
1 russet potato *(cut in 1" chunks)*
1 clove garlic *(smashed and chopped)*
1 medium yellow onion *(chopped)*
1 large carrot *(chopped)*
2 stalks celery *(chopped)*
1/2 red bell pepper *(chopped)*
1 bay leaf
1/4 C. frozen corn
1/2 C. frozen peas
1 C. turkey meat *(Use the small broken pieces that can't be used anywhere else.)*
fresh-ground black pepper

8 oz. dry egg noodles *(cook before adding to soup)*

2 T. fresh parsley *(chopped fine)*

- **Wrap bread in foil and place in warm oven.**
- **Place water on to boil for noodles.**
- **Mix all soup ingredients** *(shaded area)* **in large kettle and bring to boil. Reduce heat to low, cover and cook 20 minutes.**
- **Drop noodles into boiling water and cook 8 minutes. Drain and add to soup.**
- **Add parsley. Reduce heat to low. Cook 5 minutes.**

Serve with hearty bread.

Notes

____
____
____
____
____
____
____
____

MONDAY

December/Week One

Notes

Plan to pick up some whole grain dinner rolls at your bakery today.

Turkey Hash

A great way to enliven leftover turkey!

Preparation time: 30 minutes
Servings: 3-4
Ingredients:

2-4 whole grain rolls

4-5 baby red potatoes

1 large carrot *(peeled and cut diagonally in 1/8" slices)*
2 slices medium yellow onion *(quartered)*
1/2 C. celery *(chopped)*
1/2 red bell pepper *(cut in 1" cubes)*

1 T. olive oil
1 clove garlic *(smashed and chopped)*
1 C. leftover turkey *(chopped)*
2 T. Worcestershire sauce

- **Wrap rolls in foil and place in warm oven.**
- **Wash potatoes and slice in quarters. Drop in 3 C. boiling water with 1/2 tsp. salt. Cook 15 minutes.**
- **When potatoes are tender, drop vegetables into boiling water with potatoes for one minute. Drain.**
- **Spread oil and garlic in large non-stick fry pan. Sauté all ingredients** *(including turkey)* **over high heat with Worcestershire sauce. Cook 2-3 minutes.**

Serve on individual plates with warm rolls.

Turkey Mushroom Omelet

TUESDAY
December/Week One

Here's a tasty way to use a little leftover turkey.

Preparation time: 20 minutes

Servings: 2

Ingredients:

1/3 lb. mushrooms *(sliced)*
1/4 red bell pepper *(sliced and cut in 1" pieces)*
2 slices of a medium onion *(chopped)*
1 clove garlic *(smashed and chopped)*
3/4 C. white wine

6 eggs *(2 whole eggs and 4 egg whites)*
1/2 C. plain, nonfat yogurt *(stirred smooth)*
black pepper
1 T. olive oil *(or vegetable oil spray)*

1/2 C. leftover chopped turkey
3 T. fancy-shred Parmesan

1/2 C. broth
1/2 tsp. dry oregano leaves
1 tsp. dry basil leaves
1 T. corn starch dissolved in 1/8 C. water
1/4 C. plain, nonfat yogurt *(stirred smooth)*

2-4 slices of bread for toast *(use leftover hearty bread)*
2 oranges *(sliced)*

Notes

- **Sauté mushrooms, red pepper, onion, and garlic in white wine** *(about 3 minutes).*
- **Remove from pan and place in strainer.** *Save liquid.*
- **Break 2 eggs into medium-sized bowl. Separate yolks from remaining eggs and throw away. Add whites to bowl and beat with wire whisk about 30 seconds.**
- **Beat yogurt into eggs and season with black pepper.**
- **Place a 10" non-stick fry pan over medium heat and spread olive oil evenly around pan** *(or spray pan with vegetable oil spray before placing on burner).*
- **Pour egg mixture into hot pan. Cook 1 minute.**
- **Place mushroom/pepper mixture, chopped turkey, and Parmesan on one side of omelet leaving 1/2 the surface area open. Reduce heat to medium.**
- **Cook 2 minutes and fold plain half over filling.**
- **Cook one more minute. Loosen omelet from pan with spatula. Place a serving plate over omelet pan. Hold plate firmly in place and turn pan upside down so that omelet falls onto plate. Slide omelet off plate back into pan to cook other side. Cook 2 minutes. Remove from pan and place in warm oven on plate.**
- **Place liquid from mushrooms plus 1/2 C. broth in small sauce pan. Add spices, bring to boil and thicken with corn starch mixture. Reduce heat and cook 5 minutes. Stir in yogurt.**

Serve 1/2 omelet per serving. Spoon sauce over omelet. Serve toast and orange slices on side.

WEDNESDAY
December/Week One

Notes

"Creamy" Pasta Prima Vera

We're in need of a meatless dish, so here's that lovely light "cream" sauce entree.

Preparation time: 30 minutes
Servings: 3
Ingredients:

2 1/2 C. dry whole wheat spiral pasta

1 carrot *(peeled and sliced)*
1 C. chicken broth
6 medium mushrooms *(sliced)*
2 slices medium yellow onion *(quartered)*
1/2 green bell pepper *(cut into 1" chunks)*
1 clove garlic *(smashed and chopped) or 1 tsp. prepared chopped garlic*
fresh-ground black pepper
one 6"- 8" long zucchini *(cut into 1/4" rounds)*

1/4 C. plain, nonfat yogurt *(stirred smooth)*
2 T. pesto
dash of Tabasco® *(optional)*

2 T. corn starch dissolved into 1/8 C. water

2-4 T. fancy-shred Parmesan
2 T. toasted pine nuts *(chopped)*
1 large Roma tomato *(chopped into 1" chunks)*

- **Place pasta water on to boil in large, heavy-bottomed kettle. When water boils, add dry pasta and cook.** *Set timer for 8 minutes.* **Drain and rinse.**
- **In same kettle used for pasta, sauté carrot in 1/4 C. broth 2 minutes.**
- **Add mushrooms, onions, green pepper, and garlic. Sauté 2 minutes. Season with about 4 turns of fresh-ground pepper.**
- **Add zucchini and sauté another 2 minutes.** *If pan cooks dry, add another 1/4 cup broth.*
- **Remove all vegetables from kettle with perforated spoon and set aside. Add remaining broth to kettle and bring to boil over high heat.**
- **Mix yogurt, pesto and optional Tabasco® in small bowl.**
- **Thicken liquid in kettle with corn starch/water mixture, reduce heat to low, and cook 2-3 minutes. Remove from heat and add pesto/yogurt mixture.**
- **Add all vegetables and cooked pasta to thickened sauce and gently stir over medium-high heat until coated. Cover and remove from heat.** ***Do not boil.***
- **Divide into 2-3 servings on individual plates.**

Garnish with Parmesan, chopped pine nuts, and tomato.

Thank you! I needed that!

Turkey à l'orange

Here is a delicious stir fry which uses the leftover dark meat from Thanksgiving (in the freezer). This dish has a hint of a wild game quality. Set frozen turkey out to thaw in the morning.

THURSDAY
December/Week One

Preparation time: 30 minutes
Servings: 3-4
Ingredients:

Notes

Orange Sauce
- 1/4 tsp. grated orange rind
- juice from 2 oranges *(or 1 C. orange juice)*
- 1/4 tsp. sesame oil
- 2 cloves garlic *(smashed and chopped)*
- 3 slices medium onion *(chopped)*
- one 15 oz. can low-sodium chicken broth
- 2 T. white wine vinegar
- 1 T. white sugar
- 2 T. low-sodium soy sauce
- 1/4 tsp. rosemary *(finely broken)*
- 1/8 tsp. ceyenne pepper *(optional)*

- 4 T. corn starch mixed with 1/4 C. water

- 1 C. cooked dark meat turkey *(thawed, boned, and chopped)*
- 12 mushrooms *(sliced)*
- 8 oz. fresh or frozen snow peas

- 2-3 C. cooked rice

- 1 medium tomato *(chopped)*

"Quick cook" some rice before work this morning. *(see page 237)*

- **Mix Orange Sauce ingredients in large sauce pan. Bring to boil over medium-high heat.**
- **Thicken with corn starch mixture. Cook 5 minutes.**
- **Wrap chopped dark meat turkey in paper towel and place in covered, shallow dish. Cook 2 minutes in microwave. Press towel firmly against meat to absorb fat.**
- **Add turkey, mushrooms, and snow peas to sauce. Return to boil. Cook 3 minutes.**
- **Warm rice in microwave.**
- **Add chopped tomato. Return to boil and serve immediately.**
- **Spoon Orange Sauce over 3/4 C. rice per serving.**

Eat with chopsticks if you wish.

FRIDAY

December/Week One

Notes

Tortellini with "Creamy" Red Sauce

Very simple and very quick. Even when making a new batch of Red Sauce.

Preparation time: 20 minutes
Servings: 2
Ingredients:

1 1/2 C. Red Sauce *(see page 331)*
8 oz . fresh tortellini
1/4 C. plain, nonfat yogurt *(stirred smooth)*
green salad fixings
3 T. fancy-shred Parmesan
1 T. fresh chopped parsley

- **Place pasta water on to boil in large kettle.**
- **Prepare Red Sauce.**
- **Drop tortellini into boiling water.** *Set timer for 10 minutes.*
- **Measure 1 1/2 C. Red Sauce and set aside.** *Store remaining Red Sauce in fridge.*
- **Pour measured Red Sauce back into same pan. Stir in yogurt.** *Blend over low heat but do not boil.* **Remove from heat when thoroughly heated.**
- **Drain and rinse pasta.**
- **Prepare green salads.**
- **Spoon sauce over tortellini on individual plates and garnish with Parmesan and fresh chopped parsley.**

Serve with a crisp green salad.

SHOPPING DAY

SATURDAY

December/Week Two

Does someone have a cold in your household? *A daily 45-minute walk can help get rid of a cold. The exercise stimulates the immune system. Take an easy pace. Quit if you feel worse.*
Prevention Guide to the Best Home Remedies, 33 E. Minor St., Emmaus, PA 18098

When buying garlic, *choose firm heads that have not sprouted. Avoid soft, mushy heads. Store them in a cool, dry place.*
Parenting, 301 Howard St., 17th Floor, San Francisco, CA 94105

A diet rich in vitamin A *may decrease a woman's risk of breast cancer. Good sources include carrots, spinach, sweet potatoes, and cantaloupe. However, if you're taking supplements, be careful! Vitamin A can be toxic in large doses.*
Environmental Nutrition, 2112 Broadway, New York, NY 10019

This week I've introduced orzo to the menu. Although it looks like rice, it's actually the pasta of choice in Northern Italy. This is a most versatile pasta which can soak up lots of sauce. Don't buy packages of preseasoned "Risotto."

Notes

GROCERY LIST

Produce

1 medium yellow onion
1 green bell pepper
1 red bell pepper
1/4 lb. white mushrooms
1 large carrot
3/4 lb. fresh broccoli
one head Romaine lettuce
1 bunch green onions
one package prewashed spinach
red leaf lettuce
green salad fixings
one large cucumber
8 Roma tomatoes
1 tart apple
1 fresh lemon
firm tofu

Frozen Foods

nonfat frozen yogurt
frozen orange juice

Meat/Fish/Poultry

1 lb. ground turkey breast
4-6 boneless, skinless chicken breasts
2 fresh or frozen snapper fillets

Canned or Dry Foods

one 29 oz. can tomato sauce
three 15 oz. cans chicken broth
one 15 oz. can vegetable broth
one 6 oz. can sliced water chestnuts
one 6 oz. can sliced bamboo shoots
one 16 oz. bag orzo *(in pasta section)*
8 oz. fresh fettuccine
12 oz. dry whole wheat spiral pasta
one 16 oz. can sour pie cherries
or 1 bag frozen pie cherries
one 6 oz. bottle cherry juice
or 1 small bottle cranberry juice
pecan halves

Chilled Foods and Dairy

plain, nonfat yogurt
nonfat milk

Buy if you're out

1 head garlic
celery
1 bunch parsley
olive oil
dry dill weed
ground anise
brown rice
white cooking wine
red cooking wine
canola, peanut or corn oil

SUNDAY

December/Week Two

Notes

Chicken Breasts with Sour Cherry Sauce

An elegant and hearty encore! This time I've added orzo as the starch. It's wonderful for sopping up a delicious sauce. The ingredients below assume you're cooking for two. If you have extra orzo, it makes great leftovers. Cooked orzo also freezes well.

Preparation time: 30 minutes

Servings: 2

Ingredients:

one 16 oz. bag orzo *(Use 2 C. cooked orzo tonight and store the rest.)*

3 T. chopped parsley
1 clove garlic *(smashed and chopped)*
5 green onions *(chopped)*

2-4 boneless, skinless chicken breasts
1 clove garlic *(smashed and chopped)*
1 T. olive oil

1/2 lb. broccoli *(cut in 2" lengths)*

1/4 C. dry white wine
1/4 C. cherry juice or cranberry juice

2 T. corn starch dissolved in 1/8 C. water

1 C. sour pie cherries *(plus juice from can)*

1/2 lemon split into wedges

- **Preheat oven to 300 degrees.**
- **Cook orzo in boiling water 8 minutes, stirring occasionally. Drain and rinse.**
- **Mix 2 C. orzo with parsley, garlic, and onions. Cover and microwave 3 minutes. Set aside.**
- **Sauté chicken breasts in garlic and oil in non-stick fry pan over medium-high heat,** *(about 5 minutes per side).* **If pan gets dry, add water or white wine** *(about 1/4 C.).* **When browned, place on an oven-safe plate in 300 degree oven. Set pan aside. You will use it as is.**
- **Place broccoli and steamer basket in large sauce pan with 1/2 C. water.** *Do not turn on burner yet.*
- **Pour wine into pan in which chicken was cooked. Rub bottom gently with fork over medium-high heat until wine boils. Add cherry juice and return to boil.**
- **Thicken sauce with corn starch mixture and reduce heat to low. Cook 5 minutes.**
- **Add cherries with juice and cook 1 more minute.**
- **Turn heat on high under broccoli now. When water boils, cover and cook 2 minutes.**
- **Serve breasts on individual serving plates. Spoon cherry sauce over breasts and flank breasts with 3/4 C. orzo and broccoli. Set a lemon wedge on each plate to dress the broccoli.**

Light a candle tonight! Have a glass of your favorite dry white wine.

Snapper with Dill

MONDAY

December/Week Two

Different fish have different personalities with similar spices. It's dill with snapper tonight.

Preparation time: 25 minutes
Servings: 2
Ingredients:

2 cups cooked rice *("quick cooked" this morning)*
6-8 toasted pecan halves *(chopped – toast under broiler)*
1/4 C. white wine
2 slices medium onion *(chopped)*
3 T. chopped parsley *(fresh or dried)*

1 clove garlic *(smashed and chopped)*
1 tsp. olive oil
1/2 package prewashed spinach or 1 bunch washed spinach *(coarsely chopped)*
1/2 C. chicken broth
5-6 mushrooms *(sliced)*

1 tsp. butter
4 T. flour shaken with 1/4 C. nonfat milk
dash of nutmeg

1/2 C. white wine
1 clove garlic *(smashed and chopped)*
1/2 - 3/4 C. chicken or vegetable broth

2 small snapper fillets *(2/3 lb.)*
black pepper
a couple pinches of dill weed

1/4 C. plain, nonfat yogurt *(stirred smooth)*

1/2 fresh lemon *(cut in wedges)*

- **Measure 2 C. rice into medium-sized bowl. Add pecans, wine, onion, and parsley. Cover and microwave 2 1/2 minutes on high.**
- **Place garlic and oil in large, heavy-bottomed kettle over medium-high heat. Add spinach, 1/4 C. broth, and sliced mushrooms. Toss until spinach is wilted. Remove veggies with perforated spoon and add remaining broth to liquid in pan.**
- **Bring liquid to boil, add butter, and thicken with flour/milk mixture.** *Be sure to shake flour/milk mixture thoroughly to remove all lumps.* **Season with dash of nutmeg and cook over low heat 5 minutes. Stir often.**
- **Place wine, garlic, and 1/2 C. broth in sauté pan and bring to boil.**
- **Slide fish fillets into boiling mixture and season with black pepper. Cook about 3 minutes per side. When you turn fillets, sprinkle dill weed over each.** *If liquid in pan cooks away, add another 1/4 C. broth.*
- **Add spinach to cream sauce and return to boil. Remove from heat and stir in yogurt.**

Serve fillets flanked by "Creamed" Spinach and Nutty Rice on individual serving plates.

Notes

"Quick cook" some rice this morning before you leave for work. *(see page 237)*

TUESDAY

December/Week Two

Notes

Hot Chicken Salad

Here's some lighter fare as the week continues. We've just about recuperated from Thanksgiving!

Preparation time: 20 minutes
Servings: 2
Ingredients:

a loaf of your favorite hearty bread

3 boneless, skinless chicken breasts
1 T. olive oil
1 clove garlic *(smashed and chopped)*

1/4 C. broth
1/8 lb. broccoli *(chopped in 1" pieces)*

Dressing:
1/4 C. orange juice
1 clove garlic *(smashed and chopped)*
1/2 tsp. dry basil leaves
2 T. olive oil
1 T. balsamic vinegar
1/2 tsp. sesame oil

4 leaves Romaine lettuce
4 leaves green or red leaf lettuce
1/2 green pepper *(cut in thin slices)*
2 slices yellow onion *(quartered)*
2-3 Roma tomatoes *(chopped)*
1 tart apple *(cored and chopped in small pieces)*

Pick up a loaf of your favorite hearty bread on the way home from work.

- **Wrap bread in foil and place in warm oven.**
- **Sauté chicken breast in oil and garlic in non-stick pan over medium-high heat 4 minutes per side.**
- **Add broth and chopped broccoli to pan. Sauté another 2 minutes. Remove pan from heat and set aside.**
- **Combine salad dressing ingredients in glass dish and microwave on high 1 minute or combine in small sauce pan and bring to boil over medium-high heat. Remove from burner. Set aside.**
- **Tear lettuce into large bite-sized pieces and arrange on two large serving plates.**
- **Add all cold vegetables and apple.**
- **Thin slice one chicken breast and arrange with hot broccoli on top of each salad.** *Store extra breasts in fridge for next Sunday's meal.*

Top with warm salad dressing and serve with hearty bread.

Leftover Night

"Soup's on"- among other things. Time to eat the free food.

WEDNESDAY

December/Week Two

Preparation time: 20 minutes
Servings: 2-3
Ingredients:

Whatever you have in the fridge.
leftover Turkey Noodle Soup
leftover pasta
leftover orzo

Notes

Liven up *leftovers with a crisp green salad and toast from leftover hearty bread.*

Try to incorporate plenty of vitamin C and E into your diet. *A Finnish study published in the British Medical Journal found that low blood levels of vitamin E were associated with higher risk of developing cataracts. Vitamin C also is important in the prevention of cataracts, as eye fluids are normally rich in vitamin C. Good sources for the vitamins are.*

Vitamin C	*Vitamin E*
citrus fruits	*leafy greens*
tomatoes	*seeds*
broccoli	*olives*
peppers	*asparagus*
cauliflower	*almonds*
cantaloupe	*vegetable oil*

Holiday weight control. *Before going to Holiday parties, have a glass of nonfat milk and a piece of fruit, or drink a tall glass of cold water and eat a handful of fat-free crackers. This will slow down your intake of fat-filled goodies at the party. While at the party, alternate between alcoholic beverages and soda with lemon or lime.*

THURSDAY

December/Week Two

Notes

"Quick cook" some rice before leaving for work this morning.

"Quick cooked" rice
In medium sauce pan, mix 1 C. brown rice and 2 1/4 C. cold water. Bring to boil over high heat. Turn off heat, leave on burner and don't lift cover. Leave it for the day.

Vegetarian Stir Fry

A stir fry loaded with nutrients. This is a most rewarding meatless meal.

Preparation time: 30 minutes
Servings: 2-3
Ingredients:

1 T. canola, peanut, or corn oil
1 tsp. sesame oil
1/4 C. vegetable broth
3 slices medium onion *(chopped)*
2 cloves garlic *(smashed and chopped)*
1 carrot *(sliced diagonally)*
1/2 C. broccoli *(cut in 1" pieces)*

6 mushrooms *(sliced)*
1/2 green bell pepper *(cubed)*
1/2 red bell pepper *(cubed)*
1/2 C. sliced, peeled water chestnuts *(drained)*
1/2 C. sliced bamboo shoots *(drained)*
2 T. low-sodium soy sauce

1 C. vegetable broth
2 T. corn starch mixed with 1/4 C. water
1 T. soy sauce
(optional) dash of cayenne pepper

1/2 C. thin sliced firm tofu
1 medium tomato *(chopped)*

1 1/2 C. cooked rice

- **Place oils and broth in large heavy-bottomed sauce pan or wok over high heat. Sauté onion, garlic, carrot, and broccoli 2 minutes stirring constantly.**
- **Add mushrooms, peppers, water chestnuts, bamboo shoots, and soy sauce. Sauté an additional 2 minutes. Remove all ingredients from pan with perforated ladle or spoon and set aside on large plate.**
- **Using same pan, add remaining broth and bring to boil. Thicken with corn starch/water mixture. Add additional soy sauce and cayenne pepper. Reduce heat and cook 3-4 minutes.**
- **Return vegetables to pan. Add tofu and tomatoes. Stir to coat with sauce until liquid begins to bubble. Remove from heat.**
- **Serve immediately on individual plates over warm rice.**

Chopsticks? You know the drill.

Pasta Bolognese

A simple favorite. You will have great leftover Red Sauce as well as Italian Turkey Sausage.

FRIDAY

December/Week Two

Preparation time: 30 minutes
Servings: 2-3
Ingredients:

8 oz. fresh fettucine

Italian Turkey Sausage
1 T. olive oil
1 lb. ground turkey
2 slices medium yellow onion *(chopped)*
2 large cloves garlic *(smashed and chopped)*
2 tsp. dry basil leaves
1 tsp. dry oregano leaves
1/2 tsp. ground anise
dash of Tabasco® sauce
1/8 C. red wine

Red Sauce
one 29 oz. can tomato sauce
2 cloves garlic *(smashed and chopped)*
1/4 C. red wine
1 T. dry oregano
1 1/2 T. dry basil leaves
4 slices medium yellow onion *(chopped)*
a few dashes of Tabasco® sauce *(optional)*

1/3 lb. cooked Italian Turkey Sausage
1/8 C. red wine
1 1/2 C. Red Sauce

green salad fixings

3 T. fancy-shred Parmesan

Notes

- **Place pasta water on to boil in large kettle. Drop pasta into water and cook 2 1/2 minutes. Drain and rinse.**
- **Place oil in sauté pan over medium-high heat.**
- **Add ground turkey and the rest of the Italian Sausage Ingredients.**
- **Prepare Red Sauce at the same time. Place all ingredients in medium sauce pan and bring to boil. Cover, reduce heat to low, and cook 10 minutes.** *(When Red Sauce is cooked, measure 1 1/2 C. for tonight's recipe and put remainder away in fridge.)*
- **Sauté sausage mix until browned.** *(Reserve 1/3 of the sausage for tonight's recipe and put remainder away in fridge.)*
- **Combine Italian Sausage, wine and Red Sauce in same pan used to cook Red Sauce.** *Bring to boil. Reduce heat to low and cover while finishing dinner preparations.*
- **Prepare green salads.**
- **Divide pasta on two plates and spoon Bolognese Sauce over each serving.**
- **Garnish with Parmesan cheese.**

Serve with crisp green salad. Pretty simple! Bravo! Bravissima!

SATURDAY
December/Week Three

Notes

SHOPPING DAY

Common New Year's resolutions include: *improve finances, stop smoking, eat right and lose weight, exercise more, and improve personal relationships. Most Americans don't stick with it: 55% lose motivation in one month, and 40% give up in six months.*
Research by John Norcross, Professor of Psychology, University of Scranton, PA

The season of excess? *Over the holidays 1.7 billion cookies will be consumed, 15 million pounds of fruit cake will be baked, 120 million pounds of eggnog will be consumed, 20 million ties will be sold, 22 million people will drive more than 100 miles, and 5 million people will travel by plane, train or bus.*
Gallup Polls and USDA nutritional information

Make sure you have "Happy Holidays" - *never drink and drive.*

When traveling by plane, *always call the airline 24 hours ahead of departure and order special meals. There are many choices: low sodium, vegetarian, fruit plates, low cholesterol, lowfat, etc. There is no extra cost, and the nutrition level is much better than normal airline fare.*

The holiday season is upon us. Happy Hanukkah *to all who will celebrate The Feast of the Dedication as this blessed eight day celebration gets it all started.*

GROCERY LIST

Produce

2 large russet potatoes
one 6" zucchini
2 medium yellow onions
1 lb. fresh mushrooms
1 green bell pepper
1 red bell pepper
1 large carrot
2 large, fresh beets
one head iceberg lettuce
one head red or green leaf lettuce
6-8 Roma tomatoes
1 fresh lemon

Frozen Foods

green beans

Meat/Fish/Poultry

1/2 lb. ground turkey breast
6 fresh or frozen scallops
2 boneless, skinless chicken breasts

Canned or Dry Foods

one 29 oz. can tomato sauce
12 oz. dry split peas
five 15 oz. cans chicken broth
16 oz. dry whole wheat spiral pasta
8 oz. fresh fettuccine
a loaf of your favorite hearty bread

Chilled Foods and Dairy

4 oz. sharp cheddar cheese
large wheat tortillas
fresh salsa
fresh pesto

Buy if you're out

1 head garlic
one bunch green onions
celery
parsley
frozen corn
turkey bacon
brown rice
red cooking wine
white cooking wine
plain, nonfat yogurt
butter

Split Pea Soup

Here's more welcome cold weather fare.

SUNDAY

December/Week Three

Preparation time: 45 minutes
Servings: 3-4
Ingredients:

Soup Ingredients
1 1/2 C. split peas
3/4 C. Italian Turkey Sausage *(leftover from last week)*
1 bay leaf
three 15 oz. cans chicken or vegetable broth
1 clove garlic *(smashed and chopped)*
1 medium yellow onion *(chopped)*
1 large carrot *(chopped)*
2 stalks celery *(chopped)*
1/2 red bell pepper *(chopped)*

5 T. flour shaken with 1/2 C. nonfat milk

hearty bread

fresh-ground black pepper
2-3 dashes Tabasco®
2 T. fresh parsley *(chopped fine)*

3/4 C. plain, nonfat yogurt *(stirred smooth)*

- **Wash and sort split peas in colander.**
- **Place Italian Sausage, split peas, and all other Soup Ingredients** *(shaded box)* **in large, heavy-bottomed sauce pan. Bring to boil over high heat. Reduce heat to low, cover and cook 20 minutes.**
- **Shake flour and milk vigorously in container with tight-fitting lid.** *Shake until all lumps have disappeared.* **Stir gradually into boiling mixture.**
- **Wrap bread in foil and place in warm oven.**
- **Reduce heat under soup to low. Cook 10 minutes. Stir often.**
- **Add pepper, Tabasco®, and parsley. Cook 5 minutes.**
- **Stir in yogurt just prior to serving. Remove from heat.**

Serve with warm hearty bread.

Notes

MONDAY

December/Week Three

Notes

Pasta with Scallops

A return to the "pasta della mare" theme. (You'll also use up some leftover Red Sauce.)

Preparation time: 30 minutes
Servings: 2-3
Ingredients:

6 large frozen scallops *(thaw just prior to cooking)*
1 T. olive oil
3 slices medium onion *(quartered)*
1 clove garlic *(smashed and chopped)*
2 stalks celery *(chopped in 1" pieces)*
1/4 C. chicken broth

1 1/2 C. Red Sauce *(leftovers from last Friday, or see page 349)*
dash of Tabasco®
1/4 C. red wine

green salad fixings

8 oz. fresh fettuccine

3 T. fancy-shred Parmesan

- **Place pasta water on to boil in large kettle.**
- **Place scallops in large fry pan with oil, onion, garlic, celery, and broth. Sauté 3 minutes over medium-high heat.**
- **Add 1 1/2 C. Red Sauce, Tabasco®, and wine. Return to boil. Remove from heat.**
- **Prepare green salads.**
- **Drop pasta into water. Cook 2 1/2 minutes. Drain and rinse.**

Divide pasta onto plates. Spoon Red Sauce with scallops over each serving. Garnish with Parmesan cheese and serve with crisp green salad.

Chicken with Rice and Mushrooms

TUESDAY
December/Week Three

This is a slightly different twist to chicken breasts with mushroom sauce.

Preparation time: 30 minutes
Servings: 2-3
Ingredients:

Notes

1/2 lb. fresh white mushrooms
1/2 red bell pepper *(cut in thin 1" strips)*
2 thin slices of a medium yellow onion *(quartered)*
2 cloves garlic *(smashed and chopped)*
1/4 C. chicken broth

2 boneless, skinless chicken breasts
1/4 C. chicken broth

1/2 lb. frozen green beans
2 thin slices medium onion *(quartered)*
one slice turkey bacon *(from freezer - chopped fine)*
1/2 C. broth

1/4 C. broth
1/4 C. white wine
2 T. corn starch *(dissolved in 1/4 C. water)*

2 C. cooked rice

- **In 12" fry pan, sauté mushrooms, red pepper, onion and garlic in broth - 3 minutes. Remove from pan with perforated spoon and set aside.**
- **Place chicken breasts in same pan. Sauté over medium-high heat 3 minutes, turning once. Add broth and sauté another 3 minutes until lightly browned. Reduce heat to low, add a little water to pan. Cover and cook 5 minutes per side.**
- **Place beans, onions, turkey bacon and broth in large covered sauce pan.** *Do not begin cooking yet.*
- **Remove chicken from pan. Add broth and wine. Bring to boil and stir to bring up drippings. Thicken with corn starch. Reduce heat. Cook 5 minutes.**
- **Add mushrooms to sauce.**
- **Turn on heat under beans. Bring to boil. Reduce heat to low, cover, and cook 2 minutes.**
- **Warm rice 1 1/2 minutes on high in microwave.**
- **Chop chicken and add to mushroom mixture. Bring to boil. Remove from heat.**

"Quick cook" rice before work this morning. *(see page 348)*

Serve rice covered with chicken/mushroom sauce. Arrange beans on both sides.

WEDNESDAY
December/Week Three

Notes

Leftover Soup Night

Do you have leftover pea soup plus at least one other leftover soup in the freezer? Tonight could be a soup adventure.

Preparation time: 20 minutes
Servings: 2-3
Ingredients:

Whatever you have in the fridge.
leftover pasta
leftover soup
leftover Chicken with Mushrooms and Rice

Cut a little fresh fruit, *even if it's only an apple, and serve it with leftovers.*

Nonfat or lowfat cookies are better, but beware *of how many you eat in one serving. Reduced fat cookies may be lower in fat, but they are still high in sugar. Sugar, of course, has lots of calories; if you're not burning them, you'll store them. Some old favorites like graham crackers, ginger snaps, and fig bars have always been low in fat.*
University of California at Berkeley Wellness Letter, PO Box 420148, Palm Coast, Florida 32142

More holiday weight control. *I used to bake lots of goodies during the holidays and send them as gift boxes to friends. However, I have a sweet tooth too, and many of the cookies never made it to the gift box. Every holiday season I had trouble maintaining my weight. Hmmmmm? Now, if I plan to give a gift of sweets, I bake several recipes over the course of a weekend: fudge, almond roca, butter cookies, etc. Then I make sure I pack them all in boxes and give them away.*

Watch your stress level *at this time of year. You don't have to get Christmas cards out, bake Christmas goodies, spend lots of money, and live up to mythical memories of your childhood. If we try to live up to "Madison Avenue's" version of the holidays, we can lose sight of the warmth of the season.*

Pick up a loaf of good bread or use leftover bread as needed. If leftover bread is several days old, toast and spread with a whisper of butter to freshen it up.

Baked Potato with Beets

Time to load up on multiple vitamins with this meal.

THURSDAY

December/Week Three

Notes

Preparation time: 15-20 minutes
Servings: 2
Ingredients:

2 large russet baking potatoes *(washed, rubbed with olive oil and poked with a fork)*
2 large fresh beets
1/2 C. frozen corn
juice from 1/2 a lemon mixed with 1/2 tsp. melted butter
3/4 C. plain, nonfat yogurt *(stirred smooth)*
salsa
2-3 strips cooked turkey bacon *(chopped)*

- **If you don't have the luxury of "time bake" on your oven, try microwaving this meal. Place potatoes and beets** *(unwrapped)* **in shallow dish in microwave. Cook for three 5-minute cycles at full power. Turn to a different position after each cycle.**
- **Set beets out of oven** *(or microwave)* **to cool. Let stand 5 minutes.**
- **Microwave corn in covered glass dish for 1 minute on high. Set aside.**
- **Using a pair of rubber gloves, unwrap beets and vigorously rub them under cold water. This will remove the outer skin. Slice or chop them for serving. Place beets in bowl and pour lemon/ butter mixture over them. Stir to coat well.**
- **Stir yogurt and set out salsa and bacon.**

Split potatoes and place on serving plates. Top with corn, yogurt, bacon, and salsa. Serve beets on same plate.

Some quick preparation this morning: wash potatoes and beets. Wrap beets in foil and prick potatoes with a fork. Place all in a shallow baking pan in oven. Set "time bake" to start oven (350°) 1 hour before you arrive home this evening. You should have some turkey bacon in the freezer. If you don't, the meal will survive without it!

FRIDAY

December/Week Three

Notes

Taco Salad

Quick fixin's and most satisfying! (The only cooking needed is the ground turkey).

Preparation time: 15-20 minutes

Servings: 3-4

Ingredients:

1/4 C. Red Sauce *(page 349)*

1/2 lb. ground turkey breast
1 T. olive oil
2 slices medium yellow onion *(chopped)*
1 clove garlic *(smashed and chopped)*
1 tsp. oregano leaves
1/2 tsp. ground cumin
1 T. mild chili powder
dash of Tabasco®

1/2 green pepper *(cut in 1" cubes)*
1 clove garlic *(smashed and chopped)*
2 slices yellow onion *(quartered)*
1 T. chili powder
1/4 C. broth or water

6-8 leaves washed red leaf lettuce
1/2 head chopped iceberg lettuce

sharp cheddar cheese
2-3 Roma tomatoes *(chopped)*

flour or corn tortillas

1/2 C. plain, nonfat yogurt *(stirred smooth)*
salsa

- **Make a fresh batch of Red Sauce.** *(Use 1/4 C. for this meal and reserve the rest.)*
- **Sauté ground turkey in olive oil along with onion, garlic, and spices in large non-stick fry pan over medium-high heat. Sauté 5 minutes stirring constantly. Add 1/4 C. Red Sauce. Cover, reduce heat to low, and cook an additional 5 minutes.**
- **When meat is done, remove to bowl and set aside.**
- **Using same fry pan, sauté green pepper, garlic, and onions with chili powder and broth. Sauté 2 minutes over high heat. Remove from pan and set aside.**
- **Place 2 washed leaves red leaf lettuce on each plate as bed for salad. Top with chopped iceberg lettuce.**
- **Divide meat and sautéed vegetables onto beds of lettuce.**
- **Garnish with a grating of sharp cheese and chopped tomato.** *Go easy on the cheese! Only two or three draws across the grater per salad are needed.*
- **Warm tortillas by setting them, one at a time, in large fry pan for about 30 seconds per side over medium-high heat.**
- **Spoon yogurt and salsa over salad to suit your taste.**

Serve with tortillas on the side.

SATURDAY
December/Week Four

SHOPPING DAY

Check your list and supplies carefully. This is a Holiday week and you'll be happy you're well prepared.

By cooking the meals from these recipes this year, *you have probably reduced your fat intake. It may interest you to know that in one study, people who obtained 40% of their calories from fat had a 39% chance of developing a lesion on their arteries. On the other hand, those who obtained only 20% of their calories from fat had a 19% chance of a lesion forming.*
American College of Cardiology, Bethesda, MD

Dark green leafy vegetables *like collard greens and spinach can lower your risk of macular degeneration, a leading cause of age-related blindness.*
American Medical Association, Chicago, IL

Fresh fish *should be refrigerated immediately and cooked within 24 hours. Cook it fast and thoroughly. Smoked fish should be refrigerated as well.*
Working Women, 230 Park Avenue, New York, NY 10069

Not all health foods are low in fat. *A half cup of granola can have 50% calories from fat - 7% more than is found in a candy bar.*
The PDR Family Guide to Nutrition and Health, Medical Economics, 1995

Notes

GROCERY LIST

Produce

one 6" zucchini
9 medium russet potatoes
1 large russet potato
10 baby red potatoes
2 medium yellow onions
1 sweet onion
3/4 lb. fresh mushrooms
2 green bell peppers
2 red bell peppers
2 large carrots
1 lb. fresh broccoli
1 head Romaine lettuce
1 head green leaf lettuce
green salad fixings
one cucumber
2 packages
prewashed spinach
8 Roma tomatoes
2 fresh oranges
fresh oranges or Satsumas
1 fresh lemon

Frozen Foods

Meat/Fish/Poultry

2 Italian chicken or
turkey sausages
1 lb. ground turkey breast, or 1
lb. lean ground pork
* *If you are opting for the fresh Salmon dinner on Christmas Day, you will need to pick up fresh fish on Christmas Eve.*

Canned or Dry Foods

one 29 oz. can tomato sauce
six 15 oz. cans chicken broth
two 15 oz. cans whole cranberries
one 6 oz. can chopped black olives
16 oz. dry multi-colored spiral pasta
8 oz. fresh cheese tortellini

Chilled Foods and Dairy

plain, nonfat yogurt
nonfat milk

Buy if you're out

1 head garlic
1 bunch green onions
saltine crackers
dried thyme
brown sugar
Worcestershire sauce
Dijon mustard
white cooking wine
fresh pesto
shredded Parmesan
eggs

SUNDAY

December/Week Four

"Cossack" Red Potatoes and Sausage

Revisit this delicious one-dish meal.

Preparation time: 30 minutes
Servings: 2-3
Ingredients:

10 baby red potatoes
1 T. olive oil

2 links Italian chicken or turkey sausage
2 T. broth

1/4 C. chicken broth with 2 dashes Tabasco® sauce
1 clove garlic *(smashed and chopped)*
1 large carrot *(peeled and sliced in 1/8" slices)*

1/2 green bell pepper *(chopped in 1" pieces)*
1/2 red bell pepper *(chopped in 1" pieces)*
one slice medium yellow onion *(quartered)*

2 T. pesto
3 T. broth
dash of Tabasco®

4 Roma tomatoes *(chopped in large pieces)*
4-6 T. fancy-shred Parmesan cheese

- **Preheat oven to 400 degrees.**
- **Wash potatoes, cut in half and place face down on oiled cookie sheet in oven.**
- **Prick sausage several times with fork. Wrap in paper towel, place in covered dish and microwave 2 minutes on high. Repeat process twice. Cool slightly and slice in 1/8" rounds.**
- **Place sausage in large fry pan and sauté with 2 T. broth 3 minutes.**
- **Add remaining broth** *(with Tabasco®)*, **garlic, and carrots. Sauté 2 minutes.**
- **Add peppers and onion and sauté an additional 3 minutes.**
- **Remove potatoes from oven and add to sausage/vegetable mixture.**
- **Mix pesto, broth, and Tabasco®.**
- **Stir chopped tomatoes and pesto mixture into sausage/vegetable/ potato mixture.**

Serve immediately on individual plates and garnish with Parmesan cheese.

Notes

Loaded Rice

One last time before the year ends - and you'll use up your pesto!

MONDAY

December/Week Four

Notes

Preparation time: 25 minutes
Servings: 2
Ingredients:

8-10 baby red potatoes or 1 large russet potato
1 T. olive oil

1/2 lb. mushrooms *(sliced)*
1/4 red bell pepper *(thin-sliced)*
1 T. olive oil
1 large clove garlic *(smashed and chopped)*
1/4 C. white wine
2 slices medium onion *(quartered)*

3/4 C. chicken or vegetable broth
3 T. corn starch dissolved in 1/8 C. cold water

1 1/2 C. cooked brown rice

1 C. plain, nonfat yogurt
1 T. pesto
dash of Tabasco®

2 Roma tomatoes *(chopped)*

- **Preheat oven to 400 degrees.**
- **Wash and halve baby red potatoes. If using russet potato, wash and slice** *(unpeeled)* **in 1/2" slices. Place potatoes, flat side down, on cookie sheet oiled with one tablespoon olive oil.**
- **Sauté sliced mushrooms and bell pepper in oil with garlic, wine, and onion** *(about 4 minutes).* **When done, remove mushroom mixture from pan with perforated spoon. Set aside.**
- **Add broth to pan. Return to boil.**
- **If cooking russet potato slices, turn them now.**
- **Slowly stir corn starch mixture into boiling liquid. Reduce heat to low. Cook 5 minutes, stirring often.**
- **Add mushrooms to thickened mixture. Return to boil. Remove from heat.**
- **Warm 1 1/2 C. cooked rice 2 minutes on high in microwave on individual serving plates.**
- **Remove potatoes from oven. If using baby reds, push them into rice. If using russets, chop into 1" pieces before sprinkling over rice.**
- **Stir yogurt, pesto, and Tabasco® together until smooth. Microwave 30 seconds on high. Stir again, and add to thickened mushroom sauce.**

"Quick cook" some rice this morning. *(see page 348)*

Pour sauce over potato/rice mixture and garnish with fresh chopped tomato. Enjoy!

TUESDAY

December/Week Four

Notes

____

____

____

____

____

____

____

Merry Christmas, Everyone!

My sincere wishes to you and your loved ones for a warm, safe, and stress-free holiday. The greatest of gifts has already been given when one has given the gift of love.

Swedish Meatballs

(or Your Favorite Christmas Meal)

Perhaps you have a traditional Christmas Eve meal. If you don't have a traditional favorite, perhaps you would like to start one. (Swedish Meatballs has been the traditional dinner in our house for years.)

Preparation time: 1 hour and 30 minutes

Servings: 3-4

Ingredients:

Meatballs

1 lb. ground turkey breast or lean ground pork	1 tsp. dry oregano leaves
1 C. crushed saltine crackers	2 tsp. dry basil leaves
1 clove garlic *(smashed and chopped)*	1/2 tsp. ground black pepper
2 thin slices onion *(chopped very fine)*	1/4 tsp. thyme leaves
two egg whites	1/8 tsp. nutmeg
1/8 C. fresh chopped parsley *(or 3 T. dry parsley)*	1/3 C. chicken broth

one 15 oz. can whole cranberry sauce

5 medium-sized russet potatoes *(quartered)*

1/2 red bell pepper *(sliced in thin strips)*
1 clove garlic *(smashed and chopped)*
2 tsp. olive oil

1 lb. fresh broccoli

- **In large bowl, mix all meatball ingredients. Mix with hands until will blended.**
- **Heat 1 T. oil in large cast iron skillet 1 minute over medium-high heat. Remove pan from heat.**
- **Form meat balls** *(slightly smaller than a golf ball)* **with rolling motion between hands, and place in hot skillet. Return to heat. Turn often until well browned. Remove from pan and place in uncovered pan in oven at 300 degrees for about 30 minutes.**
- **Open a can of cranberries and spoon into serving dish,** *(save can).*
- **Pour excess grease or liquid from meatballs into empty can and discard.** *Set skillet aside. Drippings will be used to finish meal.*
- **Peel potatoes, quarter and place in large, covered, sauce pan with 3/4 C. water. Bring to boil, reduce heat to med. and cook 15 minutes. Remove from heat when cooked. Drain and reserve cooking water. Serve in bowl as plain boiled potatoes.**
- **Make white gravy.** *(See recipe in box on left.)*
- **Sauté pepper slices in garlic and oil in bottom of medium sauce pan 1 minute. Remove from pan.**
- **Add 3 C. water and a pinch of salt. Bring to boil.**
- **Drop broccoli into water just before serving meal and boil 1 minute. Drain. Toss with peppers in pan.**

Serve family style, and allow everyone to help themselves.

White Gravy

1/2 C. white wine
one 15 oz. can chicken broth
1/4 C. flour blended with 1/2 C. nonfat milk
fresh-ground black pepper
dash of nutmeg

1/2 C. nonfat yogurt *(stirred smooth)*

- *Add wine to pan used to cook meatballs. Rub bottom of pan with fork as it boils to bring up drippings on the bottom. Add broth and leftover water from cooking potatoes. Return to boil. Shake flour mixture vigorously to be sure there are no lumps and slowly stir into boiling liquid. As gravy thickens reduce heat to low, season with a few turns of fresh-ground black pepper and a dash of nutmeg. Cook 5 minutes.*
- *Add meatballs to gravy and cook another 5 minutes. Stir in yogurt just prior to serving.*

Baked Salmon Dinner

WEDNESDAY

December/Week Four

This dinner comes together easily once the salmon and potatoes are in the oven. You can leisurely prepare the potatoes and salmon during the day. The spinach preparation will take about 15 minutes if you're using prewashed, packaged spinach.

Preparation time: 30 minutes *(once salmon is in oven)*
Servings: 4
Ingredients:

4 medium russet potatoes *(sliced)*
1 T. olive oil
1/2 sweet onion *(sliced thin)*

one 3-4 lb. whole, fresh salmon *(cleaned, filleted, and head removed)*

Salmon Baste
1/4 C. white wine
1 small clove garlic *(smashed and chopped)*
2 T. brown sugar
2 T. Worcestershire sauce

black pepper
4-5 slices yellow onion
one orange *(sliced in rounds with rind)*

3 T. Parmesan cheese

one 15 oz. can whole cranberry sauce *(stir well and place in glass dish)*

- **Preheat oven to 450 degrees.**
- **Place sliced potatoes face down in oiled loaf pan or 9" X 13" glass dish. Layer potatoes/onion/potatoes. Season each layer with black pepper.**
- **Rinse salmon to clean thoroughly. Open salmon and place flat** *(skin side down)* **on cookie sheet lined with foil.**
- **Mix wine, garlic, sugar and Worcestershire in bowl. Microwave 1 minute on high.**
- **Spread Baste over both sides of salmon, and season with black pepper. Lay onion slices and oranges on one side. Place halves together and cover loosely with foil** *(leave plenty of space for steam to escape).*
- **Place salmon and potatoes in oven at same time. Set timer for 30 minutes.** *You will need to cook the salmon 15 minutes for every inch of thickness of the flesh. Check the salmon after 30 minutes. As the flesh cooks, it becomes lighter in color. The salmon is done when the flesh is consistently light in color. If more cooking is required, lay salmon open (skin side down), loosely cover again, and return to oven.*
- **Remove potatoes from oven after 30 minutes of cooking.**
- **When salmon is cooked, begin Creamed Spinach.** *(see box)*
- **Remove salmon skin, onion and orange slices from salmon and sprinkle Parmesan on potatoes.**

Serve salmon wedge flanked by potatoes and "Creamed" Spinach. Set dish of cranberries on table. (Save about 5 oz. salmon for Friday's salad.)

"Creamed" Spinach

2 bags prewashed spinach
1 clove garlic *(smashed and chopped)*
1/2 red bell pepper *(sliced thin)*
2 slices medium onion *(chopped fine)*
1/4 C. white wine
1/2 C. broth
4 T. flour *(shaken with 1/4 C. nonfat milk)*
1/8 tsp. nutmeg
1/4 C. plain, nonfat yogurt *(stirred smooth)*

- *Sauté first six ingredients in large heavy-bottomed kettle until wilted. Remove vegetables with perforated spoon and set aside. Pour any excess liquid back into pan.*
- *Thicken liquid with flour mixture. Reduce heat to low. Cook 5 minutes.*
- *Add nutmeg and return spinach to kettle. Bring to boil and remove from heat. Add stirred yogurt.*

THURSDAY

December/Week Four

Notes

Pasta Prima Vera

Yummm! Red Sauce prima vera. You will need to make fresh Red Sauce.

Preparation Time: 30 minutes
Serves: 2
Ingredients:

2 1/2 C. dry spiral pasta

1 1/2 C. Red Sauce *(see page 349)*

1 T. olive oil
1/2 tsp. crushed garlic
1 large carrot *(peeled and sliced)*
2 slices medium onion *(quartered)*

1/4 C. broth *(use vegetable if you are cooking vegetarian)*
1/2 medium green pepper *(cubed in 1" chunks)*
1 small zucchini 6" long *(cut in rounds)*
6 medium mushrooms *(sliced)*

2 Roma tomatoes *(cut in 1" chunks)*

2-4 T. fancy-shred Parmesan cheese
4 T. chopped black olives

- **Place pasta water on to boil in large sauce pan.**
- **Drop dry pasta into boiling water and cook 8 minutes.** *(Set a timer so you don't forget.)*
- **Make Red Sauce.**
- **Measure olive oil and garlic into sauté pan over medium-high heat. Start with carrot and onion. Sauté 1 minute.**
- **Add broth, green pepper, zucchini, and mushrooms - sauté 2 minutes. Remove veggies from pan and set aside.**
- **Drain and rinse pasta.**
- **Pour 1 1/2 C. Red Sauce into same pan used to cook pasta. Bring to boil.**
- **Add all vegetables** *(including Roma tomatoes)* **to sauce and remove from heat.**
- **If necessary, microwave cooked pasta 1 minute on high to re-heat, or measure 1 to 1 1/2 C. per serving and place in bowl with boiling water for 1 minute prior to serving. Drain and rinse in colander.**
- **Divide pasta onto separate plates and ladle veggie sauce over it.**

Garnish with Parmesan and chopped olives and serve immediately.

Caesar Salad with Salmon

FRIDAY

December/Week Four

Lighter fare after heavier holiday meals. You should have a little salmon leftover from Christmas dinner.

Preparation time: 25 minutes
Servings: 2
Ingredients:

Notes

Salad
7 large leaves Romaine lettuce *(broken)*
3 large leaves green leaf lettuce *(broken)*
1/2 cucumber *(peeled, sliced in 1/4" rounds and quartered)*
3 green onions *(chopped)*
1/2 red bell pepper *(thin sliced and quartered)*
4 Roma tomatoes *(chopped)*
4 mushrooms *(thin-sliced)*

Dressing
1/2 tsp. fresh-ground black pepper
3 T. vegetable broth
1 T. balsamic vinegar
2 cloves garlic *(smashed and chopped)*
1 tsp. Dijon mustard
5 T. lemon juice
1 1/2 tsp. Worcestershire sauce

5 oz. baked salmon fillet *(broken into pieces)*

2-3 T. fancy-shred Parmesan

1 apple *(cored and sliced)*
1 loaf of your favorite hearty bread

Pick up a loaf of hearty bread today.

- **Toss vegetables in large bowl with broken lettuce leaves.**
- **Whisk dressing ingredients together.**
- **Pour dressing into bowl with vegetables and toss.**
- **Serve salads on large individual plates. Sprinkle with salmon pieces.**

Garnish with Parmesan cheese, serve with sliced apple and hearty bread.

SATURDAY

December/January

Notes

SHOPPING DAY

This will be your final shopping day of the year!

Which juices are best? *Orange juice is a winner! One glass supplies the following adult requirements: 100% vitamin C; 20% folic acid; 10% potassium; and 6% magnesium, copper, and vitamins A and B6. Other good choices: grapefruit, lemon, prune, pineapple, cranberry, and grape juice.*
Nutrition Action Health Letter, July-August, 1995, 1875 Connecticut Ave., Suite 300, Washington, DC

Fight colds before they get a grip. *Wash your hands and your children's hands often. Clean phones and door knobs with disinfectant. If you have more than one child, clean toys often. Use disposable tissue and toss after each use. Empty waste baskets often. Drink lots of liquids, particularly water.*
Gallup Polls and USDA nutritional information

Among other benefits, *beans work to suppress the appetite. Why? Beans digest slowly, which causes a gradual increase in blood sugar.*
Prevention's Guide to Weight Loss, 33 E. Minor St., Emmaus, PA 19098

Stay fresh during the holidays. *Schedule regular exercise, even if it's a walk before dinner. Don't drink alcohol or caffeine before bed. Switch to soda during the later hours of holiday parties and drink decaf with any dessert that's served late in the evening. Get plenty of rest. (This may mean going to fewer holiday parties!)*

GROCERY LIST

Produce

one head red cabbage
8-10 baby red potatoes
2 medium yellow onions
1/2 lb. fresh mushrooms
2 green bell peppers
1 red bell pepper
1 large carrot
3 tart apples
1/2 lb. fresh broccoli
iceberg lettuce
green salad fixings
6-8 Roma tomatoes
1 fresh lemon

Frozen Foods

Meat/Fish/Poultry

2 lb. ground turkey breast
4-6 boneless, skinless chicken breasts
1/2 lb. turkey breast fillets

Canned or Dry Foods

two 29 oz. cans tomato sauce
one 29 oz. can "Ready-cut" tomatoes
12 oz. dry kidney beans or
two 28 oz cans kidney beans
two 15 oz. cans chicken broth
16 oz. dry whole wheat spiral pasta
8 oz. fresh fettuccine
1 large thin-crust Boboli®
a loaf of your favorite hearty bread

Chilled Foods and Dairy

4 oz. sharp cheddar cheese
large wheat tortillas
fresh salsa

Buy if you're out

1 head garlic
one bunch cilantro
celery
parsley
brown rice
ground anise
ground cloves
chili powder
ground cumin
Greek or Italian olives
capers
red cooking wine
white cooking wine
plain, nonfat yogurt
butter

Red Bean Chili and Brown Rice

SUNDAY

December/January

More great cold weather fare. The chili is wonderful on its own, but I love it in combination with rice. Cook the kidney beans during the day. Cook brown rice 1/2 hour before dinner. Freeze the leftovers for a busy night....next year!

Preparation time: 2-3 hours
Servings: 3-6
Ingredients:

Notes

4 C. cooked kidney beans *(you may use two 28 oz. cans beans)*
Sometimes I use a combination of one 15 oz. can garbanzo beans, one 15 oz. can kidney beans and one 28 oz. can kidney beans.

1 lb. ground turkey breast
1 medium onion *(chopped)*
2 stalks celery *(chopped)*
1 clove garlic *(smashed and chopped)*
1/4 C. broth

1 green bell pepper *(chopped)*
1 red bell pepper *(chopped)*
1/4 C. fresh cilantro *(chopped) You may substitute 3 T. dry cilantro leaves.*
one 29 oz. can "Ready-cut" tomatoes
one 29 oz. can tomato sauce
2 cloves garlic *(smashed and chopped)*
2 T. dried oregano leaves
2 tsp. ground cumin
1/4 tsp. ground cloves
8 T. chili powder
1/4 tsp. cayenne pepper *(optional)*

2 C. cooked brown rice
sharp cheddar cheese

a loaf of your favorite hearty bread

- **Cook beans as described** *(see page 295)* **or use canned beans.**
- **Brown turkey with onion, celery, and garlic in 1/4 C. broth in large heavy-bottomed kettle.** *About 7 minutes over medium-high heat.* **When liquid boils away, keep stirring until turkey meat is golden brown.**
- **Remove pan from heat and add all remaining ingredients** *(in shaded box.)*
- **Bring to boil, cover, reduce heat to low, and cook one hour.**
- **Cook rice.**
- **Place 1/2 C. rice in bowl. Fill bowl with chili. Garnish with a grating of sharp cheddar cheese.**

Serve with a slice of your favorite bread.

MONDAY

December/January

Notes

Leftover Night

Do you have leftover stuff in the fridge? Clean it out and start the year right.

Preparation time: 20 minutes
Servings: 2-3
Ingredients:

Whatever you have in the fridge.
leftover Pasta Prima Vera
leftover Red Bean Chili

Make a green salad *to go with leftovers tonight.*

More on holiday get-togethers and office parties. *Eat a small meal before heading off to a party if you know dinner will be served late.*
1995 Providence Heart Diet, Providence Heart Center, Seattle, WA

Eat a small breakfast at home. *Fast food breakfasts are a "no-no". A biscuit and sausage at MacDonald's has about the same number of calories as an order of large French fries, Quarter Pounder, and side salad with 1000 Island dressing.*
Nutrition Action Health Letter, Center for Science in the Public Interest, 1875 Connecticut Ave. NW, Washington, D. C.

Keep cheese fresh longer. *Store cheese in a sealed plastic bag in the fridge after opening. If mold appears, simply slice off the moldy portions. The cheese underneath is fine and carries no flavor of the mold.*

Pasta Putanesca

Spicy pasta night. Finish the year with a blast!

TUESDAY

December/January

Preparation time: 30 minutes
Servings: 2-3
Ingredients:

Italian Turkey Sausage
1 T. olive oil
1 lb. ground turkey breast
2 slices medium yellow onion *(chopped)*
2 tsp. dry basil leaves
1 tsp. dry oregano leaves
1/2 tsp. ground anise
2 large cloves garlic *(smashed and chopped)*
dash of Tabasco® sauce

1 1/2 C. Red Sauce *(leftovers or see page 349)*
1/8 C. red wine
2 cloves garlic *(smashed and chopped)*
2 T. green capers *I like the larger capers, they're softer and more flavorful.*
5 Italian or Greek olives *(chopped)*

green salad fixings

12 oz. dry whole wheat pasta

3 T. fancy-shred Parmesan
1 T. chopped parsley

Notes

- **Place pasta water on to boil in large kettle.**
- **Place all Italian Sausage ingredients in fry pan and cook until browned over medium-high heat** *(about 10 minutes)*. **Remove from heat and set aside.** *Use 1/3 of the Italian Sausage in tonight's recipe and save remainder for another time.*
- **Prepare Red Sauce.** *Reserve 1 1/2 C. for tonight's meal and save the rest for a future meal.*
- **Prepare green salads on individual plates.**
- **To 1 1/2 C. Red Sauce, add wine, 1/3 of the cooked Italian Sausage, 2 cloves garlic, capers, and olives.**
- **Cover sauce and place over low heat while finishing dinner preparations.**
- **Drop dry pasta into boiling water. Cook 8 minutes. Drain and rinse.**
- **Divide pasta onto plates and cover with Putanesca Sauce.**

A new year is born!

Garnish with Parmesan cheese and chopped parsley. Light a candle and open a nice bottle of red wine to toast in the new year!

Index

GROCERY LIST
January/Week Two

Produce

2 medium russet potatoes
3 medium white potatoes
8-10 baby red potatoes
2 medium yellow onions
1 lb. fresh mushrooms
1 green bell pepper
1 red bell pepper
3 laege carrots
1/2 lb. fresh broccoli
green salad fixings
one bunch chard
6-8 Roma tomatoes
4 tart apples
1 fresh lemon
ginger root

Frozen Foods

1 package frozen spinach

Meat/Fish/Poultry

1 lb. ground turkey breast
1 package thin sliced turkey breast fillets
2 frozen halibut fillets *(If you prefer fresh* fish, buy on the day you plan to cook it.)

Canned or Dry Foods

one 29 oz. can tomato sauce
one 15 oz. can chicken broth
one 6 oz. can sliced water chestnuts
one 6 oz. can sliced bamboo shoots
8 oz. fresh fettuccine
8 oz. fresh (or dry) cheese tortellini
1 box old fashioned rolled oats
1 C. package shelled walnut halves
graham crackers
raisins
dried fennel seed
ground nutmeg
ground anise
red cooking wine

Chilled Foods and Dairy

1 dozen eggs

Buy if you're out

1 head garlic
frozen corn
12-16 oz. brown rice

GROCERY LIST
Getting Started

Produce

1 lb. fresh broccoli
12-15 baby red potatoes
2 heads garlic
one 6" zucchini
2 medium yellow onions
2 large carrots
1/2 lb. white mushrooms
5-6 tart apples
1 head iceberg lettuce
1 head red leaf lettuce
10-12 Roma tomatoes
2 green bell peppers
2 red bell peppers
1 cucumber
pine nuts
1 fresh lemon

Canned or Dry Foods

12 oz. dry spaghetti
12 oz. dry spiral pasta
16 oz. brown rice
two 15 oz. cans chicken broth
one 29 oz. can tomato sauce
1 small jar Dijon mustard
1 small jar honey mustard
1 bottle low or nonfat salad dressing
Tabasco® sauce
chili powder
cumin powder
dry basil leaves
dry oregano leaves
one 16 oz. box corn starch
5 lb. unbleached flour
5 lb. white sugar
1 C. package pecan halves
one 17 oz. bottle olive oil
one 6 oz. bottle sesame oil
one 17 oz. bottle white vinegar
one 17 oz. bottle balsamic vinegar
6 oz. vegetable oil spray *(pump style)*
1 liter white cooking wine
breakfast cereal
1 large thin-crust Boboli®
1 loaf whole wheat bread

Frozen Foods

one 12 oz. can orange juice
12 oz. frozen peas
12 oz. frozen corn

Meat/Fish/Poultry

2 boneless, skinless chicken breasts
1 lb. Italian chicken or turkey sausage links
2 fresh snapper fillets
1 lb. turkey breast fillets

Chilled Foods and Dairy

1/2 gallon nonfat milk
32 oz. plain, nonfat yogurt
14 oz. fresh salsa
6 oz. fancy-shred Parmesan
3 oz. sharp cheddar cheese
7 oz. fresh pesto
1 package whole wheat tortillas
8 oz. fresh egg fettuccine

Notes

Notes

Notes

GROCERY LIST
January/February

Produce
1 medium yellow onion
8-10 baby red potatoes
1/2 lb. fresh mushrooms
1 green bell pepper
1 red bell pepper
1 large carrot or 2 medium carrots
1 bunch celery
1/2 lb. fresh broccoli
1 bunch red leaf lettuce
one head iceberg lettuce
one bunch green onions
green salad fixings
8 Roma tomatoes
1 large tart apple
1 bunch fresh basil
1 fresh lemon

Frozen Foods
1 package frozen spinach

Meat/Fish/Poultry
1 1/2 lb. ground turkey breast
1 boneless, skinless chicken breast
6-8 slices barbecued pork

Canned or Dry Foods
one 29 oz. can tomato sauce
two 15 oz. cans chicken broth
one 15 oz. can vegetable broth
one 6 oz. can sliced bamboo shoots
12 oz. dry penne or mastaciolli pasta
8 oz. fresh cheese tortellini

Chilled Foods and Dairy
plain, nonfat yogurt
4 oz. sharp cheddar cheese
whole wheat flour tortillas
or corn tortillas

Buy if you're out
1 head fresh garlic
frozen corn
frozen peas
sesame oil
low-sodium soy sauce
brown rice
saltine crackers
fresh pesto
fresh salsa
eggs

GROCERY LIST
March/Week One

Produce
one 6" zucchini
1 medium yellow onions
1 1/2 lb. fresh mushrooms
1 green bell pepper
1 red bell pepper
1 large carrot
1 acorn squash
1/2 lb. fresh broccoli
green salad fixings
8 Roma tomatoes
2 oranges
1 tart apple
2 fresh lemons
1 bunch fresh cilantro

Frozen Foods

Meat/Fish/Poultry
1 1/2 fresh true cod fillets *(you may wish to buy fresh fish on Thursday.)*
1 lb. turkey breast fillets
1/2 lb. ground turkey breast

Canned or Dry Foods
one 29 oz. can tomato sauce
one 15 oz. can chicken broth
one 6 oz. can chopped black olives
16 oz. dry whole wheat spaghetti
16 oz. whole wheat spiral pasta
1 lb. dry black beans *or two 15 oz. cans black beans*
one large thin-crust Boboli®

Chilled Foods and Dairy
plain, nonfat yogurt
nonfat milk

Buy if you're out
1 head garlic
1 bunch fresh parsley
frozen corn
1 jar garlic dill pickles
Worcestershire sauce
balsamic vinegar
whole wheat flour tortillas

GROCERY LIST
February/March

Produce
2 medium yellow onions
1/2 lb. fresh mushrooms
2 green bell peppers
2 red bell peppers
2 large carrots
celery
1/8 lb. fresh broccoli
one head green cabbage
iceberg lettuce
one bunch green onions
green salad fixings
10-12 Roma tomatoes
1 large slicing tomato
1 fresh lemon

Frozen Foods
frozen concentrated orange juice
16 oz. frozen peas

Meat/Fish/Poultry
1 lb. turkey breast fillets
5 boneless, skinless chicken breasts
2 frozen orange roughy fillets *(do not thaw)*
6 frozen scallops *(do not thaw)*

Canned or Dry Foods
one 29 oz. can tomato sauce
two 15 oz. cans chicken broth
12 oz. dry whole wheat spiral pasta
8 oz. fresh cheese or hazelnut tortellini
1/2 C. package pecan halves
6-8 hazelnuts
a loaf of your favorite Italian bread

Chilled Foods and Dairy
4 oz. sharp cheddar cheese
whole wheat tortillas
plain, nonfat yogurt

Buy if you're out
1 head garlic
fresh ginger root
1 bunch fresh parsley
brown rice
brown sugar
red cooking wine
white cooking wine
fresh pesto

Notes

Notes

Notes

GROCERY LIST
March/April

Produce

one 6" zucchini
one 6" crooked neck squash
3 medium russet potatoes
3 medium yellow onions
1 1/2 lb. fresh mushrooms
1 green bell pepper
2 red bell peppers
1 yellow bell pepper
1 large carrot
bok choy
1/2 lb. fresh broccoli
green salad fixings
1 head red or green leaf lettuce
1 cucumber
8-10 Roma tomatoes
one bunch fresh parsley
2 oranges
1 lemon
1 lime
1 package firm, plain tofu

Frozen Foods

1 package cooked, shelled, large shrimp (buy frozen shrimp if fresh are unavailable)

Meat/Fish/Poultry

1 lb. boneless, skinless chicken breasts
1 Italian sausage link
2 chorizo sausage links
5 large raw shrimp *(you may wish to pick up on Friday)*

Canned or Dry Foods

one 29 oz. can tomato sauce
four 15 oz. cans chicken broth
one 15 oz. can vegetable broth
saffron threads
one 6 oz. can sliced water chestnuts
one 6 oz. can sliced bamboo shoots
white rice
1 lb. dry navy beans or four 15 oz. cans beans
12 oz. dry multi-colored spiral pasta
8 oz. fresh cheese ravioli
one 6 oz. can black olives
8 oz. roasted cashews
one box fortune cookies
a loaf of hearty bread

Chilled Foods and Dairy

pesto sauce

Buy if you're out

1 head garlic
celery
frozen corn
sesame oil
low-sodium soy sauce
white vinegar
white cooking wine

GROCERY LIST
March/Week Four

Produce

one 6" zucchini
2 medium yellow onions
1/2 lb. fresh mushrooms
1 green bell pepper
1 red bell pepper
3 large carrots
1/4 lb. fresh broccoli
1/8 lb. fresh green beans
one head Romaine lettuce
green salad fixings
iceberg lettuce
one bunch green onions
one large cucumber
6-8 Roma tomatoes
4 lemons

Frozen Foods

Meat/Fish/Poultry

3 fresh halibut fillets
turkey bacon
2 boneless, skinless chicken breasts

Canned or Dry Foods

one 29 oz. can tomato sauce
one 29 oz. can chopped tomatoes
one 29 oz. can "Ready-cut" tomatoes
two 15 oz. cans chicken broth
four 15 oz. cans vegetable broth
16 oz. dry whole wheat penne pasta
12 oz. dry spiral pasta or spaghetti *(get whole wheat if you can find it)*
one 15 oz. can garbanzo beans
one 15 oz. can kidney beans
a loaf of your favorite hearty bread

Chilled Foods and Dairy

1 dozen eggs
fancy-shred Parmesan
fresh pesto

Buy if you're out

1 head garlic
celery
frozen corn
frozen peas
sesame oil
low-sodium soy sauce
brown rice
dry red wine
fumé blanc (wine)
butter

GROCERY LIST
March/Week Three

Produce

2 large russet potatoes
2 medium russet potatoes
one 6" zucchini
3 medium yellow onions
1/2 lb. fresh mushrooms
1 green bell pepper
2 red bell peppers
4 large carrots
celery
1/4 lb. fresh green beans
1/2 lb. broccoli
2 bunches fresh spinach *(or 1 package fresh, prewashed spinach)*
green salad fixings
one large cucumber
one bunch green onions
one bunch fresh cilantro
one bunch fresh parsley
6-8 Roma tomatoes
1 tart apple
2 dozen pistachios
1 ripe cantaloupe
1 lemon
1 lime
1 package plain, firm tofu
hearty bread

Frozen Foods

frozen spinach

Meat/Fish/Poultry

1 1/2 lb. turkey breast fillets
1 lb. boneless, skinless chicken breasts
1 1/4 lb. fresh salmon fillets
(You may wish to buy fresh fish *the day it is to be cooked.)*

Canned or Dry Foods

four 15 oz. cans chicken broth
one 6 oz. can sliced water chestnuts
12 oz. dry spinach spiral pasta
8 oz. fresh cheese tortellini
1 small jar Italian or Greek olives
a loaf of hearty bread

Chilled Foods and Dairy

1 dozen eggs
plain, nonfat yogurt

Buy if you're out

1 head garlic
1/2 C. pine nuts
frozen peas
brown rice
dry dill weed
cayenne pepper
Dijon mustard

Notes

Notes

Notes

GROCERY LIST
April/Week Three

Produce
2 medium yellow onions
10 baby red potatoes
6-8 small white potatoes
6 fresh mushrooms
2 green bell peppers
2 red bell peppers
1 yellow or orange bell pepper
2 large carrots
1/8 lb. fresh broccoli
one head green cabbage
green salad fixings
1 bunch beet greens *(or available greens)*
6-8 Roma tomatoes
1 lemon
1 lime
1 tart apple
1 bunch fresh parsley

Frozen Foods
frozen orange juice
1 package large, shelled, cooked shrimp

Meat/Fish/Poultry
3 Italian turkey or chicken sausage links
2 frozen orange roughy fillets

Canned or Dry Foods
one 29 oz. can tomato sauce
one 29 oz. can "Ready-cut" tomatoes
two 15 oz. cans chicken broth
1 lb. dry navy beans or
two 15 oz. cans cooked white beans
buy canned beans if you are not cooking dry beans
12 oz. dry bow tie pasta
8 oz. fresh cheese ravioli
a loaf of hearty bread

Chilled Foods and Dairy

Buy if you're out
1 head garlic
frozen peas
corn starch
brown sugar
brown rice
Dijon mustard
red cooking wine
shredded Parmesan
plain, nonfat yogurt
butter

GROCERY LIST
April/Week Two

Produce
6 medium russet potatoes
10 baby red potatoes
4-6 fresh turnips
one 6" zucchini
2 medium yellow onions
1 lb. fresh mushrooms
1 green bell pepper
1 red bell pepper
2 large carrots
green salad fixings
green leaf lettuce
one cucumber
3-4 bunches fresh spinach *or two bags prewashed spinach*
6-8 Roma tomatoes
1 head red cabbage
1 tart apple
1 fresh lemon

Frozen Foods

Meat/Fish/Poultry
1 lb. ground turkey breast
2-3 lb. turkey breast fillets

Canned or Dry Foods
two 29 oz. cans tomato sauce
three 15 oz. cans chicken broth
one 6 oz. can tuna packed in water
one 15 oz. can whole cranberries
8 oz. fresh fettuccine
12 oz. dry penne pasta
lowfat Italian salad dressing

Chilled Foods and Dairy
plain, nonfat yogurt
pesto sauce
butter

Buy if you're out
1 head garlic
toasted sunflower meats
sesame oil
extra-virgin olive oil
ground anise
brown rice
red cooking wine

Notes

Notes

GROCERY LIST
May/Week Two

Produce

2 large russet potatoes
one 6" zucchini
2 yellow onions
1/8 lb. fresh broccoli
1/2 lb. fresh mushrooms
2 green bell peppers
one each - yellow
and red bell pepper
bok choy
1 orange
1/4 lb. dried cranberries
green salad fixings
6-8 Roma tomatoes

Frozen Foods

frozen corn

Meat/Fish/Poultry

1 lb. ground turkey breast
8-10 large frozen, cooked, shelled shrimp
2 boneless, skinless chicken breasts

Canned or Dry Foods

1/2 C. package chopped walnuts
1/2 C. package whole, blanched almonds
one 6 oz. can sliced water chestnuts
one 6 oz. can sliced bamboo shoots
one 15 oz. can apple sauce
one 29 oz. can tomato sauce
two 29 oz. cans "Ready-cut" tomatoes
two 15 oz. cans chicken broth
2 C. dry black beans *(or two 15 oz. cans black beans)*
2 C. dry navy beans *(or two 15 oz. cans navy beans)*
12 oz. dry whole wheat or spinach spaghetti
12 oz. dry multi-colored spiral pasta
red cooking wine
one loaf of your favorite hearty bread
1 box fortune cookies

Chilled Foods and Dairy

3 oz. sharp Cheddar cheese

Buy if you're out

one head garlic
dried thyme leaves
ground cumin
chili powder
ground cloves
old-fashioned oats
plain, nonfat yogurt
fancy shred Parmesan

GROCERY LIST
May/Week One

Produce

8-10 baby red potatoes
or 1 large russet potato
4 tart apples
2 yellow onions
1/2 lb. fresh broccoli
1 lb. fresh mushrooms
2 green bell peppers
2 red bell peppers
12 medium carrots
1 bunch green onions
2 bunches fresh spinach
or 1 package prewashed spinach
green salad fixings
1 cucumber
6-8 Roma tomatoes
one lemon
firm tofu

Frozen Foods

Meat/Fish/Poultry

1 lb. ground turkey breast
2 boneless, skinless chicken breasts
2 fresh snapper or cod fillets *(You will not cook the fish until Thursday. You may wish to wait and purchase freshfish on Thursday.)*

Canned or Dry Foods

1/2 C. package sliced almonds
1/2 C. package pecan halves
one small bottle Greek or Italian olives
one small bottle capers
one small can sliced black olives
one 29 oz. can tomato sauce
five 15 oz. cans chicken broth
one 15 oz. can vegetable broth
12 oz. dry spiral or penne pasta
(whole wheat if you can find it)
one loaf of your favorite hearty bread
2 large thin-crust Boboli® or frozen pizza shells

Chilled Foods and Dairy

1 dozen eggs

Buy if you're out

pine nuts
garlic
one package turkey bacon
(Check the freezer. You'll only need a couple pieces.)
ground cinnamon
dry basil leaves
dry oregano leaves
dry tarragon leaves
ground anise
brown rice
Tabasco®
olive oil
Dijon mustard
red cooking wine
white cooking wine
plain, nonfat yogurt
fresh pesto
butter

GROCERY LIST
April/May

Produce

6-8 baby red or white potatoes
2-4 medium baking potatoes
2 medium yellow onions
4 tart apples
fresh ginger
1 green bell pepper
1 red bell pepper
1 yellow bell pepper
2 large carrots
one bunch green onions
green salad fixings
2 ripe kiwi
6-8 Roma tomatoes
fresh parsley
4 oz. fresh snow peas
1 lemon
1 lime

Frozen Foods

1 package frozen snow peas
(if fresh snow peas are unavailable)

Meat/Fish/Poultry

1 lb. ground turkey breast
1 package thin-sliced turkey fillets
(you may also use whole fillets and slice them yourself)
6-10 boneless, skinless chicken breasts
8-10 large, cooked cocktail shrimp

Canned or Dry Foods

one 29 oz. can tomato sauce
two 15 oz. cans chicken broth
one 15 oz. can black beans
one small bottle barbecue sauce
whole wheat or saltine crackers
8 oz. fresh cheese tortellini
white cooking wine

Chilled Foods and Dairy

6 oz. sharp cheddar cheese
nonfat milk
tortillas

Buy if you're out

garlic
frozen corn
one 15 oz. can navy beans
(if you have no leftover beans)
dried rosemary
chili powder
cumin powder
sesame oil
low-salt soy sauce
corn starch
balsamic vinegar
cornmeal
brown rice
Parmesan cheese
eggs
plain, nonfat yogurt

Notes

Notes

Notes

GROCERY LIST
May/June

Produce

1 6" zucchini
1 medium yellow onion
1/2 lb. fresh asparagus
1/8 lb. broccoli
1 lb. fresh mushrooms
2 green bell peppers
2 red bell peppers
2 tart apples (Granny Smith)
1 bunch fresh parsley
1 head red leaf lettuce
1 head Romaine lettuce
1 large cucumber
3 oz. pine nuts
10 Roma tomatoes
1 fresh lemon
celery

Frozen Foods

one package large, frozen scallops
You may choose to buy fresh scallops later in the week. If so, buy 10 small scallops.
orange juice

Meat/Fish/Poultry

3 boneless, skinless chicken breasts
8-10 oz. snapper *(you may wish to buy fresh fish on Wednesday)*

Canned or Dry Foods

1/2 C. pecan halves
one 29 oz. cans tomato sauce
two 15 oz. cans chicken broth
12 oz. dry spinach spiral pasta
12 oz. dry whole wheat spaghetti
8 oz. fresh egg fettuccine
1 loaf of your favorite hearty bread

Chilled Foods and Dairy

nonfat milk
3 oz. Gorgonzola cheese

Buy if you're out

brown rice
stone ground cornmeal
dried dill weed
dried rosemary
dried basil leaves
balsamic vinegar
sesame oil
corn starch
white cooking wine
red cooking wine
plain, nonfat yogurt
fancy-shred Parmesan

GROCERY LIST
May/Week Four

Produce

6-7 large russet potatoes
one 6" zucchini
3 large carrots
2 yellow onions
1/2 lb. fresh broccoli
1/2 lb. fresh mushrooms
1 green bell pepper
2 red bell peppers
one bunch red seedless grapes
1 pink grapefruit
1 white grapefruit
2-3 tart apples
one bunch fresh parsley
green salad fixings
one head red leaf lettuce
iceberg lettuce
cucumber
6-8 Roma tomatoes
2 fresh lemons

Frozen Foods

Meat/Fish/Poultry

1 lb. turkey breast fillets
10 -12 boneless, skinless chicken breasts

Canned or Dry Foods

one 15 oz. can whole beets
two 6 oz. cans chopped clams
one 29 oz. can tomato sauce
one 15 oz. can chicken broth
12 oz. dry spinach linguini
12 oz. dry penne pasta *(whole wheat)* or multi-colored spiral pasta
one large, thin-crust Boboli® shell
a loaf of your favorite crusty bread
You may wish to pick this up fresh from *the bakery on Thursday.*

Chilled Foods and Dairy

Buy if you're out

one head garlic
one 10 oz. package frozen corn
brown sugar
ground cinnamon
balsamic vinegar
Worcestershire sauce
honey
plain, nonfat yogurt
fancy-shred Parmesan

GROCERY LIST
May/Week Three

Produce

4-5 baby red potatoes
3 medium white potatoes
3 large carrots
one parsnip
2 yellow onions
1 sweet onion
1/2 lb. fresh broccoli
3/4 lb. fresh mushrooms
2 green bell peppers
2 red bell peppers
1 cucumber
two 6" zucchini
fresh ginger root
one bunch fresh parsley
green salad fixings
one head red leaf lettuce
iceberg lettuce
3 oz. toasted sunflower seeds *(shelled)*
6-8 Roma tomatoes
1 lemon
1 orange

Frozen Foods

one 3 lb. package frozen, boneless, skinless chicken breasts
frozen halibut fillets or steaks
Buy if fresh halibut is too expensive.

Meat/Fish/Poultry

1 lb. turkey breast fillets
2 halibut fillets *You may wish to buy fresh fish on Wednesday.*

Canned or Dry Foods

dried fennel seeds
paprika
ground cumin
whole bay leaf
brown sugar
white cooking wine
red cooking wine
two 6 oz. cans chopped clams
one 29 oz. can tomato sauce
two 15 oz. cans chicken broth
one small can sliced black olives
8 oz. fresh or dry linguini
12 oz. dry spiral pasta *(multi-colored or spinach)*
one loaf of your favorite hearty bread

Chilled Foods and Dairy

3 oz. sharp cheddar cheese
plain, nonfat yogurt
nonfat milk
whole wheat tortillas
fresh salsa

Buy if you're out

one head garlic
dried thyme leaves
ground cumin
chili powder
ground cloves
old-fashioned oats
plain, nonfat yogurt
fancy-shred Parmesan

Notes

Notes

Notes

GROCERY LIST
June/Week Three

Produce

2 large baking potatoes
1/4 lb. fresh snow peas *(buy frozen peas if fresh snow peas are not available)*
3 medium yellow onions
1/2 lb. fresh broccoli
1 head red cabbage
1 tart apple
1 lb. fresh mushrooms
1 green bell pepper
1 red bell pepper
green salad fixings
one large cucumber
2 slicing tomatoes
1 fresh lemon
1 orange
fresh strawberries

Frozen Foods

frozen corn

Meat/Fish/Poultry

2 boneless, skinless chicken breasts
one Chorizo sausage *(Italian sausage will do)*
4 oz. smoked salmon

Canned or Dry Foods

2 C. dry white beans
one 29 oz. can tomato sauce
two 15 oz. cans chicken broth
8 oz. fresh fettuccine
1 loaf of your favorite hearty bread

Chilled Foods and Dairy

3 oz. sharp cheddar cheese
fresh salsa

Buy if you're out

1 head fresh garlic
powdered cumin
caraway seed
nonfat Italian dressing
plain, nonfat yogurt
shredded Parmesan
1/2 dozen fresh eggs

GROCERY LIST
June/Week Two

Produce

2 large russet potatoes
10 baby red potatoes
one head broccoflower
1/2 lb. baby asparagus
one 8" and one 6" zucchini
one 8" yellow crooked neck squash
one medium yellow onion
1/2 lb. fresh mushrooms
2 green bell peppers
2 red bell peppers
one bunch green onions
one carrot
green salad fixings
one small piece ginger root
2 fresh lemons
one fresh lime
one orange
dried cranberries

Frozen Foods

Meat/Fish/Poultry

3-4 boneless, skinless chicken breasts
turkey bacon
8-12 oz. fresh tuna fillets (4 oz. per person)
If tuna fillets are not available or too expensive, use halibut.
2 Italian turkey sausage links
10 oz. fresh fillet of sole or orange roughy
Buy frozen roughy fillets and keep them frozen.

Canned or Dry Foods

one 29 oz. can tomato sauce
one 29 oz. can "Ready-cut" tomatoes
one 15 oz. can chicken broth
16 oz. dry penne pasta
12 oz. dry spiral pasta *(whole wheat)*
one 6 oz. can sliced black olives
1 large, thin-crust Boboli® shell
1 jar of your favorite jam

Chilled Foods and Dairy

nonfat cream cheese

Buy if you're out

1 head fresh garlic
shelled walnuts or pecans
sliced almonds
old-fashioned rolled oats
dried dill weed
low-salt soy sauce
wheat germ
white cooking wine
red cooking wine
plain, nonfat yogurt
1/2 dozen eggs
pesto

GROCERY LIST
June/Week One

Produce

10 baby red potatoes
1 medium yellow onion
1 red onion
2 bunches spinach or
1 package prewashed spinach
1 lb. fresh broccoli
1 lb. fresh mushrooms
1 green bell pepper
3 red bell peppers
1 large cucumber
1 head celery
bok choy
one head red leaf lettuce
1 head Romaine lettuce
one head green leaf lettuce
2 large cucumbers
8 Roma tomatoes
2 ripe peach or nectarines
1 pint fresh strawberries
1 tart apple
2 ripe pears *(if available)*
1 C. fresh blueberries
2 bananas
1 fresh lemon

Frozen Foods

frozen concentrated apple juice

Meat/Fish/Poultry

2 boneless, skinless chicken breasts
6 oz. frozen or fresh scallops

Canned or Dry Foods

1 C. package sliced almonds
one 29 oz. can tomato sauce
two 15 oz. cans chicken broth
one 15 oz. can vegetable broth
one 6 oz. can water chestnuts
one 6 oz. can sliced bamboo shoots
one small can sliced black olives
24 oz. dry spinach spiral pasta
12 oz. dry penne pasta
1 box fortune cookies
a loaf of your favorite hearty bread

Chilled Foods and Dairy

3 oz. feta cheese
1 package pita bread
fresh pesto

Buy if you're out

1 head garlic
1 bunch fresh parsley
balsamic vinegar
Greek olives
caraway seeds
curry powder
powdered nutmeg
sesame oil
corn starch
nonfat mayonnaise
white cooking wine
red cooking wine
plain, nonfat yogurt

Notes

Notes

Notes

GROCERY LIST
July/Week Two

Produce

6-8 baby red potatoes
2 large russet potatoes
one 6" zucchini
1 medium yellow onion
1/2 lb. fresh mushrooms
2 green bell peppers
2 red bell peppers
2 large carrots
celery
1/4 lb. fresh green beans
1/2 lb. fresh asparagus
1 head iceberg lettuce
1 head red leaf lettuce
1 head green leaf lettuce
2 bunches spinach
two large cucumbers
10-12 Roma tomatoes
1 bunch fresh parsley
1 bunch green onions
fresh chives
fresh mint leaves
1 lemon
2 tart apples
unflavored, firm tofu

Frozen Foods

Meat/Fish/Poultry

6 - 8 oz. fresh or frozen crab meat *(if available)*
1/2 lb. ground turkey breast
turkey bacon

Canned or Dry Foods

1 small jar dried chives *(if fresh* are unavailable)
one 15 oz. can vegetable broth
three 15 oz. cans chicken broth
one 29 oz. can tomato sauce
two 6 oz. cans tuna packed in water
one 6 oz. can crab meat *(if fresh* is unavailable)
12 oz. dry spinach spiral pasta
8 oz. fresh cheese tortellini
1/2 lb. bulgar
a loaf of your favorite hearty bread

Chilled Foods and Dairy

4 oz. sharp cheddar cheese
tortillas (wheat or corn)

Buy if you're out

1 head garlic
pine nuts
bulgar
olive oil
Greek olives
capers
balsamic vinegar
Dijon mustard
paprika
white cooking wine
saltine crackers
Tabasco sauce®
plain, nonfat yogurt
nonfat milk
fancy-shred Parmesan
fresh salsa
eggs
fresh pesto

GROCERY LIST
July/Week One

Produce

10 baby red potatoes
one large russet potato
one 6" zucchini
2 medium yellow onions
1 lb. fresh mushrooms
1/2 lb. broccoli
1 green bell pepper
1 red bell pepper
1 head broccoflower
1/2 lb. carrots
1/4 lb. fresh snow peas
2 fresh nectarines or peaches
one bunch fresh parsley
green salad fixings
one large cucumber
3 oz. pine nuts
6 Roma tomatoes
one bunch green onions
1 fresh lemon
firm tofu *(unflavored)*

Frozen Foods

Meat/Fish/Poultry

2 boneless, skinless chicken breasts
1 lb. ground turkey breast
2 small or 1 large orange roughy fillet *(Buy frozen fillets. Do not thaw.)*

Canned or Dry Foods

1 C. package shelled pecan halves
two 29 oz. cans tomato sauce
two 15 oz. cans chicken broth
one 6 oz. can chopped black olives
one package 18" *(or standard)* lasagna noodles
12 oz. dry whole wheat pasta
one box bulgar
1 loaf of your favorite Italian bread

Chilled Foods and Dairy

5 oz. part-skim mozzarella cheese
1 pint lowfat Ricotta cheese
1 dozen eggs
fresh salsa
pesto

Buy if you're out

1 head garlic
celery
brown rice
dried rosemary leaves
dried oregano leaves
dried dill weed
ground anise
honey mustard
red cooking wine
white cooking wine
plain, nonfat yogurt
fancy-shred Parmesan

Notes

Notes

GROCERY LIST
August/Week One

Produce
2 medium yellow onions
1 large sweet onion
8-10 baby red potatoes
2 green bell peppers
2 red bell peppers
1/2 lb. carrots
1 head iceberg lettuce
1 head red leaf lettuce
1 head green leaf lettuce
1 head Romaine lettuce
1 bunch fresh parsley
1 bunch green onions
celery
one red cabbage
1/2 lb. fresh mushrooms
1/2 lb. fresh asparagus
green salad fixings
one large cucumber
6-8 Roma tomatoes
1 ripe cantaloupe
4 fresh lemons

Frozen Foods

Meat/Fish/Poultry
5 boneless, skinless chicken breasts
6-8 large, cooked, shelled shrimp
1/2 lb. true cod fillet *(You may wish to* buy the cod fillets on Tuesday.)
turkey bacon

Canned or Dry Foods
one 29 oz. can tomato sauce
two 15 oz. cans black beans
1 small can sliced black olives
three 15 oz. cans chicken broth
one 6 oz. can sliced water chestnuts
one 6 oz. can sliced bamboo shoots
16 oz. dry penne pasta

Chilled Foods and Dairy
4 oz. sharp cheddar cheese
4 oz. mozzarella cheese
whole wheat tortillas
salsa

Buy if you're out
1 head garlic
toasted sunflower meats
frozen corn
turkey bacon
sesame oil
white cooking wine
low or nonfat salad dressing
1 dozen eggs

GROCERY LIST
July/August

Produce
one 6" zucchini
4 large russet potatoes
1 medium yellow onion
1 large sweet onion
1/2 lb. fresh mushrooms
1 green bell pepper
1 red bell pepper
3 large carrots
1 butternut squash
1/2 lb. fresh broccoli
1 head Romaine lettuce
1 head green leaf lettuce
green salad fixings
1 bunch green onions
1 large cucumber
6-8 Roma tomatoes
3 fresh peaches or nectarines
1/2 pint fresh raspberries
1 fresh lemon

Frozen Foods
orange juice
frozen raspberries *(if fresh unavailable)*

Meat/Fish/Poultry
1 lb. fresh salmon fillets
3 boneless, skinless chicken breasts

Canned or Dry Foods
chopped black olives
one 29 oz. can tomato sauce
three 15 oz. cans chicken broth
one 15 oz. can vegetable broth
one small can artichoke hearts
one 6 oz. can sliced water chestnuts
one 6 oz. can sliced bamboo shoots
16 oz. dry whole wheat spiral pasta
16 oz. dry radiatore pasta
8 oz. fresh cheese tortellini
1/4 lb. roasted cashews
fortune cookies

Chilled Foods and Dairy
1 dozen eggs

Buy if you're out
1 head garlic
frozen corn
sesame oil
low-sodium soy sauce
brown rice
Italian or Greek olives
corn starch
red wine vinegar
plain, nonfat yogurt

GROCERY LIST
July/Week Three

Produce
one 6" zucchini
1 medium red onion
2 medium yellow onions
1/2 lb. fresh mushrooms
1/2 lb. fresh broccoli
2 green bell peppers
2 red bell peppers
2 large carrots
1 head cabbage
1 head Romaine lettuce
1 head green leaf lettuce
2 large cucumbers
10-12 Roma tomatoes
2 medium tomatoes
1 bunch fresh cilantro
1 bunch green onions
fresh ginger root
1 lemon and 1 lime
1/2 C. toasted sunflower meats
1 fresh nectarine or peach
1 tart apple

Frozen Foods
one can frozen orange juice

Meat/Fish/Poultry
6 - 8 oz. fresh or frozen baby shrimp *(if available)*
4-5 boneless, skinless chicken breasts

Canned or Dry Foods
1/2 C. package sliced almonds
1 small jar dried chives *(if fresh are unavailable)*
three 15 oz. cans chicken broth
one 29 oz. can tomato sauce
two 6 oz. cans sliced water chestnuts
two 6 oz. cans chopped clams
one 6 oz. can baby shrimp *(if fresh is unavailable)*
12 oz. dry spiral pasta
8 oz. fresh angel hair pasta
16 oz. dry sea shell pasta

Chilled Foods and Dairy
4 oz. feta cheese
pita bread
fresh hummus

Buy if you're out
1 head garlic
1 bunch fresh parsley
frozen peas
low-sodium soy sauce
sesame oil
brown sugar
Dijon mustard
nonfat mayonnaise
1 small bottle Greek olives
white cooking wine
sliced almonds
brown rice
Tabasco® sauce
plain, nonfat yogurt

Notes

Notes

Notes

GROCERY LIST
August/Week Four

Produce
one 6" zucchini
10-12 baby white potatoes
2 medium yellow onions
1/2 lb. fresh mushrooms
2 green bell peppers
2 red bell peppers
1 yellow bell pepper
celery
1 bunch collard or other greens
8-10 ears fresh sweet corn
1/2 lb. fresh broccoli
1 head Romaine lettuce
1 head green leaf lettuce
green salad fixings
1 bunch green onions
one large cucumber
8-10 Roma tomatoes
one pear and 1/2 pt. berries
2 fresh lemons
1 lb. fresh peas *(in the pod)*
plain, firm tofu
1 fresh peach or nectarine

Frozen Foods
2 frozen snapper fillets *(if you are unable to buy fresh fish)*
frozen peas *(if fresh unavailable)*

Meat/Fish/Poultry
8-10 boneless, skinless chicken breasts
6-9 large, cooked, shelled shrimp
2 fresh snapper fillets *(You may wish to purchase fresh fish on Wednesday.)*

Canned or Dry Foods
one 29 oz. can tomato sauce
one 29 oz. can "Ready-cut" tomatoes
one 15 oz. can chicken broth
one 15 oz. can vegetable broth
one 6 oz. can sliced water chestnuts
16 oz. bow-tie pasta
16 oz. whole wheat spiral pasta
one 1/2 C. package slivered almonds
a loaf of your favorite hearty bread

Chilled Foods and Dairy
flour tortillas

Buy if you're out
1 head garlic
1 bunch fresh parsley
brown rice
brown sugar
sesame oil
Dijon mustard
red cooking wine
Tabasco®
fancy-shred Parmesan
1 dozen eggs

GROCERY LIST
August/Week Three

Produce
one 6" zucchini
10-12 small baby red potatoes
3 medium russet potatoes
2 medium yellow onions
1 lb. fresh mushrooms
1 green bell pepper
1 red bell pepper
3 large carrots
1 lb. fresh broccoli
green salad fixings
1 bunch green onions
1 package prewashed spinach or 2 bunches fresh spinach
1 large cucumber
8-10 Roma tomatoes
2 fresh lemons
1 tart apple
3/4 C. dried apricots
banana, strawberries, nectarine, seedless grapes, and blueberries *(for Sat. brunch)*
firm, unflavored tofu

Frozen Foods
concentrated apple juice

Meat/Fish/Poultry
12 oz. fresh or frozen halibut fillets
6-8 large cooked, shelled shrimp *(frozen is OK)*
2 boneless, skinless chicken breasts

Canned or Dry Foods
three 15 oz. cans chicken broth
one 6 oz. can sliced water chestnuts
one 6 oz. can sliced bamboo shoots
12 oz. dry whole wheat spiral pasta
apricot jam
a loaf of your favorite hearty bread

Chilled Foods and Dairy
plain, nonfat cream cheese
butter

Buy if you're out
one head garlic
pine nuts
frozen peas
turkey bacon
1/2 C. package pecan halves
1/2 C. package shelled walnuts
shredded coconut
brown rice
old-fashioned oats
white cooking wine
Dijon mustard
Worcestershire sauce
sesame oil
low-sodium soy sauce
bran flakes
pesto
plain, nonfat yogurt
nonfat milk

GROCERY LIST
August/Week Two

Produce
3 medium russet potatoes or 8-10 baby red potatoes
1 medium yellow onion
1 lb. fresh mushrooms
2 green bell peppers
2 red bell peppers
3 large carrots
1/2 lb. fresh broccoli
one head green leaf lettuce
green salad fixings
1 head iceberg lettuce
fresh cucumber
10-12 Roma tomatoes
one bunch fresh basil
one bunch fresh parsley
1 fresh lemon

Frozen Foods

Meat/Fish/Poultry
2 boneless, skinless chicken breasts
1/2 lb. ground turkey breast
one Italian turkey or chicken sausage link

Canned or Dry Foods
one 29 oz. can tomato sauce
one 15 oz. can black beans
1 small can chopped black olives
two 15 oz. cans chicken broth
one 15 oz. can vegetable broth
12-16 oz. dry penne pasta
8 oz. fresh fettuccine
one large, thin-crust Boboli®

Chilled Foods and Dairy
salsa
3 oz. sharp cheddar cheese

Buy if you're out
1 head garlic
frozen corn
powdered cumin
chili powder
cornmeal
brown rice
white cooking wine
pesto
tortillas
Parmesan cheese
plain, nonfat yogurt

Notes

Notes

Notes

GROCERY LIST
September/Week Two

Produce

6 medium russet potatoes
8-10 baby red potatoes
2 medium yellow onions
1/4 lb. fresh mushrooms
1 green bell pepper
2 red bell peppers
1/2 lb. fresh broccoli
green salad fixings
1/4 lb. pistachios
4-5 Roma tomatoes
one bunch green onions
2 fresh peaches or nectarines
3-4 tart apples
one bunch fresh cilantro
one bunch fresh parsley
1 fresh lemon
1 fresh lime

Frozen Foods

one package frozen spinach

Meat/Fish/Poultry

2 boneless, skinless chicken breasts
1 lb. thin sliced turkey breast fillets
(or buy unsliced fillets)
1 1/2 lb. ground turkey breast

Canned or Dry Foods

one 29 oz. can tomato sauce
two 15 oz. cans chicken broth
12 oz. dry bow tie pasta
one 15 oz. can sliced beets *(not pickled)*

Chilled Foods and Dairy

1 dozen eggs

Buy if you're out

one head garlic
celery
frozen corn
frozen peas
dried rosemary
dried fennel seed
brown sugar
sesame oil
brown rice
saltine crackers
white cooking wine
plain, nonfat yogurt

GROCERY LIST
September/Week One

Produce

4-5 large russet potatoes
3-4 oz. fresh snow peas
one 6" zucchini
1 medium yellow onion
1/2 lb. fresh mushrooms
2 green bell peppers
2 red bell peppers
2 jalapeno peppers
5 medium carrots
1/2 lb. fresh broccoli
1 head iceberg lettuce
1 head red leaf lettuce
1 bunch fresh parsley
1 cucumber
green salad fixings
10-12 Roma tomatoes
1 ripe cantaloupe
2 ripe kiwis
1 fresh lime
1 ginger root
6-8 ears corn *(You may wish to pick up fresh corn on the way home from work Tuesday evening.)*

Frozen Foods

Meat/Fish/Poultry

6 boneless, skinless chicken breasts
1 lb. ground turkey breast
8-10 large, cooked, shelled shrimp
(frozen shrimp are OK)
1 lb. turkey breast fillets

Canned or Dry Foods

one 29 oz. can tomato sauce
one 29 oz. can chopped tomatoes
one 15 oz. can tomato sauce
oat bran or bran flake cereal
1/2 lb. dry kidney beans or
three 15 oz. cans kidney beans
two 15 oz. cans vegetable broth
two 15 oz. cans chicken broth
12 oz. dry whole wheat spaghetti
a loaf of hearty bread

Chilled Foods and Dairy

plain, nonfat yogurt
whole wheat tortillas

Buy if you're out

garlic
celery
toasted sunflower meats
pine nuts
cornmeal
ground anise
ground cloves
ground sage
paprika
cayenne pepper
capers
Greek olives
Dijon mustard
red cooking wine
eggs
salsa

GROCERY LIST
August/September

Produce

2 large sweet onions
1/2 lb. fresh broccoli
3/4 lb. fresh mushrooms
2 green bell peppers
2 red bell peppers
8-10 baby red potatoes
1 bunch fresh parsley
1/4 lb. fresh snow peas
1 head iceberg lettuce
1 head leaf lettuce
green salad fixings
1 large cucumber
4 Roma tomatoes
fresh peaches, pears, strawberries, blueberries and bananas

Frozen Foods

frozen concentrated apple juice
frozen snow peas *(if fresh unavailable)*

Meat/Fish/Poultry

1 lb. ground turkey breast
2 boneless, skinless chicken breasts
3-5 oz. smoked salmon

Canned or Dry Foods

1/2 C. package sliced almonds
one 29 oz. can tomato sauce
two 15 oz. cans chicken broth
one 6 oz can sliced water chestnuts'
12 oz. dry multi-colored spiral pasta
12 oz. dry whole wheat spiral pasta
12 oz. dry sea shell pasta
8 oz. fresh fettuccine
loaf of hearty bread

Chilled Foods and Dairy

3 oz. sharp cheddar cheese

Buy if you're out

one head garlic
celery
nonfat mayonnaise
ground anise
white cooking wine
red cooking wine
whole wheat tortillas
fresh salsa
pesto

Notes

Notes

Notes

GROCERY LIST
October/Week One

Produce

2 large baking potatoes
one 6" zucchini
2 medium yellow onions
1 lb. fresh mushrooms
1 green bell pepper
1 red bell pepper
2 large carrots
celery
1 head broccoflower
1 head Romaine lettuce
green salad fixings
1 bunch green onions
2 cucumbers
8 Roma tomatoes
1 orange
1 fresh lemon

Frozen Foods

one package frozen spinach
2 frozen sole or roughy fillets *(If you don't have time to buy fresh fish during the week)*

Meat/Fish/Poultry

2 lb. boneless, skinless chicken breasts

Canned or Dry Foods

curry powder
ground cloves
ground coriander
powdered ginger
raisins
one 29 oz. can tomato sauce
one 15 oz. can chicken broth
one 15 oz. can cooked pumpkin
one 6 oz. can chopped black olives
one 15 oz. can whole beets *(don't buy pickled)*
16 oz. dry whole wheat penne pasta
white rice
1 C. package chopped pecans
one large, thin-crust Boboli®
1 package pita bread

Chilled Foods and Dairy

one dozen eggs
3 oz. sharp cheddar cheese
1% buttermilk *(1 quart)*

Buy if you're out

1 head garlic
1 bunch fresh parsley
pine nuts
frozen corn
frozen peas
ground anise
dry dill weed
old-fashioned rolled oats
molasses
white cooking wine
red cooking wine
part-skim mozzarella
plain, nonfat yogurt
salsa
butter

GROCERY LIST
September/October

Produce

8-10 baby red potatoes
2 medium yellow onions
1 lb. fresh mushrooms
2 green bell peppers
2 red bell peppers
2 large carrots
1/8 lb. fresh broccoli
green salad fixings
one head iceberg lettuce
6-8 Roma tomatoes
1 fresh lemon

Frozen Foods

Meat/Fish/Poultry

1/2 lb. turkey breast fillets
2 boneless, skinless chicken breasts
1 lb. ground turkey breast

Canned or Dry Foods

one 29 oz. can "Ready-cut" tomatoes
three 15 oz. cans chicken broth
one 6 oz. can sliced water chestnuts
one 6 oz. can sliced bamboo shoots
16 oz. dry penne pasta
1/2 C. package whole blanched almonds
12 oz. package large egg noodles
1 loaf fresh rye bread

Chilled Foods and Dairy

3 oz. sharp cheddar cheese
whole wheat tortillas
1 bottle of beer

Buy if you're out

1 head garlic
bok choy
turkey bacon
brown rice
corn starch
paprika
cayenne pepper
dry mustard
beer
red cooking wine
pesto
salsa

GROCERY LIST
September/Week Three

Produce

3 white potatoes
20 baby red potatoes
2 medium red potatoes
2 medium yellow onions
1/2 lb. fresh mushrooms
2 green bell peppers
2 red bell peppers
one head bok choy
one acorn squash
1 bunch spinach
1 bunch Swiss chard
1/8 lb. fresh broccoli
green salad fixings
one large cucumber
8-10 Roma tomatoes
2 tart apples
1 fresh lemon
fresh ginger root
8 oz. dried cranberries
one orange
firm tofu
dried cranberries

Frozen Foods

3 frozen halibut fillets
If unable to purchase fresh fish or if frozen is easier for you.

Meat/Fish/Poultry

3 fresh halibut fillets *(if available) or purchase on Wednesday*
2 Italian turkey sausage links
1 lb. ground turkey breast
6-8 large, cooked, shelled shrimp
1 boneless, skinless chicken breast

Canned or Dry Foods

one 29 oz. can tomato sauce
two 15 oz. cans navy beans
two 15 oz. cans chicken broth
one 6 oz. can sliced water chestnuts
one 6 oz. can sliced bamboo shoots
12 oz. dry whole wheat spaghetti
12 oz. dry whole wheat spiral pasta
wheat germ
1/2 C. package chopped pecans or walnuts
1/2 C. package sliced almonds

Chilled Foods and Dairy

nonfat cream cheese

Buy if you're out

garlic
celery
fresh parsley
dried fennel seed
nutmeg
saltine crackers
brown rice
sesame oil
sliced almonds
fortune cookies
fresh pesto
fancy-shred Parmesan
plain, nonfat yogurt

Notes

Notes

Notes

GROCERY LIST
October/Week Four

Produce
2 large russet baking potatoes
2 medium potatoes
4-5 baby red potatoes
one 6" zucchini
2 small turnips
3 medium yellow onions
3/4 lb. fresh mushrooms
one head broccoflower
2 green bell peppers
2 red bell peppers
3 large carrots
1/2 head green cabbage
green salad fixings
1 tart apple
6-8 Roma tomatoes
1 bunch fresh parsley
2 fresh lemons

Frozen Foods

Meat/Fish/Poultry
1 lb. turkey breast fillets
2 boneless, skinless chicken breasts
1/2 lb. ground turkey breast

Canned or Dry Foods
one 29 oz. can tomato sauce
one 29 oz. can "Ready-cut" tomatoes
one 15 oz. can "Ready-cut" tomatoes
one 15 oz. can tomato sauce
one 15 oz. can kidney beans
two 15 oz. cans chicken broth
two 6 oz. cans minced clams
8 oz. fresh angel hair pasta
12 oz. dry egg noodles
a loaf of your favorite hearty bread

Chilled Foods and Dairy
nonfat milk
3 oz. sharp cheddar cheese

Buy if you're out
one head garlic
frozen corn
dry dill weed
paprika
chili powder
powdered cumin
nonfat mayonnaise
Dijon mustard
dill pickles
honey
red and white cooking wine
plain nonfat yogurt

GROCERY LIST
October/Week Three

Produce
one 6" zucchini
3/4 lb. fresh broccoli
1/2 head green cabbage
2 medium yellow onions
1 1/2 lb. fresh mushrooms
2 green bell peppers
2 red bell peppers
1 yellow or orange bell pepper
4 large carrots
one head bok choy
green salad fixings
one large cucumber
5-6 Roma tomatoes
fresh ginger root
1 fresh lemon
1 fresh lime

Frozen Foods
frozen, concentrated orange juice
8 oz. frozen snapper *(if no access to fresh fish)*

Meat/Fish/Poultry
2-3 boneless, skinless chicken breasts
5-6 cooked, deveined shrimp
8 oz. fresh snapper *(you may wish to pick up fresh fish the day you cook it)*

Canned or Dry Foods
one 29 oz. can tomato sauce
two 15 oz. cans chicken broth
one 6 oz. can sliced water chestnuts
one 6 oz. can sliced bamboo shoots
1 small can chopped black olives
1/2 lb. dry navy beans or two 15 oz. cans beans
12-16 oz. dry whole wheat spiral pasta
8 oz. fresh cheese ravioli
fortune cookies

Chilled Foods and Dairy

Buy if you're out
one head garlic
fresh parsley
celery
frozen peas
low-sodium soy sauce
cayenne pepper
sesame oil
brown rice
brown sugar
fresh pesto
fancy-shred Parmesan

GROCERY LIST
October/Week Two

Produce
1 lb. large red potatoes
2 medium yellow onions
1 white onion
celery
1/2 lb. fresh mushrooms
1 green bell pepper
2 red bell peppers
2 heads red cabbage
1/8 lb. fresh broccoli
1 bunch fresh parsley
1 head Romaine lettuce
green salad fixings
green or red leaf lettuce
6-8 Roma tomatoes
1 fresh slicing tomato
1 large fresh cucumber
3 tart apples
2 fresh Bartlett pears
1 fresh lime
1 fresh lemon
8-10 dried apricots

Frozen Foods
one package frozen raspberries
frozen concentrated orange juice
5 large frozen scallops
frozen nonfat vanilla yogurt

Meat/Fish/Poultry
1 lb. assorted German-style sausages (knockwurst, bratwurst etc.)
2 chorizo sausages
5 boneless, skinless chicken breasts
6 large, shelled, raw shrimp

Canned or Dry Foods
one 29 oz. can tomato sauce
four 15 oz. cans chicken broth
one 6 oz. can apricot nectar
grainy mustard
1/2 C package pecan halves
12 oz. dry whole wheat spaghetti
1 small box wild rice
chocolate sauce
a loaf of hearty bread

Chilled Foods and Dairy
plain, nonfat yogurt

Buy if you're out
1 head garlic
toasted sunflower meats
frozen peas
turkey bacon
garlic dill pickles
red and white cooking wine
caraway seed
saffron threads
sesame oil
brown rice
white rice

Notes

Notes

Notes

GROCERY LIST
November/Week Three

Produce

6-8 medium russet potatoes
8-10 baby red potatoes
1 medium yellow onion
1 bunch green onions
1 1/2 lb. fresh mushrooms
1 acorn squash
1 green bell pepper
1 red bell pepper
1 lb. fresh broccoli
green salad fixings
4 Roma tomatoes
1 mediium tomato
2-4 tart apples
one bunch fresh parsley
1 fresh lemon

Frozen Foods

Meat/Fish/Poultry

1 lb. ground turkey breast
2 boneless, skinless chicken breasts
10 oz. orange roughy fillets *(keep frozen)*

Canned or Dry Foods

one 29 oz. can tomato sauce
two 15 oz. cans chicken broth
one 15 oz. can vegetable broth
one 6 oz. can sliced water chestnuts
one 6 oz. can sliced bamboo shoots
12 oz. dry bow tie pasta
1/2 C. package pecan halves
1/2 C. package roasted cashews
raisins

Chilled Foods and Dairy

3 oz. sharp cheddar cheese
plain, nonfat yogurt
eggs
shredded Parmesan

Buy if you're out

1 head garlic
frozen corn
frozen peas
saltine crackers
brown rice
low-sodium soy sauce
sesame oil
Worcestershire sauce
brown sugar
cinnamon
dried rosemary leaves
white cooking wine
pesto

GROCERY LIST
November/Week Two

Produce

one 6" zucchini
8-10 baby red potatoes
2 medium yellow onions
1 lb. fresh mushrooms
2 green bell peppers
2 red bell peppers
celery
one bunch collard greens or kale
3 large carrots
1/2 lb. fresh broccoli
bok choy
1/8 lb. fresh green beans
one head iceberg lettuce
red leaf lettuce
green salad fixings
one head green cabbage
7-9 Roma tomatoes
1 cucumber
3 oz. fresh green beans
1 fresh lemon
1 fresh lime
2 crisp apples
fresh ginger root
toasted sunflower meats

Frozen Foods

orange juice
1 frozen halibut fillet *(if you don't have a leftover fillet in freezer)*

Meat/Fish/Poultry

5 boneless, skinless chicken breasts
2 links hot Italian sausage
1 lb. turkey breast fillets

Canned or Dry Foods

one 29 oz. can tomato sauce
one 29 oz. can chopped tomatoes
two 15 oz. cans chicken broth
three 15 oz. cans vegetable broth
one 15 oz. can kidney beans
one 15 oz. can garbanzo beans
12 oz. dry penne pasta
12 oz. dry whole wheat spiral pasta
a loaf of your favorite hearty bread *(olive or seed bread if you can find it)*

Chilled Foods and Dairy

whole wheat tortillas
3 oz. sharp cheddar cheese
fresh salsa

Buy if you're out

1 head garlic
1 bunch parsley
frozen corn
frozen peas
ground cumin
dried rosemary
chili powder
honey mustard
sesame oil
brown rice
capers
white cooking wine
plain, nonfat yogurt

GROCERY LIST
November/Week One

Produce

one 6" zucchini
8-10 baby red potatoes
3 medium russet potatoes
2 large beets
2 medium yellow onions
1 lb. fresh mushrooms
1 green bell pepper
1 red bell pepper
3 large carrots
1 lb. fresh broccoli
green salad fixings
8 Roma tomatoes
1 tart apple
1 fresh lemon

Frozen Foods

3 frozen halibut fillets or steaks
(if you don't have access to good fresh fish)

Meat/Fish/Poultry

1 lb. ground turkey breast
1 boneless, skinless chicken breast
3 fresh halibut fillets *(You may wish to buy fresh fish on Thursday.)*

Canned or Dry Foods

one 29 oz. can tomato sauce
one 29 oz. can "Ready-cut" tomatoes
two 15 oz. cans chicken broth
12 oz. dry multi-colored spiral pasta
1 package spinach lasagna noodles
1 package egg lasagna noodles
one 6 oz. can chopped black olives
one large, thin-crust Boboli®
loaf of hearty Italian bread

Chilled Foods and Dairy

4 oz. part-skim mozzarella
one dozen eggs
plain, nonfat yogurt
lowfat Ricotta cheese

Buy if you're out

1 head garlic
1 bunch fresh parsley
brown rice
fancy-shred Parmesan
rubber gloves *(You'll need them to handle beets this week.)*

Notes

Notes

Notes

GROCERY LIST
December/Week Two

Produce
1 medium yellow onion
1 green bell pepper
1 red bell pepper
1/4 lb. white mushrooms
1 large carrot
3/4 lb. fresh broccoli
one head Romaine lettuce
1 bunch green onions
one package prewashed spinach
red leaf lettuce
green salad fixings
one large cucumber
8 Roma tomatoes
1 tart apple
1 fresh lemon
firm tofu

Frozen Foods
nonfat frozen yogurt
frozen orange juice

Meat/Fish/Poultry
1 lb. ground turkey breast
4-6 boneless, skinless chicken breasts
2 fresh or frozen snapper fillets

Canned or Dry Foods
one 29 oz. can tomato sauce
three 15 oz. cans chicken broth
one 15 oz. can vegetable broth
one 6 oz. can sliced water chestnuts
one 6 oz. can sliced bamboo shoots
one 16 oz. bag orzo *(in pasta section)*
8 oz. fresh fettuccine
12 oz. dry whole wheat spiral pasta
one 16 oz. can sour pie cherries
or 1 bag frozen pie cherries
one 6 oz. bottle cherry juice
or 1 small bottle cranberry juice
pecan halves

Chilled Foods and Dairy
plain, nonfat yogurt
nonfat milk

Buy if you're out
1 head garlic
celery
1 bunch parsley
olive oil
dry dill weed
ground anise
brown rice
white cooking wine
red cooking wine
canola, peanut or corn oil

GROCERY LIST
December/Week One

Produce
2 medium yellow onions
one 8" zucchini
2 medium white potatoes
4-5 baby red potatoes
1 lb. fresh mushrooms
1 green bell pepper
1 red bell pepper
4 large carrots
1 lb. fresh broccoli
green salad fixings
4-5 Roma tomatoes
4 oranges
1 fresh lemon
pine nuts

Frozen Foods
8 oz. package snow peas

Meat/Fish/Poultry

Canned or Dry Foods
one 29 oz. can tomato sauce
seven 15 oz. cans chicken broth
12 oz. dry whole wheat spiral pasta
8 oz. fresh cheese tortellini
12 oz. package egg noodles
loaf of hearty bread

Chilled Foods and Dairy
1/2 dozen eggs
fresh pesto
plain, nonfat yogurt

Buy if you're out
1 head garlic
fresh parsley
celery
frozen corn
frozen peas
brown rice
sesame oil
chopped black olives
Worcestershire sauce
white wine vinegar
white cooking wine

GROCERY LIST
November/Week Four

Produce
5 lb. russet potatoes
3 sweet potatoes or yams
3 large yellow onions
celery
1/2 lb. fresh mushrooms
1 green bell pepper
2 red bell peppers
1 lb. carrots
1 lb. fresh broccoli
4-6 tart apples
green salad fixings
red leaf lettuce
green leaf lettuce
one large cucumber
4 Roma tomatoes
1/4 lb. dried cranberries
1 fresh lemon

Frozen Foods
frozen corn

Meat/Fish/Poultry
1 frozen turkey *(if not ordering a fresh bird)*
1/2 lb. turkey breast fillet
2 lb. ground turkey breast
or 1 lb. ground turkey breast and
1 lb. lean ground pork
turkey bacon
2 boneless, skinless chicken breasts

Canned or Dry Foods
one 29 oz. can tomato sauce
2 bags or boxes dried bread for stuffing *about 32 oz. (buy unseasoned and unbuttered)*
1 C. package slivered almonds
one 15 oz. can pickled beets
one 15 oz. can pitted black olives
six 15 oz. cans chicken broth
two 15 oz. cans whole cranberries
two 6 oz. cans sliced water chestnuts
12 oz. dry spinach spiral pasta
8 oz. fresh fettuccine
a loaf of hearty bread
dinner rolls *you may wish to pick them up fresh on Wed.*

Chilled Foods and Dairy
nonfat milk

Buy if you're out
1 head garlic
dried thyme
dried bay leaf
dried sage
dried rosemary
butter-flavor cooking spray
gravy separator
eggs

Notes

Notes

Notes

GROCERY LIST
December/January

Produce

one 6" zucchini
9 medium russet potatoes
1 large russet potato
10 baby red potatoes
2 medium yellow onions
1 sweet onion
3/4 lb. fresh mushrooms
2 green bell peppers
2 red bell peppers
2 large carrots
1 lb. fresh broccoli
1 head Romaine lettuce
1 head green leaf lettuce
green salad fixings
one cucumber
2 packages
prewashed spinach
8 Roma tomatoes
2 fresh oranges
fresh oranges or Satsumas
1 fresh lemon

Frozen Foods

Meat/Fish/Poultry

1-2 Italian chicken or
turkey sausages
1 lb. ground turkey breast, or 1
lb. lean ground pork
* If you are opting for the fresh
Salmon dinner on Christmas
Day, you will need to pick up
fresh fish on Christmas Eve.

Canned or Dry Foods

one 29 oz. can tomato sauce
six 15 oz. cans chicken broth
two 15 oz. cans whole cranberries
one 6 oz. can chopped black olives
16 oz. dry multi-colored spiral pasta
8 oz. fresh cheese tortellini

Chilled Foods and Dairy

plain, nonfat yogurt
nonfat milk

Buy if you're out

1 head garlic
1 bunch green onions
saltine crackers
dried thyme
brown sugar
Worcestershire sauce
Dijon mustard
white cooking wine
fresh pesto
shredded Parmesan
eggs

GROCERY LIST
December/Week Four

Produce

one 6" zucchini
9 medium russet potatoes
1 large russet potato
10 baby red potatoes
2 medium yellow onions
1 sweet onion
3/4 lb. fresh mushrooms
2 green bell peppers
2 red bell peppers
2 large carrots
1 lb. fresh broccoli
1 head Romaine lettuce
1 head green leaf lettuce
green salad fixings
one cucumber
2 packages
prewashed spinach
8 Roma tomatoes
2 fresh oranges
fresh oranges or Satsumas
1 fresh lemon

Frozen Foods

Meat/Fish/Poultry

2 Italian chicken or
turkey sausages
1 lb. ground turkey breast, or 1
lb. lean ground pork
* If you are opting for the fresh
Salmon dinner on Christmas
Day, you will need to pick up
fresh fish on Christmas Eve.

Canned or Dry Foods

one 29 oz. can tomato sauce
six 15 oz. cans chicken broth
two 15 oz. cans whole cranberries
one 6 oz. can chopped black olives
16 oz. dry multi-colored spiral pasta
8 oz. fresh cheese tortellini

Chilled Foods and Dairy

plain, nonfat yogurt
nonfat milk

Buy if you're out

1 head garlic
1 bunch green onions
saltine crackers
dried thyme
brown sugar
Worcestershire sauce
Dijon mustard
white cooking wine
fresh pesto
shredded Parmesan
eggs

GROCERY LIST
December/Week Three

Produce

2 large russet potatoes
one 6" zucchini
2 medium yellow onions
1 lb. fresh mushrooms
1 green bell pepper
1 red bell pepper
1 large carrot
2 large, fresh beets
one head iceberg lettuce
one head red or green leaf lettuce
6-8 Roma tomatoes
1 fresh lemon

Frozen Foods

green beans

Meat/Fish/Poultry

1/2 lb. ground turkey breast
6 fresh or frozen scallops
2 boneless, skinless chicken breasts

Canned or Dry Foods

one 29 oz. can tomato sauce
12 oz. dry split peas
five 15 oz. cans chicken broth
16 oz. dry whole wheat spiral pasta
8 oz. fresh fettuccine
a loaf of your favorite hearty bread

Chilled Foods and Dairy

4 oz. sharp cheddar cheese
large wheat tortillas
fresh salsa
fresh pesto

Buy if you're out

1 head garlic
one bunch green onions
celery
parsley
frozen corn
turkey bacon
brown rice
red cooking wine
white cooking wine
plain, nonfat yogurt
butter

Notes

Notes

Notes

ORDER FORM

Qty.	Title	Price	Can. Price	Total
	COOKBOOK OF THE YEAR	**$21.95**	**$28.95**	
	GROCERY LISTS	**$4.95**	**$6.50**	
Shipping and handling (add $4.50 for first book, $3.00 for each additonal book)				
Sales tax (WA residents only, add 8.2%)				
Total enclosed				

Telephone Orders:
Call (800) 461-1931
Have your VISA or
MasterCard ready.

Fax Orders:
(206) 672-8597
Fill out order
blank and fax.

Postal Orders:
Hara Publishing
P.O. Box 19732
Seattle, WA 98109

Payment:Please Check One

☐ Check

☐ VISA

☐ MasterCard

Expiration Date:_______/_______

Card #:____________________

Name on Card:____________________

Name______________________________________

Address______________________________________

City________________ **State**______ **Zip**______

Daytime Phone(**)** ____________________

5-Quantity discounts are available.
For more information, call (206) 775-1481.

Thank you for your order!

I understand that I may return any books
for a full refund if not satisfied.